# FIVE  MISSION

## THE LABOUR PARTY UNDER ED MILIBAND

TIM BALE

OXFORD
UNIVERSITY PRESS

# OXFORD
## UNIVERSITY PRESS

Great Clarendon Street, Oxford, OX2 6DP,
United Kingdom

Oxford University Press is a department of the University of Oxford.
It furthers the University's objective of excellence in research, scholarship,
and education by publishing worldwide. Oxford is a registered trade mark of
Oxford University Press in the UK and in certain other countries

Published in the United States of America by Oxford University Press
198 Madison Avenue, New York, NY 10016, United States of America

British Library Cataloguing in Publication Data
Data available

Library of Congress Control Number: 2014959992

ISBN 978-0-19-870296-2

Printed in Great Britain by
Clays Ltd, St Ives plc

# Acknowledgements

Many people have contributed to this book—some knowingly, some unknowingly, some whom I interviewed, some whose work I read from afar, often on a daily basis. Since the interviews for the book were conducted on an off-the-record basis, the words of those who were kind enough to talk to me are quoted or paraphrased without attribution. Although I have tried hard to show where that occurs in the text, I do not mark those occasions with myriad endnotes reading, say, 'private information' or 'unattributed interview'. As a reader, they drive me mad, so as a writer I prefer not to make use of them. The notes I do include therefore refer only to publicly available sources, some relating to books, some relating to articles in newspapers and magazines and blogs, some referring to speeches and broadcasts, and a fair few to opinion polls. Finally, in addition to acknowledging the sterling efforts of all those at OUP who have helped produce this book, I would like to thank my colleagues, my friends, and my family—especially my immediate family—for putting up with me while I wrote it.

Tim Bale

*London*
*2015*

Our politics in Britain is not led and shaped by leaders alone, but also by political parties; and our leaders are bred and trained by political parties. A party has a pulse; it is an animal with a memory and reflexes; it has hopes and dreams, drives and phobias. From party are our leaders drawn; and within a party's culture are their beliefs and instincts incubated. Party inhabits them.

It may not always show. In the daily grind, the thousand common-sense decisions that a leader has to make, usually on advice and always within the narrow constraints of the possible, he will not appear driven by the religion of party; and he'll take care not to seem so. But under pressure, in moments of crisis or passion—in those unre-hearsed responses that play such an important part in history—the old Adam will out . . . Party matters. Leaders of different parties are in their hearts marching to the beats of different drums. If you want to know what's going to happen you must listen to the drumbeats; go into their caves and study the nature of the beast.

Matthew Parris, The Times 6 October 2012

# Contents

# Introduction

Sitting around in Number Ten on the afternoon of Tuesday, 11 May 2010, while they waited for their boss to walk out into Downing Street and formally announce the end of thirteen years of Labour government, Gordon Brown's staff and colleagues could be forgiven for thinking back to what might have been. Certainly, the contrasts with the summer of 2007 could not have been sharper. Back then, everyone who had stuck with Brown felt vindicated rather than vanquished. It had not been easy. For all his faults, Tony Blair had been the only leader most of them had ever known. Not only that, but he was the man who had transformed the party and persuaded voters—at least until the invasion of Iraq in 2003—that its head, as well as its heart, was in the right place. But enough was enough. It had gone on too long. Labour's greatest asset had become its biggest liability. It was time for him to give way gracefully to the man whose economic and social policies had done almost as much as he himself had done to secure the party three general election victories in a row.

Anyone who had worked with Brown knew, of course, that he could be a nightmare to work with. And voters had their doubts, too, even before he finally made it into Number Ten. They may have respected him, but they could never really connect with him. They also wondered whether he was actually up to the top job, even though, as Blair's Number Two, he had a record of making the right calls on the big issues—raising extra revenue to fix the NHS, refusing to join the euro, keeping the economy bubbling along nicely. On the other hand, he seemed to exude substance, where his younger, far less-experienced Tory opponent, David Cameron, had only style. And the first few months seemed to confirm it. Floods, terrorist attacks: Brown seemed to have taken all of them in his stride, while Cameron, who at that point had been Conservative leader for only a year and a half, was coming under mounting pressure. The polls had turned around. Labour was on course for victory. The 'Brown bounce' had put the spring—no, the swagger—back into their step. It was surely only a matter of when, not if.[1]

Fast forward again to Friday, 7 May 2010, and it all looked very different. Things could have been worse—but not much. The elation of 1997 was a distant memory, the hope suddenly rekindled in the summer of 2007 utterly hollow, blown apart by their boss's failure that autumn to call 'the election that never was', by the chapter of accidents that had followed it, and by the banking crisis and the ensuing economic crash. Brown had spent years doing everything he could to force Labour's most successful leader to step down and let him take over. But his eventual victory in that war of attrition had turned to ashes in his mouth. His political style and his personality—brooding, bitter, introverted, obsessive—had famously led one of his colleagues to predict to journalists before he took over that he would make 'a fucking awful prime minister'.[2] Looking back over the three years he was in charge, very few people now disagreed.

It is, of course, possible to make the case, as Steve Richards and Bill Keegan have done, that there was rather more to it (and rather more to Gordon Brown) than that.[3] And it is certainly true that Brown, with the help of his Chancellor, Alistair Darling, actually handled the truly terrifying possibilities thrown up by the global financial meltdown as well as—maybe even better than—any other world leader. No British banks failed; credit did not dry up completely; and the inevitable recession was shorter and shallower—in the UK at least—than pessimists had predicted. Moreover, the way Brown brought together fellow heads of government and international organizations to coordinate their responses rather than play beggar-my-neighbour deservedly earned him plaudits from all those involved. The domestic politics, however, he got badly wrong. The new Prime Minister was already in trouble after running away from an early election and trying to pretend otherwise. But, instead of confessing to the country that belts would need tightening, he resorted to repeating a line that had always worked well for him as Chancellor but now sounded not only tired but also delusional—namely, that the choice for the country lay between 'Labour investment' and 'Tory Cuts'. The prospect of the latter, it was true, worried many people. David Cameron had tried to convince voters that key public services were safe in Tory hands, but had ultimately failed, in the language routinely employed by journalists and politicians, to 'seal the deal' with voters. Even though he was preferred to Brown as Prime Minister, that support did not translate into trust in his party.[4] The problem for Labour was that nobody believed Brown's story either: indeed, he was held in contempt and ridicule in equal measure.

Things might have improved for Labour if his colleagues could somehow have replaced Brown. But the party has never been as willing or able to rid itself of lame duck leaders as its Conservative rival. In any case, the only people who seemed to fit the bill on this occasion declined even to step in once the deed was done, let alone do the deed themselves—Home Secretary Alan Johnson, because he was not sure he wanted the top job, Foreign Secretary David Miliband, because he believed he had a better chance of succeeding after rather than before a general election. As a result, Labour found itself stuck in the proverbial slow motion car crash as it slid to one of its worst showings at a general election since the Second World War. But, while its vote share, at under 30 per cent, was woeful, the sheer scale of its rejection by the electorate was disguised by the pro-Labour 'bias' in the electoral system and mitigated by some heroic efforts on the ground in the constituencies. Partly as a consequence, Cameron's Conservative Party had failed to win an overall majority, meaning that the day after it lost the election Labour was somehow still in the game. Whether it would remain in office, however, was much more doubtful. It all depended on the Liberal Democrats—Britain's third party and one that Labour politicians had never really taken very seriously.

Admittedly, Labour's chance of retaining power was a slim one, given that only Cameron could offer Nick Clegg a shot at a majority coalition in May 2015. But it was a chance nonetheless.[5] Three men were desperate to try and seize it: Brown because, even after he had realized he could not remain Prime Minister, he was genuinely afraid of the economic and social consequences of a Tory government; Peter Mandelson and Andrew Adonis, because a coalition with Clegg would provide not only the opportunity to keep the Conservatives out but also the chance to heal the century-long split in Britain's 'progressive majority'. Others, while they could just about see the logic, were unimpressed and unpersuaded. David Miliband seemed detached, although that was probably, thought most of his colleagues, because he was now focused on taking over after Brown stepped down—something everyone knew he had been planning long before the election. Alistair Darling, like Jack Straw and Andy Burnham, was adamant: the game was up; it was better to go with dignity than to hang on as bad losers; whatever the electorate wanted, it clearly was not Labour; if the numbers had made a Lib–Lab coalition possible, things might have been different, but they were what they were. Tony was giving Gordon the same advice. Others, especially those who knew how dreadful the Treasury figures were, were not convinced that, even if the parliamentary arithmetic had been different, a Lib–Lab coalition could survive—not because of the Lib Dems but because of the difficulty they knew they would have persuading their more left-wing backbenchers to approve the kind of austerity measures that any Comprehensive Spending Review worth the name would inevitably have entailed. The two Eds—Balls and Miliband—were slightly more equivocal; but only slightly. They, like so many of their colleagues, were exhausted and inclined to throw in the towel, but they were prepared at least to listen to what the Lib Dems wanted. What they would not do was allow themselves to be sucked into a Dutch auction whose sole purpose was to persuade Cameron to offer Clegg more than he had initially intended.

This, in fact, was exactly what the Lib Dems were playing at. Labour's representatives in secret weekend talks with Clegg's negotiating team—Ed Balls, Ed Miliband, Peter Mandelson, and Andrew Adonis—had done little or no preparation themselves, and, without a document setting out some sort of basis for an agreement, they had no choice but to spend most of their time listening to what amounted to a Lib Dem shopping list. By the time the two sides met again on the Monday—this time with the full knowledge of the media and, just as the Lib Dems wanted, the Conservatives—the two Eds were all but convinced there was no point carrying on. Most of the parliamentary party seemed to agree, with even those who had every reason to despise Brown hating Clegg for having the temerity to do what they should have done before the election and demand that the Labour Leader step down. Adonis and Mandelson tried to take a more positive stance, but could do little to disguise the ebbing enthusiasm of their younger colleagues—both of whom were inevitably beginning to think about the leadership contest that Brown's decision to step down (one taken, ironically enough, to make a Lib–Lab deal possible) had now made inevitable and in which they had already made up their minds to stand. In any case, by now the Lib Dems were in way too deep with the Tories to turn to Labour without securing the sort of concessions on electoral reform and deficit reduction that not even the most flexible of the latter's negotiating team could seriously consider. The fact that the Lib Dem team then began to whisper to the media that their Labour counterparts were supposedly being obstructive confirmed to all concerned that the talks were little more than a charade designed, first, to convince the Lib Dems' rank and file that there was no alternative but to do a deal with the Conservatives and, second, to convince Team Cameron that he needed to offer Clegg just that little bit more. It was at that point, sick of being made to look as if he were somehow clinging to office by his fingernails, Brown decided that he was going and went outside—together with his family—to tell the press that he was resigning as Prime Minister and bringing to an end thirteen years of Labour government.

This book tells the story of what happened next and what has happened since. It begins with a leadership contest in which heir apparent, David Miliband, found himself unexpectedly challenged and eventually pipped at the post by his younger brother, Ed. After explaining exactly how and why that happened, it then goes on to show how Labour, despite its leader being written off as a fratricidal freak, a hopeless geek, and even a dead-man-walking, has managed to give itself at least a chance of returning to office at the first time of asking. If that does happen, it would be a trick that very few British Leaders of the Opposition have ever been able to pull off and a miracle even more remarkable given that it is operating in an environment increasingly hostile to politicians and mainstream parties—and given the parlous state into which so many traditional parties of the centre-left have fallen throughout the rest of Europe.[6]

Key to all this has been Labour's remarkable refusal, despite being wracked during most of its thirteen years in government by unresolved and bitter conflicts between 'Blairites' and 'Brownites', to see history repeat itself. Although the party has had its moments—most obviously in the autumn of 2014 when Miliband's leadership itself was called seriously into question—it has never come close to descending into the near civil war that followed equally crushing defeats in the early 1950s, the early 1970s, and the early 1980s. How, the book asks, has this happened? Just as importantly, has there been a price to pay? Has unity come at the cost of a wider appeal, of a stronger sense of direction, of tough decisions postponed? Has Ed Miliband in particular tried to square too many circles? And has he pretended to be something he is not, ensuring that he is bound to disappoint people—not least those whose faith in him has challenged the common wisdom that, barring the odd brave move and the occasional impressive speech, he simply is not up to the job of leading the opposition let alone the country as a whole? Why, if that really is the case, has the party not dumped him in favour of someone who looks and sounds like a Prime Minister—or at least a winner? Finally, is Labour's unity far more fragile than it looks, disguising profound personal, strategic, and ideological tensions that may well explode if Miliband fails in his five-year mission to return the party to power in May 2015? And what if he succeeds? 'Sartre', notes journalist and former Conservative frontbencher Paul Goodman, 'said that hell is other people, and Eliot that hell is oneself. Both', he concludes from bitter experience, 'were wrong. Hell is opposition . . .'. Governing, however, is twice as hard.[7]

# I

# Strangers and Brothers:
# Spring–Autumn 2010

By the time the five candidates for the Labour leadership filed into the hall at Manchester's Central Convention Complex for the formal declaration of results, they already knew which one of them had triumphed. Not so most of the assembled delegates, staffers, and journalists. Having sat through promotional videos and speeches by former leader Gordon Brown and acting leader Harriet Harman, they were forced to wait even longer as the master of ceremonies, Ann Black, instead of simply announcing and anointing the winner, let the tension build by taking her audience through the voting in the party's three-way electoral college round-by-round.[1]

The first set of results produced few surprises. The left's token candidate, Diane Abbott, had made it into the contest in the first place only because a number of Labour MPs who shared little or nothing in common with her politically had nominated her in order to ensure the leadership race would not be fought over by four, 30–40-something, white men. Since only seven of the thirty-three MPs who had nominated Abbott actually voted for her, and since she failed even to win the plurality of votes cast by members of her own constituency party, she finished, as everyone knew she would, a poor fifth in all three of the college's equally weighted components—the parliamentary section (made up of Labour MPs and MEPs), the constituency section (made up of grass-roots members), and the affiliates section (dominated by trade unionists). Meanwhile, former Foreign Secretary, David Miliband, much as expected, topped the voting in the first and second sections, followed by his younger brother Ed, also an ex-Cabinet Minister (albeit at the rather less prestigious Department for Energy and Climate Change), who—again much as expected—garnered most support in the third.

So far, so predictable. What mattered now were second preferences. In each round, the candidate finishing last would be eliminated and their votes duly redistributed to those still in the contest. In a close race like this one, the winner would very likely be the candidate who persuaded those voters who had not ranked them number one to make them their second choice. And so it turned out. Next to be eliminated was Andy Burnham, the former Health Secretary, whose campaign had centred on his vision of a national care service and on the fact that, although he was an Oxbridge graduate like all the other candidates, he was the only one of the men standing who could lay claim to a working-class background. As the detailed results of round two flashed onto the huge screens in the hall, it became obvious—at least to the cognoscenti if not the majority of the audience—that Ed had not only extended his lead among trade unionists but had made up serious ground on his brother in the other two sections as well. Everything now hinged on those MPs and MEPs, as well as those grass-roots members, who had voted for Ed Balls.

Balls had spent years at the Treasury advising Gordon Brown before becoming an MP and, in short order, a Cabinet Minister. His attacks on the Coalition's austerity programme, along with his combative Commons performances against Tory Education Secretary Michael Gove, may have reinforced his reputation as an opposition heavyweight capable of taking on the Conservatives, but his campaign had failed to establish his credentials for the top spot. Worse, its implicit criticism of the fiscal consolidation plan put together by Alistair Darling before Labour lost office rankled with those worried that it would only make restoring the party's battered reputation for economic competence even more difficult. He was also, rightly or wrongly, seen by many MPs—especially those who thought they knew what he had got up to at the Treasury—not just as a bruiser but as a bully.[2] Balls was therefore the third candidate to be eliminated. Would enough of those who chose him as their number one give their second preferences to David, the front runner, to see him through? Or would they plump instead for his younger brother, Ed, whose leadership campaign had started slowly but had gathered momentum over the summer—so much so that, on the day before the result was due, bookmakers had declared him, rather than David, the punters' favourite? Just five or six MPs could make all the difference.

After what seemed like an age but was really only a moment, the figures for the final round appeared on screen. The result could not have been much closer: 50.65 per cent of the vote versus 49.35. But it was nevertheless decisive. The big lead Ed Miliband had built up in the trade-union section of the electoral college, combined with the number of second preferences he had managed to garner from those who had initially favoured Abbott, Burnham, and Balls in the other sections, meant that he, and not his brother, was declared the winner. From the moment he had talked seriously to his closest friends in the Brown government about standing for the leadership, he had been confident that the arithmetic stacked up. He had retained that confidence all the way through, even in the early days of the contest when, as one of those working on his campaign later put it, his team 'were tied together with bits of string' and the enthusiasm of young volunteers.[3] All their hard work had now paid off.

Rather than releasing the tension, however, the announcement of a winner only seemed to add to it. Ed's team—backroom 'boys' such as Polly Billington, Greg Beales, Katie Myler, Stewart Wood, Lucy Powell, Anna Yearley, Marcus Roberts, James Morris, and Alex Smith—were ecstatic, but also anxious. Their worries focused not so much on David: he was probably enough of a professional (and enough of a brother) to react gracefully to defeat, at least in the short term. His supporters, however, were another matter. Tears were inevitable, fair enough even: it is never easy to learn that months of work for a cause you passionately believe in has all been for nothing. The danger, however, was that some of those who were most passionate would not leave it there. Rather than pulling themselves together or else walking away and sulking in silence, they would begin badmouthing the 'wrong brother', telling anyone who would listen (and there were plenty of journalists who were happy to oblige) that his victory was illegitimate, that it had been won only by cosying up to the unions and telling the party what it wanted to hear, and that Labour had made a terrible mistake—one that it would live to regret, one that would see it leave behind New Labour, 'lurch to the left', and lose the next election.[4]

Whether or not it might have been prevented by a more determined attempt by 'Team Ed' to avoid people on their side celebrating his win as signalling the end of New Labour, this was exactly what happened.

As well as reporting the joy with which his election had apparently been greeted in Conservative Campaign Headquarters (CCHQ), and the fact that bookmakers had duly lengthened the odds on Labour winning in 2015, Sunday's and Monday's papers were shot through with unattributed critical comment from those on the losing side, much of it centring on the role of the unions in delivering Ed what some clearly saw as an illegitimate victory. According to the *Guardian*, for example, one 'Labour figure' had privately dubbed the result 'the doomsday scenario', while another described it as 'a gothic horror'. The day before, its sister paper, the *Observer*, had quoted a plaintive (but anonymous) Shadow Cabinet Minister to the effect that 'Had David won, we were back in the game'. In the *Mail on Sunday*, meanwhile, a nameless former Cabinet Minister had declared:

This is catastrophic for the Labour Party. I've worked with Ed in government. He could not make a decision to save his life . . . When Labour elected Tony Blair, they voted with their heads over their hearts. With Ed, they've voted with their hearts over their heads. David Miliband did not win the contest but that doesn't change the fact that he was undoubtedly the right person to win it . . . Ed is a therapist, not a leader. He will make the Labour Party feel good about itself again but that's not important to the country.

Alan Johnson, the man whom many had hoped might be persuaded to replace Gordon Brown either before or after the general election but who had demurred and declared himself for David, probably understood such feelings. Yet, ever the pragmatist and unwilling to join those prepared simply to carp anonymously from the sidelines, he instead penned a piece for the *Independent on Sunday* in which he warned Ed to stay in the centre ground and to resist some sort of 'core vote strategy'. Not completely helpful, but at least a signal that he was prepared to stay in the game. Others, it appeared were less sure. Monday's *Times* not only joined other papers in speculating that David might turn down a place in his brother's Shadow Cabinet, but also noted that major donors to the Labour Party, including Lord Sainsbury, had cancelled their plans to attend conference after hearing the result.

How had it all gone so wrong? How had the man who they, along with many MPs, party members, and media commentators, regarded as the rightful heir to the crown and the sure-fire winner of any contest managed to lose it? It was not as if David Miliband had failed to convince people that he would make a better fist of the job than his rivals. Indeed, if one looks at the polling of party members and Labour-voting, Labour-affiliated trade unionists carried out at the end of July and again at the beginning of September 2010 by YouGov, the front runner retained or actually improved his ratings.[5] In July, some 40 per cent of party members and some 31 per cent of trade unionists said he would be the most effective of the rival candidates as Leader of the Opposition, putting him way ahead of the field. In September the figures were 44 per cent and 31 per cent. When it came to being most likely to lead Labour to victory at the next general election, the figures were 52 per cent (members) and 41 per cent (unions) in July and 55 per cent and 42 per cent respectively in September—more than twice the proportion who said the same of his younger brother, Ed. The gap between them when it came to being best Prime Minister was not quite as yawning, but it was big nonetheless—and it had grown. In July, 41 per cent of members told YouGov that David would make the best PM, compared to 27 per cent who said Ed. In September, the figures were 45 and 28 per cent respectively. The figures for the trade-union members were not very different. How, then, in spite of all this, did Labour contrive not to pick as its leader the candidate who outscored all his opponents on the criteria that one might reasonably have assumed were most crucial?

The answer to that question may be multi-layered but, at root, revolves around three, fairly simple truths. The first is that, although a candidate's assumed ability to win elections and do a good job in government are clearly crucial, the number one priority for most political parties when choosing a leader is actually unity—which is why, when it comes to deciding on how (rather than who) they choose, so many of them, like Labour, eschew first-past-the-post systems in favour of electoral arrangements that reward candidates whose support is wide as well as deep. The second is that parties, especially when they have run into trouble, normally try to find a leader who seems to represent a break with the past. The third is that victory and defeat in leadership contests often turns on a wicked combination of personal chemistry and, rather more prosaically, the rules of the game.

Those rules in Labour's case meant an electoral college divided into three, equally weighted sections, meaning that a sufficiently big win in one of the sections can quite easily outweigh any disadvantage suffered

in either or both of the other two. This is exactly what happened in
2010. Ed Miliband lost out to his brother in the section containing
MPs and MEPs and the section containing ordinary grass-roots members. But David's wins in those sections, while clear-cut at 53:47 and
54:46 respectively, were ultimately insufficient to allow him to overhaul his brother's even more convincing, 60:40 win in the affiliates
section dominated by the votes of trade-union levy-payers.

The rules of the game also meant a preferential system of voting that,
unless one candidate is more popular than all his or her rivals put
together and can therefore deliver a knockout blow in the very first
round, makes it vital for anyone standing to garner second- as well as
first-preference votes. While David was indeed able to convince many
of those whose number one choice was one of his rivals to put him
down as their number two, Ed was able to do so as well—and,
crucially, he was able to do even better than his brother when it
came to attracting the second preferences of the third candidate to be
eliminated from the race, Ed Balls. In the constituency section, Balls's
second-preference votes split in favour of Ed by a ratio of 59–41—
higher in fact than in the affiliates section, where the split favoured Ed
but only by 55–45. In the MPs and MEP's section, the ratio in favour
of Ed rose to 63–37. This was enough to ensure that, although David
ended up winning both the MPs and MEPs and the Constituency
Labour Party (CLP) sections, his wins were simply insufficient to make
a difference to the overall result.

The rules of the game mattered in other respects, too—and right
from the start. David was probably better known than his rivals and
had certainly done a much bigger job in government than they had.
He also got his campaign up and running, and raised money much
faster and in far larger amounts, than they did: indeed, figures released
by the electoral commission showed that by the end of July he had
raised £185,265—more than six times as much as Ed Balls, who at that
stage was his nearest rival on the financial front. The fact that this was
actually more than the £156,000 spending limit allowed by the party
was immaterial—the cost of staff to stuff envelopes, make calls, and
write messages was not included in that figure. As a result David would
have been very well placed indeed to fight a contest lasting only as long
as the six-week affair that had seen Tony Blair win in 1994. Sadly for
him, it was not to be. Despite the fact that, when the Shadow Cabinet
was asked for its opinion by the acting leader, Harriet Harman, a

majority had opted for short and sweet, the 2010 contest stretched out over four long months. This hiatus presented the Tories with a huge opportunity to establish their narrative that the country's economic problems were primarily down to their opponent's profligacy rather than the global financial crisis—one they brilliantly seized with endless references to Labour 'maxing out the nation's credit card'. It also gave Ed Miliband a much better chance than he otherwise would have had to overhaul his brother's early lead.

Doubtless the decision to play it long was taken partly because some of those charged with determining the timetable hoped a longer contest would slow and maybe reverse David Miliband's early momentum. But that was by no means the only reason. Those responsible for the decision also believed a lengthy contest would give the party time to work out and talk about why it had lost its way—something that, because leadership contests (and contestants) tend to look to the future rather than engage in post-mortems, never really came to pass: notwithstanding a couple of potentially useful pamphlets on the subject by Chris Bryant (*Tidy Britain*) and Liam Byrne (*Why did Labour Lose, and How Can We Win Again*), there was, for example, no equivalent of Michael Ashcroft's *Smell the Coffee*, which brilliantly exploited extensive (and expensive!) opinion research to make the case for Conservative modernization after 2005.[6] Secondly, it was thought that playing it long might gain Labour a modicum of media exposure when journalists would otherwise pay it no attention, pre-occupied as they were with a new government that, because it was a coalition, would probably provide most of the inter- and intra-party tension on which newspapers in particular thrived. As National Executive Committee (NEC) member Ann Black noted in her contemporary record of events:

The NEC discussed the process of electing a new leader at length. A hastily-convened meeting of the procedures committee (comprising the NEC officers, the Chair of the conference arrangements committee, and the general secretary) had recommended a timetable ending with the party conference in September, rather than in July ... There were valid arguments for both main options. July would be seen as decisive and outward-looking, a new shadow team could start preparing for the return of parliament, and we would be ready for a snap election. September would allow fuller involvement of rank-and-file members and trade unionists, the new leader would be launched in media prime-time instead of during the holidays, combining the ballot with other internal elections would save money, members could judge candidates by how effectively they attacked the ConDems.[7]

The rules also counted when it came to candidates contacting their electorate. MPs and MEPs, of course, were no problem, although there were some who insisted that David's campaign must somehow have been told which parliamentarians had already voted so they could concentrate on those yet to cast their ballot. CLP members and trade unionists, however, were a different matter. David's better-funded campaign undoubtedly enjoyed an advantage in contacting grass-roots members, even if Ed's team may have evened things up a little by its arguably more creative use of text messages and social media. But, when it came to the trade unions, the boot was very much on the other foot: Ed's campaign found it much easier than his brother's to come by the contact details of levy-payers, which must have contributed to his big win in the affiliates section.

Painstaking research by the academic Mark Wickham-Jones and his colleagues also strongly suggests that Ed received a huge boost from the fact that trade unions could nominate particular candidates.[8] Local constituency parties were also free to nominate their favourite candidate, but in their case there is little or no evidence that their doing so swayed the votes of individual party members: had they done so, David Miliband, who may not have been quite as popular among more ideologically motivated activists as he was among more moderate, passive grass-roots members, may have found the latter voting for him in lesser numbers than they actually did. Trade-union levy-payers, however—possibly because many of them were less personally invested in the whole process, possibly because there is a tradition of their doing so—seemed far more inclined to follow the advice given to them by their leaders.

This tendency might have had only a limited impact if there had been a greater variety of trade unions affiliated to the party and if their leaders had confined their backing of a particular candidate to the initial nomination process. However, recent years had seen significant mergers, with super-unions such as Unite, Unison, and the GMB in the vanguard.[9] Meanwhile, although most British people work in the private sector, trade unions have found it much easier to recruit in the public sector, thereby ensuring, argue critics, that its vested interests are disproportionately represented in the labour movement. Even this might not have mattered had the leaders of the three biggest unions not decided enthusiastically and continually to endorse candidates other than David Miliband. But that was exactly what they did—allegedly in concerted fashion following a 'secret' meeting between them at London's Commonwealth Club in early July. Unite in particular made full use of its formidable e-campaigning machine to remind its levy-payers to vote for Ed, whose role in putting together Labour's manifesto in 2010 had brought him into far more contact with union leaders than his brother had enjoyed as Foreign Secretary.

Moreover, in one or two cases, unions' decisions to endorse Ed Miliband as the best-placed 'stop-David' candidate saw them, at least in the view of some on David's campaign, depart from the spirit if not the letter of the guidelines sent out by the party. The guidelines warned unions and other affiliated societies that they 'should not include any information in the ballot envelope indicating support for individual candidates'—a ruling that left open the possibility that such information could be included *along*side rather than *in*side the said envelope. The GMB, the country's third biggest union, placed the envelope containing the ballot papers inside a bigger envelope on which was printed a call to vote for Ed, and which also carried inside it a magazine whose front cover contained another endorsement and a letter from General Secretary Paul Kenny to the same effect. Britain's biggest union, Unite, sent out a transparent envelope that contained not just the ballot envelope but a recommendation that the recipient vote for Ed from joint General Secretaries Tony Woodley and Derek Simpson. The fact that Ed had both these unions—and Britain's second biggest, Unison—going into bat for him so strongly must have made a difference. So must the fact that the big unions, as well as restricting access to their membership lists to the other campaigns, and donating directly to Ed's, were able to fork out the equivalent of hundreds of thousands of pounds to help him without it counting against his official spending limit of £156,000, since it could be classified as internal communications expenditure. Given how vital Ed's big win in the affiliates section of the electoral college actually was, their efforts on his behalf may well have been decisive.

It is possible to argue, of course, that all this rather begs the question—in other words, that David lost, not because the he was the victim of sharp practice by the trade unions with the largest number of levy-payers (or, for that matter, because the turnout among those unions whose support he did manage to secure, such as USDAW and Community, was no more impressive than the paltry proportion mobilized by their much bigger counterparts) but because he failed to win their support in the first place. To understand why, we need to go beyond matters of process and ask what exactly was it about David Miliband, and about the Labour Party (and indeed the wider labour movement), that prevented the contest's clear front runner from finishing first in the end?

One seemingly inescapable problem was that David Miliband was closely associated with Tony Blair, having been his Head of Policy for seven years between 1994 and 2001, when he was elected to Parliament and then promoted into the Cabinet less than five years later. This meant that a significant proportion of those voting, and in particular a significant proportion of trade-union leaders who were urging their members to vote as directed, regarded him not simply with suspicion but as an anathema—in much the same way that David's most loyal supporters regarded the 'Brownite' Ed Balls. They acknowledged that Blair had been brilliant at winning elections, but he had also taken the party in directions that many thought were ideologically disgraceful, organizationally divisive, and ultimately electorally disastrous. It was not just the Iraq war, although that was bad enough, or the way 'tough on crime, tough on the causes of crime' had morphed into ID cards and 42-days detention without trial for terrorist suspects, although that made some on the liberal left very, very uncomfortable. It was the stress on reform of the public services, which, as far as most of the sector's trade unions were concerned, seemed to be mainly about outsourcing, competition, and private finance rather than doing something about low pay and preserving jobs. The way in which the City of London and financial services generally seemed to be more important than the renewal of Britain's manufacturing and small business base also rankled. And university tuition fees—despite all the evidence suggesting that they had not, as many on the left had feared, put lower-income students off higher education—also remained a huge bone of contention.

So, while YouGov polls of Labour Party members and Labour-voting, Labour-affiliated trade unionists in the summer of 2010 showed that the vast majority of them (81 per cent of party members and 77 per cent of trade unionists) regarded Blair as having done a good job as Prime Minister—and certainly a better job than Gordon

Brown—they also showed that he was considered, on balance, a liability, as was the self-styled 'third man' in the New Labour trio, Peter Mandelson. Indeed, while Brown (worryingly, perhaps, given the contrast with voters' views) was regarded as a net asset, with 51 per cent of party members seeing him as an asset and 40 per cent seeing him as a liability, Blair's ratings were 34 and 58 per cent and Mandelson's were 27 and 64 per cent. Blair was also seen as way to the right of where trade unionists and party members located themselves on a left–right scale. Presented with a continuum running from −100 (very left wing) to +100 (very right wing), Labour members placed themselves at −51 and Labour trade unionists placed themselves at −45; their figures for Blair, though, were +9 and +11—somewhere to the right of centre. Interestingly, however, those who said they would rather be led by Ed regarded Labour's former leader as far more right wing than did those who preferred David, placing Blair at +20 (members) and +21 (trade unionists) rather than, as David's supporters did, at −2 and 0 (dead centre). The other striking difference between supporters of Ed and supporters of David was in their reaction to Blair's saying that the party should not move a millimetre from New Labour's approach. Of those supporting Ed rather than David, only 20 per cent of members and 31 per cent of trade unionists thought Blair was correct, compared to 64 per cent and 57 per cent of those who preferred David to Ed.[10]

In short, David, was seen—ideologically at least—as the Blairite, New Labour, 'continuity' candidate, which suited Ed's team perfectly. In David's camp this was greatly resented—not least because the weight of residual sympathy for Gordon Brown in the party made it tricky for them to counter with the obvious point that Ed represented continuity, too, but with Blair's far less successful rival. Ed was also fortunate in this respect in that Balls's decision to run allowed him to position himself as neither Blairite nor Brownite. This was not too much of a stretch: as one of those who had worked with Ed in government confided, they had felt even then that 'there was something not quite right: Gordon was a social democrat who lost his social democracy on the way and had a way of doing politics that we didn't take quite to'. They were also careful during the leadership campaign to talk about things that had worked neither under Brown nor under Blair, most obviously, for example, the fact that the costly system of tax credits had never really managed to get to the root of the problem of poverty and inequality. Ed's generally sunny rather than saturnine disposition, as well as his self-declared interest in the importance of ideas in politics, also made it much easier to believe his offer of both a new style of politics and an end to what someone who worked closely with him on his leadership campaign called 'the desiccated triangulation' of the last decade.

David Miliband's team clearly recognized the obvious threat his brother's positioning posed to their man, even if none of them realized till far too late that their champion's politically correct gesture to 'lend' some of his supporters to Diane Abbott in order to ensure she got nominated was an act of unthinking idiocy that made it much, much easier for Ed than it should have been to avoid being branded the stand-out left-winger in the contest. Left to their own devices, they might have pursued a more aggressive strategy: mounting a more determined effort, for instance, to undermine what one of his supporters later told the journalist John Rentoul was 'a Brownite coup dressed up as an Obama insurgency'.[11] David, however, was reluctant to see attack as the best form of defence. This was largely because part of his pitch was that he was running a positive rather than a negative campaign, although, in the view of those working for Ed, it was also because, fundamentally, 'David never ever, ever took Ed seriously . . . There is something there about the psychology of a senior sibling.' The older of the two brothers tried hard, however, and not altogether in vain, to shake off the Blairite label that his opponents were busy trying to pin on him. As he made clear in his Keir Hardie lecture on 9 July, although he was not going to take what he regarded as the easy way out and simply disown all the downsides of the Blair–Brown era, he nevertheless acknowledged that the 1997–2010 governments had made mistakes (not least the fact that it was 'too hands on with the state and too hands off with the market') and that it was time to move on—to what he had already referred to as 'next Labour' rather than New Labour. He also surprised many—and in the view of some of his supporters wasted valuable time—by getting involved with 'Movement for Change', an organization that aimed to build the capacity of ordinary people to campaign for change on issues in their locality and that he claimed to see as the way to renew the party's grass roots.

This sort of stuff, which drew heavily on the work (and, in the speech's case, the words) of academic and community organizer Maurice Glasman, may well have helped—but not enough, especially when some of his highest-profile supporters insisted on criticizing Ed in ways that openly framed the debate in terms of keeping the Blairite flame alive. Indeed, Peter Mandelson's comments in *The Times* at the end of August to the effect that Ed risked 'slamming the door in the faces of millions of voters who voted for our party because we were New Labour' and warning of the 'electoral cul-de-sac' that faced anyone who wanted 'to create a pre-new-Labour future' may well have done David more harm than good.[12] His intervention did not, it should be said, have Ed's team punching the air: Mandelson, after all, was a prototypical 'big beast' famous for backing winners. But many in David's team believed—and continue to believe—that it was one of the things that scuppered his chances. However true this was, it seemed he had become, in the words of one of Ed's closest advisers, 'the embodiment of the hopes of Blair continuity people [even] when he himself didn't want that'. He might have avoided that had he been prepared, for instance, to do what most Democratic contenders in the USA do and feint left to secure the nomination before returning to the centre straight afterwards. But he was not—partly because he thought he could win anyway and partly because he thought it might be a difficult trick to pull off in the British context.

Still, in the wake of Mandelson's intervention, David sent a public email to all his supporters a couple of days afterwards in which he promised 'I will move us on from Blair–Brown. I am sick and tired of the caricature that this leadership election is a choice between rejecting and retaining New Labour.' And there is some evidence to suggest that he managed to achieve at least some distance from his former boss. Asked by YouGov just a few days later to place David on the same left–right scale as themselves, party members (who, remember, put themselves at −51), put him just to the left of centre at −2 and Labour-voting union members (whose self-location was −45) put him just to the right at +4—significantly less right-wing than Blair. The problem was, however, that it was all relative: Ed, with his willingness to come out against the Iraq war and for civil liberties as well as the 'living wage' and an assault on high pay, was placed at −31 by members and −23 by trade unionists, while, with the exception of people such as Jon Cruddas and Dennis Skinner (who declared for David on the grounds that he was the candidate who most scared the Tories), nearly all of David's highest-profile supporters were right-wingers. For conservative and centrist media commentators, nearly all of whom favoured

David, the fact that Ed was publicly backed by Neil Kinnock (and possibly Gordon Brown) and David by Peter Mandelson (and probably Tony Blair) told you all you needed to know. Sadly for David, the same was true of Labour members and Labour-supporting trade unionists, whose leaders had their suspicions about him confirmed when, at a hustings held at the 2010 Trades Union Congress (TUC) Conference in Manchester, he was the only candidate to hesitate when asked about his attendance at a big anti-cuts rally planned for the following month.

But—whatever David's supporters might argue—it was not just that the party itself worried about where he would take it. Many of those voting in the leadership contest were also worried that the electorate at large would be ambivalent about, even antipathetic towards, some of the policies he might insist on promoting and defending. Labour people knew that David enjoyed far greater popularity and credibility with the electorate than did his rivals. And, if they needed reminding in the run-up to the ballot, they could consult a widely reported YouGov poll commissioned by David's campaign, which found, as the *Guardian* noted, that '47% of respondents who had a view believe the shadow foreign secretary is the most effective alternative to Cameron—a 28 point lead over his nearest rival, his brother Ed, who scored 19%', although (rather soberingly for those who take an interest in the minutiae of politics) their ratings when shorn of the 'don't knows' and 'none-of-the-aboves' were just 20 per cent and 8 per cent respectively. The fly-in-the-ointment, however, was neatly summed up by a YouGov poll, commissioned by Ed, and which appeared the very next day. This could be spun as showing '72% of uncommitted voters would be less likely to back a Labour leader' who followed Tony Blair's advice not to depart a millimetre from New Labour, with similarly large majorities saying they would be more likely to back a leader who had been opposed to the Iraq war, who wanted to retain the 50p top rate of tax on incomes over 150,000, who wanted to scrap tuition fees in favour of a graduate tax, and who pledged to 'depart from the Blair and Brown years and move on from New Labour with a different approach'.[13]

So, while Ed clearly looked and sounded less like a leader than his brother, at least in the eyes of the wider electorate and, indeed, Labour Party members, he could claim—with at least a degree of credibility—that the direction in which he was promising to take the party was actually the one in which floating voters (and, just as importantly, all those on the liberal left who felt betrayed by Nick Clegg) wanted it to go. To Ed's detractors, of course, he was trying to win by telling the party what it wanted to hear. This was no doubt true—but only up to a point. To Ed's supporters he also happened to be telling it like it was. In other words, he was the only one of the candidates to appreciate that the international and domestic political economy had not simply ground to a temporary halt but had been exposed as fundamentally flawed and, because it was not delivering to the majority of people, required re-engineering rather than simply running repairs. As he put it in a keynote article for the *Observer* at the end of August, the main thrust of which was not so very far away from some of the things David had said in his Keir Hardie lecture even if couched in more populist and more consciously socialist terms:

New Labour's political economy—highly flexible, liberal markets and a stronger welfare state—achieved great things: continuous growth with low inflation and the tax revenues which could be used to redistribute resources to invest in public services and tackle child poverty. But in the end, some of the limitations in our approach were exposed. We must be for the creation of wealth as well as its distribution, but we were too late to recognise this required government to act. We left our economy too exposed to the financial crash because we didn't build a diverse enough industrial base. And our faith in maximum flexibility and a hands-off approach to the responsibilities of the rich meant that we became more unequal as a country and many middle- and low-income families were left feeling squeezed and insecure, part of a society where we work the longest hours in western Europe.

We need a different approach. Britain's big question of the next decade is whether we head towards an increasingly US-style capitalism—more unequal, more brutish, more unjust—or whether we can build a different model—a capitalism that works for people and not the other way around. For Labour to . . . reconnect with those who turned their backs on our party, this is the project on which we must embark.[14]

This sort of stuff pressed several specific buttons, not least one that hinted at an argument made on the left (but also some psephologists) that Labour, while it had to continue appealing to the middle class, needed to think even more about the four million to five million largely working-class voters who had deserted it between 1997 and 2010—a point made for Miliband in a Fabian essay drafted for him by the MP John Trickett and Ed's young pollster, James Morris, and that was published in mid-August. Significantly, however, the particular points were also woven into a more general argument, urged on Ed by Morris and others in his team. This was that Ed was 'the change candidate', supposedly in marked contrast to his rivals (especially, if only by implication, David), who were stuck in what he called, in an interview with *LabourList*'s editor, the blogger Mark Ferguson, 'a comfort zone, a New Labour comfort zone'.[15] This was ironic, Ed suggested, not so much because he was the one being accused by Blairites of wanting to wind back the clock but because the party's modernization in the mid-1990s came about only because people had found 'the courage to change'. Indeed, as he put it in his Fabian essay, it was precisely because, unlike the purveyors of 'New Labour nostalgia', he took the 'crisis of working-class representation for Labour' seriously that he could fairly claim to be 'the modernising candidate in this election'.[16]

All this meant that those who were charged with choosing Labour's next leader were simply unable to have their cake and eat it too. If they could have voted for someone who combined David's top-flight experience and charisma and Ed's fresh-start, slightly more social democratic and socially liberal approach to policy and politics, they would have done so in their droves. However, that was not what was on offer. It was either–or. David was in some ways the obvious choice, and it is a testament to his considerable qualities that he won over a majority of Labour Party members despite refusing to backtrack on Iraq (even though he was apparently far less convinced of its wisdom in private than in public) and being widely seen as the 'Blairite' candidate in an era where that was far from an obvious advantage. However, a substantial minority of members worried about him 'doing a Blair' and taking on the party—perhaps by signing up to rather than resisting the Coalition's austerity programme. Ed did not quite seem to have what it takes to be a leader, but perhaps the unpopularity of the government would give him time to grow into the role and give the public the chance to appreciate what many saw as the manifest superiority of the policies he was espousing.

But there was something else that mattered, too—and mattered more at Westminster than anywhere else. Ed's lead in the affiliates' section of the electoral college was significant but it need not have been overwhelming had David been able to persuade just a few more of his colleagues at Westminster to give him either their first or second preference. He was unable to do so, of course, partly for the same reasons he was unable to persuade some of those voting in the other sections. And, according to one of his supporters, the decision to hand the management of his campaign to 'two Scots MPs from similar wings of the Labour Party was not very wise—and two men at that'. But there was another reason—one referred to only obliquely, at least in public, during the campaign. It had to do with the assertion by Ed's supporters that their candidate 'spoke human'.

That jibe referred in part to the way Ed was in his element when doing off-the-cuff, interactive appearances in front of small to medium-sized audiences—a talent for communication that had seen him touted as a possible contender by journalists like the *Guardian*'s Jenni Russell as early as autumn 2009 and that clearly did him no harm during the fifty-six hustings held all around the country during the contest itself.[17] But the 'Ed speaks human' jibe also touched on something more sensitive and, in public at least, largely unspoken— namely, that a fair few Labour MPs felt (or at least claimed) that, over the years, David had made little or no effort to cultivate or, in some cases, even treat them like equals. This may have been unfair—shyness, after all, afflicts over- as well as under-achievers. As one of his supporters who knew him well noted: 'He's socially awkward, and he's had to learn to be more outgoing. He's turned into someone who can be extremely sweet and extremely caring and all the rest of it. But it's not his default position.' Unfortunately for those who knew David less well or had only just met him in person, that default position was all-too-easily misinterpreted as smugness, self-satisfaction, or even a superiority complex. As a result, tales of his supposed tendency to patronize people or simply blank them rang true enough around Westminster to have damaged his chances.

And this was not all. There was also a feeling among some MPs that David's failure to challenge Gordon Brown for the leadership when presented with multiple opportunities to do so in 2007, 2008, and 2009 suggested he lacked not just the courage and the hunger for the top job but the decisiveness needed to do it well. The fact that, after much humming and hawing, he had stayed in the Brown government made it harder for him to criticize it during the leadership contest. But even more of a problem was the fact that, as one of his supporters later lamented, 'the pissing about, will-he-won't-he conspiracies made him look weak and pathetic'. Conversely, while Ed's decision to challenge his older brother was portrayed as bordering on the pathological by

David's supporters, there were many—even among those who vaguely disapproved of what he was doing—who acknowledged that it did at least demonstrate that he possessed the killer instinct that all leaders probably need. Indeed, it was all the more impressive because the younger Miliband had a bit of a reputation among his colleagues as someone who had trouble making up his mind and was too inclined to square circles—or, as one of them put it more bluntly, 'indecisive, weak, always looking over his shoulder at the party, no clarity of vision'. Ed's decision to stand in the first place, and then the ruthless way his campaign helped position his brother as a Blairite who would find it difficult to connect with ordinary people, was also striking because, ordinarily, he came over as one of life's nice guys—a tad wonkish perhaps but somebody who was not, generally speaking, too busy or else too convinced of his own importance to stop and chat, not least to the new intake. As one of David's supporters observed,

David is not always great at sitting there and listening to people who are much less intelligent than he is—which is most people! . . . Ed's got much greater *emotional* intelligence than his brother . . . Moderate, 2010 newly elected MPs went to see David and went to see Ed. David would give them ten minutes, looking over their shoulder, clearly impatient. Ed would listen to every little thing they wanted to talk to him about. Surprise, surprise, they voted for Ed.

Ed's nice-guy reputation obviously came in useful when soliciting votes. That was partly because it meant that nobody accused him of simply turning on the charm when it suited him, once again providing a sharp contrast with his brother. As one of his team recalled, when describing how MPs reacted to their canvassing: 'OK, I'll take Ed's call, but only because he'll ask me nicely—unlike his fucking brother' or 'You wouldn't believe the voicemail message David left me yesterday—as though I was his best mate. He hasn't spoken to me since I arrived here.'

Ed's reputation as a decent bloke also mattered because it was buttressed by a deliberate decision on the part of his campaign team—even when strong characters like Tom Watson were doing their damnedest to persuade fellow MPs who were supporting Balls to give their second preferences to Ed—to eschew anything that smacked of the strong-arm, 'You'll never work in this town again' tactics that some of his brother's supporters were rumoured to be trying on. There is a fine line between, on the one hand, reminding colleagues that the candidate you are canvassing for is the front runner and therefore likely to be the man who will be deciding who gets a front-bench job in a few weeks' time and, on the other, hinting that such a job might not be forthcoming unless said colleagues vote the right way. Whether or not that line was crossed in reality, some Labour MPs certainly seem to have believed that it had been. That may have been irrelevant had David gone for a shock and awe, 'inevitability' approach right from the start, coupling visuals that demonstrated he had the support of many of the great and the good with a full declaration of the impressive number of pledges he already had. Instead, his team chose to release the names of his supporters in tranches to convey a sense of momentum. This gave the impression that Ed was not initially as far behind him as, in fact, he was, persuading some who might otherwise have written him off that he was in with a chance.

Ed Miliband's team were hardly in a position to warn colleagues of the risks involved in not supporting their candidate, but they were willing to hint that supporting him might lead to bigger and better things. David's team, however, were under strict instructions not to do anything that smacked of swapping jobs for votes. But, sadly for David, few were impressed by his high-mindedness. Instead, they saw it as all of a piece with what they regarded as hauteur and his sense of entitlement. Or they saw it, not unreasonably, as the act of someone determined not to be tied down as a leader by his party. Whatever, because David's stance extended to big beasts as well as lowly back-benchers, it meant it was impossible to do the one thing that some of his supporters privately suggested he could and should do in order to guarantee victory—namely, to offer Ed Balls the post of Shadow Chancellor in return for his second preferences. Apparently, this was simply impossible—not just because David did not want to compromise (or be compromised) but because, in the words of one of his supporters, 'he hated Ed Balls'.

This sort of stuff also stirred up memories of the poisonous atmosphere that had developed between and around Blair and Brown and that continued when Brown, having finally achieved his ambition to replace Blair as Prime Minister, proved so hopeless at the job that people were soon plotting to get rid of him as well. Very few people wanted a return to that kind of thing—including David Miliband and Ed Balls. However, they (once again, not necessarily fairly) had become more associated with it than was Ed Miliband. This was partly because Ed's campaign was careful to distance him from both Prime Ministers. But it was also because Ed had been seen as one of the few politicians close to Brown that those closer to Blair (who, according to his biographers, referred to Ed as 'the emissary from Planet Fuck') were happy to deal with—a decent bloke unwilling to dabble in the dark arts employed by those who were even closer to his master than he was. Because of all this, Ed was seen by many inside Westminster as the candidate with the best chance of moving the party on from the Blair–Brown era, in terms not just of big-P Politics but of small-p politics, too.

But if one of the reasons why Ed Miliband beat David Miliband was because he was seen as the unity as well as the change candidate, there was one split that his win was likely to precipitate rather than prevent—namely, the rift between the two brothers themselves. As his biographers, James Macintyre and Mehdi Hasan, quite rightly suggest, Ed had made up his mind to stand, assuming a vacancy occurred, by the New Year of 2010. Like the other candidates, he did no canvassing before the general election, although some of his colleagues at Westminster noted that he seemed surprisingly keen to accept their invites to constituency fundraisers, whereas, in the run-up to the election, he (like his brother) did not seem to be quite as willing as some thought he should be to defend the government on television and radio. Once the election was over, however, and even as he was joining the team picked by Brown to negotiate a possible coalition with the Lib Dems, his friends were putting out feelers on his behalf. His decision to run was rooted, naturally, in a genuine belief on his part that he was best placed to provide the fresh start and different style needed to put Labour back in contention. But he also knew that, were he to stand aside and effectively allow his older brother a free run, then the likelihood of the party electing a second Miliband as leader was vanishingly small. This, then, was the only shot he would ever get—but one he could take only if he set aside all concerns of what his entering the race might do to his relationship with David. He must, of course, have hoped that any damage done could be repaired—at least in the long term. On the other hand, deep down, he must have known there was a risk that, however much they tried to ensure that their two campaigns fought a clean fight, what he was doing might end up ripping the family apart.

Despite their best efforts, the tensions between the two men, and their wives, had grown ominously as the summer wore on, sparked by sniping (more often indirect than direct) between their two staffs.

Certainly there was suspicion among many of those working for Ed that many of those employed in top jobs at the Party's Headquarters in Victoria Street (most of whom were appointed during the Blair era) were rooting for David, although quite what they could have done actively to help him win is hard to say. These suspicions were only heightened in hindsight by rumours that, when the results were announced in Manchester, many of those officials who were supposed to take care of the new leader were suddenly nowhere to be found. In fact, those involved had tried but failed, in the run-up to conference, to get either Team Ed or Team David to plan exactly what they wanted to happen in the minutes and hours after their man had been declared the winner. Indeed, in marked contrast to the rumours, those who had to run Ed Miliband's operation generally had only good things to say about the help they got from party staff in the early weeks and months of his leadership. Moreover, most of them were grown up enough to realize that what was widely reported as some-thing akin to a mass exodus from Victoria Street in those weeks and months actually had as much to do with the inevitable departure of overworked and underpaid young staffers for jobs in the private sector (and, in some cases, less lucrative work in Shadow Ministerial teams) as it did with ideologically inspired disappointment.

The most immediate question for Ed, however, at least as far as journalists were concerned, was whether David was prepared, as he had claimed during the campaign, to serve in his first Shadow Cabinet. Ed's first full speech to conference as leader, then, not only had to make a good first impression on both the audience in the hall and the journalists who would edit and interpret it for the audience at home; it also had to be carefully calibrated so as to leave open the door for his brother. These aims were not necessarily mutually exclusive: acknow-ledging that Labour in government had not got everything right and had grown remote from those it sought to represent, promoting the need to undertake a radical rethink yet also 'to fight for the centre ground, not allow it to be dominated or defined by our opponents', was something David had himself done several times over the course of the leadership contest. And Ed's decision to balance his acknowledge-ment of the role of trade unions with his opposition to 'irresponsible strikes', while it might have irritated the leaders who had helped him get elected, did his cause no harm either. The same probably went for his admission that 'I won't oppose every cut the coalition proposes. There will be some things the coalition does that we won't like as a party but we will have to support...the fiscal credibility we earned before 1997 was hard won and we must win it back by the time of the next general election.'[18]

Some areas of disagreement with David could not, however, be so easily elided, notably their different takes on tuition fees, on anti-terrorist legislation, and, most awkwardly of all, on Iraq. Ed's assertion in his speech that 'I do believe that we were wrong. Wrong to take Britain to war and we need to be honest about that' went down well with most of the audience—but not with his brother. Mortifyingly but, given the level of media speculation about his feelings and future, hardly surprisingly, David was caught by TV cameras turning to Harriet Harman, who (unlike him and Jack Straw and Alistair Darling) had joined in the applause, and asking, rather too pointedly, 'You voted for it. Why are you clapping?'

It was the realization that there were bound to be many more moments like this, as well as the racing certainty that his own hopes of ever leading Labour had effectively gone up in smoke, that persuaded David not to accept a post—even the shadow chancellorship that was proffered—in his brother's team. By the time it was made official, his announcement came as no surprise. Indeed, in some quarters, and even in parts of what could now be called Ed Miliband's office, it was greeted as much with relief as with regret. There was still some speculation that David might return to the fray at some point, but that was a bridge that could be crossed when they came to it. The more pressing issues were the composition and the configuration of Ed's Shadow Cabinet. There was little that he could do about the former: Labour MPs elected most of its members and there was insufficient time or, indeed, energy to try to persuade them to back particular colleagues. What mattered most at that stage, anyway, was that high-profile MPs who had backed David agree to stand and to serve—something that may have been achieved at least in part by Ed successfully persuading Gordon Brown's Chief Whip, Nick Brown, not to run for re-election to the post, leaving the way clear for his preferred candidate, and someone with far less baggage, Rosie Winterton. The task now was to put together a front bench that would be seen as neither Brownite nor Blairite and capable of taking on a coalition government that, while Labour had been busy looking the other way, had done its best to determine the terrain on which the party and its new leader would have to fight for the next five years.

# 2

# No Honeymoon: Autumn 2010–Spring 2011

Labour has long prided itself on being more democratic than its main rival, the Conservative Party. Tory leaders, beyond the need to strike a balance between right and left, between old hands and young Turks, and between different parts of the country, have always enjoyed a free hand when it comes to selecting their Shadow Cabinet. Not so Labour leaders. In government, they might enjoy a little more room for manœuvre. In opposition, however, they have to play the hand dealt them by their fellow MPs, who would get together, traditionally on an annual basis, to elect nineteen people out of whom leaders were obliged to build a team to fulfil the constitutional function of scrutinizing the government and to do the equally important, but more political, job of persuading the public that Labour was a credible alternative. It was always open to Labour leaders to bring in people who had not been elected—from the Lords as well as the Commons—but it did not do to appoint too many such people. October 2010 offered a couple of new twists. This time, thanks to a Parliamentary Labour Party (PLP) vote in September, the gender quota (another big difference with the Conservatives) would be raised from four to six, while Ed Miliband would apparently be stuck with whoever was foisted on him for two years rather than one—which made his refreshing refusal (or was it simply his inability?) to organize a slate of placemen and women for the elections all the more risky. Otherwise, however, it was business as usual.

When the results were announced, it was immediately obvious that none of those in the top ten places had given Ed his or her first preference in the leadership election. Even then there was speculation as to whether the new leader would be pleased or disappointed at who had made the cut and who had not. Defeated leadership contenders Ed Balls and Andy Burnham, not surprisingly, were elected, coming in at number three and number four, respectively—rather better than the thirty-fifth place managed by Diane Abbott (who was later given a front-bench job shadowing public health). Top spot, however, went to someone who had declined to stand—Balls's wife, Yvette Cooper—and second place went to John Healey, one of those who had backed Balls but then swung it for Ed by giving him his second preference. Cooper was one of eight women to be elected, six of them for the first time, including, in tenth place, Caroline Flint, who had famously quit Gordon Brown's government complaining of pressure, bullying, and being treated as 'window dressing'. The other female incumbent was the supposedly 'ultra-Blairite', former Olympics minister Tessa Jowell. MPs also found room for other prominent supporters of David Miliband, such as Alan Johnson, Douglas Alexander, and Jim Murphy, although out went Blairites Pat McFadden and Ben Bradshaw. Ed's campaign manager, Sadiq Khan, was one of the new boys, and Ed-supporting incumbents such as Hilary Benn and John Denham remained *in situ*. Another Ed supporter, Peter Hain, finished in twenty-first place but was co-opted as Shadow Welsh Secretary, as well as Chair of the party's National Policy Forum (NPF) and Miliband's link man with its NEC.

To an old hand like Jack Straw, who had announced his retirement from the front bench over the summer, the whole process was 'barking mad' and meant the inclusion of 'half a dozen' people who were not up to the job. Miliband, however, as he was duty-bound to do, confessed himself delighted. He then immediately surprised everybody by naming as Shadow Chancellor Alan Johnson, rather than Ed Balls (who went to shadow the Home Office) or the equally well-qualified Yvette Cooper (who, after refusing to shadow Vince Cable at Business, became Shadow Foreign Secretary). This move looked in some ways like a canny one. Johnson was one of the few Labour politicians to whom (in the minds of journalists anyway) the public warmed, and he had been very much a cheerleader for David during the leadership campaign—so much so that he had not held back from firing a few warning shots across Ed's bows not long after the results were announced. The appointment of a man not known for taking much of an interest in economic policy was risky, but at least it limited the potential for a Blair–Brown scenario—something that might have arisen had he appointed Balls, who had very decided views of his own and who knew all about building an alternative powerbase to a party leader.

The decision not to have Balls shadow the Treasury also suggested that Miliband was alive to concerns that Balls's forthright, Keynesian critique of the government's austerity programme could be painted— indeed, was already being painted—as 'deficit denial'. To Conservatives and their friends in the media, such an approach typified Labour's refusal to acknowledge that its enthusiasm for borrowing even in good times, while it might not have caused the global financial meltdown, was at least partly to blame for the mess in which it had left the nation's finances. Clearly, Johnson, as a Cabinet Minister, bore some collective responsibility for the economic policy of the Labour government. But he was nowhere near as closely associated with it as Balls (or even, for that matter, Miliband). He was also acknowledged as 'a safe pair of hands' in parliament and good on broadcast media. There was also every chance that, as well as providing some much-needed variety in a Shadow Cabinet that contained at least ten people who had been privately educated as well as nine Oxbridge graduates, Johnson's very ordinary origins would provide a politically useful contrast with those of Conservative Chancellor George Osborne, heir to a baronetcy. In the meantime, it was announced that the new Shadow Chancellor and Leader of the Opposition would, as Osborne and Cameron had done, supposedly work in offices with a shared anteroom so as to allow their teams to work closely together.

There were other bits and pieces of good news, too. Miliband's decision to persuade the Chief Whip, Nick Brown, not to stand for re-election seemed to have paid off. Although he was unable to persuade Andy Burnham (whom he eventually installed at Education) to take the job, he had nevertheless taken one of the more controversial figures of the old regime out of the game, replacing him with Rosie Winterton—a far less divisive pick. The need to fill junior places on the front bench also allowed for the fast-track promotion of MPs from the new intake who were seen as loyalists as well as potential rising stars, most obviously Rachel Reeves, who went to the Department of Work and Pensions (DWP), and Chuka Umunna, who was made Ed's Parliamentary Private Secretary (PPS). Meanwhile, the Tories were in trouble over their decision to remove child benefit from households that contained a higher-rate taxpayer. The move would save the Treasury a lot of money, and was regarded with equanimity by most voters, the vast majority of whom were in no danger of losing any money on the deal. However, as well as hitting a group of people well able to complain about being hit, it also undermined the principle that this was a benefit that should go to all mothers, regardless of income. And it created an absurd anomaly whereby a two-parent family whose joint income was actually quite high would hang onto the benefit as long as each partner earned under the limit, whereas a single-parent earning just over the limit would lose it.

Although it could be, and was, pointed to as evidence that 'we're all in this together', the government's child-benefit announcement went down badly with some of its natural supporters, with the *Daily Mail*—always keen to defend family values—in the vanguard. The hostile reaction eventually led to some (arguably cosmetic) adjustments being made. In the meantime, however, the announcement created an opportunity that Miliband eagerly—perhaps too eagerly—seized in order to emphasize a point he had made immediately following his victory—namely, that, as he put it in the Tory-supporting *Sunday Telegraph* the morning after the night before, his aim was 'to show that our party is on the side of the squeezed middle in our country and everyone who has worked hard and wants to get on'.[1] This was a line that Miliband's team—and few could criticize their message discipline on this one at least—was to turn into something approaching a mantra over the coming weeks and months.

In fact, the idea of the squeezed middle was actually nothing new. Work done by Liam Byrne in the last year or so of the Labour government had revealed that the British economy had not actually been delivering the rise in living standards for ordinary people that, given its steady growth until 2007–8, one would have expected. This was also familiar to policy people such as Gavin Kelly and Nick Pearce, formerly of Number Ten but now back in think tanks. In an article published in the centre-left magazine *Prospect* in August, they had pointed to mounting evidence on both sides of the Atlantic that showed that the real incomes of ordinary people had been stagnating over the long term and not just since the global financial crisis.[2] It should also have had a familiar ring to anyone who recalled Gordon Brown's last party conference speech as Prime Minister in 2009, when he noted: 'When markets falter and banks fail it's the jobs and the homes and the security of the squeezed middle that are hit the hardest. It's the hard pressed, hard working majority—the person with a trade, the small business owner, the self-employed. It's the class room assistant, the worker in the shop, the builder on the site.' That Brown had used the phrase and Miliband had simply recycled it would have come as no surprise to those who had backed his brother in the leadership contest, many of whom bemoaned (even if they understood) David's decision during it not to tar Ed as a Brownite in the same way that some of Ed's supporters had tarred him as a Blairite. More importantly, there was the issue, evident in the inclusion of almost every walk of life in Brown's use of the term, of defining exactly who it was supposed to refer to—an obvious question that journalists did not take long to pursue, and one on which Miliband famously floundered when tackled on it by combative *Today Programme* presenter John Humphrys later on in the autumn.[3] Still, the fact that so many people saw themselves as struggling while the super-rich, at one end, and those in receipt of welfare benefits, at the other, carried on regardless, meant the term caught on with journalists. Because of the row over child benefit it also helped Miliband to get off to a respectable, if not a flying, start at his first Prime Minister's Questions (PMQs) as Leader of the Opposition—an occasion that over the course of the next four-and-a-half years was, on balance, to provide him with more lows than highs.

If the government's withdrawal of child benefit allowed Miliband something of a free hit, at least initially, one of the next items in its in-tray—what to do about university funding—was a much more obviously double-edged sword. True, the recommendation in the Browne report (commissioned by the Labour government) that student tuition fees be increased substantially was clearly going to pose problems for the Coalition, especially for the Lib Dems. Nick Clegg had been unable to persuade his party before the election to drop its pledge to abolish fees entirely and had therefore campaigned on it—which was one reason why, along with his performance in the televised leadership debates and the Lib Dems' opposition to the Iraq war, they had done well among younger voters. The party had already shed a significant amount of support purely as a result of joining the Conservatives in coalition. The announcement, in the wake of the Browne report, that fees would not only stay but would have to rise—and that the Lib Dems would not in fact be exercising their right to vote against the policy—was the final straw for those Lib Dem voters who had been unsure about the Coalition but were initially willing to give it the benefit of the doubt. The fact that Clegg's parliamentary party then split three ways on the vote (27 voting for, 21 against, and 8 abstaining) only made matters worse. By early December, a poll of 2010 Lib Dem voters conducted for Lord Ashcroft, the Conservative peer who had decided to expand his range of political interests into opinion research, was suggesting that just over half of them had abandoned the party, with just over one in five saying they were intending now to vote Labour.[4]

This was ostensibly good news for Miliband, and not just for his party. After all, he had openly declared during the leadership contest, not least in response to polling evidence that supported the idea, that one way Labour could turn things around was to make a pitch for disaffected Lib Dems—a strategy that was bound to appeal to those who had been brought up on the notion, beautifully encapsulated in David Marquand's book *The Progressive Dilemma*, that reuniting the two sides of the centre-left would unlock a latent anti-Tory majority.[5] Its new-found scepticism towards ID cards, the Iraq war, and tuition fees (which were now the trigger for student riots in central London) were at the very heart of that pitch. As long as Miliband did not allow Labour's enthusiasm for attacking Clegg to distract it from attacking Cameron, too—which was one reason why the word had gone out from the leader's office that Labour spokespeople were henceforth to refer to the Coalition as the Tory-led government—then tuition fees provided the party with a golden opportunity to pick up support. But there was one big problem: Alan Johnson, as Shadow Chancellor, was, to say the least, highly sceptical about his leader's policy of replacing fees (which, after all, he had personally steered through the Commons in 2004 as Higher Education Minister) with a graduate tax. Indeed, on the very same day that Ed was advocating the latter in one newspaper, another carried an interview with Johnson in which he confessed he was doubtful it could work.[6]

Had that been the only difference of opinion between the two men, it might have been less a topic of gossip and concern, especially after Johnson publicly bowed to pressure and penned an article for *The Times* a few days later arguing that 'there is a strong case for a graduate tax, which may offer a fairer way of sharing costs between individuals and government'.[7] Unfortunately, it was also well known, not least because Johnson, who must have known what he was doing, was happy to tell print and broadcast journalists that the Shadow Chancellor did not agree with his leader that the 50p top rate for the highest earners should be made permanent rather than a temporary response to hard times. Like tuition fees, tax was a totemic issue—one that, in the case of the top rate anyway, symbolized New Labour's commitment (or, if you were on the left, capitulation) to the vision of a liberal, aspirational society where people were welcome to get 'filthy rich' (as Peter Mandelson had once put it) as long as that meant the economy carried on growing at a rate sufficient to pay for improvements to public services. That said, as Johnson himself stressed on several occasions, there was time enough to make a decision on such matters. The party's main aim had to be to restore voters' faith in its economic competence. Despite its presiding over a decade of respectable growth, high employment, and low inflation and interest rates, Labour's reputation on the issue had been destroyed by a combination of the global financial meltdown and the Coalition taking every opportunity, especially while the opposition had its eye off the ball during its leadership contest, to blame the UK's debt and deficit on its supposed profligacy in power between 1997 and 2010.

Quite how the restoration of Labour's 'economic credibility' that commentators sagely agreed was vital could be achieved in opposition was by no means clear, however. Obviously, a start could be, and was, made. For one thing, Labour spokespeople could admit—as Miliband himself did in a speech to the Fabian Society's Conference in the New Year—to making 'serious mistakes' in government, although even this was trickier than it sounded. First, unless they thought they would be able get away with repeating *ad nauseam* 'failing properly to regulate the banks', then they would inevitably be asked for more specific instances and hence provide even more sticks with which the party could then be beaten. Second, some sort of 'masochism strategy' left little or no opportunity to combat the prevailing belief among voters—one naturally encouraged by the government and its friends in the media—that Labour had recklessly 'maxed out the nation's credit card' (as the Conservatives cleverly put it) when the truth (as least as most Labour people saw it) was that the hole in the nation's finances was largely down to propping up the banks, paying out benefits to the casualties of the downturn, and a collapse in tax revenues. Realizing, as Alistair Darling and others had told Gordon Brown at the time, that the Labour government's refusal to talk about the need for cuts was counterproductive and expressing an appropriate degree of contrition was one thing. Effectively helping your opponents to trash your own record, and thus your brand, was another.

Whatever, the Tories' success in embedding their narrative 'led us to conclude early on', a close adviser to Miliband admitted 'that there was no point trying to contest their account of the past—that we had to be future-oriented'. In his view, 'that helped us because we wanted a change-message anyway'. But there was a downside—and one that did not do Miliband any favours with some of his colleagues. Such a strategy may have been wholly consistent with Ed's determination to distance himself from both Blair and Brown during the leadership campaign. But it also seemed to mean making no serious attempt to defend any of the achievements of its thirteen years in government— something that drove lots of MPs to distraction, especially if they were Blairites and especially if they represented deprived constituencies that, in the words of one of them, were 'absolutely transformed' after 1997.

There were other things that could be done, of course, to counter Tory propaganda. Labour spokespeople could be careful not to dismiss the need to make savings, stressing they would be selective in their response to the Coalition's ideas for making them. On the other hand, it was far too early to start coming up with a list of additional cuts, not least because the only ones worth any serious money—pensions, welfare, housing, and defence, say—were questionable in principle and bound to alienate large numbers of voters. And, in any case, advocating them so soon after being in office would have prompted journalists to ask why, if they were such a great idea, Labour had not implemented them when it had had the chance? Moreover, since Labour—and Johnson himself—was convinced that the scale of the cuts proposed by the Coalition would choke off the nascent recovery over which the Brown government had presided, it did not make much sense to argue that the opposition was urging the government to go further and faster. The policy response required from the party was obviously going to be rather different if the economy tipped into recession, which was considered unlikely but could not be ruled out. Even worse, whether another recession did or did not happen, the likelihood was that some sort of recovery would be underway by the next general election. If and when that happened, Labour's policy would have to shift again, although whether such a shift would make much of a difference if the government were able to generate some sort of feel-good factor was surely a moot point.

Furthermore, all this presumes that the electorate were interested in anything Labour had to say anyway. Seeing as it was only a matter of months since they had given the party its marching orders, this was surely unlikely. Indeed, it was more likely that stories about Miliband's forgetting to get himself registered as the father of his first child and his decision to take paternity leave after the birth of his second child in early November gained greater cut-through than the detail of Labour's stance (or lack of one) on the debt and the deficit. The truth, however prosaic, was that what the party most needed to do was to avoid giving hostages to fortune while it gave itself time to think and to allow the effects of the Coalition's fiscal consolidation strategy to become clear. In any case, unless the Coalition collapsed early (which could not be completely ruled out but which was deemed unlikely), Labour was in for a five-year long haul.

Alan Johnson was in some ways the perfect man to oversee that holding operation—or would have been had he not, rather uncharacteristically given his reputation as the ultimate 'safe pair of hands', begun to make one or two silly mistakes in interviews, which, while they would have passed the average citizen by completely, were pounced on by the Conservatives to stoke speculation that he was not up to this particular job. Just before Christmas, Miliband had announced the appointment of not one but two people to oversee Labour's media operation, both from print journalism. Having tried and failed to tempt Steve Richards, journalist, broadcaster, and author of a revisionist book on Gordon Brown, to take the job, Miliband chose to split it.[8] Bob Roberts, Political Editor of the *Mirror*, the Labour-supporting tabloid, was brought in as Director of News, primarily to handle the lobby at Westminster, while Tom Baldwin, the more controversial *Times* Chief Reporter, was appointed Director of Strategy and Communications—a role that inevitably saw him billed as Miliband's very own Alastair Campbell. The need to do something in this area had become increasingly obvious—glaring, some said, in the light of the messy way Labour handled the admittedly difficult case of immigration spokesperson Phil Woolas, whose parliamentary career was ended after an investigation into electoral malpractice.[9] Getting the right people, however, had been far harder than it should have been—not least because Fleet Street's finest were far from sure that, if they took the job, they would be joining the winning side.

The first big test for the new media team came almost immediately. Not long after Christmas, the Shadow Chancellor had managed to distract from Labour's otherwise successful attack on bankers' bonuses and the government's VAT rise as 'the wrong tax at the wrong time' by making another couple of unforced errors in interviews. Those closest to him put it down to the fact that 'AJ just hated the job', but it transpired that there was more to it even than that: Johnson's ten-year marriage was falling apart. After giving his boss a week's notice—a long time in the circumstances—Johnson announced his resignation. This left Miliband and his advisers anxiously weighing up an obvious choice. If he appointed Ed Balls as Shadow Chancellor, Balls's combative personality and command of economics would sharpen Labour's attack: the first duty of an opposition, after all, is to oppose and in so doing undermine the government's case for re-election. Another point in the idea's favour—not to be underestimated, given the need to project an image of calm decision—was that it would make an instant reshuffle relatively easy. Yvette Cooper could take over the Home Office brief from her husband, and could hand over the Foreign Affairs portfolio (where many thought she was wasted) to Douglas Alexander. Fears that this would represent some sort of belated triumph for the Brownites could be assuaged by appointing the Blairite Liam Byrne to take on the DWP brief and adding him to a select group of Shadow Cabinet Ministers who would supposedly oversee strategy. In any case, other than Balls, who else was there? Moreover, not appointing him surely risked being seen either as a calculated snub or else as evidence that Miliband was too scared of his rival to make him, effectively, his number two?

But the downsides were considerable. This could turn out to be what economists and political scientists are fond of calling a 'critical juncture'—an event that effectively commits one to accepting a course of action even though it begins to look as if an alternative might have been better. For a start, Balls would find it next to impossible, both temperamentally and intellectually, to concede Labour made serious mistakes, and would be portrayed by Osborne not just as a 'deficit denier' but also as one of the architects of Gordon Brown's manifestly deluded claim to have 'abolished boom and bust'. Moreover, if Miliband did move Balls into the job he seemed to feel was his by right, he would lose any realistic hope of controlling the party's strategy on the issue that was more likely than any other to decide the next election. Balls was convinced—and any number of economists agreed with him—that, even if the UK economy eventually recovered, it would be severely and unnecessarily damaged by the government's austerity policies. He would, therefore, be bound to emphasize the message that the government was going 'too far, too fast'—a line that risked crowding out other messages and leaving Labour high and dry if the economy did recover, however unimpressive that recovery might be. And then, inevitably, there was the question of Balls's collegiality: he had certainly tried his best during the leadership contest, but could he work together as part of a team, especially when he himself was not the leader (or the leader's *éminence grise*) and when he had long regarded the man who was the leader as his junior?[10]

In the end, having got Balls's agreement that the so-called Darling plan would continue (as it had under Johnson) to form the basis of Labour's deficit reduction strategy, Miliband and his inner circle decided to risk it—comforted, perhaps, by the fact that, unlike Brown, who never fought and lost a leadership contest against Blair, Balls, who had fought such a contest and come a poor third, could hardly harbour the illusion that he was owed big-time for supposedly gifting the top job to another man. Few believed for a moment all the stuff about 'two Eds being better than one' or that sharing a suite of offices would prevent any independent briefing. But maybe Balls's appointment might see the two men working in harness, if not in complete harmony. Indeed there was one very good reason why the whole thing might not turn into a Blair–Brown-style psychodrama: as Miliband put it to the *Independent*'s Andrew Grice in an interview shortly afterwards: 'We have seen that movie before and had front row seats. We are determined that there will be no sequel. It was a formative experience for both of us. It is something we are absolutely determined to avoid.'[11] More immediately, Miliband may also have believed that Balls's wiggle-room was now smaller than it might have been, since, on the weekend prior to the Johnson story breaking, and after ensuring Shadow Cabinet buy-in, the Labour leader had followed up his Fabian conference speech by a round of interviews in which, as well as admitting his party should have done more to regulate the City and to reduce the country's reliance on financial services, he confessed it should have been clearer about the need to reduce the deficit and to do so by making spending cuts.

In some ways, however, that speech illustrated Labour's central problem—one that Balls's appointment was likely to exacerbate rather than alleviate. Milband's moderate *mea culpa* was supposed to help earn the party 'permission to be heard' by an electorate that up till now had been too angry to listen. Yet it was balanced by the simultaneous insistence that it was the financial crisis rather than Labour's excessive debt-fuelled spending that had blown a hole in the nation's finances. The fact was that the public believed that it was both—and that the likelihood that they could ever be dissuaded from thinking that was vanishingly small. It was (and this was arguably something David Miliband would have grasped intuitively) a waste of time trying. Indeed, like every 'sorry, but', qualified apology, it was counterproductive, because it muddied the waters and prevented the main message being heard. Ironically, it was all there in *The Unfinished Revolution* by Philip Gould—New Labour's bible-cum-playbook in the early years and one that also had a profound impact on Conservative modernizers: if you have lost the argument, then, almost irrespective of who was right and who was wrong, you should 'concede and move on'.[12]

What Cameron and his colleagues did appreciate, however, was that opposition was one thing, office another. Out of power, parties are price-takers. Only in it can they be price-makers. Opportunities fundamentally to shape events and voter preferences are few and far between and have to be grabbed with both hands on those rare occasions when, because of some crisis or another, they arise—just as they were grabbed by Attlee in 1945 and Thatcher in 1979, but not by Blair, who allowed a combination of his initial inexperience, his overriding fear of the country's right-wing media, his inability to control his Chancellor of the Exchequer, and his commitment to standing 'shoulder to shoulder' with the USA, to derail his dream of persuading British voters that the facts of life (as Thatcher once put it) were not Tory but essentially progressive and inevitably European. Cameron and Osborne (even more so, perhaps) were clearly determined, however, just as their role model had been thirty years before, to use the economic disaster that had befallen Britain to reshape or even shrink the state—particularly, in their case, when it came to welfare spending.

If the debate about which aspects of the massive consolidation proposed by the Coalition to accept and which to reject had been merely a matter of political positioning, it would have been hard enough. Neither Miliband nor Balls, for instance, seemed to want to acknowledge that, for every £10 billion worth of cuts Osborne was proposing, the Darling plan had committed Labour to £8 billion, meaning that—if they had decided to level with the electorate and get specific (which they were singularly reluctant to do)—all manner of supposedly worthy initiatives would have to go. But it was not merely a matter of positioning. The government's consolidation pro-gramme was also bound to have a huge, and in many cases almost immediate, impact on the interests of trade unions, which had not only helped Miliband to win the leadership but were now providing the party with the majority of its funding. As George Eaton of the *New Statesman* reminded readers: 'Back in 1994, when Tony Blair became Labour leader, trade unions accounted for just a third of the party's annual income.'[13] However, as he went on to point out, recently released figures from the Electoral Commission showed how this has changed.

In quarter four of 2010, the party received £2,545,611 in donations (exclud-ing public funds or 'short money'), £2,231,741.90 or 88 per cent of which came from the unions, compared to 36 per cent in the final quarter of 2009. Private donations have all but collapsed since Ed Miliband became leader, with just £39,286 raised from individual donations to CLPs. In total, the unions were responsible for 62 per cent of all Labour funding last year (up from 60 per cent in 2009), with one union, Unite, providing nearly a quarter (23 per cent) of all donations.

Miliband could hardly afford to ignore such figures, especially because, at the very same conference at which he had been declared Labour's new leader, it was revealed that the 2010 election, during which it had been heavily outspent by the Conservatives, had left the party £12 million in debt. This was probably why, when he was weighing up whether to address the TUC's anti-cuts 'March for the Alternative', which attracted between a quarter and a half a million protesters to central London on 26 March 2011, he eventually decided to attend—even if, in the end, he tried to have it both ways by admitting the 'need for difficult choices, and some cuts' at the same time as arguing that 'we are standing on the shoulders of those who have marched and struggled for great causes in the past' and were part not of a minority but of the 'mainstream majority'.[14] Unfortunately for him, however, it was the actions of the minority—a group of masked, self-styled anarchists who began attacking police, banks, and shops in the capital's wealthy West End—that attracted headlines, the only consolation being that few voters would have been watching live and therefore seen the split-screen juxtaposition of his speech to the rally in Hyde Park and the violence, which kicked off just as he was speaking.

The speech—apart from the passing acknowledgement that savings were needed—actually went down reasonably well. But, to some, that was all part of the problem. Miliband was, in effect, preaching to the converted—or, rather, the unconverted in the sense that his audience, unlike the majority of the country if the polls were to be believed, could see neither rhyme nor reason for the cuts the government was making. Their mood was actually caught by the *Economist*'s Bagehot blogging from a 'People's Policy Forum', organized the previous day in Nottingham not by the unions but by the Labour Party itself:

For hour after hour, in policy session after policy session, Mr Miliband and his shadow ministerial team were bombarded with angry, self-righteous demands for Labour to wave a magic wand and make the cuts go away. Denial does not begin to cover the mood . . . This was more like a gathering of exiled loyalists after a revolution, demanding to be led back to the promised homeland by their battered, bloodied chiefs . . . Of all the scores of people who raised their hands to ask questions or make mini-speeches, not one appeared to be from the private sector. There were no entrepreneurs, no small businessmen, no big businessmen. Instead, this was the living, breathing incarnation of what happens when you expand public spending from 40% of GDP to something close to 50%, in the space of a decade.[15]

There was, of course, an upside to all this. Not only did it mean that unions were likely to go on giving to Labour as the only party that stood any conceivable chance of defeating the Coalition at the next election. It also meant that at least some of those who were so enraged by its austerity programme might consider joining Labour as members. As such, as well as giving the impression that the party was, in some vague way, on the up, they might make some small contribution to improving the party's finances, too: in 2010, for example, membership subscriptions and related giving had raised over £7 million. More important, however, was the possibility that they might provide proverbial 'boots on the ground' for Labour, both in local campaigns and at the general election scheduled (in the new Fixed Term Parliaments Bill) for May 2015. Labour sources were already boasting about an influx of members over the summer (confirmed as an additional 46,000 by November 2010)—some of them presumably disgruntled Lib Dem supporters. However, it was well aware that, like other parties in the UK, and Europe more generally, it had been haemorrhaging members for years—indeed, its losses may well have been higher than those of its rivals, since it had been in government for thirteen years and was therefore as likely to have disappointed as to have delighted its supporters. And even those who had stuck with the party through thick and thin had felt that it had largely taken them for granted after taking office back in 1997. David Miliband's response to all this—inspired by former Cabinet Minister James Purnell—had been to try to integrate lessons learned from campaigning organization Citizens UK into an organization called Movement for Change, which had been set up during the leadership contest but which he hoped, if and when he became leader, he could use to re-energize the party itself. Ed Miliband's response, once he had become leader, was, in November 2010, to invite veteran MP and former Cabinet Minister Peter Hain (one of his earliest backers in the leadership contest) to conduct a stock-taking exercise.

In May 2011 Hain produced a consultation paper entitled *Refounding Labour*.[16] Rather than setting out any kind of vision, it focused on setting out the challenges Labour was facing and soliciting suggestions. It did not, however, mince its words, arguing that the party 'still looks inward rather than outward, is stuck in its structures, and is not engaged with local communities or national civil society'. The influx of new joiners since 2010 was noted, as was the fact that some 130,000 members (around 70 per cent of the total membership) had voted in the leadership contest. But so too was the fact that, when Labour lost power, membership was just 40 per cent of what it had been when the party had entered office in 1997 and it was also ageing and in many cases inactive. As a result, the paper went on to note, 'we are still spread pretty thinly on the ground, and with a weak base from which to develop contacts in the community and build popular support'. Getting people to help out on the phone during elections was not so much a problem—indeed the incentives provided to CLPs had meant that volunteers had made a big contribution to the voter identification effort that helped the party turn what could have been a complete meltdown in 2010 into something slightly less catastrophic. But persuading people to do the traditional, 'doorstep' stuff—canvassing, leafleting, and so on—was getting more and more difficult. This mattered because, as 2010 and the very different outcomes around the country showed, local effort between and during election campaigns could make a real difference.

In these circumstances, the paper argued, the party had to think hard about both recruitment and retention. Already, many who did join quickly came to believe that, despite the existence of the party's various Policy Forums and the tradition of sending in resolutions, they had no tangible impact on policy. Conference was less and less well attended by constituency delegates and was seen by many as a corporate event rather than Labour's constitutionally supreme decision-making body. It was prohibitively expensive to go to, and membership itself was not that cheap either: true, in 2011 under-19s and all new members under 27 (for the first year only) paid just £1, and there was a £20.50 rate for the unwaged, retired, and political levy-paying union members; but the standard rate was £41. Would making it less expensive help—or would it simply sacrifice valuable income, since the real problem was not cost but motivation, especially in an era where politics could find expression in so many different ways and there were so many competing temptations and demands on people's time? Potential and actual members clearly were not keen on procedurally focused branch meetings, meaning that the burden was falling on a dwindling band of activists, who understandably found it hard to cope. 'Too often', the paper lamented, 'members join up, pitch in and burn out'.

Social media, Hain went on to suggest, offered considerable opportunities, both when it came to 'closing the gap between leaders and led' and when it came to campaigning. Indeed, the party's use of ICT in 2010 had contributed to the fact that, despite having only a third of the paid staff it had employed during the 2005 contest, Labour had actually managed to make three times the number of contacts with voters. However, it was no panacea. As the party had found in 2010, it was one thing to contact your supporters, another to get them to the polls. Nor was it always easy for an organization built geographically to know how best to use technology that knew no such boundaries—something that a party whose leader (and the brother he had defeated) was keen on 'community organizing' (genuine, two way, hyper-local effort based on discovering people's concerns and helping them to mobilize collectively to address them) had to figure out. Critics could legitimately ask just how interactive electronic communication between 'leaders and led' really was, and just how representative those who got involved 'virtually', rather than in person, really were. As the paper put it, 'many of those engaged in blogging and posting comments on websites seem at least as remote from the concerns of everyday voters as the most rules-obsessed General Committee delegate'.

This willingness to rethink something so fundamental was, superficially at least, encouraging. But it was far from an immediate priority—not when there were elections coming up that were bound to be seen by the media as Miliband's first big test. In the event, it was one he was deemed to have passed, but only narrowly. Labour made gains as the Lib Dems suffered at the hands of voters unimpressed by their decision to go into coalition with a Conservative Party whose vote share held up depressingly well, partly perhaps because it was doing its best to ensure that local authorities made cuts to services rather than impose big increases in council tax. Where the Tories did not do well, of course, was in Scotland, which, however, managed to provide an even bigger blow to Labour. Alex Salmond's Scottish National Party (SNP) managed to do what many had imagined was the impossible—namely, winning an overall majority in a parliament elected using proportional representation. That win could be—and was—discounted down in London by Labour by portraying it as a reaction to the Tory-led government at Westminster and by pointing out that Scottish voters had always proved themselves more willing to lend their support to the SNP at elections to Holyrood than they were at general elections. Nonetheless, for a party that had been concerned for decades about losing what had once been its iron grip north of the border, and that supplied a fair few frontbenchers at Westminster, it was a worrying development: there was nothing now that could stop Salmond calling a referendum on independence, which, even if lost, would make it much, much harder for Labour to win a majority in what remained of the United Kingdom.

Constitutional questions were also the flavour of the month in the country as a whole—although, as always, more for those heavily involved or interested in politics than for the bulk of the electorate.

On 5 May 2011, as well as local elections, there was also the nation-wide referendum on the Lib Dems' proposal to change the system used for general elections from First Past the Post to the Alternative Vote (AV)—a system that, while not proportional, supposedly achieved a greater modicum of fairness by allowing electors to rank order their preferences. Labour's position on the issue was theoretically clear but in practice highly ambivalent. At the fag-end of the last parliament, the Brown government, casting around for some means of demonstrating its commitment to political renewal in the wake of the MPs expenses scandal, had pledged itself to hold a referendum on the voting system. For reasons that had more to do with securing grudging agreement within the party than principled consideration, it had lighted on AV as its preferred alternative—much to the disgust, at the time, of the Lib Dems, whose leader Nick Clegg had called it a 'miserable little compromise'. When negotiating his coalition with David Cameron, however, it had soon become clear to Clegg that AV—or rather a referendum on AV—was the best he was going to be able to get from the Conservatives, whose resistance to change meant they would be campaigning on the 'no' side. Given Labour's support for AV in its manifesto, it would have been logical for it to have campaigned for a yes. However, there were well over 100 Labour MPs (out of around 250) publicly opposed to the change. Electoral reform had long been seen by many Labour people as something only the 'chattering classes' were really interested in, and now it been rendered virtually untouch-able by virtue of its being backed by Clegg, whose reputation with the public was sinking even further and faster than his worst enemies had predicted.

As a result, Miliband, even though he (along with over fifty parlia-mentary colleagues) had publicly declared himself in favour of the change, knew that it would be impossible to establish a party line on the issue. He had therefore effectively allowed Labour both inside and outside Westminster a free vote. This had allowed some 200 Labour MPs and peers to sign up to the no-holds-barred *NotoAV* campaign, notwithstanding the fact that the vast bulk of its funding came from Conservative Party donors. And, as it became more and more obvious that AV was going down to defeat, even some of those Labour people who were in favour—including Miliband himself—were accused of not putting much effort or enthusiasm into efforts to turn things around. If they were right, then Miliband could hardly be blamed:

why on earth waste time and political capital on a doomed cause that had proved unpopular with the public—especially when supporting it would place him in the same camp as the Deputy Prime Minister, now the nation's least favourite politician? Indeed, so toxic had Clegg become that the Labour leader had simply refused to share a platform with him throughout the campaign.

Inasmuch as Labour supporters were, as some polls suggested, the swing voters in the referendum, then these mixed signals were hardly likely to inspire sufficient numbers of them to vote yes. Accordingly, the referendum was defeated 68:32. Since most academic research suggested that AV might well have favoured the Lib Dems, whose candidates would have attracted the second preferences of both Labour and Tory voters, the result was far from disastrous for Miliband. Moreover, he had polished his credentials as a progressive—no bad thing given his determination to win over disillusioned Lib Dem supporters—but without putting either his own reputation or that of his party on the line.

But what was Miliband's reputation after six months or so in the job? How was he seen by the voters? As a succession of Tory leaders who had tried and failed to beat Blair before David Cameron had come along in 2005 could attest, first impressions count—if only because they often prove very difficult to shift. If this really was so, then Miliband was in serious trouble. He had begun, in late September 2010, in positive territory, according to YouGov, which asks its respondents to rate how well or badly party leaders are doing. However, by the end of November his ratings were negative, and in their first polling conducted after the local and Scottish elections and the AV referendum, just 33 per cent of people thought he was doing well against 49 per cent who thought he was doing badly—a net figure of −16, which was much lower than Cameron's current net rating of −4, although nowhere near as bad as Clegg's −45![17] A better comparison, however, may be with recent Leaders of the Opposition. In May 2011, Mori recorded Miliband as having a net satisfaction rating of −8 with voters as a whole and +24 with voters intending to support Labour. This was, of course, nowhere near Tony Blair, who scored +30 and +60 respectively, but no one really expected that. However, it did put him above William Hague in 1997, who scored −23 and −13, Iain Duncan Smith in 2002 (−9 and +21), and Michael Howard in 2004 (−12 and +48). On the other hand, Miliband ranked just below David

Cameron, who at the same point in his leadership in 2006 had had a net positive rating from the public (albeit only of +2) and party supporters (+28) alike. It was not a terrible start, then, but it was hardly auspicious.[18]

Perhaps more worrying, however, were the leaks from Tory focus groups purporting to show that voters' abiding impression of Miliband so far was of someone who not only looked too young to do the job and was best known for shafting his older brother, but who looked and sounded 'odd'. One could argue that this was hardly his fault and ask rhetorically what exactly was he expected to do about it? Sure, a voice coach might help—and maybe an operation that Miliband underwent in August 2011 to correct a nasal problem might help too. But his face? That was his face. What did people want? Cosmetic surgery and all-American dentistry?

That said, it is possible to argue that Miliband and those advising him had only himself—and themselves—to blame. He had made a point of rejecting the idea that he should follow David Cameron's example and provide the press and public with eye-catching images of himself: a trip to the frozen north, cycling to work, and relaxing with his photogenic family. In November 2010, just a couple of months after taking up the leadership, Miliband insisted to the *Guardian*'s Allegra Stratton and Patrick Wintour that opposition was 'about digging in', not about huskies, 'short-term fixes nor short cuts to success'.[19]

To those closest to him, Miliband's self-denying ordinance was only sensible: after all, Gordon Brown had tried all sorts of gimmicks to no great effect, and had the Tories not just tried and failed to win themselves a majority by opting for a makeover rather than a root-and-branch rethink? To his critics, however, Miliband's words betrayed an astonishing arrogance: did he really think he could single-handedly reshape how politics had come to be covered in the twenty-first century? Cameron, for all his famous self-confidence and supposed superficiality, had not, they argued, made the same mistake. True, the fact that he had fought a long-run contest against an opponent he had already effectively beaten had given him considerably more time than Miliband had had between effectively knowing the top job was his and actually starting it. But, as a former public-relations (PR) man, he had nevertheless used that time well, thinking a great deal about how to communicate to the public in the most basic way possible that here was an engaging fresh face, a family man, a 'new man' even, who was willing and able to do things very differently from those who had gone before him.[20] On the upside, Miliband's camera-shyness meant that he avoided the disastrous mistakes made by William Hague, whose gauche attempts to look trendy, or even just like a regular guy, by posing at the Notting Hill Carnival and Alton Towers had instead made him a laughing stock. On the other hand, the Labour leader's decision not to provide the media with arresting visual images *à la* Cameron was surely a missed opportunity to help define himself rather than allow others—often with malign intent—to define him instead.

As with personality, so with policies. In the run-up to a 'we've got to change to win' speech to the Party's NPF at the end of November 2010, Miliband let it be known that he would be commissioning a panoply of policy reviews, coordinated by Liam Byrne, and that he wanted them to start with 'a blank piece of paper'—hence the Forum's slogan 'New Politics: Fresh Ideas'. This approach was intended to be inspiring; but it was risky, too, inevitably prompting the accusation that he did not really know what he wanted and therefore had no strategy. In some ways of course, the policy reviews *were* the strategy, or at least part of it, providing him, as similar exercises had provided his predecessors, both with some breathing space and (if credible, well-known outsiders could be brought in to help with them, as they were by Cameron) a chance to persuade the public that Labour really was doing some fresh (and non-dogmatic, non-tribal) thinking. But this was not really what happened.

For a start, Miliband announced that, as well as the six policy commissions normally association with the NPF and the nationwide consultation exercise that allowed members and non-members alike to attend events or write in with ideas, there would be twenty-two working groups. This was not necessarily fatal—Margaret Thatcher had allowed far more than that to be set up in her years in opposition. However, it was bound to increase the demands on Liam Byrne—demands that became even more acute after he was moved from the relatively light Cabinet Office portfolio to DWP in the post-Johnson reshuffle. The sheer number of groups also guaranteed that many of them—even assuming they did get off the ground and do some valuable nitty-gritty work that could be pulled together in a 'state of the nation' document a year later—would make little impact on the public consciousness.

That the bulk of the groups were to be led by familiar Labour faces—most of them the Shadow Cabinet members responsible for that particular area—was not necessarily a disadvantage, however. Indeed, this, and the fact that the first phase of the Policy Review was all about frontbenchers (some of whom had been cocooned in Whitehall for years as members of the government) getting out and listening to voters and party members made it more likely that their work would be anchored in both public opinion and real-world experience than in ideological abstraction. This mini-'masochism strategy' exposed the politicians involved to the full force of voter disillusion with Labour's position on, say, welfare and immigration—'a sheet anchor', in the words of one of those heavily involved, that would hopefully mean that it 'would become impossible for Labour to veer off into madness', as it had done in the 1980s. And, because so many MPs were involved, sometimes travelling to and from events around the country together, it meant that pretty much the same messages were internalized by all of them. So while the first, 'listening' stage of Byrne's Policy Review process did not result in much in terms of concrete policy prescriptions, it did contribute to the surprisingly broad agreement at Westminster about both the need for change and the direction it should probably take. This in turn helped preserve and promote party unity at the same time as preventing Labour drifting to the left in the same way that the Tories (who did not start seriously listening to the public until 2005) had drifted off to the right after 1997. Indeed, the Conservative Party's time in opposition under Hague, Duncan Smith, and Howard was almost as important a guide to what not to do for some Labour politicians as their own party's experience under Callaghan and then Foot and Kinnock in the early 1980s.

Labour's first crack at a policy review could not, however, boast an equivalent of Cameron's enlisting Bob Geldof (as much for the sake of achieving 'cut-through' to the public as any substantive contribution he could make) to advise one of the thematic, cross-departmental policy reviews he set up early on in his leadership. Still, keeping things relatively 'in house' would prevent some of the minor headaches experienced by Cameron when, despite his best efforts to maintain some behind-the-scenes control of the process, some of the review groups (most obviously the one on the environment) produced recommendations that the press seized on. And, who knows, it might mean that more of what was produced—assuming anything meaningful was produced—might actually be usable. Cameron's policy groups, for instance, made 782 recommendations in total, of which 120 made it into the manifesto (and 88 into the Coalition agreement)—a 'hit rate' of 15 per cent, which may not look too bad at first glance but would have been even lower if minor suggestions had been excluded from the calculations.

But, if policy would be some time coming—perhaps sensibly so, given the danger of generating ideas that could be either stolen or ridiculed by the government—then Labour could at least make a reasonably convincing claim that some in its ranks were thinking appropriately big thoughts. It was tempting, naturally, to divide them into rival camps. In the blue corner was a collection of academics, politicos, and academics-turned-politicos who in May 2011 released an e-book, *The Labour Tradition and the Politics of Paradox*, featuring so-called Blue Labour essays that seemed to want to reach back beyond New Labour to the party's communitarian, self-organizing, and less statist tradition in the hope of finding inspiration for the future.[21] In the purple corner (or at least in *The Purple Book: A Progressive Future for Labour*), and publishing a few months later in September, were people (for the most part politicians) brought together under the banner of Progress—a Blairite ginger group founded back in the late 1990s by Liam Byrne, Paul Richards, and Derek Draper, funded in part by Labour peer David Sainsbury, chaired by Andrew Adonis, a fellow peer who had been responsible for driving through education reforms in the outgoing Labour government.[22] Anyone actually reading both books, however, would quickly have questioned the boxing analogy. In fact, the Blairites, although they were wary of Blue Labour's nationalism and its nostalgia for traditional family and community structures, seemed every bit as willing to contemplate a radical decentralization of power. This was not just because the evidence suggested that the limits to the party's traditional use of state power had been reached. It was also because both sets of contributors were in some ways looking for an answer to David Cameron's espousal of 'the big society'—the belief that communities could do more and the state less—which, while it attracted little interest on the part of the public (or indeed the bulk of the Conservative Party), attracted the attention of progressives who believed that it might gain traction in the longer term.

The 'face' of Blue Labour (whose ideas and development are help-fully chronicled by journalist and Labour candidate Rowenna Davis in her book *Tangled up in Blue*) was Maurice Glasman, a London academic with a background in community organizing.[23] Miliband had got to know him just as he was looking for some inspiration for Labour's 2010 manifesto, which he was charged with putting together. Glasman, through his friendship with James Purnell and Jon Cruddas, the MP for Dagenham and Rainham, had actually helped David more during the leadership contest, drafting his much-admired Keir Hardie lecture. Nevertheless, Ed had still decided to nominate him as a member of the House of Lords in November 2010 on the grounds that he would help stir up some much needed debate in the party.

A romantic at heart, Glasman believed that Labour—not just in 1997 but all the way back to 1945—had turned itself from a pluralistic movement rooted in the real-life experience of its supporters into a technocratic, managerial machine bent on big government, comprom-ised by its reliance on the tax revenues from finance capital required to pay for it, and captured by a liberal-oriented, change-obsessed agenda that alienated small-c conservative voters and hollowed the party out organizationally. The financial crisis and its election defeat merely exposed problems with Labour's political economy and dysfunctional structure that were there already. It needed to think more long term and 'relationally' and learn from places that already did, not least Germany, whose regional banking, apprenticeship, co-decision, and occupational welfare models had much to teach the UK, and the USA, where community organizing—the idea that politics had to begin by helping to empower communities before it could mobilize votes—first took off. To Miliband, who was temperamentally inclined to believe in the power of ideas and collective action, and who had likewise concluded that Labour could not simply carry on where it had left off, all this was highly attractive. Embracing it also allowed him to differentiate himself not just from Blair but also from Brown. That said, Miliband's embrace of Blue Labour was far from total—he was (and is) too much of a Fabian for that. As his biographers make clear: 'He sees the state as a benevolent but not infallible force, in need of reform and democratisation but, above all else, a crucial instrument for achieving social justice. And the issue that . . . drives his leadership and defines his social democracy is the issue of inequality.'[24]

Those beliefs did not, however, prevent Ed Miliband contributing a foreword to Blue Labour's e-book. Nor did the fact that it was the product of a series of seminars held in London and Oxford that were organized by David-supporter Jon Cruddas, and Jonathan Rutherford, editor of the left-wing journal *Soundings* and an academic at Middlesex University. The other MPs invited were all well-known Blairites, and David Miliband himself attended some of the sessions. His brother's involvement, however, was facilitated by the fact that another of the academics involved, Marc Stears, of University College Oxford, was a friend from his undergraduate days, and by the fact that the seminars were also attended by Stewart Wood, an academic who had worked for Gordon Brown and whom Miliband had elevated to the Lords and appointed as his strategy adviser. It was Wood who drafted Miliband's foreword to the e-book that grew out of the seminars. And, despite the fact that (with the exception of the chapter by the think-tanker Graeme Cooke) the contributions were generally longer on diagnosis than on prescription, the collection managed to attract tens of thousands of downloads and a fair degree of attention from the print media.

Inasmuch as this contributed to a general impression that the party was doing some hard thinking and coming up with new ideas, then, irrespective of whether it was actually read or not, this was useful: one of Margaret Thatcher's biggest achievements in opposition was to convey a sense of intellectual energy that could be contrasted to a government that had supposedly run out of ideas. How much it did to influence, even indirectly, Labour's policies or its organization, however, is much less certain. For one thing, there was no manifesto as such, on either front. For another, while Miliband and his advisers were quite keen on the idea that it would be one of many voices helping to start a debate, key front-line figures (most obviously Balls, Cooper, and Alexander) and institutions (most crucially, the trade unions) showed little sign of interest. Moreover, it is possible to argue that, by acting as an outrider able to stake out 'radically conservative' positions that may have helped Miliband move beyond New Labour's supposedly naive enthusiasm for all things global, Blue Labour—on some issues at least—may not so much have sparked a debate as made discussion more difficult. A good example is Glasman's provocative remarks on immigration. One of the reasons the e-book was picked up was because its publication followed an interview that Glasman had given to Progress's eponymous magazine.[25] In it, as well as suggesting Labour had to take seriously the concerns of core voters who were tempted by the English Defence League and saw nothing fair in losing out on, say, housing to new arrivals, he argued that under the Blair and Brown governments immigration amounted to 'a real assault on the wage levels of English workers'. Labour, he claimed, had acted in a

> very supercilious, high-handed way: there was no public discussion of immigration and its benefits. There was no election that was fought on that basis. In fact there was a very, very hard rhetoric combined with a very loose policy going on. Labour lied to people about the extent of immigration and the extent of illegal immigration and there's been a massive rupture of trust.

Glasman had a point perhaps. But the language was incendiary and a gift to Labour's opponents, which is why the interview was so eagerly picked up by, among others, the *Daily Mail*. That story earned Glasman a call from Ed Miliband, and may have made it more difficult than it should have been for others to discuss openly what Labour was going to do about an issue that had caused it immense damage at the previous election, especially in the language of culture and identity (rather than simply economics) that Glasman (and Rutherford and Cruddas) were prepared to talk in. The incident also gave some of those who had taken to meeting in parliament once a week to take the Blue Labour agenda forward pause for thought. Their concerns were only compounded by an interview Glasman then gave to the *Telegraph*'s Mary Riddell in which he agreed to the need for a complete stop on immigration at least for a while, arguing that 'Britain is not an outpost of the UN. We have to put the people in this country first.'[26] Although no bridges were burned right down to the ground (Glasman was still invited for a while to so-called friends of Ed meetings and worked with the TUC's Duncan Weldon on an economic prospectus), Blue Labour, in the sense of it being a more or less concerted effort by a group of articulate public intellectuals to shift the party in their direction, was over—at least for a while.

Progress's *Purple Book*, like Blue Labour's effort, also had a foreword by Ed Miliband—one that stressed 'responsibility, our obligations to each other, a sense of solidarity, and people's ability to have a say in shaping the places where they live', as well as sounding the alarm about 'vested interests' and 'a new inequality between the rich and the rest'. But this book, even if a mischievous Matthew Parris at *The Times* may have been right to claim it was 'more brandished than read', was a very different beast.[27] Reflecting its Blairite origins, and the fact that most of its contributors had worked in government, it was more focused, once it had reminded people what the party had achieved in office, on why the party had lost momentum and support after 2005, on what it needed to do to put that right, and on brainstorming policies that would not only help it to win back power but tackle the challenges it would face once there. True, it shared Blue Labour's concerns about the party shrivelling into a statist, top-down, technocratic, target-driven, and bloodless managerialism. It also recognized, as contributors such as Douglas Alexander and Liam Byrne stressed, that New Labour's political economy relied too much on growth and the UK's under-regulated financial services sector generating tax revenue that could then be used for public services and a degree of redistribution. The latter, it noted, was based so much on need rather than on common-sense notions of desert that it led ordinary people, whose wages were not growing as fast as had originally been assumed, to question the inherent fairness of the welfare state. In addition, the interest some of its contributors took in 'pre-distribution'—the argument associated with American academic Jacob Hacker that government should try to ensure that the market provided people with sufficient incomes rather than providing them with a state hand-out after the event—was also shared by several of those associated with Blue Labour.[28] So was the interest shown in mutuals and cooperatives, in active industrial policy, and in asset-based and 'relational' welfare. Nevertheless, despite a chapter (rather presciently entitled 'One Nation Labour: Tackling the Politics of Culture and Identity') from frontbencher Ivan Lewis that dealt with some of Blue Labour's key themes, the *Purple Book* had a fundamental disagreement with what it saw as Glasman and Co.'s backward-looking nostalgia. As the volume's editor, Robert Philpot, put it: 'Rather than reassuring the public that Labour understands, and will help people to manage, the process of change, all too often Blue Labour seems to suggest that the party should attempt to persuade the electorate that it can resist it. This is a false promise and Labour should not make it.'

In reality, of course, Labour wanted to avoid making any promises at such an early stage in what would, presuming parliament ran for the full fixed term of five years, be a long, hard road. Ideas were welcome—especially if they were in tune with Miliband's own analysis of the UK's problems and his preferred solutions. These were actually very clear—and shared (indeed, influenced) by some of those closest to him, such as Stewart Wood. In their view, what went on both during the long boom under Blair and the spectacular bust under Brown was proof that Britain's economy needed what Wood came to call 'a supply side revolution from the left'—institutional and regulatory changes that had little or nothing to do with tax and spend. The latter may have been necessary to rescue public services such as health and education from decades of decline. However, not only had the money run out but, even when there was much more of it, it seemed to have made only a marginal (albeit not completely insignificant) impact on inequality, poverty, and social mobility. To make serious inroads into those underlying problems meant turning the UK from a country in which the government endlessly and ever more ingeniously compensated citizens for the consequences of their living in a relatively low-wage, low-skill, low-investment, low-productivity economy into one that paid better, that trained and educated more people, and that devoted far more resources to the kind of research and development that would enable them to produce world-class (and hopefully tradable) goods and services at least as efficiently as its competitors.

No one could pretend this would be easy. Indeed to the connoisseur it looked like an incredibly ambitious attempt to drag the country from what academic political economists such as Peter Hall and David Soskice called one 'variety of capitalism' into another—namely, from the liberal market economy typical of the Anglosphere into the coordinated market economy, the most obvious (and successful) example of which is Germany, with its *mittelstand* of highly competitive, export-oriented small and medium-sized businesses.[29] However, whatever the rights and wrongs of the ideas involved, and however difficult they would be to realize, they had several strategic advantages.

First, while they were clearly not cost-free, the emphasis was not on raising and spending huge amounts of money that, in an age of austerity, the nation clearly did not have. Second, while they were hardly a 'retail offer' to the electorate, they did constitute a reasonably coherent diagnosis and prescription that could be contrasted—if only at the elite level—to what the Conservatives (and the Lib Dems) were currently doing. Third, the ideas were to some extent future-proof. Miliband and those around him were convinced that the Coalition's spending cuts were indeed, as Ed Balls put it, going 'too far, too fast'.

However, the Labour leadership was also pretty sure that some sort of recovery would be underway by 2015, allowing the Tories to argue that they deserved to remain in government. The long-term, supply-side approach would, it was hoped, allow Labour to reframe the argument so that it was about the sustainability (as well as the tangibility) of that recovery: yes, it's the economy stupid, but what kind of economy and whose recovery?

Finally, the supply-side ideas could be married together with more than a touch of good old-fashioned populism: reforming the supply side was in part about tackling the practices of big businesses trying to protect their returns and their privileges at the expense not just of market efficiency but also of the millions of ordinary people who were their customers. Some of the most egregious examples, of course, were provided by the financial services sector, and opinion research, public and private, continued to show high levels of resentment against 'the bankers' who had played such a big part in the crash and who had been found guilty of industrial scale mis-selling, but who were still paying each other astronomical salaries and bonuses. Labour had to handle all this carefully. For one thing, as Miliband freely admitted, it had played a part in all this by its commitment to light-touch regulation while in government. For another, if it came on too strong, it would be accused of being 'anti-business' by its opponents. However, if it could manage to put itself on the side of 'the people' against 'vested interests', and claim to be doing so in the interests not just of fairness and decency but also of economic efficiency—just as Blair and Brown had done when they criticized utility company 'fat cats' when they were in opposition—who knew what could be achieved?

For the moment, however, all this was more backstage than frontstage—not so much because Miliband and his advisers did not know what they wanted to do, but because they spent much of the first few months of his leadership worrying less about the impact he would make on the public and more on making sure that the party did not fall apart. In hindsight, as some of them recognize, such fears were exaggerated, but they were entirely understandable. The historical precedents, after all, were not exactly promising. Defeat in 1931, 1951, and 1979 (and, to a lesser extent, 1970) had seen Labour descend into factional infighting. And, given the nature of the leadership contest and the years of bitter and dysfunctional division between Prime Minister and Chancellor that had preceded it, there was at least a prima facie risk that embittered Blairites would fight some sort of rearguard action against a leadership that, superficially anyway, looked almost entirely Brownite. Just because that did not, for the most part anyway, happen does not mean that it was never going to. Indeed, one of the reasons it did not may well have been the time and effort that Miliband and his staff put into managing the fallout from the contest in behind-the-scenes meetings and calls with parliamentarians and, of course, donors.

There was, however, a huge opportunity cost to all this. Time spent keeping people on board or just asking them to wait before they made up their minds was time spent not providing the public with images and positions that might have helped furnish them with a clearer and more positive impression of who Labour's new leader was and what he wanted to do. But, given voters' apparent disdain for parties whose members spend time sniping against, or even hacking great lumps out of, each other rather than taking the fight to the other side, who is to say for sure that that cost was not worth paying? Besides, the fixed-term parliament meant that Miliband could argue he had time on his side: there were four-and-a-half years in which opportunities to define himself would either present themselves or could be engineered. CCHQ had enormous fun, of course, producing a document entitled *Ed Miliband's 100 Days of Dithering and Disarray*, which featured a calendar of decisions ducked by the Labour leader since taking over in September, as well as reminding people, via three or four wounding quotations from former colleagues, that he had built up something of a reputation for indecisiveness while serving in government.[30] But even CCHQ could not control what one Tory Prime Minister famously called 'events, dear boy, events'. How was it to know, for example, that supposed 'safe pair of hands' Andrew Lansley's botched Health and Social Care Bill would run into such trouble at Westminster that, at the beginning of April, he would have to announce an unprecedented 'pause' in its parliamentary passage, boosting Labour's morale and engendering a little more confidence in a leader who could now make a better claim that he was capable of hitting the government where it hurt. True, he had needed the help of veteran Lib Dem Peer and former Labour minister Shirley Williams to do so. But, inasmuch as the local election results a month later told a story, it was Her Majesty's Loyal Opposition rather than disloyal members of the junior coalition partner who got the credit: Labour gained 857 seats; the Lib Dems lost 748.

Frustratingly for Miliband, the senior coalition partner, the Conservatives, contrived to come out of those elections wholly intact, gaining eighty-six seats. Indeed, without the chaos surrounding the Bill, and Miliband's attack on it, the Tories might have done even better. That is not to say, however, that all this was not politically important in the long term. After all, Cameron had spent much of his time in opposition doing everything he possibly could to persuade sceptical voters that his party really could be trusted with the NHS. He had not succeeded completely by the time the 2010 election came along, but had probably done just about enough to prevent the issue becoming as big an advantage for Labour as it had been in some previous contests. Now it looked as if all the Prime Minister's hard work might have been for nothing. Still, as the local election results suggested, there was at least a chance that, by taking action, the government could eventually contain some of the damage. The same could not be said, however, of what happened the day after Lansley made his climbdown in the Commons. On 5 April 2011, the Metropolitan Police arrested the News Editor and Chief Reporter of Rupert Murdoch's *News of the World*, the UK's best-selling Sunday newspaper, on suspicion of unlawfully intercepting voicemail messages—a practice now commonly known as 'phone-hacking'. In so doing they set in train a series of events that rapidly span out of control and that, by the summer of 2011, would present Ed Miliband with an opportunity, albeit a risky one, to show the country what he was really made of.

# 3

# Predators: Spring–Autumn 2011

The arrests carried out by the Met at the beginning of April 2011 were hardly a bolt from the blue. A journalist from the *News of the World* had been imprisoned for phone-hacking in 2007 and evidence marshalled by *Guardian* journalist Nick Davies and his colleagues suggested that the practice was far more widespread on News International titles than the company had been willing to admit. Celebrities who had been affected had already brought forward lawsuits or were beginning to do so. There were also rumours flying around that the Met's decision in 2009 not to reopen its investigation into what had gone on had been influenced by the unduly close relationships that some of its officers had built up with the newspapers involved. And, as if the story were not already political enough, one of the people implicated in the case was none other than Andy Coulson, former editor of the *News of the World*, who had been hired by David Cameron to head up his media team in opposition and had then become Director of Communications in Number Ten when the Tories entered government in May 2010. On 21 January, Coulson had finally departed Downing Street, his decision knocking Alan Johnson's resignation as Labour's Shadow Chancellor off the headlines. Five days later, the Met had announced it was reopening its investigation into phone-hacking at News International under the title Operation Weeting. Realizing it was now in serious trouble, the company had begun to adopt a more cooperative attitude to the investigation and a more conciliatory approach to those whose voicemail messages had been intercepted, especially those who had the money and the connections to enable them to demand legal redress.

The issue was by no means an easy one for Labour. The desperation of both Blair and Brown, whether in opposition or in government, to keep the mass circulation dailies on their side had been legendary. Their concern was understandable: in 1992 the Tory press had thrown everything it had at Neil Kinnock and supposedly helped turn imminent victory into crushing defeat. However, New Labour's craven courting of editors, columnists, and proprietors had long since become a source of dismay and embarrassment to many in the party—either because they believed it was immoral or because they believed the leadership was attributing far too much electoral influence, and therefore ceding far too much power, to people who were Eurosceptic fans of the free market with distinctly illiberal views on crime, punishment, and immigration. As one frontbencher put it: 'I always thought it was absolutely right for the Labour Party to try to neutralize Murdoch; the problem was that we went on to have an affair with him.' And for what? As soon as it became clear that the Conservative Party had a reasonable chance of winning again, those papers had rushed back home, leaving a pathetic Brown fuming impotently about the injustice of it all. And yet. And yet. While those in charge now were considerably more sceptical of the power of the press to swing voters than their predecessors, they nonetheless took its continued capacity to set the agenda for broadcast media seriously. Given that relations with the Murdoch press were difficult enough already, notwithstanding the fact that Miliband's media chief Tom Baldwin had been recruited from *The Times* partly in the hope of improving the situation, they were therefore reluctant to make things any worse. It was no surprise, then, when a leaked email, sent in January, suggested that Labour's media team was urging the party to proceed with caution on phone-hacking, which on no account should be linked to another story currently running—Rupert Murdoch's attempt to buy back control of satellite broadcaster BSkyB.

As revelation followed revelation on the phone-hacking front, however, it became increasingly difficult for Miliband to soft-peddle and stick to platitudes. For one thing, he was as concerned as anyone else in the country at what had been going on. For another, he could see, particularly in the wake of Coulson's resignation, that there might be some political advantage in taking a harder line on the issue. Besides, two of the people who had been hammering away at it for years were high-profile Labour MPs—Tom Watson (best known before then, perhaps, for trying to precipitate Tony Blair's replacement by Gordon Brown) and Chris Bryant (also a one-time 'plotter' against

Blair who had discovered that his own phone had been hacked after a parliamentary run-in with Rebekah Brooks, now News International's Chief Executive, back in 2003). By mid-April 2011, their campaigning, combined with the court cases being brought by celebrities and the fact that the Met had begun to make arrests as part of its renewed investigation, saw Miliband shift his position significantly. He was now calling for a wide-ranging independent review of the press, although only after the completion of the police inquiry and any court cases resulting from it. His insistence that 'self-regulation continues to be the right thing. We do not want the government regulating the press' suggested, however, that he was still hedging his bets rather than burning his bridges. Bryant, for example, was explicitly warned, albeit by Miliband's staff rather than by Miliband himself, not to press things too hard—even to the point, just before going into the Chamber to make yet another intervention in the affair, of receiving a phone call to remind him that he was a Shadow Minister. No surprise then that, in the middle of June, Ed Miliband, as well as Ed Balls, Yvette Cooper, and Douglas Alexander, chose to join other revellers at Murdoch's annual summer party in Kensington.[1]

In July 2011, however, everything changed. The *Guardian* splashed on the news that the *News of the World*, edited at the time by Rebekah Brooks, had hacked the mobile phone of Milly Dowler, a teenager who had gone missing and was eventually found murdered; the revelation provoked widespread disgust. Miliband, belying his reputation for indecisiveness and taking advantage of the fact that, unlike some other Labour figures, he had no real or pretended personal connection with News International people, moved fast. Choosing to ignore the continued caution of some of his colleagues about a direct attack, and now urged on rather than held back by Baldwin, he decided not only to call for Brooks to step down, but also to press the Prime Minister, a personal friend of hers, for an independent, public inquiry into the press and to refer Murdoch's bid for BSkyB to the Competition Commission. In what was widely regarded as by far his best performance at PMQs since becoming leader, Miliband not only had Cameron on the ropes but seemed to be speaking for the whole country in demanding action against a monster that many felt had now run out of control.

At long last, Miliband was not only making headlines, he was making the weather. In short order, the *News of the World* closed down, Cameron announced the setting-up of a judge-led inquiry into the press, which would not have to wait until the end of the police investigation, Murdoch's News Corp withdrew its bid, and, finally, Brooks was forced to resign. The Labour leader had played a blinder, and he had done it by being bold and trusting his instincts, deciding on more than one occasion to wing it and go beyond the rather more cautious approach he had agreed on with advisers just minutes before getting up to speak. Even better, the whole thing dovetailed with his desire strategically to position the party as the enemy of powerful vested interests. Equally important, after a difficult few weeks in which his embarrassingly convoluted response to strikes by public-sector unions had set malicious (and even some sympathetic) tongues wagging about whether he was really up to the job, he looked like a leader—one of those rare politicians capable of displaying both guts and judgement at one and the same time.

Party politics, however, is not all about what goes on in public and at Westminster. As well as what political scientists like to call 'the party in public office', there is also 'the party on the ground'—the grass-roots members and activists—and 'the party in central office'—the paid staffers who, as the party's bureaucracy, service and support both the MPs (and MEPs and councillors) and the ordinary members. In Labour's case, the head of the organizational side of things is known as the General Secretary—a post commanding a substantial salary and huge responsibilities, not least on the financial front. He or she is officially appointed by the party's NEC, a thirty-three-member body (made up of representatives of the parliamentary party, the delegation in the European Parliament, constituency parties, affiliated societies, local government, and the trade unions), which, in theory anyway, acts a bit like a board of governors. The General Secretary when Ed Miliband took over as leader, Ray Collins, had been in post since 2008 and was generally credited with having done a good job of getting the party through the 2010 election campaign albeit in extremely strait-ened financial circumstances. In January 2011, however, he had, at Miliband's urging, taken up a place in the House of Lords. As a result the search was on for a replacement.

As in any party, the choice of who runs the bureaucracy is not simply an administrative decision but a deeply political one: as Peter Watt, author of an eye-opening memoir on his time in the post between 2005 and 2007, puts it, the job is about 'building alliances and allegiances, keeping the different factions of the party happy'. The successful candidate, it was assumed, would be the man or woman in charge through to (and probably beyond) the next general election and would play a significant part in ensuring the party was in a fit state to fight it. Certainly, under New Labour, it was widely acknowledged that the General Secretary, while not necessarily a creature of the leader, needed to be able to work closely alongside him—not always an easy task, as previous incumbents (not least Peter Watt) could attest.[2] The leader, as a member of the NEC, could try to influence who was awarded the post but ultimately could not control the decision: back in 2005, for example, Blair had backed Ray Collins rather than Watt for the job, although it is worth noting that the two enjoyed a good relationship once the latter was in post.

For Miliband, the choice was finely balanced. On the one hand, it was widely assumed (not altogether fairly) that staffers at the party's Victoria Street Headquarters, most of whom had been recruited in the Blair era, had been hoping (some said banking) on his brother David winning the leadership contest. Backing a candidate who was a known quantity to them would presumably help reduce continued friction between Ed's Office and Victoria Street—friction that had as much to do with disputes over roles and responsibilities as it did with funda-mental ideological differences. In that case, the obvious man to go for was Chris Lennie, Labour's Deputy General Secretary, who had been in post for ten years. On the other hand, Lennie, although respected by many who worked with him, was not universally popular—perhaps not surprisingly, since he had often been tasked with cutting budgets (and therefore personnel), as well as handling disputes and disciplinary issues. He was also seen by many activists, rightly or wrongly, as the choice of a party 'establishment'. As far as they were concerned, those in charge in London had run things in their own interests for too long, conniving, for example, to 'parachute' leadership favourites into safe seats—the paradigmatic example of which, legend had it, being David Miliband back in 2001. Since Ed Miliband was supposed to be all about change and doing politics differently—something he had emphasized yet again in a speech to Labour's NPF at the end of June—perhaps it would be better for him to try to shake things up a bit by pushing for the appointment of someone who knew the Labour Party well but did not currently work for it. In that case, maybe he should come down instead on the side of Iain McNicol, karate black belt, bagpipe-player, and (possibly more importantly) the national political officer of the GMB, the UK's third biggest union, who had worked hard to help get him elected. The problem with doing that, however, was that it was bound to result in Miliband being accused of dancing to the tune of the union bosses who had been so instrumental in winning him the leadership less than a year before.

As so often happens, especially in the era of social media, rumours spread that the Leader's Office was attempting some kind of 'stitch-up', Miliband having apparently decided to plump for Lennie over McNicol. Perhaps inevitably—but also because they coincided with activists' worries about the transparency of both the ongoing policy review and the *Refounding Labour* consultation—those rumours duly sparked a determined campaign to ensure that McNicol's candidacy be given equal consideration. In the event, it clearly was, not least because McNicol ran a determined and characteristically efficient campaign to ensure he was in with a chance. On the same day as Rupert Murdoch was making his high-profile appearance in parliament, the NEC voted narrowly to appoint McNicol, who, as well as winning over most union members of the committee, also impressed CLP members with his promise to oversee what he called 'a dramatic decentralization of party power, decision making and resourcing to empower staff, members and candidates around the UK'.

Miliband may not have got his man on this occasion, but talk of the 'control freakery' that had supposedly characterized New Labour thereby passing into the dustbin of history was probably a little premature. Indeed, it was perfectly possible to argue that, when it came to the parliamentary party, if not the NEC, Miliband was taking it to new heights. The leadership contest and the Shadow Cabinet elections that had followed soon after had made it obvious that his support at Westminster was shallow, to say the least. Partly for this reason—and partly because relatively few people at the top had much, if any, experience of opposition, Miliband had consented to the idea that Shadow Ministers, rather than Party Headquarters, be allowed to appoint their own advisers and media people, much as if they were still in government. For those who believed this granted them way too much autonomy, this was a bad move, but now it had been done it was deemed impossible to undo without creating too much trouble. But what if, instead of opening up that particular can of worms, Miliband could tackle something even more fundamental—namely, the fact that, in opposition, Labour leaders were obliged to appoint their Shadow Cabinet largely on the basis of who the PLP decided should be in it?

Helped by his widely admired handling of the News International scandal but also by veterans who could remember the energy that Shadow Cabinet elections wasted, he had managed to persuade his MPs, who voted by a margin of 196 to 41 with 20 abstentions, to depart from a tradition stretching back to the 1920s and scrap them. Henceforth, Labour's leader, like his Tory counterpart, would be able to choose his own team, albeit with the proviso that the number of women in it should at least reflect the proportion of women in the PLP. This was a move that even Blair had been too cautious to make— yet was more evidence, claimed Miliband's supporters, that their man had no intention, as many Blairite critics alleged, of confining the party to its comfort zone. That depended, those critics responded, on what exactly he did when it came to picking his own people at the next reshuffle, as well as his extending his radicalism to other areas of the party's organization and policy.

What was happening with Peter Hain's *Refounding Labour* exercise could hardly be said to be promising in this regard. The wider party's response to the consultation phase was reasonably impressive, running to around 3,500 submissions from individuals and organizations. There had clearly been a degree of discomfort caused, however, when Dan Hodges, a former Labour staffer with a wicked turn of phrase who was now carving out a career in journalism on the back of well-sourced stories about the party's trials and tribulations, revealed that the project, far from being managed from Victoria Street, appeared to have been effectively 'outsourced' to a fledgling political consultancy.[3] Concerns were also voiced when the party (not, it must be said, those running the actual consultation) proved less than enthusiastic about publishing the submissions received and the surveys conducted and when, at the end of July, it produced an interim report, *Refounding Labour to Win*, apparently authored by the consummate insider, Deputy General Secretary Alicia Kennedy, just a few short weeks after the consultation had closed, provoking suspicions that submissions had barely been read, let alone taken seriously.[4]

Part of the problem may have been the undue raising of expectations by a leadership still keen—much to the irritation of those who had been around at the time and remembered things slightly differently—to contrast itself with the old regime. Miliband, for example, had told Labour's NPF at the end of *Refounding Labour*'s consultation phase:

let's be honest, the leadership believed its role was to protect the public from the party. It never really believed the party could provide the connection to the British people. And we didn't build a genuine movement. By the end, it was our party members that were trying to tell the leadership what people wanted it to hear... But the leadership did not listen enough. So we went from six people making decisions in a smoke-filled committee room in the 1980s to six people making the decisions from a sofa in Whitehall. Old Labour forgot about the public. New Labour forgot about the party. And, by the time we left office, we had lost touch with both.

Had *Refounding Labour*'s interim report lived up to this kind of billing, then activists' concerns about the project's management might have been set aside. Unfortunately it turned out to be far from earth-shattering. Its focus on local innovation, community organizing, and the possibility (but no more than that) of various organizational reforms (including the idea—eventually approved—that either the leader or the deputy leader should always be a woman), certainly provided little that Labour could use to persuade voters that it had taken a long hard look at itself and was now determined to pursue fundamental change. Existing members, the report suggested, were clearly prepared to countenance the idea of 'registered supporters' who could be 'mobilized to back local campaigns and add to local party efforts at election time; be invited to local events and be consulted on local and national matters by email'—but not if they were granted the same formal rights as ordinary members. However, the party seemed keen to keep open the possibility that in time they be allowed to vote in leadership elections, although ideally in the affiliated section of the electoral college, where they would therefore dilute the influence of trade unions. On the latter, there was little more than a vague promise to explore reciprocal invitations to each other's events. Questions of financing, including membership fees, were effectively put off for another time, as were those pertaining to the policy process (about which there were clearly widespread concerns) and in particular the weighting of votes at conference.

All this was pretty thin stuff. And even then, giving the lie to the idea of Labour somehow practising 'the new politics', its suggestions were simply bundled into a package on which, in September, and following a climbdown in the face of union intransigence, Conference was given a good old-fashioned take-it-or-leave it, Yes–No vote. Despite delegates having hardly any time to digest a new 100-page rule book, page-upon-page of amendments being tabled, and just a couple of hours of debate, they duly voted by an overwhelming majority to approve a compromise package—one that, at the last-minute insistence of the unions, ditched the leadership's proposal to include registered supporters in the affiliates section of the electoral college in favour of a complex scheme that would see the creation of a new, fourth section of the college should their numbers go over 50,000.

That Miliband blinked before the unions did on party reform was perhaps understandable. Relations with them had been uneasy since the end of June when the Labour leader had expressed his reservations about public-service strikes over pay and pensions—reservations that he repeated in his address to the TUC Conference in mid-September and that earned him a few boos and heckles in the process. Little wonder, then, that he would not commit either to condemn or to support more planned stoppages in November. Or that incoming General Secretary, Iain McNicol, as well as telling conference about his plans to turn Labour into 'a party which takes action, not just minutes', took the trouble to burnish his union as well as his grass-roots credentials: 'I haven't read every pamphlet by Compass and Progress. I'm not absolutely sure what the differences are between Blue Labour, Red Labour and Purple Labour. But I've always paid my union dues and my party subs. I've never ducked a leaflet round. And I've never crossed a picket line.'

This sort of stuff went down a treat in the hall, of course. And it is doubtful, given the vanishingly small proportion of voters who would have been paying attention to what was going on in Liverpool, that it did much harm. That said, there may have been an opportunity cost. Annual conferences provide one of the few chances British parties get maybe to hog the headlines for a few days. Using them to announce big (and ideally controversial) organizational and policy changes is therefore one of the few means available to an opposition to demonstrate to voters that it is changing. Frankly, the announcement that, at some point in the future, registered supporters might play a minor role in electing Labour's next leader or, for that matter, that Labour's leader in Scotland would now be chosen by all its members north of the border rather than solely by Members of the Scottish Parliament, did not really cut it. Likewise, McNicol's speech was worthy enough, but, in common with most of the contributions from both the floor and the podium, neither its content nor its tone was going to do much to address the serious perception problem with which the party—and particularly its leader—clearly still had to contend.

Labour could take some comfort in the fact that, despite the drubbing it had received in 2010, its brand appeared to be less 'toxic' than the Tories. A poll taken just before conference for the left-leaning Institute of Public Policy Research (IPPR) found that only 30 per cent of people said they would 'never' vote Labour, compared to 42 per cent who said the same about voting Conservative, with the difference between the two being particularly pronounced among the much-coveted C2 voters.[5] However, the same poll suggested that in the south of England the position was reversed—a point hammered home in a more detailed analysis of Labour's image problem outside its northern and Scottish heartlands by Patrick Diamond and Giles Radice in their pamphlet Southern Discomfort: One Year On, published just in time for conference by the social democratic think tank Policy Network.[6] Other polling released before and during conference was a reminder that, for all his work on phone-hacking in July and his reasonably deft handling of the media during the urban riots that took place later in the summer, Miliband was still a long way from convincing most voters that he had what it took to run the country. A Populus poll for The Times, for instance, showed that even half of those intending to vote Labour had difficulty imagining him as PM.[7]

Even more worrying for the party, perhaps, was the qualitative work done on behalf of Conservative peer (and now increasingly well-respected pollster) Lord Ashcroft, based on focus groups of floating voters. Groups were shown cards bearing words, phrases, and images, out of which they constructed 'mood boards' that summed up their impression of each party leader. Cameron came out as 'determined', 'ruthless', and 'competent'—a bit of an action man as well as a family man, sometimes inclined to rush things but a strong leader at least. The mood boards for Miliband were not as encouraging: more positive groups thought they might be able to see light at the end of the tunnel and believed that he understood ordinary people, but others chose either blank cards or an image of clouds to express the fact that they did not really feel they knew him. Others lighted on an image that showed a little boy playing at being a businessman to convey an apparently widespread concern that the Labour leader was 'out of his depth'. They also seemed to see him as 'lucky', but not in a good way; to quote from Ashcroft's report: 'Participants knew that the result [of the leadership contest] had been very close. Several thought he also seemed lucky in that he had apparently been chosen by the unions to do their bidding, and in the sense that he was lucky to have become leader given how unqualified he seemed.' Ultimately, however, 'weird'

was the most commonly chosen word or phrase to describe Mr Miliband—several said they felt rather unkind choosing it but that it simply summed up their view. As well as being an overall impression, several examples of perceived weirdness were cited, including the contest with his demeanour and the way he spoke, and his apparently reluctant marriage. The decision to stand against his brother, whom nearly all thought was better qualified, also seemed to many to be distinctly odd (as well as being the single best known fact about him).[8]

In other words, despite all the talk of his 'ripping up the rule book' and going after News International being some sort of game-changer, both quantitative and qualitative research suggested that the electorate's underlying view of Ed Miliband had barely shifted and that (in common with most opposition leaders) he had lost rather than gained support during his first year in the job, meaning he was now a drag on, rather than a draw for, his party.

Concerns about all this undoubtedly played a part in Labour's leader deciding to set aside his initial reluctance to involve his children in contact with the media. In what was naturally interpreted as a blatant attempt to show that he was just as much a normal family man as Cameron, Labour's conference began with Miliband providing photographers with the opportunity to snap him (suitably attired in a apparently casual grey v-neck sweater) not just with his wife, Justine, but his two infant sons, Daniel and Samuel. He nevertheless continued to insist that, although, as he told the *New Statesman*'s Mehdi Hasan in a pre-conference interview, 'it would be crackers to say you don't care' about your image, what really mattered was 'the big picture'—in particular whether you, as Leader of the Opposition, had 'a clear sense of what's wrong with the country and what needs to change'.[9] Perhaps he was right. However, any such analysis, irrespective of whether it was more Blue Labour than New Labour, would be truly useful, electorally speaking, only if it could help convince the country that the opposition had better answers than the government on the economy. Sadly, for the moment anyway, this was patently not the case. The very same polls that showed Labour either just behind or just in front of the Tories in terms of vote intention also showed that it needed to do much more to persuade people that it could be trusted to look after their money. The problem—at least as some gloomy insiders (as well as many gloating outsiders) saw it—was that this depended not just on Miliband himself but also on Ed Balls.

Balls, being Balls, naturally had a plan—on this occasion a five-point one. But whether it (and whether he) was capable of convincing voters that Labour had better answers on the economy than the Tories was another matter. That was because it concentrated on telling voters not what the party planned to do if it won an election scheduled for 2015 but what it would be doing right now if it, rather than the current coalition, were in office. The ideas all made perfect sense, especially if one were a Keynesian economist: temporary action on VAT and small business National Insurance contributions, bringing forward infra-structure projects, and a levy on bank bonuses to fund youth employ-ment and house building initiatives would all help kick-start a stuttering economy, and might persuade people that Labour had more of a sense than the Tories of how to restore growth. On the other hand, they could easily be portrayed by Labour's opponents—especially given the widespread assumption that, when in a hole, governments should stop, not start, digging—as evidence that, as ever, the party's solution to everything was to spend more and let up on deficit reduction. Moreover, persuading voters that this was not the case was arguably made all the more easy by Balls's refusal to issue a sufficiently fulsome apology, not just for the odd 'mistake' he was prepared to admit to (on bank regulation, on the 10p tax rate, on East European immigration, and on industrial training), but for Labour having messed things up on the economy more generally—particularly in respect of having over-borrowed and over-spent during the good times.

The fact that well-known Blairites like Tessa Jowell were giving media interviews that appeared to be endorsing the idea of a more wide-ranging apology probably made it less rather than more likely that Balls would 'concede and move on'. In any case, he may well have been right to argue in various media interviews that it was absurd to argue that the cause of the nation's fiscal problems was anything other than the global financial meltdown and the consequent recession—just as commentators like the *Independent*'s Steve Richards were right to ask, as did Balls, 'whether the headlines about apologies will reassure voters or reinforce a view of incompetence': as he noted: 'Sorry we screwed up the economy—Vote Labour' was hardly a winning slogan.[10] However, what Balls was doing arguably sounded even worse. Like it or not, people were convinced that, even if the bankers had played a big part in the crisis, Labour was to blame too—and that the only way out of it now was for the country to tighten its belt, grit its teeth, and get through the pain. If they could ever have been persuaded to think otherwise, the moment was long gone. Not saying sorry suggested that the party still believed that it, rather than the voters, knew best. Worse, focusing on its plans to reduce revenue and spend more money in response to the Coalition's austerity programme, rather than coming up with alternative cuts of its own, suggested that Labour had failed to grasp the gravity of the situation. It also lent credence to the idea that, like so many of its sister parties on the centre-left, it seemed to believe social democracy and spending had to go together and therefore did not really know what to do when the money ran out—a message driven home a couple of months after conference in a pamphlet for Policy Network by Graeme Cook, Adam Lent, Anthony Painter, and Hopi Sen called *In the Black Labour: Why Fiscal Conservatism and Social Justice Go Hand-in-Hand*. As the authors (think tankers who had worked for the Labour movement) put it:

Taxpayers, voters and lenders to the British state feel they have a right to know what the main opposition party would do about high levels of borrowing and when they would do it by. Satisfying this demand is fundamental to being regarded as a credible alternative government . . . It is precisely the vagueness of Labour's position over its short to medium term plans for the deficit that confirms the voters' worst suspicions about the Party's lack of commitment to addressing the fiscal crisis.[11]

Of course, Balls's decision to focus on what Labour would do were it in office right now rather than what it hoped to do in 2015 was in some ways perfectly rational. Even if the much talked about double-dip recession had never actually happened, the economy had slowed, just as he had predicted. In any case, who knew what the state of the public finances or, indeed, the economy as a whole would be in three-

and-a-half years' time? Was there really any point in making commitments that might look badly out of date by then or else give the Tories
plenty of time to work out how to counter them? Yet in trying to
avoid this at the same time as trying to look as though he knew what
needed doing, Balls was all-too-obviously trying to have his cake and
eat it too. Then again, so was his leader. Deciding that he had best not
go into conference talking too abstractedly about 'a new centre ground'
revolving around inequality between the rich and the rest and a 'new
bargain for Britain', Miliband needed something a little more concrete.
So, on the eve of conference, Labour briefed its intention to cap
university tuition fees at £6,000 rather than the current £9,000, paid
for by not scrapping taxes on the finance sector and changing rules on
repayments. But the announcement impressed no one when, after some
confusion, it became clear that this was yet another 'promise' that was in
fact no such thing. Rather than a commitment, it was one of those things
that Labour would do if it were in office right now, not in 2015. As for
what it might do in the real world, it had apparently not given up the
idea of a graduate tax—a method of funding higher education that
famously had failed to convince Alan Johnson when he was Shadow
Chancellor and, for what it was worth, did not convince many people
actually working in the sector either.

   The kerfuffle over tuition fees, however, probably did not do quite
as much damage to Labour's high hopes for the 2011 conference as
another 'policy' that had to be clarified almost as soon as it was
announced. The party had clearly made the running on phone-hacking
over the summer, even if its claim for the moral high ground had
almost come unstuck after Gordon Brown, in his first Commons
speech since leaving Number Ten, had attacked what he called the
'sewer rats' at News International in terms that were at best hyperbolic
and at worst hypocritical. 'Hackgate' had not only boosted Miliband
personally, but offered some support for the notion that, as its conference banners declared, Labour was up for 'New Politics. Fresh Ideas'.
Shadow Culture Secretary Ivan Lewis clearly sought to build on all this
at conference by proposing tougher laws on media cross-ownership
and like-for-like rights of reply, both of which were guaranteed to
enrage proprietors and editors alike. But he also floated the idea that,
'as with other professions, the industry should consider whether
people guilty of gross malpractice should be struck off'—a suggestion
that immediately saw him accused of proposing a state licensing

scheme for journalists. This in turn forced Miliband to insist that this was not Labour policy, only to find himself then mocked for executing the 'fastest U-turn in history'. It also meant that, by the time the Labour leader got up to deliver his big set-piece speech to conference, the Tory Party in the media was more desperate than ever to declare it a flop.

They did not have to try too hard. Even discounting for the irony that the live television transmission was interrupted just as he got to 'My message to the public is . . .', Miliband did not deliver the speech well, leading to yet another rash of speculation, even among sympathetic or neutral commentators, on whether voters could ever be persuaded to elect a man who, despite undergoing corrective nasal surgery in the summer, simply did not sound the part and who, as one of his colleagues put it to the *Guardian*'s Simon Hoggart, looked 'like a schoolboy who's been caught hiding in a cupboard to get out of games'.[12] Just as damagingly, he also made a couple of unforced errors that would have shamed a student debater.

First, presumably because the whole thing was partly about trying to establish the fact that he was his 'own man', anxious to set out what Labour now stood for, Miliband somehow persuaded himself that it would be a good idea to say, 'You know, I'm not Tony Blair. I'm not Gordon Brown either'—something he might just about have got away with had he not paused momentarily between the two sentences, thereby allowing sufficient time for some members of the audience, apparently (and therefore even more damagingly) from the Unite union, to register their noisy disdain for the first of the aforenamed. Miliband was clearly discomfited, but rather than rounding on them, he simply ploughed on. Then, in interviews afterwards, as the clip was played again and again, he chose to register no more than polite disagreement, inevitably provoking hostile print journalists to ask whether a party that clearly thought so little of the only man ever to lead it to three successive victories could really be serious about regaining office. As the *Telegraph*'s Ben Brogan, put it:

Time-stopping moments don't come often in politics, but that was one. Imagine David Cameron standing powerless . . . as the hall boos Margaret Thatcher, and you get an inkling of the monumental denial now gripping a party that used to be one of the most formidable election-winning machines since the war.[13]

However, this was not the Tory media's only (or even their most effective) attack line. That was reserved for what it decided was Miliband's second schoolboy error—namely, the distinction he decided to draw, as a means of highlighting the difference between his kind of 'ethical' capitalism (long-termist, cooperative, high skill, high wage) and the government's more neo-liberal version, between firms that were 'predators' and those that were 'producers'. The strategy underlying the distinction may have been just about coherent, but it was also risky. Whatever the Tories and their friends in the media liked to argue, Miliband's closest advisers were perfectly well aware that the British economy was bound eventually to recover—indeed, if truth be told, it actually took rather longer to do so than they had initially expected. They were, accordingly, pinning their hopes not on recession delivering victory but on Labour being able to convince the country that the nation's economic problems were so deep-seated that it would require more than a temporary return to growth to solve them. They saw his 2011 speech as the one that would stir up controversy, his 2012 speech as the one that would articulate a vision, and his 2013 speech as the one that would provide practical solutions. The biggest risk was that this relied on getting voters to agree with Miliband that the system as a whole (rather than particular parts of it) was broken—something he had not yet managed to do.

Alliteration, in other words, was no substitute for a well-prepared argument—something that became very clear very quickly. As soon as he had finished speaking Miliband and his aides were being pumped by journalists for examples and asked whether this or that firm was naughty or nice—a line of enquiry that was entirely predictable given that, when Labour pre-tested the idea with focus groups, one of the first questions that came up was 'Which one is Alan Sugar?' Understandably (but also unforgivably) 'Team Ed' was not willing to get into naming names, and nor were other frontbenchers. It did not help either that the Shadow BIS team, who knew the arguments better, were not tasked with the briefing for the speech. And things were made even worse by the noticeable lack of willingness on the part of other high-profile spokespeople in the wake of the speech (with the partial exception of the Shadow Health Minister John Healey) to make a concerted attempt to use the predators–producers distinction, thus making it obvious that people were uncomfortable with it. Lib Dem Secretary of State for Business Vince Cable texted the Labour leader following the speech to congratulate him on making one of the best arguments for social democracy he had heard in years. Very few of Miliband's own colleagues agreed with him.

As a result of all this, any good that Miliband's speech tried to do—for instance, admitting to Britain's responsible, 'hard-working majority' that a Labour government would not be able afford to reverse many of the Coalition's cuts and would need to be just as hard-headed when it came to those on benefits and in social housing as it would be with the bankers—went right out of the window. Miliband and his team (taking their cue perhaps from a *New York Times* piece on 'Why Voters Tune Out Democrats' penned the previous July by one of Labour's favourite US pollsters, Stan Greenberg) had hoped to temper the stress on responsibility with a touch of radical populism, putting the party on the side of the people against various fat-cats and vested interests.[14] But the speech simply ended up making it easier than ever for Miliband's enemies—inside and outside the Labour fold—to paint him into a corner. Blair's former speechwriter Phil Collins, writing in *The Times*, said out loud what many Blairites thought privately about a speech that in their view, for all that it channelled continuing public anger against bankers and bosses, virtually guaranteed that the party would find it impossible to drum up significant support from the business community—the sector that most voters, whether they liked it or not, knew was ultimately responsible for providing their livelihoods. Miliband, wrote Collins, by outing himself as 'the last gasp, the dying breath of vintage social democracy in which state action directs the nation towards moral betterment', had 'surely accelerated his demise'.[15] If anyone had any doubts, he concluded, it was now clear that Labour's leader was 'going to fight from the Left and he is going to lose from the Left'. Danny Finkelstein, another *Times* columnist and previously an adviser to the Tories during William Hague's darkest days, thought pretty much the same—and, even more woundingly, delivered the blow as much in sorrow as in anger: 'First, most people don't think Ed Miliband is up to being prime minister. And second, he is too left-wing. And there's not a lot Labour can do about either of those things. That's the signal, the rest is just noise.'[16]

Almost inevitably, a handful of Finkelstein's and Collins's fellow journalists attempted to leverage all this into renewed leadership speculation, with Shadow Home Secretary Yvette Cooper most frequently named as favourite to take over. They also afforded her contribution to conference a rather warmer welcome—not just because she seemed much more willing than some of her colleagues to admit that the party had made mistakes while in office, but because the mistakes she owned up to were precisely those that the media were particularly fond of highlighting when criticizing the last Labour government. She noted, for instance, that

we didn't need 90-day detention, we didn't need 42-day detention. They were never justified by the evidence. On immigration, we should have had transitional controls for Eastern Europe and we should have brought in a points-based system earlier. Managed migration has benefits for our economy and our culture, but we also need to recognize its impact on communities. And that means strong, fair controls that are properly enforced.

However, there was no sense in which this—any more than her announcement that the Met's former Commissioner, John (now Lord) Stevens, had agreed to head up her review of the future of policing—was actually driven by some fiendish plan on Cooper's part to ensure she outshone her leader. Rather, it was the latest move in an attempt on the part of the leadership as a whole to reposition Labour on immigration. Since, as Maurice Glasman had reminded people over the summer, this was the issue that, along with the economy and the belief that the party was a soft touch on welfare, had done it most damage at the last election, Cooper, then, was simply doing what most Labour people thought needed to be done, not taking the kind of lonely, brave, and counter-intuitive stand against an imagined liberal elite that might have put her at odds with Miliband. In any case, although there were many MPs who were worried about their leader, and some who were also worried about how far to the left he was taking the party, the vast majority were prepared to give him—for the moment at least—the benefit of the doubt.

And with good reason perhaps. After all, the Tories did not seem any closer, now that they were in power, to convincing people that they could be trusted with it, while plenty of disillusioned Lib Dem left-wingers seemed to have made up their minds that Labour was the only alternative. Put that together with the vagaries of the electoral system, which meant that the Conservatives probably needed to be somewhere between five and ten percentage points ahead of Labour at a general election to win an overall majority, and victory was far from a forlorn hope. As a result, many of those who had served on the front bench under Brown, as well as many of those who hoped to make progress through the ranks in opposition, realized that there was a chance—and maybe not an outside chance at that—that they might be waiting on a call from Prime Minister Miliband (however, unlikely that sounded) in May 2015. Indeed, there was no guarantee that the Coalition would even last that long. That possibility (albeit one that began to grow fainter as it became clear that the Lib Dems genuinely believed that their interests were best served by sticking with the Tories till the bitter end) meant that a spot of good old-fashioned Labour infighting might prove even more fatal to the party's chances than usual. One reason, perhaps, why, as the *Guardian*'s political columnist Michael White, veteran of many an annual conference over the years, noted, Labour was 'in better shape . . . than the party's internecine history would have predicted'. In contrast, he observed, to what had happened in the wake of 'past historic defeats . . . the party of brotherly love has not resorted to what Douglas Alexander cheerfully calls "the circular firing squad" where, like the last scene in Hamlet, almost everyone ends up dead'. This, he concluded, constituted 'progress of a sort and owes much to Ed Miliband's emollient style of leadership'.[17]

Substance as well as style may also have played a part in keeping the peace. Not only did Miliband's refusal to go with what he called 'the conventional opposition playbook' and pick a fight with his party help avoid trouble, but his feint to the left (if that is what it was) was also sufficient—just about—to satisfy activists who wanted a lot more socialism than they felt they had been getting for the last decade and a half. That said, that was not what was on offer from everybody responsible for the direction of the party. Douglas Alexander, for instance, faced with demands from the floor for something a little redder in tooth and claw at a fringe event on 'What Must Labour Do Next', could only slip into the sort of language that infuriated plain-speakers: 'I think', he admitted, 'there is new space opening up for a conversation about inequality that wasn't there when we were in office', before going on to ask: 'What should Labour's response be? What is the exact characterization of inequality? . . . What are the policy instruments that can be most effective?'

On the other hand, by no means everyone in the party outside Westminster would have scorned such vagaries and demanded instead that its elected representatives immediately mount the barricades

waving red flags and shrouds. Indeed, another reason why Labour after
2010 managed to avoid a swift descent into the faction fighting that
characterized its response to defeat in, say, 1979 was that New Labour
had been more than simply a superficial makeover: disciplined pragmatism had not completely snuffed out ideological zeal, but it had
percolated a long way down the party. The contrast, for instance,
between how Conservative spending measures had been handled by
Labour people in local government in the 1980s and how they were
handling them now was not simply marked; it was massive. Labour
authorities such as Lambeth, which in the 1980s had been a byword for
ideologically inspired posturing that did nothing to protect those who
were most in need of protecting from cuts, were now renowned
innovators, seeking to empower citizens to help pick a responsive
and responsible path through centrally imposed austerity. Indeed, the
'cooperative council' model it pioneered would, like other local
innovations, eventually feed into the party's NPF—a shining example
rather than a dire warning. If there was still anything identifiable as 'the
left', then, it no longer had an institutional base from which to attack
the leadership by pretending to attack the Tories. Had Ken Livingstone not lost the London Mayoralty to Boris Johnson back in 2008,
maybe things would have been different. But probably not: after all,
Ken had mellowed considerably over the decades, and, even though
Labour had retained control of many London boroughs, the Tory
tabloids had long since given up even looking for the 'loony left'. As
Councillor David Sparks, the leader of the Local Government Association's Labour group, told conference:

Contrary to when we fought . . . the Thatcher cuts, we haven't descended in
local government into the insanity we had last time. We've had difficult
decisions, we've had agonising decisions, but we've stayed together in unity
to protect, as much as we possibly can, our communities. We must maintain
that unity, beyond councillors, to the whole of the party, to the whole of the
movement, to the trade union movement as well . . . Labour local government
is continuing to innovate. It's absolutely critically important for the health of
the party that we never lose sight of that. We must not just ossify into some
static, retrograde, going-back, siege mentality that can actually happen when
you are under threat.[18]

Labour, then, appeared to have learned some important lessons from
the 1980s—and not just in local government. It was facing a government every bit as inimical to its values and interests as Margaret

Thatcher's. Indeed, even those who were thought of (and who thought of themselves) as on Labour's right could see very little to admire in it or, indeed, in David Cameron as a Prime Minister. Nor, given the failure of the SDP in the 1980s, and given the way the Lib Dems had behaved in the aftermath of the 2010 election, were they under any illusions regarding the possibility of a 'progressive' alternative to an overall Labour majority. If the party were to stand any chance of defeating the Coalition, then it simply had to avoid imploding and indulging in the kind of infighting that had helped deliver the Tories four consecutive terms in office between 1979 and 1997.

But it was not just the marginalization of the hard (or for that matter the soft) left, or the dire warning provided by Labour's last period in opposition, or the fact that neither of the coalition partners was itself that popular, that made for the party's unusual, if sometimes uneasy, unity. After all, Labour might no longer be riven on profound ideological lines, but that did not mean that the factions that had developed around the Prime Minister and Chancellor between 1997 and 2007 had suddenly ceased to matter. Why, then, were Blairites and Brownites not fighting each other like cats in a sack, as many had predicted?

The absence of war had many causes, some of them already discussed. But it also had a lot to do with both factions becoming disillusioned with their figureheads. The mixture of jeering and cheering that greeted Miliband's mention of Tony Blair, and the fact that Labour's leader continued to insist on distancing himself from his electorally successful predecessor, inevitably put some Blairites' noses out of joint. But it would be wrong to imagine that they held the former Prime Minister in the same kind of unthinking regard as Conservative acolytes of Margaret Thatcher held their icon. Even for many of his biggest fans, whatever Blair had done for the party and delivered for Britain on the domestic front, he would be for ever tainted by his decision to join the USA in invading Iraq—an invasion that not only failed to turn up any weapons of mass destruction but left that country even more unstable, deadly, and dangerous than it had been under Saddam. Meanwhile, for their part, Brownites, as well as those on the left of the party who had hoped forlornly that the transition from Blair would give them more of what they wanted, had been let down by their man, too. It might have been different had Blair somehow clung on to Downing Street in 2007 and therefore been the one to lead Labour to a big defeat at the 2010 election.

Instead, Brown had been given his long-awaited chance and had utterly blown it.

In the leadership contest that followed, the old enmities were rarely too far beneath the surface, but they were nonetheless sublimated. The Brownites had split three ways, with those most closely identified with the regime rooting for Ed Balls, the rather less zealous supporting Ed Miliband, and the rest backing David. Moreover, for all the talk that the contest had taken on an extra edge because of the rivalry between two brothers, the fact that they *were* brothers reduced the chance that some sort of civil war would break out in its aftermath. It was unlikely, should one Miliband win the leadership and then bomb badly with the country, that the party would turn straight away to another. Meanwhile, anything other than exemplary behaviour from the loser was bound to be written off as personal pique rather than political disagreement. Whoever lost therefore had little or no incentive over the next few years to undermine the winner and remain a focus for internal discontent. If David won, Ed would almost certainly serve under his brother. If David lost, then, even if he did not return the favour, he was unlikely to set out to cause Ed trouble in the same way as he might have done otherwise.

In the event, Ed's victory and David's defeat meant that Labour was being led by the more acceptable face of Brownism, while the Blairites had suddenly lost their champion, had no one very obvious to turn to as an alternative, and anyway were being offered jobs under the new dispensation. It was not game over: differences—particularly differences of emphasis—remained. But there was at least the possibility that now, rather than festering, they could contribute to a creative tension that might actually help the party make smarter decisions about its positioning and what exactly it needed to focus on to win back power. One contribution at the 2011 conference illustrated this nicely. Ed Miliband had made much of the idea that Labour was not lurching to the left, as his detractors alleged, but that the centre ground of British politics had itself shifted: people wanted an economy that worked for everyone, not just a few at the top. Liam Byrne, the Blairite Shadow Work and Pensions Secretary, whom Miliband had put in charge of Labour's policy review (perhaps as penance for leaving an infamous note telling his successor as Chief Secretary that 'there is no money'), appeared to use the same idea in his platform speech in Liverpool. But there were subtle differences. Talking about the feedback that Labour had received from the hundreds of events it had held, and the thousands of submissions it had received, Byrne made it pretty clear to anyone listening carefully that the public's main beef was not just the economy but welfare and immigration, too. And on those issues, Labour had clearly lost touch with public opinion. Members might not like it, but any 'new centre ground' was not 'a place that the party gets to pick'; it was 'where voters say it is'. As he said in a speech to the Blairite think tank Progress in the summer, Labour would need 'tough, costed, forward-looking proposals that put the welfare state on the side of the hard-working majority'. This meant that it would have to 'get tough on those who are consistently found shirking their responsibilities'. Miliband himself might not have gone quite so far, or used quite such tough language—not at that time anyway. But it was a message that he, or at least the party as a whole, really needed to take on board. When it came to the Shadow Cabinet reshuffle carried out in early October, then, Byrne—Blairite or not—retained his post both as Policy Coordinator and as Shadow Secretary of State.

Miliband's first reshuffle may have provided few fireworks but it was important—and not just because it was the first in which a Labour leader in opposition was not hamstrung by having to find places for colleagues elected by the PLP. It was not a time for bloodletting—never his style anyway—but it was a chance to surround himself with more colleagues who were hopefully a little more likely to go out to bat for him. As one of his advisers later observed:

No one ever thinks that Ed is out to get scalps from bits of the Party he doesn't like. The problem we had was, because Ed came out of relative obscurity to being leader, he never had time to create a following. David had a following. Ed Balls had a following. But Ed never did. You can't create a following once you're leader because that would be divisive. So how do you create a base of support which isn't a factional group? The answer is you can't so you have to make the Shadow Cabinet your base.

This began with promotions for two MPs from the 2010 intake, with Chuka Umunna, formerly Ed Miliband's PPS, becoming Shadow Business Secretary and Rachel Reeves becoming Shadow Chief Secretary to the Treasury. Both had impressed as media performers and had therefore featured already in the lists of 'rising stars' occasionally compiled by journalists. Umunna stood out as a young, black, privately educated lawyer who had originally been associated with the left-wing group Compass but had since migrated rightwards—one reason (another may have been jealousy, pure and simple) why his rapid progress was not greeted with universal acclaim on the back benches. Reeves, an economist who exuded competence as much as charisma, came from a more ordinary background and, as such, did not attract the same degree of scepticism. The other appointments that attracted attention were those of Michael Dugher and Tom Watson, the scourge of Tony Blair and, more recently, Rupert Murdoch, who was given the role of Campaign Coordinator. Both men were associated with the Brown machine and, as such, expected to bring a more worldly-wise but also harder edge to Labour's communications and organization. Naturally some Blairites were none too impressed. It was not, however, the case that they had no one at the top table (or near it anyway): Stephen Twigg was appointed Shadow Secretary of State for Education, taking over from Andy Burnham, who—perhaps rather riskily in terms of some of the unfinished business from the last government—moved to Shadow his old job as Health Secretary. Also promoted were other members of the new intake like Liz Kendall, who, like Umunna and Reeves, were not so easy to pigeonhole. Perhaps inevitably, however, many observers were determined to portray the reshuffle as Ed Miliband taking the opportunity to bring the old gang back together. While that narrative may have been too harsh, or simply too pat, the fact that it gained traction was testimony to how difficult, or even impossible, it is for any leader to make a clean break with the past.

# 4

# Omnishambles: Autumn 2011–Spring 2012

Sadly for party leaders who are not also prime ministers, pretty much the only way the media are able to measure how well they are doing is to look at (and of course commission) opinion polls. This almost inevitably puts those leaders at a disadvantage. Inasmuch as polls are influenced by politicians at all, at least in the short run, then it is politicians in government rather than out of it who are more likely to shift them. They are afforded far more coverage, and they are in a much better position actually to do things rather than simply talk about doing them. The second week of December 2011 is a case in point. Through the autumn, the biggest political event of which was George Osborne's admission that he would miss his deficit and debt reduction targets, Labour had maintained a small lead over the Conservatives, even if, as the *Sun* took great delight in reminding its readers at the end of the first week of December, polls showed that many of those intending to vote for the party were distinctly unimpressed with Miliband himself. A few days later, however, the Tories received a sudden boost in their ratings. The reason? David Cameron was hailed a hero for vetoing a European Treaty in Brussels, and promptly returned to Westminster to wipe the floor with Labour's leader when the matter was discussed in the Commons. Cue renewed questions about whether Ed was up to the job, which an excruciating three-page, 'Christmas with the Milibands' photo shoot in the *Mirror* did nothing, oddly enough, to dampen down.[1] Indeed, it being the festive season, there was little else for journalists to do other than, first, enjoy the fact that Ed Balls, unaware of the *Mirror* feature, had talked publicly about how he would never allow *his* kids to appear in that sort of story and, secondly, to try to parlay what was admittedly genuine concern about Miliband in Labour's ranks into something approaching a leadership crisis—complete, of course, with speculation about who might take over, their clear favourite being Balls's wife, Yvette Cooper.

The way in which the media move swiftly through their register of stock phrases in order to conjure something out of nothing (or almost nothing) is laid bare by political correspondent Rob Hutton in his marvellously satirical book *Romps, Tots and Boffins*.[2] But it has to be said that, on this occasion, Labour—or at least parts of the Labour coalition—ensured that the hacks did not have to work too hard. Both front- and backbenchers had been happy, off the record of course, to share their dismay at Miliband's morale-sapping performance in parliament before Christmas.[3] And, in the New Year, Blue Labour 'guru' Maurice Glasman—this time very much on the record—waded into the fray, penning a piece for the *New Statesman* that managed to combine an apparent declaration of support for Miliband with a caustic critique of the lack of progress Labour had made since the election. Unlike his New Labour counterparts, he saw nothing wrong with predators and producers—indeed, he called on Ed, who in his view had so far 'flickered rather than shone, nudged not led', to be even bolder on that score. At the moment, he complained:

There seems to be no strategy, no narrative and little energy. Old faces from the Brown era still dominate the shadow cabinet and they seem stuck in defending Labour's record in all the wrong ways—we didn't spend too much money, we'll cut less fast and less far, but we can't tell you how. Labour is apparently pursuing a sectional agenda based on the idea that disaffected Liberal Democrats and public-sector employees will give Labour a majority next time around. But we have not won, and show no signs of winning, the economic argument. We have not articulated a constructive alternative capable of recognising our weaknesses in government and taking the argument to the coalition. We show no relish for reconfiguring the relationship between the state, the market and society. The world is on the turn, yet we do not seem equal to the challenge.[4]

Glasman's comments made such a splash because they came from someone who believed that the party had chosen the right brother back in 2010 and because they related to substance as well as style: it clearly was not just Blairites who believed that Labour had to address the fact that voters were at least as (if not more) worried about the deficit as they were about growth. And at least he had the guts to say in public what other Labour politicians seemed happy to let slip to journalists in private, notwithstanding their receiving a memo from Tom Baldwin, then leaked to his old employer, *The Times*, providing them with ample defensive and offensive 'lines to take'—including a clear steer that the leadership was now planning, in response to voter research, a big push on 'the cost of living'.[5] That Glasman's views were aired openly and honestly did not exactly help matters, however. They contributed, for instance, to a gruelling New Year interview for Miliband with the *Today Programme*'s John Humphrys, who, on the back of his poor personal ratings, challenged Labour's leader directly on whether he had the qualities—and even perhaps the looks—to do the job.[6]

Whether or not Humphrys had, as many Labour supporters claimed, gone too far, it was a tough time for Miliband. And things got even tougher when he made what was inevitably billed as a speech to 'relaunch' his leadership by acknowledging that Labour would face 'difficult choices' if it were to deliver fairness when there was no additional money to spend. In a coordinated move, Balls then used an interview with the *Guardian* to signal (in advance of a keynote speech to the Fabian Society Conference) that, whatever his position on Labour's responsibility for the deficit, the party was going to have to accept its consequences now that Osborne had admitted in his Autumn Statement that he would not be able to eliminate the deficit by 2015. Labour might not like cuts; it might even believe that, had the government not cut too far, too fast, some of them might have been unnecessary; but, Balls said, it had to live with them. 'My starting point', he confessed, 'is, I am afraid, [that] we are going to have [to] keep all these cuts. There is a big squeeze happening on budgets across the piece . . . At this stage, we can make no commitments to reverse any of that, on spending or on tax.' He then went on to insist:

It is now inevitable that public sector pay restraint will have to continue through this parliament. Labour cannot duck that reality and won't. There is no way we should be arguing for higher pay when the choice is between higher pay and bringing unemployment down. I know there will be some people in the trade union movement and the Labour party who will think, of course, Labour has got to oppose that pay restraint in 2014 and 2015. That's something we cannot do, should not do and will not do.[7]

Talking not merely of being unable to reverse the Coalition's cuts but of having to keep all of them, as well as insisting on the need for pay restraint, was a significant—though arguably belated—shift on Balls's part, even if his characteristic insistence that what he was saying now was what he had always thought effectively prevented Labour making more of a virtue out of necessity. Pretty soon, however, people were questioning whether Balls was speaking for the whole party. Rumours circulated that he had gone a little further on cuts than Miliband had assumed he was going to. Then Deputy Leader Harriet Harman went on the radio a couple of days later and insisted that, while the two Eds were right to remind people that a future Labour government would need to make plenty of proverbial hard choices, 'it's simply not the case that we're accepting the government's spending cuts. That couldn't be further from the truth. We think that the government's austerity spending cuts are making a bad situation worse; we think that they're too far and too fast. And actually we're fighting the cuts.' Labour, it appeared, was still trying to have its cake and eat it too. Cameron promptly made the most of the confusion at a session of PMQs that would otherwise have proved pretty difficult for him, given the fact that official figures now showed unemployment rising to a seventeen-year high. Last year, crowed the Prime Minister, the Leader of the Opposition 'wanted to march against the cuts, now he tells us he accepts them' yet at the same time 'he's telling us he wants to spend more and borrow more. He's so incompetent he can't even do a U-turn properly.'[8]

Then, of course, there was the question of whether, even if people could see past the knockabout and the mixed messaging and appreciate that some sort of shift had occurred, whether that shift went anything like far enough. Certainly, it came nowhere near meeting calls from people who had worked alongside both Balls and Miliband in government for Labour to do some deeper thinking about how social democracy could work now it could no longer rely on sharing the proceeds of growth as it had done between 1997 and 2007. A good example was Gavin Kelly, a former senior adviser to both Blair and Brown in Number Ten, who had since become Chief Executive of the Resolution Foundation, a think tank focusing on practical measures to improve living standards people on low and middle incomes. Writing for the *New Statesman*, Kelly insisted that Labour needed not only to ponder but also to declare more openly 'what [the state] should do less of, more of, and differently, given the realities of the next decade and beyond'. He suggested, for example:

It could, for instance, offer less generous support for affluent baby boomers in terms of universal benefits at the same time as it puts in place a proper... system of social care, overwhelmingly paid for by the ageing generation itself rather than their working age counterparts.

It could invest far more in childcare supporting more women to work, raising family living standards, and spreading opportunity; and far less in supporting the most affluent in our society to build up larger pensions. It could invest more in growth-enhancing capital investment and new housing even if this means a longer era of low or no growth in current expenditure.[9]

Achieving 'clarity about who will be the winners and losers from Labour's fiscal decisions, and the need to build widespread public consent for these choices', would not of course be easy, Kelly admitted. But it needed to begin the process, and more immediately needed to move from a general admission that cuts would be necessary to levelling with the public about where exactly it would hope to make savings and (just as trickily) raise revenue. 'There will be no prizes', he wrote, 'for sounding more hawkish in the abstract and dovish when it comes to specifics'. Whether or not he was right about this—voters, after all, do not have that big a reputation for rewarding honesty if it will cost them dear—Kelly was spot-on when he suggested that following his recommendations would inevitably arouse anger among interest groups that might lose out. Ed Balls, after all, was proposing something pretty mild in comparison, as was Miliband by backing him. But both took flak almost straight away—and from a very predictable direction.

Len McCluskey of Unite, one of the unions that had done so much to help Ed rather than David win the leadership back in 2010, claimed in a *Guardian* column that it represented 'a victory for discredited Blairism at the expense of the party's core supporters' and challenged 'the whole course Ed Miliband has set for the party, and perhaps his leadership itself'. As for Balls himself, he had, as far as McCluskey was concerned, joined Blairites Liam Byrne (who had recently talked about getting back to Beveridge), Stephen Twigg (who had talked about introducing longer school days), and Jim Murphy (who had declared a willingness to see defence cuts and remarked on Labour's need to demonstrate 'credibility' rather than 'shallow and temporary' populism) as the 'four horsemen of the austerity apocalypse'. Expressing outrage that 'no effort was made by Labour to consult with trade unions before making the shift', Unite's leader claimed Miliband was being 'dragged back into the swamp of bond market orthodoxy. And this policy coup', he warned, 'may not be the end of the matter. Having won on the measures, new Labour will likely come for the man sooner or later.' For those who wanted 'a real alternative' to the Coalition, however, it was time, he insisted rather ominously, 'to get organised in parliament and outside'.[10]

McCluskey's words were followed up by the general secretaries of the other big unions. Dave Prentis of Unison, the UK's second biggest and predominantly public-sector union, claimed 'Our members needed hope and a reason to vote Labour. They have been snatched away.' He went on to declare that 'Ed Miliband's naivety is breath-taking'. Instead of standing by those struggling on low wages, Labour had 'chosen instead to play cheap politics with their lives'. The Labour leader's 'ill-thought-through comments' would, he warned, 'have unintended consequences', although he declined to spell them out.[11] The leader of the UK's third biggest union, the GMB's Paul Kenny, was more direct. The media were given sight of a letter he had written to his officials assuring them that he had 'spoken to Ed Milliband and Ed Balls to ensure they were aware of how wrong I think the policy they are now following is' and suggesting: 'It is now time for careful consideration and thought before the wider discussions begin on the long-term implications this new stance by the party has on GMB affiliation.' A few weeks later, the union's executive released a state-ment to the effect that 'relations with the Labour Party and what GMB members expect and want from the party will form a major plank in the debate at GMB Congress in Brighton in June', when a resolution on disaffiliation might well be voted on.[12]

This was hardly subtle. Labour, after all, was millions of pounds in debt—so much so that it had made changes to the way it uprated staff pensions so as to reduce its liabilities. Indeed, it was even in the process of getting its constituency parties to transfer any properties they owned to it so as to allow loans to be raised against them if necessary. But the general secretaries' intervention did at least offer Miliband, despite his genuine distaste for the idea that demonstrating leadership meant taking on the party or the unions, a chance to do precisely that. In a series of broadcast interviews he insisted: 'I am not going to change my policy in the face of threats, I am going to do the right thing. Of course there are going to be some people in the party who don't like it but I'm afraid that's tough. We need to do the right thing, the responsible thing.' Unions had to accept that in 'tough times' there may be a trade-off between preserving jobs and services, on the one hand, and paying rises, on the other. And, when it came to reversing government cuts, he was not going to make promises he could not keep, since his priority 'must be to show that Labour can be trusted with the nation's finances'.[13]

Rushing to his defence, Blairite former Shadow Chancellor (and former union leader) Alan Johnson was even blunter: Labour was going to win only if it could demonstrate, as the two Eds were now doing, that it was 'living in the real world, not some fantasy utopia based on outdated ideology and a distorted view of which vested interests should be immune to radical change'.[14] A pamphlet on *The New Centre Ground* by one of McCluskey's *bêtes noires*, Liam Byrne, similarly stressed the need for adaptation, albeit in less charged language.[15] And, writing a fortnight later for the *New Statesman*, David Miliband likewise warned of the dangers of the party becoming little more than 'Reassurance Labour'—an organization that felt good about itself but refused to change with the times—although inevitably (but almost certainly wrongly) his words were interpreted by many as coded criticism of his brother rather than of those who insisted that nothing good had come out of the New Labour years.[16]

The extent to which the genuine row with the unions helped Labour's policy shift cut through to voters is debateable, however. Less so is the extent to which, along with the imagined row with his brother, it deflected attention from Miliband's nascent attempt to open up another front in the war to win them over—namely, the positioning of Labour as some sort of consumer champion. 'People's living standards are squeezed as never before', he told the *Telegraph* in an interview, 'and we have to do everything we can to relieve that burden' by combating exploitation by 'predatory' (that word again) companies.[17] The problem was widespread, but he pointed to some obvious and particularly egregious examples, including inflated management fees for pensions, undisclosed but unavoidable levies from budget airlines, the perennial problem of bank charges and extortionate 'customer care' helplines, railway station car park charges, and overly complex (as well as expensive) energy bills. Regarding the latter, it was even revealed a few weeks later that Labour, in an attempt to prove that it could make a real difference even in opposition, was looking at a scheme pioneered by some continental socialist parties, which had hooked up with internet switching agents to help consumers to get better deals—an initiative that was actually taken further but ultimately appears to have attracted little or no uptake.

All this consumer-focused campaigning had the advantage of being about tangible issues that would probably feature on many voters' lists of pet peeves—unlike the debate about the 'short-termism' apparently 'hard-wired' into British capitalism that Miliband was simultaneously conducting in the pages of the *Financial Times*.[18] The question, of course, was whether, even if voters had not blinked and missed it, this sort of initiative was almost too retail, too micro-level. It was no doubt worthy, both in and of itself, and as the first skirmish in what the Labour leadership had decided would be a much bigger campaign on the cost of living. With real wages for the 'squeezed middle' having first stagnated and then fallen, the latter was becoming a huge concern, as a widely reported piece of research from Gavin Kelly's Resolution Foundation made abundantly clear.[19] And the specific examples of ripoffs cited by Miliband were also the sort of stuff that tested well in focus groups. But were they seriously going to change the way people thought about a party still seen by many as a spendthrift soft touch— especially when the government was in effect making the running on 'fairness' by introducing a 'benefits cap' in its Welfare Reform Bill to ensure that households dependent entirely on benefits could no longer receive support greater than an amount equivalent to the median after-tax household income of £26,000?

Polling suggested that about three-quarters of voters (and well over two-thirds of Labour voters) supported such a cap, notwithstanding what its opponents suggested were its glaring practical flaws. Labour, however, was equivocal. Shadow Secretary of State for Work and Pensions Liam Byrne declared he was willing to consider a cap that took into account local variations in housing costs and protected the vulnerable from homelessness. However, when it became clear a large number of Labour peers were determined to resist the idea come what may, the party eventually supported what was in effect a wrecking amendment introduced in the House of Lords to exclude child benefit from the calculation. The amendment, along with others (including one that tried to overturn the under-occupancy charge or 'bedroom tax' on people in social housing deemed to have more rooms than they needed), was duly overturned by the government's majority in the Commons and the Bill was granted Royal Assent at the beginning of

March. The Chancellor, George Osborne, had learned all about dividing lines from Gordon Brown. Just as he hoped, Labour, despite the leadership trying (and ultimately failing) to reconcile its concern for those families affected with its need to take into account public opinion, looked like ending up on the wrong side of this one.

Labour was not totally without a response, of course. Its aim, not surprisingly or indeed unreasonably, was to try to reframe the largely negative debate about welfare into one about positive moves to help get people back into work, at the same time stressing that these would involve an element of compulsion that showed that Labour could be tough, too. The second week of March saw Byrne, coming off the back of a think-tank pamphlet produced by one of his shadow team, Stephen Timms, introduce the idea of a 'real jobs guarantee'.[20] Building on the example of the Labour government's Future Jobs Fund, which had been scrapped by the Coalition in spite of independent assessments that it had been reasonably effective, it would offer six months' work and training to anyone between 18 and 24 who had been unemployed for a year, with the bulk of employers' costs being subsidized by government, paid for (yet again, insisted sceptical government spokesmen) by a tax on bankers' bonuses. Miliband followed up with a speech stressing that there would be 'tough consequences' for those who did not take up the offer, including benefit sanctions. Unfortunately, the whole thing rather fell apart when a clearly poorly briefed Deputy Leader Harriet Harman gave what was widely derided as a 'car-crash' television interview on the scheme with the BBC's Jo Coburn.[21] This was a pity, since the idea itself was not necessarily a bad one and it was not as if Labour, at that stage, had many ideas to go round. Indeed, as the *Sun* rather cruelly put it in a headline announcing news of a break-in at Miliband's office: 'Ed's HQ Burgled . . . No Policies Found'.

Still, even those dark days were punctuated by the odd ray of light—both organizationally and politically. In many ways, Miliband's first year had been a real struggle. For a start, his wafer-thin majority, and the fact that he was not the first choice of the PLP, the Shadow Cabinet, or, indeed, most of the party's non-union donors and its professional staff meant a lot of time had to be spent on what is known euphemistically as 'political management'—in other words, trying to reassure doubters that, as one of Miliband's advisers later put it, his team was more than merely 'a Brownite cabal, reinvented'. The fact that so many people remained so sceptical for so long only increased the sense of vulnerability felt by many in the Leader's Office and by Ed himself. And this in turn led to a degree of hypersensitivity, which made things even harder than perhaps they needed to have been. As one insider later observed:

The thing about the Labour Party is it's a gossip machine. It lives on gossip. It lives on people slagging each other off... That's how it copes with the stress of it all. It's like any work place but bigger and... in the papers every day. They should have realized sooner that, at the end of the day, you might have one or two people who are genuinely out to sabotage you but 99 per cent of them will maybe slag you off yet still want to get Labour elected.

Just as importantly, whereas David had spent a lot of time over the summer of 2010 working out how he was going to run things when he won, Ed had kept the focus on winning, leaving him no time to think about what sort of operation he would put in place if he won. Partly as a result, and partly because so many of the obvious candidates had wanted David to win and/or were desperate for a break from politics, he had simply peopled the Leader's Office with staff from his campaign team, one or two of whom were, to put it mildly, not well suited to the administrative demands placed upon them. It was, therefore, a huge relief to all concerned when Miliband eventually found someone to take on the Chief of Staff role on a permanent basis. Tim Livesey had been working as an adviser to the Archbishop of Canterbury for six years, although before that he had worked as a career diplomat and as a press officer in Downing Street. It was hoped that what he lacked in experience of the Labour Party he would more than make up for in his ability to bring calm and order to a Leader's Office that lacked both— so much so that people who dealt with it talked of emails, letters, and telephone calls simply going unanswered.

Meanwhile, on the political front, Miliband could claim a victory of sorts when (in addition to Peter Mandelson telling the *Today Programme* that New Labour had overstated the extent to which globalization, without more government intervention, would spread wealth as well as generate growth), David Cameron appeared to feel the need to move on to what the Labour leader liked to think of as his chosen battleground. Appearing on BBCTV's *Andrew Marr Show*, the week after Miliband had taken a pounding on the very same sofa on tax and spend, the Prime Minister talked of the need to deal with excessive pay and the companies involved who were 'frankly ripping off the share-holder and the customer'.[22] Rewarding top executives for failure made 'people's blood boil'. It was, he claimed, 'crony capitalism' (a phrase he had borrowed from the philosopher-turned-Tory MP Jesse Norman) and it was 'wrong'. Perhaps, then, Miliband's attack at conference on 'predators'—one he had followed up in mid-November in a speech on 'responsible capitalism' at the Social Market Foundation and was about to follow up again with a call for 'one nation banking'—had not been such a bad idea after all?[23] Sure, it may have been a slower-burn success than his response to Hackgate—an event from which he still seemed to draw so much confidence. But was he not setting the agenda in the way that ultimately successful leaders of the opposition such as Thatcher and Blair had done? Why else would the government be so keen to be seen to be doing something on the subject?

Miliband's renewed confidence that he was onto something was strengthened by the controversy that blew up at the end of January around the million-pound bonus to be paid to Stephen Hester, head of RBS—a bank in which the government had taken a majority stake in order to rescue it after the crash—in spite of its share price declining markedly over the year and it sacking thousands of staff. Again, the Labour leader proved himself tactically acute as well as strategically astute. When it became clear that, notwithstanding media and public disquiet on the issue, the government was unwilling to step in to block the bonus, Milband declared that Labour would force a Commons vote on the issue, at which point Hester decided—much to David Cameron's relief—to forgo the payout but also to stay on in his job.

Even this, though, was not enough for some of Miliband's critics, who made the point that one of the reasons Cameron (and indeed Clegg and Cable) had decided, albeit belatedly, to move onto his territory was because the Labour leader, while he had clearly tapped into public concern about excess and exploitation, had failed to back up his 'producers versus predators' speech with a handful of memorable measures designed to tackle the situation. True, Cameron's ideas on limiting executive pay were mainly for show only, just as his announcement a few days later that Fred 'the Shred' Goodwin would be stripped of his knighthood provided a convenient distraction from news that the veto he had wielded in Brussels in December turned out, in Miliband's words, not to be for life, just for Christmas, since the twenty-five member states that had signed the Fiscal

Compact were going to be able to use EU institutions to enforce it after all. True, too, that Labour's Shadow Business Secretary, Chuka Umunna, had now come up with some rather more convincing proposals of his own on remuneration. But, as far as Miliband's critics were concerned—some of them, ironically, the very same people who had initially expressed concerns about him making Labour appear anti-business—none of that made up for the fact that the government had been allowed to get there first.

Arguably, some of the party's problems frontstage had their roots in problems backstage, which the appointment of Tim Livesey could not on its own hope to solve. Miliband had managed, via Tessa Jowell, the Blairite former Minister for the Olympics, to persuade Charles Allen, ex-Chief Executive of ITV, to work part-time (and unpaid) alongside whoever was appointed Labour's new General Secretary. His role would be to provide advice on organizational reform based on his extensive experience in the corporate world and on the Common-wealth and Olympic Games. Fortunately, although things had not gone strictly according to plan and the job had gone to Iain McNicol rather than Chris Lennie, the arrangement went ahead anyway, McNicol concluding that it would do the cause of reform no harm to have Labour looked over by a businessman of Allen's calibre, and Allen (who had already assisted Miliband by helping to land Tim Livesey for the Chief of Staff job) was happy to carry on if McNicol was happy to work with him.

The first thing they did was to conduct a series of face-to-face interviews with well over 100 elected politicians, volunteers, and professional staff in order to get a sense of where the land lay and what might be done to reform an organization that, they both knew, badly needed to change. They were especially keen to overcome what was generally seen as a dysfunctional and damaging divide between the political operation located in the Leader's Office based in parliament and the professional operation in Party Headquarters, initially located in Victoria Street opposite New Scotland Yard but due, in April, to move to new premises at One Brewer's Green—a fortunate move in the sense that the latter (a) was cheaper, (b) was rather more welcom-ing, (c) had room where people from the Leader's Office could work if they wanted to, and (d) would hopefully convey the sense of a fresh start. Allen's recommendation had been for a Board comprised of six Executive Directors covering, respectively, Members and Supporters,

Governance and Party Services, Field Operations, Commercial, Policy and Rebuttal, and Communications. Approved by the NEC, adverts had gone out in the New Year, even though it was not entirely clear at that stage whether the new Board would be accountable to it. Nor, for that matter, was it clear whether the new structure at the top would entail wholesale reorganization of staff working at Party Headquarters—staff who were already coping with McNicol's openly declared determination to see Labour decentralize in order to reanimate its relationship with its volunteers and field organizers in the provinces.

Allen had deliberately chosen not to go down the route of authoring a long, formal report for fear that, like others of its ilk, it would be subject to multiple (and often malign) interpretation and, as a result, fail to result in anything changing. The downside of such a strategy was that it was bound, like all attempts to apply a new structure to a multi-layered, culturally complex organization, to attract accusations that changes were being railroaded through. Hopes that all this could all be ironed out in time and with a spirit of cooperation, however, received a severe blow when, in the second week of March, it was announced that the new Board would not only include an additional Director, whose post had not been advertised, but that three of the (now) seven posts were to be filled from within the Leader's Office: Bob Roberts as Executive Director, Communications; Torsten Bell as Executive Director, Policy and Rebuttal; and—most controversially because his was the post supposedly conjured out of nowhere—Greg Beales as Executive Director, Strategy and Planning. Even more worryingly, at least for those determined to see the whole thing as a sectarian power grab by a Brownite clique in the Leader's Office rather than a genuine attempt to integrate the political and the professional operation, the seven Directors would be joined on the Board by Tim Livesey and Lucy Powell, Miliband's Chief and Deputy Chief of Staff. Not only that, but the Board would be chaired by Charles Allen himself.

Quite where this left Iain McNicol, Labour's General Secretary, who would be on the Board but not perhaps in charge like his predecessors, left many confused—perhaps unnecessarily so: Allen was a busy man and saw his continued role as very much that of a non-executive Chairman; meanwhile the Board was intended, at least from his point of view, mainly as a coordination and communication forum rather than a locus of decision and control, the latter resting ultimately with the leader and, when it came to organizational (as opposed to political) matters, with Tim Livesey and Iain McNicol, who reported on the Board to the NEC. As in any big organization, those in its various divisions were prone to lose sight not just of the overall picture but of what the others were up to. Equally importantly, they were inclined to spend money as if they were the only ones doing it. The Board, and the obligation imposed on directors to table regular reports to it, as well as read those tabled by their fellow directors, would it was hoped counteract that tendency—something that was particularly important to McNicol, since the party, which had literally been on the verge of bankruptcy towards the end of the Blair/Brown years, was still running up a £1.7 million deficit even in 2011.

The situation was not helped by the fact that the news of the new appointments leaked to bloggers, including the notorious (and at Westminster much-read) Guido Fawkes and Dan Hodges, as well as the more friendly LabourList, run by Mark Ferguson. Things were made even worse when detailed accounts of a fraught meeting between staffers at Party Headquarters in Victoria Street and Allen, Livesey, and Powell also found their way into the blogosphere and the left-leaning *Guardian*. So, too, did a letter from staff representatives outlining their concerns both about what was to happen to their jobs in the future and about the way the whole thing had been handled, with one passage revealing their disappointment at being given the news, not by their boss, McNicol, but in a letter from Ed Miliband, who had apparently not been near Victoria Street in months. In addition to all this, there were concerns raised in the wider party about the fact that the Board contained no one from an ethnic minority and that only one of the seven Executive Directors was a woman—Emilie Oldknow, in charge of Governance and Party Services. There was also a continuing lack of clarity, some felt, about the campaigns role being played by Tom Watson, hero of Hackgate, who would now, it was announced, be assisted by outgoing Deputy General Secretary, Alicia Kennedy, employed as 'Strategic Adviser (Campaigns and Elections)' and located in the Leader's Office. Meanwhile, her former deputy, Patrick Heneghan, and not the widely respected Caroline Badley (who had masterminded Gisela Stuart's remarkable 2010 win in Edgbaston), took over as Executive Director in charge of Field Operations—an appointment that seemed to many to confirm that, in the words of one critic, 'the machine continued to pick the machine'. The other outgoing Deputy General Secretary, and the man who had lost out to McNicol when it came to the top job (or at least what had been the top job!), Chris Lennie, was also staying on to help out with fundraising and external relations, the post of Executive Director, Commercial, remaining as yet unfilled. Nor was it entirely clear where all this left Tom Baldwin in terms of the hierarchy. Bob Roberts had been appointed Executive Director of Communications, which presumably meant that he would be doing a lot more than handling the Lobby. Did the fact that Baldwin was now to be called 'Senior Adviser (Communications and Strategy)' mean he was now the junior of the two? Or was he still doing pretty much the same job with a different title? Nobody quite seemed to know what was going on, and morale, in Victoria Street/Brewer's Green if not in the Leader's Office, was low.

Had the mood across the road in the Commons been equally downbeat, then Miliband might have been in serious trouble. Fortunately, however, things were about to look up—courtesy of the Coalition and the Conservative Party. For starters, parliament was once again considering the government's controversial Health Bill, which had managed to alienate virtually all the organized interests involved in the NHS and trigger an e-petition signed by nearly 175,000 people. It also led to a number of prominent Lib Dems, especially in the Lords, siding with Labour. Many Tories were equally concerned, and were briefing endlessly against Health Secretary Andrew Lansley even as the Prime Minister was holding a summit in Number Ten to try to convince stakeholders that the massively amended Bill would not result in the dislocation and disaster that many were forecasting. Very few Labour politicians at Westminster thought that they could actually stop the Bill going through. But they could see that they had Cameron, who after all had spent much of his time in opposition trying to convince voters that the Tories could be trusted on the NHS, on the run—and that Miliband, who was careful to stress that Labour was not against reform per se, just what he called 'a misguided attempt to impose a free market free-for-all on our National Health Service', was pressing home Labour's natural advantage on the issue pretty effectively.

The government, desperate to clear the decks before the Chancellor announced what it hoped would be a game-changing Budget on 21 March, therefore breathed a huge sigh of relief when the NHS Bill finally passed the previous day. The Labour-supporting *Daily Mirror*'s decision to mark the occasion with a huge front-page photo of a gravestone bearing the inscription NHS 1948–2012, KILLED BY THE COALITION could be discounted.[24] The Tories had endured a week or so on the back foot over health, as well as over 'Horsegate'—David Cameron's belated admission that he had become such a close friend of News International's Rebekah Brooks that he had, indeed, ridden a mare bizarrely loaned to her by the Metropolitan Police. They were now about to regain the initiative—or so they thought. In fact, far from the worst being over, it was actually yet to come. Sometimes in politics, as Labour had found when, having called off 'the election that never was' in October 2007, it stumbled straight into a series of policy and operational disasters that shredded what remained of its reputation for competence, it never rains but it pours.

The Budget of 2012, at least in the short term, can lay claim to being one of the most unsuccessful in recent political history. The Chancellor had announced in his Autumn Statement that he was going to miss his targets for reducing both the national debt and the government's deficit. But the economy was also flatlining. Osborne had little option, therefore, but to try to keep things fiscally neutral. He was, however, facing pressure from the Lib Dems to raise income-tax thresholds—a measure that Clegg and his colleagues seemed to have decided was now their signature policy but that most Tories could also agree to, since it reduced taxation not just for the lowest earners but for everyone else, too. Some of the money to pay for that change could come by continuing not to raise the threshold at which people would begin to pay the higher, 40p rate of taxation, thereby ensuring that a million or so people that year would be dragged into that bracket. But that sleight of hand would not be enough in and of itself, not least because Osborne had also decided to reduce the top rate of tax (paid by those on incomes over £150,000) from 50p to 45p in the pound.

Osborne had made that decision partly because he wanted to send a signal that Britain under the Tories was 'open for business', partly because he bought the argument that 50p was ultimately counterproductive in financial terms, and partly because he was so confident he had the measure of Ed Balls. He was also seeking to curry favour with parliamentarians and party members who might one day be deciding on whether to back him as Tory leader. Any shortfall occasioned by the reduction of the top rate, Osborne concluded, could be made up by sticking with planned rises in fuel duty, by increasing VAT on various items previously taxed at a lower rate, and by bringing down the threshold at which pensioners were liable for income tax. If he thought this was all terribly clever, however, he was wrong. There were popular and compensatory measures, including the higher allowance for basic-rate taxpayers, the raising of stamp duty on houses sold for over £2 million, and the introduction of a 25 per cent minimum tax rate for the super-rich. But, partly because the government wanted those measures leaked, partly because, being a coalition, leaking was part of the negotiation process, many of them were already well known to journalists. As a result, the media were even more on the look-out for nasty surprises than usual.

Some of those nasty surprises took a little time to find, of course, even with Labour's help. But, while the hunt was going on, Miliband managed to put on quite a show in his own right. By convention, the Leader of the Opposition is required to respond immediately after the Chancellor. Normally this is no easy task, but it was one made much, much easier on this occasion by all the briefing that had gone on beforehand. Almost unable to believe his luck that Osborne had indeed decided to make a mockery of his frequent boast that 'we are all in this together' by giving a tax cut to the rich, he was effectively able to pull out of his back pocket a speech that he and Torsten Bell had written earlier. As the late, great Simon Hoggart noted in the *Guardian*, the Labour leader 'concentrated almost entirely on the 5p cut in the top tax rate. The 14,000 people in Britain who earned £1m or more a year would each be richer by at least £40,000. It was the government's own bankers' bonus!' Then, Hoggart continued, Miliband 'launched into manic pantomime. "Hands up in the cabinet if you get a benefit from the income tax cut! Come on!" . . . Nobody budged. "One more chance!" The cabinet sat morose and resentful. "Well, it's good news for him!" he said, pointing wildly at the Prime Minister. "Now he can afford his own horse!"'[25]

On its own, that bravura performance, combined with the fact that one of the Conservatives quintessential modernizers appeared to have single-handedly 'retoxified' the Tory brand, would have garnered Miliband the cheers of his backbenchers, some usefully positive coverage on the six and ten o'clock news, and perhaps a percentage point or two in the polls. It might even have helped to help people forget that, in the run-up to the Budget, Ed Balls, despite his supposed conversion to prudence in the New Year, had, in true Keynesian fashion, insisted on calling on the Chancellor to reverse his VAT increase—a move that would have added some £12 billion to the deficit. But, on its own, Miliband's performance would probably not have been much more than a temporary boost or distraction. No, the real problem for Osborne was the reaction of the media (including, most worryingly, the Tory media) to some of the other measures in his budget, in particular the so-called granny tax and then, a day or so later, as journalists, ably assisted by Labour's spinners, began to dig deeper, the so-called pasty tax—the decision to levy VAT on formerly exempt hot-food items sold in bakeries around Britain, including those run by Greggs, which saw millions wiped off its share price overnight. The message from the polling was unequivocal: the year before, YouGov had found that 44 per cent of those asked thought the Budget fair as opposed to 31 per cent who thought it unfair; in 2012, the figures were 32 per cent and 48 per cent respectively; meanwhile, on the Monday following the Budget, ComRes found that two-thirds of respondents agreed with the statement that 'the measures announced in the Budget show that the Conservatives are the party of the rich', while only a quarter disagreed.[26] Overall, the Tories' standing as measured by various polling companies dropped by between two and four percentage points, with Labour's standing rising by roughly the same amount.

Then, as if all this were not bad enough for Osborne, a few days later the *Sunday Times* ran a story (with accompanying video footage) that purported to show the Conservative Party's newly appointed Treasurer, Peter Cruddas, offering prospective Tory donors a chance to influence government policy.[27] While protesting his innocence (something he later proved in court), Cruddas stepped down immediately, and Cameron agreed to restart talks on party funding, but the damage was done. The Conservatives looked dodgy. They also looked like they were more interested in doing favours for their rich friends than they were in looking out for everyone else. And trying harder only made things worse. While Miliband and Balls, along with Rachel Reeves, paid a visit to Greggs to buy some hot sausage rolls, Osborne told a parliamentary committee that he could not remember when he had last bought a pasty from the shop, while Cameron remembered buying one at Leeds station from a food retailer that, further investigation confirmed, had actually closed down long before he claimed to have bought it. Before all this, only aficionados of the BBC's cult political comedy *The Thick of It* had ever heard the word omnishambles, but, when Ed Miliband used it to describe the Budget in the Commons a few weeks later, it seemed to make sense to everyone—so much so that it became the *Oxford English Dictionary*'s 'word of the year' for 2012.

Suddenly, everything seemed to be going Labour's way. When tanker-drivers belonging to the Unite union voted for industrial action that threatened fuel supplies across the country, right-wing newspapers were quick to condemn what the *Sun* called Miliband's refusal to 'condemn the politically driven bullying of Britain by his paymaster, Red Len McCluskey', conveniently forgetting that only a few weeks earlier Miliband had been outspoken in his criticism of the Unite leader's suggestion that strikes could hit the Olympics.[28] Yet the story quickly turned into one that focused on the incompetence of government ministers. By sending out mixed messages about the need to prepare, they had sparked panic buying on forecourts up and down the land and had even, it was claimed, put people's lives at risk (and reminded them of quite how middle-class they were) by not only advising them to fill jerry cans full of petrol but to store them in the garage. Whether or not voters believed, as some journalists suggested, that those ministers had deliberately upped the ante in order to engineer some sort of Thatcher moment, polls showed over 80 per cent of them thought the government had created unnecessary panic over a strike that in the end never actually went ahead. Those same polls showed similarly high levels of scepticism about the pasty tax and the granny tax, notwithstanding the fact that the government could have made a very good argument that, until now, the elderly had been largely shielded from austerity and were likely to make significant gains from the decision to link pensions not just to prices but to average earnings. Polls also showed very little support for the reduction of the top rate to 45p. Even more encouragingly for Miliband, they not only showed Labour suddenly opening up a decent lead over the Tories—touching double figures according to some companies; they also put the party over what was supposedly 'the psychologically important' 40 per cent threshold.[29]

But there was more to come as the government's extraordinary run of bad luck showed no sign of stopping. Shadow Home Secretary Yvette Cooper had tried her best to raise concern about the impact of reductions in spending on 'front-line' policing, helped perhaps by

Tory-supporting media happy to build up anyone whom (however much the person concerned denied it) they could present as a rival to Miliband. But she was always going to struggle to make much of an impact when all the accepted measures suggested that most crime was continuing to fall. Immigration, however, had presented more of a target. The media—ably assisted by Cooper—had already laid into Home Secretary Theresa May back in February in the wake of a scathing official report that had revealed chronic levels of mismanagement and miscommunication in the UK Border Agency (UKBA). And now she was in even more trouble over mistakes made by the Home Office that led to yet another delay in the extradition to Jordan of the suspected Islamist terrorist Abu Qatada. Meanwhile, the Prime Minister was desperately trying to hang on to his Culture Secretary, Jeremy Hunt, after the full extent of the close relationship his office enjoyed with News International came to light during the Leveson Inquiry, prompting the *Mail*, of all newspaper groups, to give Miliband a column on its main editorial page to lambast his opponents over the affair.[30] Sadly for the Labour leader, however, efforts to gain similar traction on the access that the rich and powerful enjoyed to the Prime Minister himself did not fare quite so well. Indeed, they may even have backfired when, in an ultimately unsuccessful attempt to force the Prime Minister into publishing details of more of his meetings with wealthy party donors, Miliband published a list of his own meetings since becoming leader, which showed he had on several occasions met union leaders such as Unite's Len McCluskey (more than £5 million donated to Labour since September 2010), the GMB's Paul Kenny (£2.5 million) and Unison's Dave Prentis (£2.4 million).

Cameron's continuing support for legislation allowing gay marriage (with which very few Labour MPs had any issue) was also beginning to cause him serious problems in his own party, feeding into existing concerns that he and those around him were out of touch with the values and priorities of ordinary people—concerns summed up by the maverick Tory MP Nadine Dorries, who, much to the delight of the media right across the spectrum, told the BBC that Cameron and Osborne were not only 'two posh boys who don't know the price of milk, but . . . two arrogant posh boys who show no remorse, no contrition, and no passion to want to understand the lives of others'.[31] The day after it was the turn of government statisticians to pile on the agony: preliminary figures suggested, albeit by the slimmest of margins, that the UK economy had contracted over two consecutive quarters; it appeared that the double-dip recession that Ed Balls had warned might result from the Coalition going 'too far, too fast' on austerity had finally arrived.[32]

Quite how all this would impact on local elections to be held at the beginning of May remained to be seen. On the surface, at least, things looked good for Labour, not least in the opinion polls. Towards the end of April, ICM, whose methodology tended to give the party lower scores than other pollsters, reported the party was on 41 per cent—the highest score it had recorded since May 2003 and enough to turn what had been a 3 per cent deficit the previous month into an eye-catching eight-point lead. For Labour supporters who drilled down beneath the headline numbers, however, there was less cause for celebration.On most measures of leadership Cameron was still comfortably ahead of Miliband and any closing of the gap was for the most part down to his ratings falling sharply rather than the Labour leader's rising steeply. And, while the Conservatives had clearly lost some credibility on the question of economic competence, Cameron and Osborne were nevertheless trusted to run the economy by 44 per cent of respondents as opposed to the 31 per cent who preferred to put their trust in Miliband and Balls.[33] This gap was big enough to prevent complacency seeping in, at least at the top, although not quite big enough perhaps to maintain the pressure that had pushed Miliband and Balls into hardening their line on spending in the New Year. Certainly, it put paid to any possibility—admittedly a remote one—that Labour's Shadow Chancellor might have been persuaded (*a*) to stop insisting that his opposite number needed to spend (and therefore borrow) more in order to stimulate the economy and (*b*) to begin admitting that the previous Labour government really should not have been running deficits in the years before boom turned to bust.

The public's negative reaction to Osborne's Budget also risked reinforcing the impression in Labour circles that there were votes to be had by countering fiscal continence and consolidation with an appeal to social justice. Polling by YouGov at the end of March (that is, after the Budget) suggested otherwise. Labour led the Tories 29:21 on having the best ideas for making Britain fairer, whereas the Tories led Labour 31:24 on having the best ideas for making the economy stronger. The problem? When asked to choose which was more urgent, only 32 per cent chose making Britain fairer compared to 60 per cent who plumped for making Britain's economy stronger.[34] While Miliband, then, may have been right to claim that the Budget had been a turning point because, in his words, 'the mask has slipped and [the Conservatives] have revealed something very deep about themselves, which is that they are an unchanged party with an unchanged ideology', that Budget—and his reaction to it—reinforced rather than radically altered people's perceptions of Labour.[35] If they continued to see Labour as a party with its heart in the right place but its head in the clouds, then there was nothing, as Oxford historian Ben Jackson and Labour MP Gregg McClymont had warned in a think-tank pamphlet called *Cameron's Trap*, to stop the Conservative Party, just as it had done in both the 1930s and the 1980s, winning elections in spite of the tough economic climate—especially when, as the TUC's senior economist, Duncan Weldon, noted in a *Fabian Review* article in April, economic pain was so unevenly spread around the country.[36] It was also the case, polls in May suggested, that Labour was held responsible by just under a third of voters for the continuing economic downturn—nearly twice the proportion that blamed the Coalition's cuts. Meanwhile around a quarter of voters now blamed the crisis in the Eurozone for the UK's difficulties.[37] Whatever the rights and wrongs of Balls's analysis, it clearly cut little ice with voters.

Still, the mess the government seemed to be making of everything did mean that, at least for a while, the media paid less attention than was normally the case both to Balls's intransigence and to Labour's internal tensions. These related, in the first instance, to referendums about to be held in several cities asking residents whether they would like to follow London (and a few other places) in having a directly elected Mayor. Birmingham was one such city, and a couple of high-profile Labour MPs, Gisela Stuart and Shadow Work and Pensions Secretary Liam Byrne, had talked about standing down from the Commons in order to run for Mayor. Their expressions of interest did not go down well with some of their colleagues, partly because, especially in Byrne's case, such a course of action was inevitably interpreted as a vote of no-confidence in Ed Miliband's leadership and in the policy process that Byrne was supposed to be leading. But there was more to it than that. MPs stepping down would create uncalled-for by-elections in marginal seats that the party might find difficult to win and would cost money at a time when Labour was clearly strapped for cash. Moreover, when it came to Birmingham, there were rumours of some sort of deal having been done by Labour's election coordinator (and scourge of both Blair and Murdoch) Tom Watson to ensure that a former parliamentary colleague, Sion Simon, whose seat had gone to Deputy Leader Harriet Harman's husband, Jack Dromey, in 2010 would get the nomination on the nod.

Hard evidence for all this was, as is often the case, in short supply. But the fact that the rumours were given any currency probably owed something to unhappiness in some parts of the party at what was going on in a city that was preparing to stage its fourth Mayoral contest. London was about to see the current incumbent, the charismatic Conservative Boris Johnson, face off against his predecessor, Ken Livingstone. Long a controversial figure in the party, not least because he had stood and won against it as a left-wing independent in 2000, Livingstone was having a difficult campaign, plagued as he was by accusations of anti-Semitism, on the back foot about his complex personal tax arrangements, and criticized for having supported an independent against a Labour candidate in the London borough of Tower Hamlets—something that might have seen moves to expel him by a stronger leader than Miliband.[38] Indeed, so poorly did Livingstone seem to be faring in what, after all, was a largely Labour-voting city that many in the centre and on the right of the party were once again voicing criticisms of the way in which he had been selected in the first place, asking whether it had really been necessary to choose a candidate in the summer of 2010, two years before the Mayoral election. Miliband, characteristically, seemed to have decided that discretion was the better part of valour, probably reasoning that confronting Livingstone would have created a huge split that would have seen Labour lose London anyway. When it came to the election in the spring of 2012, however, his campaigning on Livingstone's behalf could hardly be described as full-on—and quite what he made of Ken bursting into tears as he watched his own campaign video in front of the press we may never know.

In fact, Miliband made a deliberate choice after launching his party's local election campaign at the beginning of April to do most of his campaigning in those parts of the country where the party needed to win parliamentary seats at the next general election, spending quite a lot of his time doing the interactive, 'town-hall meeting' events that played to his strengths more than did set-piece speeches. Inasmuch as he made an offer to the electorate in the run-up to the election, it focused more on what Labour would do if it were in government instead of the Coalition rather than what it would promise in three years' time. This trick apparently allowed the party to make promises without making commitments, although in the long term it may have proved counterproductive, since, presuming any voters were paying attention, the distinction would have been lost on them, leaving the impression that Labour was all about taxing and spending the country out of recession.

True, there was actually more to the Labour offer than that: the imaginary Bills in the 'alternative Queen's speech' launched by the party the week before the elections was built around the idea of a 'fair deal' for people fed up of being ripped off by government, rail operators, energy firms, and so on. But even then it rarely had much to do with anything local government could actually deliver: nursing jobs would be saved, rail fares would be capped, energy bills limited for over-75s, and Labour, as he promised at the launch in Birmingham, would 'govern for the whole country, not just for the wealthy few'— words that were spun as positioning Labour as the UK's only genuinely 'one-nation' party. Whether or not this was a deliberate retort to Nick Clegg's attempt to say exactly the same thing about the Lib Dems at his party's spring conference three weeks previously, the use of a phrase traditionally associated with the Conservatives got some pick-up in the media. This may have been because it made a change for journalists bored of being reminded yet again that Labour hoped to gain only around 350 council seats on 2 May rather than the 600 or so that most election experts figured it would gain pretty easily, given that, in the equivalent elections in 2008, it had polled just 24 per cent to the Tories' 44 and the Lib Dems' 16 per cent.

In the event, Labour unquestionably exceeded not only its laughably low expectations but the predictions of most of those who claimed to be in the know, gaining 823 councillors on a national equivalent vote of 39 per cent (up nine on 2010) with the Lib Dems on 15 per cent (also down nine) and the Conservatives on 33 per cent (down four). The party also managed to see off a widely hyped threat from the SNP in Glasgow and doubtless enjoyed the fact that, in one ward in Edinburgh, a Lib Dem won less support than an independent dressed in a bird suit calling himself Professor Pongoo. In Wales, it took back Cardiff, Newport, and Swansea from the Lib Dems and the Vale of Glamorgan from the Tories. Even more importantly, Labour also did well in what Conservative-supporting columnist Matthew D'Ancona called 'Blair country'—places such as Carlisle, Harlow, Norwich, Nuneaton and Bedworth, Reading, Rossendale, and Southampton, which mapped onto marginal parliamentary seats that the party had to win in 2015 in order to stand any chance of recovering power.[39] Tory strategists could take heart that it had not been a clean sweep, even if that gave Miliband the opportunity to stress, by travelling to Worcester where Labour had done well but not well enough, that 'we've got a lot more work ahead of us'. More worrying, perhaps, those same strategists would also have noticed that Labour's encouraging performances in other towns that could prove equally vital in 2015, such as Dudley and Thurrock, owed at least something to UKIP candidates winning votes that might normally have been expected to go to the Conservatives.

Not all of Labour's dreams came true, of course. A month before the local elections, the party's candidate in the Bradford West by-election had gone down to a stunning defeat by Respect's George Galloway, who managed by sheer force of personality and some smart campaigning to win the support of large numbers of young Muslim voters. The swing from Labour to Respect, at 37 per cent, had been alarming enough. But even more worrying had been the party's failure to notice what was going on under its nose before it was too late, either to do anything about it or to reduce the shock value of the result by managing down the media's expectations in the run-up to polling day.

That failure may have been indirectly related to the distractions created by the contested reorganization of the Party's Headquarters and its move to new premises. It also had something to do with the fact that, perhaps understandably, Labour had focused a lot of its fire on its rivals in government, as well as the fact that, as the NEC's specially commissioned postmortem suggested, it had relied rather too readily on an 'off-the-shelf by-election model'. However, as the same postmortem also acknowledged, Labour's failure to realize it was going to lose until it had actually lost probably had most to do with the atrophy of the local organization on the ground. This, according to Ed Miliband, was evidence for his long-held opinion that Labour had 'to be engaged and rooted in every community of this country', and in some ways the defeat was useful, since it leant weight to General Secretary Iain McNicol's argument that the party had to focus resources less on London and more on organizing in the regions and constituencies.

Some, however, saw a darker side, believing that the loss of the seat owed just as much to Labour having assumed it could continue to rely on the notoriously patriarchal and clan politics that pervades all too many seats with large South Asian populations.[40] Miliband later implicitly acknowledged this in a Q&A session he held in June under the auspices of the Bradford Muslim Women's Council. Unfortunately, by that time, the local elections had already taken place, and five Labour councillors, including the party's group leader, had been defeated by Respect candidates (all of whom, incidentally, subsequently became independents after being disappointed by Mr Galloway's performance as a local MP).[41]

Setbacks like this, together with the fact that both the Conservatives and the Lib Dems could claim to have held on in several key places, meant that the results overall were, in the words of the *Observer's* Andrew Rawnsley, 'a sparkling wine performance rather than a champagne one'—particularly given how badly things had gone for the Tories since the Budget.[42] Still, it was enough to quieten Miliband's critics, at least for a while. There was even a silver lining to the fact that Boris Johnson beat Ken Livingstone in London: for one thing, it reignited yet another destabilizing debate among Conservatives about who could or should succeed Cameron if things continued to go downhill; for another, Miliband would not be called on to comment day-in, day-out on what would almost certainly have been a highly charged relationship between a grandstanding Labour Mayor and a government that would have taken every opportunity offered to point to his problems as a sign of things to come should voters elect Labour to national office. There was also considerable comfort taken in the fact that the margin between Ken and Boris was not as wide as some had predicted and in Labour's improved performance in elections to the London assembly. By the same token, although Labour advocates of greater devolution were disappointed that, of ten cities outside London voting on whether to have a directly elected Mayor, only one of them, Bristol, chose to do so, even they had to admit that it relieved the party of the headache that would have been bound to occur had high-profile MPs started quitting the Commons for posts that arguably offered far more power than even a front-bench berth at Westminster.

In spite of all this, it was still the case that the results of the 2012 local elections were also worrying for Tory and Lib Dem MPs—so much so that they triggered yet another bout of public agonizing about the compromises both sides felt they were making in coalition. On the Tory side this began to crystallize around Cameron's continued insistence on supporting Nick Clegg's plan to reform the House of Lords via the phased replacement of government appointees by directly elected members. Not surprisingly, perhaps, very few Conservatives had much natural sympathy for such a move. And even more of them believed it would be seen as a complete waste of time and money by voters, who were, as polls showed, nowhere near as concerned by constitutional issues as they were by, say, the economy, public services, welfare, and immigration. Judging by some rather pointed remarks about Lords reform made by George Osborne during a television interview a few days after the local elections, the Conservative leadership was not doing a great deal to discourage their scepticism. Quite what it was playing at is difficult to say, but it was making a huge strategic error. Opposition to Lords reform on the Tory benches began not only to harden but, led by talented and articulate spokesmen like Jesse Norman, to be organized. Before very long it became apparent that, should Labour decide to make common cause with the Tory rebels, Nick Clegg's plan for a directly elected senate gradually to replace the existing upper house would be in serious trouble.

Notionally, of course, Labour—like its leader—was in favour of reform. On the other hand, this was not necessarily the scheme it would have favoured had it been in charge. Nor was there any love lost with the Lib Dems: scuppering Lords reform would not only deny Clegg what was effectively his consolation prize following the loss of the AV referendum, it would also prove once again to those Lib Dem voters who were thinking of switching to Labour that the Deputy Prime Minister simply could not deliver on his progressive promises. Moreover, there were a couple of obvious ways of doing it that would avoid Labour getting the blame, at least directly. The first was to flirt with the idea of insisting on a referendum to secure public consent for reform—something that Labour did end up doing even though it was a rather risky move that could have made it extremely tricky to reject the idea of a similar vote on the EU. The second involved the fact that Lords reform was clearly so contentious that the government would need to ensure that it could, if necessary, curtail debate and move to a vote. To do this it required a so-called programme motion. By threatening to vote against such a motion, ostensibly on the grounds that it believed that such an important constitutional change should be properly debated, Labour could maintain that it was still in favour of change at the same time as forcing the Coalition to choose between accepting major disruption to the rest of its legislative agenda or abandoning a Bill that had become a touchstone—both for the Lib Dems and for Tories who believed they had pandered to their junior partner's absurd whims long enough.

To be fair to the Labour leadership, its stance was not completely dictated by its desire to drive a wedge between the two sides of the Coalition. A highly charged meeting of the PLP towards the end of June left Miliband in no doubt that a fair few of his MPs and peers were determined to oppose not just the imposition of a timetable on the Bill but the Bill itself. And in the event, things were taken out of his hands anyway. In the second week of July, the Commons decided to postpone voting on the programme motion but to vote nonetheless on the Bill's second reading, which Miliband had eventually agreed to back. However, while it was duly approved by 462 votes to 124, some 91 Tories voted against and just under 20 abstained. By August, not only had Cameron told Clegg that there was no prospect of the Bill making further progress, but Clegg had told Cameron that, as a consequence, the Lib Dems would no longer support the Coalition's planned boundary reforms. The abandonment of those reforms, experts quickly pointed out, was likely to cost the Tories around twenty seats (some that would now stay Labour and some that would stay Lib Dem) at the general election in 2015: with the boundary reform, the Conservatives could have won an overall majority by beating Labour by around four percentage points in terms of vote share across the country; now they would need a seven-point lead.

That the Lib Dems might wreak their revenge in this way had been floated for a few weeks, so when it came it came as no surprise. It was not, however, a move that anyone in the Labour leadership had somehow brilliantly foreseen months beforehand. Nonetheless, it was a huge bonus. A reduction in the number of seats in parliament and the subsequent rationalization of constituency boundaries would not have completely removed the 'bias' in the electoral system, but it would have gone at least some way to doing so. Its delay meant that the Conservatives would still need a substantial lead in vote share over Labour to win even the tiniest overall majority in parliament. It also meant that Labour, as long as it could reach around 35 per cent of the vote and hold the Conservatives below 40 per cent, stood a chance of recovering power without needing anything like the support that Blair had achieved in 1997 and 2001.

To those diehard fans of New Labour who were convinced that Miliband was relying solely on mobilizing Labour's core vote and adding to it, first, those who had deserted the party (and indeed the entire electoral process) after 1997 and, secondly, disaffected Lib Dems, this so-called 35 per cent strategy was a source of profound concern. To Miliband and his inner circle, however, that much talked-about figure, while it may occasionally have been a crumb of comfort in times of trouble, never represented the crux of their strategy or, indeed, the summit of their ambition. Yes, they did believe there were Labour supporters who had drifted away since 1997, although they were well aware that many of the so-called missing five million had simply died rather than deserted. Yes, they did hope they could appeal disproportionately to first-time voters, even if they were well aware that the young were far less likely both to register and to turn out. And, yes, they were determined to ensure that voters who had defected to Labour following the formation of the Coalition did not dribble back to the Lib Dems. But the idea that they wanted to rely—or ever thought they could or should rely—simply on those voters without trying to convince at least some of those who had voted Tory in 2010 to give Labour a chance is patently nonsense. Likewise, while François Hollande's 'anti-austerity' victory in the French Presidential election in early May was broadly welcomed in Labour circles—David Miliband, no less, celebrated his win in an article for *The Times* a couple of days afterwards while his younger brother wasted no time in popping over to Paris to be seen with him—that did not mean that the British were about to copy everything (or even anything) that their Gallic counterparts said or did.[43] Politicians are often blinkered. They are also routinely inclined to see what they want to see, as well as to possess unwarranted optimism and confidence in their own abilities. But they are rarely completely stupid.

# 5

# One Nation: Spring–Autumn
## 2012

'Success', notes the journalist Steve Richards, whom Ed Miliband tried unsuccessfully to hire to run his media operation back in 2010, 'feeds on itself and so does failure. Leaders change almost physically depending on what is happening in the opinion polls and in elections'.[1] And so it was with Miliband himself. His parliamentary response to the government's 2012 Queen's Speech was well received, not so much, Richards argued, because of any intrinsic merit it possessed but because, in the light of encouraging election results and the party's opinion-poll lead, the Labour leader was now 'viewed through a different, more flattering prism'. It was, therefore, an opportune moment for him to deal with a problem that had been concerning him for some time—namely, the Policy Review. The original intention had been for the various groups to begin to report their recommendations and for the party to put together the makings of a comprehensive programme in 2013 or possibly even towards the end of 2012. But it had become clear that this was neither feasible nor desirable. The process—intended to be consultative and therefore split into stages involving public meetings, CLPs, PLP and Shadow Cabinet, before going on to the NPF in the summer and conference in the autumn—looked unlikely to deliver much of substance any time soon. This was not necessarily a problem: after all, the Coalition now looked likely to stay together until May 2015 and no opposition party wants to come up with fresh ideas that end up looking past their sell-by date by the time the election comes around. But it did mean there was time for a rethink—a chance to reboot the process and bring in a fresh pair of eyes.

Liam Byrne, whom Miliband had initially put in charge, was also responsible for the busy welfare brief in the Shadow Cabinet and, hardly surprisingly, had found it less than easy to do both jobs at the same time. There were also issues around communication with the Leader's Office, and Byrne had put people's noses out of joint by sticking too loudly to what some—especially in the unions—insisted on seeing as his Blairite guns. What the party really needed was somebody who could take on the task full-time, who was not too strongly associated with old factional divides, who would shake things up a bit, and who might be better able to forge what (because of Miliband's initial insistence on letting a thousand flowers bloom by setting up myriad groups) had become a rather unwieldy exercise into something more focused.

The man appointed, Jon Cruddas, fitted the bill perfectly, having worked at Labour Party Headquarters and been responsible for liaison with the trade unions in Number Ten before going on to become an MP in 2001 and to contest the Deputy Leadership of the party in 2007 as a vocal critic of Blair. The fact that he had voted for David (whom he thought 'would play better at the box office') rather than Ed only made him a more attractive choice for Miliband and his advisers, as did his association with Blue Labour and its desire to reconnect Labour with its traditions of patriotism and its white working-class base. Others were less sure, dismissing the appointment as a gesture to a group that had done little more than pique the interest of the media in order to buy time for the leadership to work up some grown-up policies for the general election: as one Labour veteran who also supported David Miliband in the leadership contest later put it, 'Jon Cruddas is interesting. He's a good talker at a seminar. But he's not the man to give you a governing agenda.' Still, within weeks of his agreeing to do the job, Cruddas decided to collapse the twenty-nine existing groups into just three (which was actually the number Liam Byrne had wanted to begin with), one focused on politics, one on society, and one on economics. He also hoped to ensure that what eventually emerged from the process (probably as late as 2014) would be less a series of disparate, discrete proposals and more the component, complementary parts of an overarching narrative based on 'rebuilding Britain'—both in the literal sense, in terms of a commitment to investment in infrastructure and housing, but also in the more emotive sense of a positive, optimistic, collective, *national* endeavour associated (in Cruddas's mind anyway) with his friend the Australian political philosopher Tim Soutphommasane.

The can-do qualities inherent in the idea of 'rebuilding Britain' (which, incidentally, became the opening slogan for the party's conference in September) resonated with Miliband, not least because he was wrestling with the fact that, as he told the journalist and author Matthew D'Ancona in an interview in mid-May, 'people want to know that you are going to be competent managers of the economy—but they also want to know you are going to make a difference'.[2] Labour, like any party that believes in the power of politics to change things, arguably stood to lose more than its Conservative rival from the disillusion and disconnect afflicting many advanced Western democracies—the idea that, since all parties are the same, and therefore equally powerless, equally untrustworthy, and equally venal, none was worth voting for. Yet, as Miliband admitted in a speech to Progress a week after local elections where the turnout barely made it over 31 per cent: 'We became one of "them" rather than one of "us".'[3] Despite being dominated at the top by figures who by background, education, or profession were part of a political establishment that many people had little or no time for, the party had to persuade those very same people that it could at one and the same time operate in the real world and work to transform it. Cruddas's appointment was part of that project. So too was the announcement that Andrew Adonis, the Blairite driving force of Labour's academy programme and someone well known for combining vision with the ability to get things done, would be taking a lead role in the party's plans for long-term sustainable growth. The only other high-profile change was the retirement of Peter Hain both from the Shadow Cabinet (his place there being taken by newcomer Owen Smith) and as Chair of the NPF—a job that went to Angela Eagle, Shadow Leader of the Commons.

Labour's attempt simultaneously to mobilize and to reassure was no more obvious than in economic policy. On the one hand, Ed Balls (who was also of course acting out of Keynesian conviction) continued to insist on the need to kickstart an economy left 'flatlining' by austerity. On the other, he was unwilling to back public-sector workers taking strike action to protest pay restraint. The former stance frustrated those in the Shadow Cabinet who believed talk of a VAT cut and borrowing to invest in growth was, along with Balls's absolute refusal to acknowledge that Labour may have overspent in the boom years, a big mistake. The latter stance enraged trade-union leaders and worried those in the party who were concerned to keep them onside. Campaigns coordinator, Tom Watson MP, who was known to be close to Unite's Len McCluskey, had even gone so far as to openly criticize the way the leadership had handled the announcement on pay restraint in January, telling the *Fabian Review* that he felt he owed it to the unions 'to disagree respectfully with them and to let them know rather than to throw it on their doorstep in their Sunday paper'—a complaint that received short shrift from Balls who told the *Telegraph* in an interview 'I don't ring up trade union leaders and get their permission [for things] I need to say...My tough stance...wasn't popular with certain parts of the trade union movement, but I'm afraid that's the nature of life.' Nor was he going to apologize for teaming up with Peter Mandelson, whose concern about Labour not alienating business he shared, to write a joint piece for the *FT* on the need for a parallel strategy for growth and deficit reduction.[4]

Despite the role he played in helping to shore up Gordon Brown's government towards the end of Labour's time in office, Mandelson remained the man whom many on the left of the party loved to hate— one reason why during the leadership campaign David Miliband and his team were as much dismayed as delighted by his support. To left-wingers in the trade unions, media rumours that relations between Mandelson and the two Eds were thawing provoked suspicions that the leader they had played such a big part in electing had been somehow tempted over to the dark side. Certainly, it provided a convenient explanation for why he now seemed more preoccupied with displaying credibility and responsibility than with supporting their largely unsuccessful campaign against 'Tory cuts' and attacks on public-sector pay and pensions. The resulting resentment, married to an underlying desire to exploit their relative strength, now led some trade-union representatives to try, as they saw it, to 'reclaim the party' from the Blairites, who had supposedly stolen it from everybody else in the 1990s. Their moves were leant added impetus by virtue of the fact that, over the next year, Labour was aiming to select candidates as early as possible in winnable and defensible seats so as to steal a march on the Conservatives, who were more inclined to wait until new boundaries were confirmed. Selections had long been a sore point for many on the left, who had come to believe that there was maybe more to their chronic failure to secure more socialist and working-class Labour MPs than met the eye. And they were now determined to do something about Progress, the modernizing ginger group generously funded by millionaire David Sainsbury. According to left-wing folklore, in February someone had sent a dossier to every CLP secretary, among others, detailing Progress's supposedly sharp practices and dodgy finances and calling on the NEC (due for re-election that year) to consider what should be done about it.[5]

Paul Kenny, the GMB's General Secretary, believed that, during thirteen years of Labour government, ordinary working people's voices had been lost in what he called a 'sea of wine-bar chatter, career-chasing, carpetbaggers'. Now, at his union's annual conference in Brighton, he made clear his unhappiness at Labour's failure, now it was back in opposition, 'to wholeheartedly support public sector workers'. If it carried on like this, and if it failed to reverse some of its policies and continued to shut the union out of the key early stages of its policy-making process, the party might find that the GMB's 'money box' was shut.[6] Moreover, there could well be a move at Labour's conference in the autumn to 'outlaw' Progress, notwithstanding the fact that it provided fora to which Labour's leader, Shadow Cabinet, and its General Secretary had all contributed recently. A few days later, the *Guardian* had got hold of a political strategy document from Unite put together in December 2011, which claimed that 'Labour party policies are often determined by a small group of advisers—far too often dominated by old thinking, neo-liberalism and the organisation Progress', and this could be stopped only if the union agreed it 'should play the fullest possible part in the struggle for Labour's soul'. Fears that this was a coordinated move were stoked further by the news that Unison had decided not to allow Progress to use one of its venues to hold a meeting at which Labour's General Secretary Iain McNicol had agreed to speak.[7]

Peter Mandelson, who had long been associated with Progress, responded by telling the media: 'We don't want a political party of intolerance, divisiveness, rancour and falling out of the sort we saw in the 1980s.' He was backed up, albeit belatedly, by Miliband publicly affirming that he was 'for a Labour Party that's reaching out to all people and all organisations'.[8] Progress itself responded by promising greater transparency about its funding and its work, including the 'limited training and mentoring role' it claimed to play 'in local

government and parliamentary selection processes'.[9] Whether, however, it was that, along with the clear signal sent by Miliband that the
leadership would have nothing to do with any witch-hunt, that
calmed things down, at least for the moment, is debatable. Arguably,
the union-based left had achieved its immediate goal—namely, to fire
a shot across the right's bows in anticipation of more close-quarter
combat at local level when it came to parliamentary selections. That it
was intending to use the latter to try to shift the party in its direction
was clear from the Unite political strategy that had leaked to the
newspapers. The plan was not only to choose and train suitable people
to stand as candidates but to recruit thousands of union members into
constituency parties in order to help them get selected—a plan that
attracted relatively little sustained attention at the time but would
garner plenty later on.

   In summer 2012, however, Ed Miliband was more concerned with
trying to make headlines himself by seeking to address what both
public and private opinion research made clear was one of Labour's
key weaknesses. Both he and Shadow Home Secretary Yvette Cooper
had made it clear on a number of occasions since 2010 that Labour had
got it wrong on immigration, particularly when it came to its failure to
impose transitional controls on the accession states in 2004 and its
belated introduction of a points-based system for non-EU migrants.
They had also made it clear that the party was working to restore the
public's trust in its willingness and capacity to respond to continued
concerns about the impact and control of so many people coming into
the country. These themes were also at the heart of Ed Miliband's
heavily trailed speech on the subject to IPPR in late June 2012. But so,
too, was the argument that, just as it had been wrong not to admit the
costs as well as the benefits of immigration and to appear to be telling
those who lost out to 'like it or lump it', so too it was wrong to pretend
to people that 'we can close Britain off from the world, when all of us
know we cannot.' Indeed, what Miliband really wanted to do (as well
as slip in a passing mention that Labour might decide to keep the
government's 'cap' on numbers as well as reintroduce exit checks) was,
first, to distance himself from Brown on the issue and, secondly, to
move the argument onto what was, for Labour anyway, far more
comfortable territory. The first he did by stressing that 'worrying
about immigration, talking about immigration, thinking about immigration, does not make [people] bigots. Not in any way,' and by

emphasizing that he was 'not going to promise British jobs for British workers'. The second he did by claiming that what was needed was to introduce 'tougher labour standards to do more to protect working people from their wages and conditions being undermined' and then to begin turning Britain into an economy that invested in its existing human capital and technology rather than simply sucking in low-skilled foreign labour.[10]

These sorts of solutions made a degree of sense, even if they reflected the wholly predictable tendency of social democratic parties to come up with an economic answer to what is to no small extent a cultural question (and therefore a much harder one to answer). As such, they might have been expected to be welcomed right across the party. Fortunately for Miliband, at least in terms of garnering a few headlines, some on the left could nevertheless be relied on to let the media know that they were, to quote John McDonnell MP, 'disappointed and saddened' with what they regarded as a shift towards 'a nuanced version of blaming the migrants for the jobs and housing crisis'. Critical comments made about the speech by Diane Abbott, the Shadow Public Health Minister and former leadership contender, were more coded but in some ways even more useful because she was better known.[11] Even so, how much the ordinary voting (or indeed non-voting) public actually noted what was still a pretty subtle shift is doubtful, especially when the media were far more taken with the Chancellor's politically astute (if fiscally irresponsible) decision to forgo a planned 3p rise in fuel duty and the Prime Minister's floating the idea that under-25s might be denied housing benefit—an idea so draconian and impracticable that even Liam Byrne, Labour's Work and Pensions spokesman, and Rachel Reeves, Labour's Shadow Chief Secretary, both of whom were normally determined to ensure that Labour not be thought a soft touch on welfare, were quick to dismiss it as 'hazy and half-baked'. They may well have been right, but, as far as the Conservatives were concerned, their reaction still left the opposition on the wrong side of a dividing line.

There were issues, of course, where, potentially anyway, the boot was on the other foot. One of these was banking. Labour, in the shape of Greg Beales, was now beginning to commission a lot more polling of its own, mainly via Greenberg Quinlan Rosner's James Morris, a veteran of Ed Miliband's leadership campaign. But even publicly available polls suggested that there was still huge resentment towards an industry that had not so very long ago effectively brought the economy crashing down around everyone's ears but seemed utterly unwilling, at least when it came to remuneration, to cut its coat to suit its cloth. So when, at the end of June, it was revealed that highly paid employees from Barclays had been colluding to fix a key interbank interest rate, resentment boiled over once again. Barclays may have been one of the few UK banks that had not had to be bailed out by the government, but its Chief Executive, Bob Diamond, had become a byword for the industry's maddening lack of remorse. Surely, even he would find it impossible to get away with it this time? Sensing another 'Leveson moment', Labour made every effort to channel public anger and call for more action than the government at first seemed willing to offer. Risking the same accusations of left-populism that had initially greeted his conference speech on predators and producers, Miliband declared in a speech to the Fabian Society:

The British people will not tolerate anything less than a full, open and independent inquiry, they will not tolerate the establishment closing ranks... They want people held to account, they do not want sticking plaster solutions.... Not one person has gone to jail for what happened during the financial crisis. Why is it that when you shoplift £50-worth of goods you go straight to jail but when you fiddle, lie and cheat your way through the system, gaining millions of pounds, you get away with a slap on the wrist—if that?[12]

This time, however, even the right-wing press appeared to be onside, although this did not prevent the Chancellor, George Osborne, effectively running interference—and driving his opposite number, Ed Balls, to understandable fury—by recalling that Libor manipulation had occurred under Labour's 'light-touch' regulation and observing to the right-wing weekly the *Spectator* that 'people around Gordon Brown' were 'clearly involved' in manipulating the Libor rate and that Balls 'had questions to answer'.[13] In the end, however, Labour agreed to a compromise parliamentary inquiry under the fiercely independent Tory Chairman of the Treasury Select Committee, Andrew Tyrie, although it later made clear that, when it came to regulating the banks more generally, it was prepared to legislate to separate their investment and retail arms if, as looked likely, the government failed to implement the recommendations of the commission set up under Sir John Vickers.

Just because Miliband's line on the bankers went down well with some right-wing titles did not, of course, mean that he got a free pass.

His decision to keep a campaign promise and become the first Labour leader since Neil Kinnock in 1989 to address the tens of thousands of labour movement devotees at the traditional Durham Miners' Gala was duly noted, although so, too, was his appearance a few days earlier at a fundraiser held at Arsenal's Emirates Stadium alongside Tony Blair, whom Miliband was keen to thank 'for what he did for our party and for our country'. Miliband could also claim to be doing his Blairite best to build a coalition of candidates that encompassed the whole country rather than the public-sector professionals and the 'never had a job outside politics' mob who had, in many people's eyes, come to dominate Labour in recent years. On the one hand, the Labour leader admitted in a speech at the Chartered Accountants' Hall that Labour was short of MPs with business backgrounds and wanted to encourage anyone interested—even if he or she was not currently a party member—to join a mentoring scheme being set up to do something about the situation. On the other hand, there was an effort, delegated to Shadow Cabinet Office Minister John Trickett, to encourage ordinary working people to become parliamentary candidates in the hope that the proportion of Labour MPs from such a background could be boosted above the 10 per cent achieved in 2010. Nothing much came, it was true, of a grass-roots proposal to create a Diversity Fund to provide direct subsidies to low-income candidates and/or to encourage CLPs to do something about the issue—despite it gaining a number of high-profile endorsements. The party did manage, however, to set up a Future Candidates Programme, funded by an external foundation, to provide training and mentoring to those interested in becoming an MP. Miliband also made a point of telling the party at his post-speech Q&A at the 2012 Manchester conference that 'You have my absolute commitment that that is a massive priority for us'. This remark, taken together with Trickett making the case for widening the candidate pool to include ordinary people and a Party Political Broadcast that contrasted the Labour leader's North London comprehensive with the PM's Eton College, provoked the *Mail* into a headline declaring 'Builders and plumbers urged to join Ed Miliband's class war against the Conservatives'.[14] It was also announced in Manchester that the NEC had agreed to add 'Sexuality, Disability and Social Class' to that section of the party's rule book dealing with equality in representation.

Whether any of this could really do much to boost working-class numbers among aspiring Labour MPs is debatable. The fact that the party was ultimately far less willing, or at least less able, to do something about class (as opposed to gender) under-representation was partly why trade unions were guaranteed a sympathetic hearing at the grass roots when they argued, as they increasingly did, that they would have to take matters into their own hands. But it was becoming clear that their ambitions to shift the party's ideological centre of gravity stretched further than candidate selection, even if their capacity to finance those ambitions was possibly less impressive than it looked. In the late spring of 2012, Unite and the GMB got together to found and fund a new left-wing think tank called Class—the Centre for Labour and Social Studies—chaired by Unite's Political Director Steve Hart and given extra public profile by support from columnists and authors such as Owen Jones, Polly Toynbee, and Seamus Milne, all of whom had a considerable following on the left. The hope was to compete for attention and, in the long term, policy influence with outfits like Demos, and in particular IPPR, which had established itself as Labour's think tank of choice since its foundation in 1988. Class's ability to do this, however, would depend on it attracting far greater funding. In 2012/13, for instance, Class's income was just over £100,000. IPPR's income in 2013 was just over £3 million.[15]

Still, for those on the right of the party, coming as it did on top of the attack in Progress, it was all very ominous—especially in the light of an interview given to a tiny left-wing outlet (but eagerly picked up by the best-selling *Sun*, which also noted how many parliamentary passes Labour MPs seemed to be giving to union representatives) by the Chair of Unite's National Political Committee, Dave Quayle. The union was determined, he said, 'to shift the balance in the party away from middle-class academics and professionals towards people who've actually represented workers and fought the boss'. In order to get a Labour government that would 'restore the right to take solidarity action and strike effectively', he continued, 'we want a firmly class-based and left-wing general election campaign in 2015. We've got to say that Labour is the party of and for workers, not for neo-liberals, bankers, and the free market. That might alienate some people, but that's tough.'[16] Certainly, when Miliband told his MPs at their end-of-term meeting that he expected a 'big change, big politics' election in three years' time, this was not quite what he had in mind—one reason why, when he and Ed Balls eventually travelled down to Brighton to the TUC Conference in mid-September, they left no one in any doubt that they opposed all talk of mass strikes on pay and pensions, with Balls prepared to get himself heckled (not for the first time at a union conference) by saying 'loud and clear: we don't want to see a return to the 1980s'.

For the moment, however, Miliband was—relatively speaking—sitting pretty. Labour's lead was touching double digits. Cameron and Osborne were being openly criticized by right-wing MPs and Tory-supporting newspapers, some of which were exploiting Boris Johnson's starring role at the London Olympics to talk him up as a contender for the Tory leadership. Then one of the higher-profile members of the Tories' new intake in 2010, the best-selling author Louise Mensch, announced she was standing down to move to New York for family reasons, triggering a by-election in the marginal seat of Corby, which, owing to Labour's determination to select early in winnable seats, conveniently had its candidate, Andy Sawford, in place and ready to go. Perhaps because of all this, the party took its foot off the gas over the next few weeks. After launching Labour's campaign in Corby, Miliband took himself and his family off to Greece and began to prepare his conference speech, leaving it to a few frontbenchers, notably Chuka Umunna, Hilary Benn, and Harriet Harman to make the odd intervention relating to their portfolios.

Since parliament was in recess, few of those interventions attracted much attention. Indeed, since the majority of titles were either implacably hostile to Labour or else simply keen to show that they had the inside dope on the party, there was probably more attention paid by the print media, first, to renewed rumours of tensions between Miliband and Balls and, secondly, to the Electoral Commission's latest figures on Labour's income for the second quarter of 2012. These showed that just over two-thirds of the £2.9 million in donations that Labour was obliged to record between April and June 2012 came from trade unions, with Unite (£840,000) in the top spot, followed by Usdaw (£430,000), the GMB (£314,000), and Unison (£213,000). All those organizations surpassed the party's most generous individual donors, the best known of whom were comedian Eddie Izzard (£32,000) and star of *The Apprentice*, the entrepreneur Alan Sugar (£13,000), but the most generous was property-developer Andrew Rosenfeld, who gave £152,000. The latter attracted particular interest, not because of his incredibly impressive record as a fundraiser over the years for the NSPCC, but because he had previously chosen to live in low-tax Switzerland. The party, however, shrugged off such criticism and decided to make use of Rosenfeld's charitable experience by appointing him to a new, unpaid post, Chair of Nations and Regions, which would see him head up Labour's effort to drum up not just donations but active support and endorsements right across the country. However, rumours that Rosenfeld's involvement was all about reducing reliance on union money, which had so far accounted for just over 80p of every pound donated to the party since Miliband had become leader, seemed a little far-fetched: after all, union representatives were due to sit alongside him on a New National Development Board, which would also include Labour's General Secretary Iain McNicol and Diana Holland, who was not only Labour Party Treasurer but Assistant General Secretary of Unite.

The only possible exception to the rule that Shadow Ministers' summer initiatives are trees that fall silently in the forest was Stephen Twigg's questioning of the amount spent on free schools that ended up not opening or that did so where there seemed to be no demand. On the other hand, since the public, while not necessarily huge fans of Michael Gove's flagship policy, were not particularly opposed to it either, there may have been a trade-off for Twigg between doing exactly what Opposition spokespeople are constitutionally supposed to do—namely, hold ministers to account—and the negative signal that such action inevitably sent about Labour's seeming lack of support for 'parent power' and innovation in education. Fortunately, however, media interest in the question was limited. In any case, it was soon drowned out by the attention paid to Cameron's supposed 'lurch to the right' in his post-summer reshuffle and then (in the higher-brow outlets anyway) discussion of the supposed conversion on the part of the two Eds to 'predistribution'. This idea, associated with American academic Jacob Hacker and outlined in a speech Miliband made at the London Stock Exchange in September 2012, proposes that, rather than focus on helping the less-well-off via welfare benefits and tax credits that top up their inadequate salaries, centre-left administrations should do all they can (for example, by making a 'living wage' a condition of government contracts and by trying to restructure the economy so that it generated high-value, high-skilled jobs) to encourage employers to pay workers well enough to ensure that they do not need those benefits and credits to make ends meet.

The 2012 party conference season opened with the traditional slew of opinion polls and more or less helpful advice for leaders hoping their speeches would either consolidate progress or turn things around. When it came to the polls, most of them repeated the pattern of the past few months by showing Labour in a comfortable headline lead but with much to worry about as soon as one delved a little deeper. Populus for *The Times* was typical. Labour may have led the Tories by 45 points to 30, but when voters were asked which leader they would prefer to see in Downing Street Cameron led Miliband by 60 points to 31. Asked to pick three words out of a list of twenty that they were invited to apply to each of the leaders, the top five chosen for Miliband were 'out of his depth', then 'weak', 'out of touch', 'indecisive', and finally 'weird'. For Cameron they were 'out of touch', followed by 'arrogant', 'doesn't listen', 'stands up for Britain', and lastly 'smug'. On managing the economy, Labour had narrowed the gap but was far from closing it altogether.[17]

When it came to advice, it was similarly predictable—a mixture of the barbed, the banal, and (in view of the fact that, with only a few days to go, the die was cast) the completely bloody useless. Even Alan Johnson, writing in the *Guardian*, could only urge Ed Miliband to show the country that he had 'what it takes to be prime minister' and to remind him that 'there is no use earning the right to be listened to if you have nothing to say'. On the other side of the fence, Len McCluskey was, predictably enough, even less helpful, telling the *Sunday Times* that the Labour leader had 'got to reject the siren voices that still might come from the Blairite dead because the truth is they offer no hope for the future'—a future, he added rather menacingly, in which 'the Labour party has no God-given right to exist' unless it ensured it represented 'the voice of ordinary working people and in particular of organised labour'.[18] Given those comments, and his call on Miliband to 'kick the New Labour cuckoos out of our nest', it was perhaps little wonder that journalists attending a fringe event organized by Progress at which lost leader David Miliband made a guest appearance alongside the likes of Ben Bradshaw, Caroline Flint, and Chuka Umunna found it 'surprisingly tribal'.

And then, of course, there were the pre-conference interviews with the Labour leadership itself, often poured over less for their intrinsic interest than for their potential to cause trouble as a result of one colleague appearing to contradict another. Harriet Harman, for instance, not only ensured the enmity of the vast majority of journalists and proprietors by confirming to the *Spectator* that Labour planned to implement the recommendations of the Leveson committee via statute rather than by voluntary code; she also appeared to rule out the party sticking to Tory spending plans, thereby obliging aides to Ed Balls to let it be known that, in fact, this might well happen in the fullness of time.[19] For the moment, however, all that had been agreed was that, in its first year in government, Labour would conduct what Balls called in a pre-conference interview with the *Guardian*'s Patrick Wintour 'a proper zero-based spending review where we say we have to justify every penny and make sure we are spending in the right way'.[20] Whether this would really convince many voters, assuming they even understood the concept of zero-based budgeting (the idea that one begins by defining from scratch exactly what it is that one wants to do rather than with last year's figures), was debateable. For one thing, the review would apparently take place after rather than before the election. It could, therefore, offer no clue as to how exactly Labour would seek to cope in what would continue to be an age of austerity. Nor, for that matter, would it allow Labour to signal to its own supporters quite how difficult things were going to be—an exercise in reducing expectations that might, at least according to the authors of a Progress pamphlet, *The Purple Papers: Real Change for Britain, Real Choices for Britain*, help the party avoid coming a cropper in government, when it really would be obliged to reveal just how bare the cupboard actually was.[21] For another, Balls added the obvious qualification that, although he would continue to ensure that his Shadow Cabinet colleagues did not make unfunded spending promises, some areas would be prioritized and commitments made to them in Labour's manifesto: since these were likely to include health and a large proportion of social security and education spending, then the areas subject to root-and-branch examination might not present much scope for significant savings.

Interestingly, Balls did not mention university tuition fees in this regard, even though Miliband appeared to repeat the pledge at the public Q&A at Manchester East Academy that kicked off conference. The areas he preferred to single out were health and social care. The latter, along with childcare, was also highlighted by Douglas Alexander. His pre-conference interview with the *Evening Standard*'s Geoff Teather and Joe Murphy confirmed him as one of the left's *bêtes noires* after he was openly critical about one of their heroes, Ken

Livingstone, and the way he had lost London for Labour.[22] But when he talked to the *New Statesman*'s Rafael Behr he spoke more about policy and in particular about Labour needing to find ways of helping a working population with responsibilities for both their offspring and their elderly relatives.[23] Inevitably, given the gendered division of domestic duties, this meant appealing in particular to women, who, figures also showed, had borne the brunt not just of public-sector job cuts but also of changes to the tax and benefits system. The fact that this offered Labour not just a chance to increase its lead as the party with the best policies for women but also an opportunity to extend its appeal from younger to older middle-aged women was not lost on strategists. In the build-up to conference, the party announced that Harman would be chairing a commission on older women that would also involve a couple of people who had recently found out the hard way just how disposable they could be—namely, former *Strictly Come Dancing* judge Arlene Phillips, and BBC presenter Miriam O'Reilly.

Harman's initiative was not, of course, untypical in combining a touch of gimmickry with genuine substance. Liam Byrne, for instance, addressed conference not in the hall but via Skype from a jobs fair at Manchester College in order to support his claim (albeit one made in language that appeared to have been written by someone more used to working on movie trailers) that 'sometimes you have to strike a balance between argument and action—and when it comes to youth unemployment what we need right now is action'. Action in this case was a new 'Youth Jobs Taskforce' involving representatives from business, enterprise, the third sector, academia, trade unions, and leaders of Labour local authorities with high youth unemployment rates sharing best practice and helping to make policy—an idea not necessarily to be sniffed at, given that well over a third of the unemployed at the time were aged 16–25. By the same token, it might have been easy to dismiss Shadow Defence Secretary Jim Murphy referring in a speech that also focused on the need for ruthless discipline in defence spending to his ongoing campaign to bring servicemen and women into the Labour Party; but, given the discrim-ination and difficulty getting into the civilian jobs market many of them clearly continue to face, it could hardly be said to be unimport-ant. Similarly, Sadiq Khan's promise to extend the Freedom of Infor-mation Act to cover businesses that signed contracts with government could be dismissed as an eye-catching sop to liberals and transparency campaigners, but only if one chooses to forget just how much public money goes into such contracts and how questionable are some of the practices of the huge firms involved.

Ed Balls, both by virtue of his job and because he was singled out for criticism by union leaders angered by his refusal to reverse Coalition cuts and his support for pay restraint, hardly found it difficult to get the media's attention. But even he was not above pointing to initiatives that linked Labour with individuals and institutions that the public trusted far more than they did politicians and parties. Apart from a suggestion that the government use money raised by the sale of the 4G spectrum to build a hundred thousand new houses, Balls's speech to conference was a familiar combination of criticism of the government's 'failed economic plan', calls on the Coalition to take immediate steps to boost growth, and assurances that Labour could be trusted with the public finances. But it also included the announcement that Sir John Armitt, Chairman of the obviously highly successful Olympic Delivery Authority, had agreed to put together plans, including an independent commission that could advise government, to improve the way the UK went about renewing its infrastructure. Again, this was eye-catching and designed both to support Balls's belief in growth-generating capital investment and to show how Labour would put the long-term needs of the country over party politics; but it was also addressing a serious problem that had dogged the British economy for years and that, unless sorted out, would impact negatively on its ability to compete with other parts of the world in attracting business. The same went for Stephen Twigg inviting Professor Chris Husbands from the Institute of Education to chair a panel on Labour's proposed technical baccalaureate. Sadly, however, this particular attempt to show that Labour was recruiting outside expertise to deal with a fundamental issue attracted less interest than it might have done. The media were understandably far more interested in the heckling from the floor that greeted a speech by a Year 11 pupil praising her academy school.

The primary purpose, of course, of the conference (at least as a media event, as opposed to the fleeting opportunity it afforded the grass roots to meet and try to influence and hold accountable party elites) was, first, to maintain the momentum Labour had picked up since the spring and, secondly, to project Ed Miliband as a leader capable of setting the agenda and commanding the respect of voters, too many of whom seemed far from convinced that he was up to the job of Prime Minister. Wednesday would see the release of a Party Election Broadcast already being spun as *Ed: The Movie*, which would not only show him at home with his family but also focus on his education at a London comprehensive, with former classmates lining up to testify that he was a warm, grounded character and not just, as the political commentator Matthew D'Ancona put it, 'the ultimate Labour policy wonk—*the wonko di tutti wonki*'.[24] The main event, as always, would be the leader's speech, crafted as much for the commentariat and television news editors as for the audience in the hall. Clearly the reaction of the latter—a mixture of long-suffering constituency activists, ambitious apparatchiks, and furiously networking lobbyists—would inevitably influence the former. But that would not in itself be enough. In 2011, for instance, Miliband's talk of predators and producers had gone down well with most of his audience, but was nonetheless hammered in the media, even though, a few months later, some commentators were prepared to wonder whether he had not in fact been on to something. In 2012, Ed and his speechwriters, the most important of whom was his old friend the Oxford academic and erstwhile 'Blue Labour' thinker Marc Stears, spent more time crafting the speech. They also worked harder to find a hook that, as well as triangulating between Old and New Labour and allowing Miliband to claim the middle ground while simultaneously calling for radical change, would unite rather than divide, ensuring it stood a better chance of being well received outside the hall as well as inside it.

That hook, appropriately enough since, as Miliband himself noted, he was speaking a stone's throw away from where Benjamin Disraeli had made one of his most famous speeches, was One Nation—defined by the Labour leader as 'a country where everyone has a stake', 'where prosperity is fairly shared', and 'where we have a shared destiny, a sense of shared endeavour and a common life that we lead together'. Disraeli may have been a Tory, but David Cameron and his Conservative colleagues had forfeited ownership of his mantle by raising taxes on ordinary families and cutting them for millionaires, by dividing the country 'between north and south. Public and private. Those who can and those who can't work.' Labour, as Tony Blair had once claimed in 1995 and as Miliband had himself pointed out in the local election campaign earlier in the year, was now the only party that deserved the name. While taking the difficult decisions required to ensure that the country lived within its means, a Labour government run by him would see to it that 'the broadest shoulders will always bear the greatest burden' and would 'never accept an economy where the gap between rich and poor just grows wider and wider'. But what, he asked, exactly did all this mean for the Labour Party?

It means we can't go back to Old Labour. We must be the party of the private sector just as much as the party of the public sector. As much the party of the small business struggling against the odds, as the home help struggling against the cuts. We must be the party of south just as much as the party of the north. And we must be the party as much of the squeezed middle as those in poverty. There is no future for this party as the party of one sectional interest of our country. But so too it is right to move on from New Labour because New Labour, despite its great achievements, was too silent about the responsibilities of those at the top, and too timid about the accountability of those with power. In One Nation responsibility goes all the way to the top of society. The richest in society have the biggest responsibility to show responsibility to the rest of our country. And I've got news for the powerful interests in our country, in One Nation no interest, from Rupert Murdoch to the banks, is too powerful to be held to account.

One Nation, he finished by assuring his audience, was about 'a country for all, with everyone playing their part. A Britain we rebuild together.'[25]

There was, beyond a few words about vocational education, little new or even old policy in the speech, which Miliband made without notes and with a confidence that belied his image as some sort of socially awkward uber-geek. Nor did the speech completely eschew knockabout. Mention was made of the controversy currently gripping Fleet Street concerning claims—vehemently denied—that Cameron's newly appointed Chief Whip, Andrew Mitchell, had called Downing Street policemen 'plebs'. Miliband also asked whether anyone had 'ever seen a more incompetent, hopeless, out of touch, u-turning, pledge-breaking, make it up as you go along, back of the envelope, miserable shower than this Prime Minister and this Government?' Nevertheless it worked, with both its content and its delivery attracting praise—some of it over-the-top, some of it offered through gritted teeth—right across the media spectrum, even if, inevitably, it could hardly compete, as far as news editors were concerned, with the huge public interest generated by the sickening abduction and murder of 5-year-old April Jones in the mid-Wales town of Machynlleth.[26]

'Team Ed' had been pretty confident that One Nation would pique the media's curiosity, because it could be presented as an audacious 'land-grab' and a direct challenge to Cameron's oft-repeated insistence that the Conservatives, despite their implementing policies that were arguably more Thatcher than Thatcher, remained camped on the hallowed 'centre ground' of British politics. That it did so still came as something of a relief, since the decision had already been taken to rejig the backdrop to the main stage in Manchester so that 'One Nation' replaced 'Rebuilding Britain'. Shadow Ministers had also been briefed to begin using the term in the same way as Blair's colleagues had been instructed to attach the word 'New' as a prefix to Labour whenever possible, although whether they would be encouraged to do so in the long term was still up in the air. The slogan was never really intended to be 'voter-facing', as one of the team put it, since it was 'more a label than a message'. As a result it had not been thought through sufficiently to ensure that there would be a ready supply of policies to which spokespeople could point as concrete examples of the new approach: the best Miliband himself could do was to repeat his call for the highest rate to return to 50p and even that, it appeared, fell into the all-too-familiar category of things-Labour-would-do-if-it-were-in-government-now-not-things-it-is-definitely-promising-to-do-if it-gets-elected-in-2015. However, if One Nation continued to get as much traction in the media as it was currently getting, then who knew?

Given the good headlines, it was hardly surprising that polls conducted in the aftermath of the speech registered something of a conference bounce. Labour's lead appeared to be indubitably in double figures, while Miliband's personal ratings, while hardly stratospheric or, indeed, necessarily better than Cameron's, did seem to have improved. Summing up the situation, YouGov's Anthony Wells, blogging on his bespoke UKPollingReport site, concluded:

his job approval rating is minus 9, a big jump from minus 29 last week and his highest since the early months of his leadership back in 2010 and early 2011. YouGov repeated the bank of questions asking people to compare David Cameron and Ed Miliband that they asked a week ago, and found significant boosts in Miliband's figures on many measures, but that he still trails Cameron in the same places he trailed him a week ago. So the proportion of people thinking Miliband is the stronger leader is up 5 to 26%, thinking he is the most decisive up 7 to 28%, more likeable up 3 to 34%, having a better strategy on the recession up 5 to 29%, however on all of these he continues to trail behind David Cameron. The biggest single increase is on having a clear vision for Britain where Miliband is up 8 points to 30%, putting him only just behind Cameron on 32%. 30% of people said that they have a more positive view of Miliband since the party conference. The majority of these are Labour supporters anyway, but given that the pattern of previous polling has been a lot of doubt about Miliband amongst Labour's own voters this is no bad thing for him. Miliband needed to be able to convince people who supported Labour but don't rate him that he is up to the job, and he is making progress.[27]

The numbers, then, did not show that the speech had been as much of a game-changer as the media narrative suggested, notwithstanding the fact that Tony Blair, who obviously knew a thing or two about making speeches and winning elections, sent Miliband a note reported to be effusive in its praise. Seen from the other end of the telescope, the whole thing had actually been one big missed opportunity. Rather than taking advantage of the fact that he had come to Manchester as the head of a party with a reasonably healthy lead in order to tell it a few home truths, Miliband had, in the words of the veteran columnist and former Tory MP Matthew Parris, dedicated most of his speech to 'telling his party that his (and their) instincts had been right all along'. The targets of his speech—the vested interests he insisted needed challenging—were all targets that his audience inside the hall were happy to see taken out. The mistakes acknowledged were those they were happy to acknowledge. No cuts were detailed. No sacred cows slaughtered. No left-wing union leaders directly confronted: indeed Miliband even announced on the day after his speech that he would be addressing a TUC march against austerity due to take place in central London on 20 October.

In reality, then, Miliband was risking precious little. Nor was he telling people outside the hall much that they did not already know. A mega poll for Lord Ashcroft conducted over the summer showed Labour already had big leads over the Conservatives when it came to people saying its heart was in the right place (43:30 per cent), that it stood for fairness (40:24), that it wanted to help ordinary people get on it life (53:28) and that it stood for equal opportunity for all (44:23). True, on representing 'the whole country, not just some types of people'—one of the key themes of Miliband's speech—Labour was on slightly shakier ground, with only 32 per cent of people identifying it as doing this. That said, only 17 per cent said the same of the Tories.

And, anyway, this was far from being Labour's biggest problem: that was on being 'willing to take tough decisions for the long term', where it scored only 29 per cent to the Conservatives' 57.[28] As Janan Ganesh of the *Financial Times* noted, doing something about this probably meant 'going against, not with, the grain of his party', because, like it or not, 'it remains true that offending one's own tribe is an inescapable stop on the journey towards the centre ground. Voters only believe a party is changing when they can see its traditional supporters are angry. They see an unruly flock as proof of a strong shepherd.'[29]

Miliband, however, did not see it this way, and nor, perhaps, could he afford to. He quite consciously rejected the model of leadership that held that the only way to prove you were in control and capable of bringing your party closer to voters was to engineer some sort of symbolic confrontation with it. That was not his style and anyway risked one of his most important achievements—namely, maintaining the surface unity of a party that, after previous defeats, had nearly always descended into such bitter internal conflict that it was incapable of fighting the real enemy, the Conservatives. And, anyway, anyone who believed that an unruly flock made for a strong shepherd only had to look at the effect Tory dissent was having on Mr Cameron. Sure, he made a strong showing at his own conference a week later with a speech that reasserted his centrist, modernizing credentials and contrasted the Conservatives' support for aspiration and their determination to equip Britain for 'the global race' with Labour as 'the party of one notion: more borrowing'. But his authority and his competence were still in question. Less than a fortnight after the Tories had returned from Birmingham, for example, the Prime Minister was being hauled over the coals for making an unscripted and undeliverable promise at PMQs to oblige energy companies to offer customers their lowest tariffs. Just as importantly, the people whom Miliband was being urged to confront in his own party—most frequently, left-wingers in the union movement—had already been told plenty of home truths, most obviously by Ed Balls. Arguably, the balance was just about right: they might not have been happy, but they had not been able to stop the leadership making it clear that a Labour government would be unable to reverse the bulk of the Coalition's cuts—and they were continuing to pay their dues.

The party's financial situation was improving, not least because it was benefiting to the tune of millions every year from the provision of taxpayer-funded 'Short money' to Her Majesty's Loyal Opposition. As Party Treasurer Diana Holland told conference, Labour remained 'saddled with huge debts', many of them dating from the 2005 election; however, 'the end is in sight. All loans', she continued, 'are covered by agreed repayment plans and the party is set to achieve its goal of being debt free in 2016'. Moreover, there was no sense in which conference itself was out of control. As usual, motions had been framed so as virtually to guarantee they could be supported by both the leadership and the majority of the delegates, even those who were critical. Even when, following on from efforts to democratize the policy-making process that had emerged from the *Refounding Labour* project, conference got to vote on those subjects to which the NPF should pay particular attention, none of them was in the least bit controversial. In view of all this, and now that Labour at last looked capable of beating a coalition that was making all sorts of mistakes (the latest of which was a fiasco over the awarding of the West Coast rail franchise), was it really worth rocking the boat?

# 6

# Benefits of the Doubt: Autumn 2012–Spring 2013

E d Miliband returned to Westminster in fairly good heart—and not just because he had decided to move Shadow Cabinet meetings from the cramped, faintly depressing room allocated for that purpose in the Palace of Westminster to a rather brighter, bigger room in the suite of offices he and his team occupied across the road in Norman Shaw South. As usual, the poll bounces achieved by each of the parties at their annual conference had largely cancelled each other out. But, since Labour had established a lead going into the conference season, this was not too worrying. Miliband's virtuoso performance had done him no harm and One Nation, though hardly on the lips of the average voter, continued to attract a degree of interest in the media, which had, after all, been its main purpose. That said, a good deal of that interest centred on trying to pin down exactly what the slogan meant for both the party's overall direction of travel and its policies. Neither off-the-record briefings nor on-the-record interviews were necessarily helpful in this respect. 'Anyone who thinks one nation means moving to the centre ground is mistaken,' the *Telegraph*'s Mary Riddell was told by one of the leader's colleagues, 'It's about meeting the public's appetite for change.'[1] This, like Miliband's insistence in an interview with the *Independent on Sunday*'s Jane Merrick in early November that 'It's not a small-c conservative notion but a really radical one, because if Britain really was One Nation, it would be a much fairer place', was the kind of clarification that only added to the confusion. Nor did it assuage the concerns of those who hoped that the speech marked a much-needed shift away from what they were convinced was a position too far to the left to stand any chance of winning over floating voters.[2] Not surprisingly, any optimism about the slogan's supposed magical powers was suitably cautious: the sympathetic *Observer* columnist and long-term Labour-watcher Andrew Rawnsley, for instance, admitted that One Nation 'could provide a useful frame for Labour's arguments and a guiding light for the formulation of policy', but noted that it depended on whether it was 'merely a rhetorical device for one afternoon in Manchester, applauded today, forgotten tomorrow' or 'the beginning of a serious strategy to capture the majority'.

As if to emphasize how difficult that might be, up stepped YouGov's Peter Kellner. Married to the Labour Peer Cathy Ashton, who was currently serving as the EU's Foreign Policy Chief, Kellner, a former journalist, was widely seen, especially on the right of the party, as someone willing to tell it like it was to the leadership. And his latest contribution in a long line of such articles—this one written for the monthly magazine *Prospect*—did exactly that.[3] An argument often made on the left of the party was that New Labour's supposed neo-liberalism had alienated a significant slice of the voter coalition it had put together to win its landslide victory in 1997. Kellner set out to find out what exactly had happened to that coalition and where it was today. His analysis found that there were around 4.5 million voters who were still alive and had 'defected' from Labour since 1997. Of that total, Labour had already won back around 1.5 million, most of whom had been voting Lib Dem up to and including the 2010 general election. That still left three million people—10 per cent of likely voters in 2015—who had voted Labour in 1997 and could perhaps be persuaded to return to the fold. But the party needed to realize that this group, although they were demographically very similar to those voters who had stuck with Labour, were significantly less likely to live in social housing, to work in the public sector, or to belong to a trade union. They were also much less likely to read a centre-left newspaper such as the *Guardian* or the *Mirror*. Moreover, he continued:

As for ideology, 60 per cent of loyalists describe themselves as left-of-centre and only 23 per cent as centre or right-of-centre. Among defectors, on the other hand, 36 per cent describe themselves as left and 48 per cent as centre or right. If we convert each person's answer into an index number, from minus 100 for very left-wing, via 0 for centre, to plus 100 for very right-wing, then the average location of the loyalists is minus 35, while that of defectors is minus six. These are big differences that cannot be wished away. The pool of left-wing defectors is just 400,000. They are outnumbered by more than six-to-one by the 2.6m defectors who do not place themselves to the left.

Those in the party claiming that New Labour had somehow burned off its core working-class voters were largely mistaken, argued Kellner. The class composition of Labour support had changed between 1997 and 2010 mainly because the working class itself had shrunk: when Blair won his landslide, there were two million more working-class voters in the electorate than middle-class voters; but nowadays there were as many as six million more middle-class than working-class voters. Given all this, the party was well advised to reject 'the language of ideology, class and social division' and turn instead to what Kellner called 'the politics of national purpose'. 'One Nation' and 'Rebuilding Britain', then, might be just the ticket, but only if, contrary to some of the spin coming from Miliband's colleagues, it involved standing on the centre ground rather than leaving it vacant on a hunch—one unsupported by polling—that voters, in some newfound desire for change over security, had shifted left.

Labour was also, of course, facing a Conservative Party that was determined to hang on to what it had and, if possible, to improve on its performance. As a result, it was prepared to do what it could to respond to rising concerns about household incomes failing to keep up with prices. It froze fuel duty. It maintained the pressure on local government to keep down the cost of council tax. And, contrary to what many believed, it was actually back-end-loading spending cuts so that they would come in when, it hoped, the economy was growing and revenues were rising again. The Conservatives were also building up an impressive war chest and were determined to build on a ground game in their target seats, which, according to a typically well-informed report by *ConservativeHome*'s Tim Montgomerie, they genuinely regarded as superior to Labour's.[4] Rightly or wrongly, the Tories believed they had won over twenty more seats than they could have expected on a uniform swing in 2010 and had now drawn up a list of forty seats—some Lib Dem, most Labour—that, with the help of paid and fully trained campaign organizers, they believed they could take and forty that, with the additional advantage of incumbency, they were confident of holding. There were clearly some concerns about their vulnerability on particular issues, not least the apparent failure of the economy to pick up, the feeling that, although cuts were necessary, they were being unfairly distributed, and, inevitably, the NHS. The long-running 'plebgate' saga, which gifted Miliband one or two sessions of PMQs before ending in the resignation of Chief Whip, Andrew Mitchell, was also unhelpful. So were media stories about the Chancellor's apparent insistence on travelling in a first-class train carriage when, initially anyway, he only had a standard class ticket. This, however, was just noise. Surveys and focus-group findings signalled that the Tories retained their underlying advantage on leadership, welfare reform, and ability to run the economy. They also continued to profit from the sense that Labour deserved a good deal of the blame for the mess the country was in and had failed to learn its lesson sufficiently to be allowed to run it again. Even better, the end of October saw the return of growth, with all that that promised: certainly, the common wisdom among Tory MPs had long held that, as an unnamed minister put it to the *Observer*'s Andrew Rawnsley: 'If the economy comes right, Labour is fucked.'[5]

To Labour, of course, all this looked—and hopefully was—both simplistic and complacent. Admittedly, the polling, and the probability that things would only get better on the economic front, were worrying. And there were many on the right of the party who winced at media coverage of Miliband addressing the TUC's anti-cuts protest: an estimated 150,000 people marched through central London, and some of them booed the Labour leader when he reminded them that any government he ran would have to make 'hard choices'. However, the party could, if it looked back to 2010, find just as many reasons to believe that its ground game was a match for the Tories. After all, to have suffered one of its worst election defeats and yet still be within fifty seats of the Conservative Party owed at least something to organization, even if much of it was provided by trade-union officials as well as party activists.

Clearly, both major parties would be investing massively in digital campaigning in the hope that they could go some way towards replicating the huge advances made in that field in the 2009 and 2012 US primary and presidential elections. Indeed, Labour was soon to enter into an arrangement with Blue State Digital, which worked on both Obama campaigns, the second of which involved a Rapid Response Unit directed by a young man from the UK, Matthew McGregor. But Labour's field operations team had reason to believe that the party's voluntary membership was younger and therefore more adept with social and other digital media than its Tory counterpart.[6] Hopefully, then, they, like the Obama campaign, were more likely than their opponents to be able to leverage any online effort at the centre into voter contacts and therefore into actual votes on the day. Labour was also pinning its hopes on (and pouring scarce resources into) the training in 'community organizing' provided to its paid organizers by its American adviser (and early mentor to Barack Obama) Arnie Graf. Their job would be to work with the candidates, who were also required to commit to the community-organizing model, to listen to local needs and build grass-roots campaigns around them. The result, if things went to plan, would be multiple networks of enthusiastic volunteers who, by the time of the election, would be able effectively to convert contacts made through those campaigns into support for the party at the ballot box, not least by the significant number of voters who, research by the Fabian Society in February 2013 seemed to show, supported Labour but had not bothered voting for it in 2010.

The news, announced by Harriet Harman at conference, that Labour would be twinning frontbenchers with candidates in Labour's rather ambitious list of just over 100 target seats (the vast majority of which were seats lost to the Tories in 2010 rather than 2005 or 2001) was also a morale booster. But it was probably rather less important in the long run than the fact that Labour was working hard on getting those candidates selected sooner rather than later in order to boost their chances of negating the incumbency advantage enjoyed by Tory MPs who took seats from Labour in 2010—an advantage that some of them may have been overestimating anyway, given that, in a number of constituencies, they would be facing a rematch with the Labour MP they had replaced and who was therefore as well known in the seat as they were. Further analysis suggested that many of the most winnable seats could probably be won simply by locking in voters who had switched from the Lib Dems, most of whom, as an Ashcroft mega poll conducted in the spring of 2013 seemed to confirm, were left-wingers who despised Clegg for putting the Tories into office and were highly unlikely ever to give him a second chance.[7] Another Ashcroft mega poll—this time of marginal constituencies conducted around the same time—suggested Labour was doing reasonably well, although it was still clearly weaker in southern and suburban seats than it would have liked. To win these seats and secure its place as the largest party or perhaps even emerge with an overall majority, Labour would need to win over previous non-voters as well as a significant number of former Tory voters. This, of course, was bound to get harder once the economy began to recover, but Labour could hold on to the possibility that any recovery might not necessarily sweep all before it. First, it might not be accompanied by a commensurate rise in household incomes—an issue Labour was planning to spend a great deal of time on between now and the next election. Secondly, the government might not get as much credit for the recovery as it was hoping for if voters believed that it had occurred despite its efforts rather than because of them. And, thirdly, a recovery may even mean that voters, sufficiently confident that the worst was over, might be all the more prepared to give Labour the benefit of the doubt.

Labour could also take some comfort in the fact that the parliamentary Conservative Party still seemed to lack the discipline necessary to ensure that its leaders could focus on getting out the good news on the economy. Cameron, it seemed, could never do enough for his Eurosceptic backbenchers, who simply banked any concession he made to them and then demanded another—and another and another. Towards the end of October, with a new round of EU Budget negotiations coming up, Tory backbencher Mark Reckless tabled an amendment calling for a cut in the budget—one that the government decided it would not support. That decision, however, assumed that Labour would do the same. Instead, however, the party imposed a three-line whip on its MPs to vote for the amendment. By no means everyone in the leadership was in favour of indulging in what the *Independent*'s John Rentoul called 'the joy of disciplined opportunism'.[8] Indeed, accounts later emerged in the press of a heated exchange on the issue between Douglas Alexander, the Shadow Foreign Secretary, and Ed Balls, who, while Alexander was away overseas, had helped persuade Miliband to cut up rough.

The disagreement between Alexander and Balls, however, resulted in the two co-authoring an article in *The Times* justifying Labour's call for a cut a couple of days before the vote was due to be held.[9] Meanwhile, those who were uneasy about the manœuvre presaging a more fundamental shift towards the more sceptical position known to be favoured by Balls and by policy coordinator Jon Cruddas were reassured that support for the Tory Euro rebels was purely a tactical wheeze. As a result, when the Commons vote was held right at the end of the month, the government was narrowly defeated. What grabbed the headlines, however, was not Labour's decision but the fact that fifty-three Tory MPs had been prepared to defy their whips. The rebellion dominated political discussion for a few days, providing a helpful short-term distraction from the embarrassing news that Labour was expelling the MP for Rotherham and former Minister Denis McShane, after a parliamentary inquiry found that he had fiddled his expenses, opening the way for the criminal charges that eventually saw him convicted of fraud. But there was a longer-term benefit, too. Polling in the aftermath of the defeat, YouGov found that 69 per cent of voters thought the Conservative Party was divided and only 14 per cent thought of it as united, with the figures for Labour being 35 and 40 respectively—a reversal of what had been found when voters were asked the exact same question a year before and a perception that was only strengthened early on in the New Year when so many Tory MPs refused to join their leader (and the vast majority of Labour MPs) in voting for gay marriage.[10]

In and of itself, the fact that Labour was seen to be less divided than its main rival was clearly nowhere near enough to deliver the party victory at a general election. But, equally clearly, anything that desta-bilized David Cameron did Ed Miliband no harm. This was why, for instance, he had no problem with the Mayor of London, Boris John-son, who was widely tipped as the man the Tories would turn to should Cameron falter, in some ways stealing Labour's thunder when, in early November, he announced his support for an increase in the Living Wage for London to £8.55. Sadly, but hardly surprisingly, Johnson could not be persuaded to share a stage with any Labour people, but his announcement was nevertheless part of a wider cam-paign in which the party was heavily involved—indeed, one that produced one or two unlikely pairings, not least David Miliband and Unison's General Secretary Dave Prentis, who penned a jointly authored article for the *Observer* singing the praises of the idea and discussing how employers might be incentivized to join a number of Labour local authorities in paying it. Ed Miliband, meanwhile, insisted in an newspaper interview—perhaps a little opportunistically, given that Labour's interest in the living wage long pre-dated his speech in Manchester—that 'This is the next step for One Nation, because One Nation is about everybody having a stake in society. It is about prosperity being fairly shared. It is about giving people a proper stake in the future of the country.' More interesting, however, was another point he made in the same interview, since it signalled Labour's strategic response to the news that the UK was once again out of recession: 'We've got a growth crisis in Britain but,' he insisted, 'we've also got a living standards crisis, because the proceeds of economic growth are not being fairly distributed anymore.'[11]

This attempt to reframe the debate made sense. As previous elections in Britain and other countries had demonstrated, it was one that had helped to topple incumbents before. But there was also a good deal of evidence that it was tapping into a real problem. Research published by the Resolution Foundation think tank headed up by former Number Ten adviser Gavin Kelly suggested that, over the next decade, millions of low-income households were unlikely to find themselves tangibly better off even as any recovery took hold. Whether, however, this would be enough to ensure that the economy would not, as most Conservatives were hoping, deliver Cameron victory in 2015 was a moot point. Barack Obama's win over Romney in the US Presidential election held at the beginning of November inevitably attracted huge interest in Labour circles: after all, the Democrats were regarded not just as Labour's sister party but also as a source of campaigning inspiration. However, most of the chatter in the aftermath of the contest revolved around the supposed superiority of the Democrats' field operations, the ability of Obama to persuade people that, unlike the plutocratic Mitt Romney, he was on their side, and of course the danger of thinking, as the Republicans had apparently done, that the combination of an economy still hungover from the crash, negative campaigning, and a vague promise of change would deliver victory. All fascinating stuff. But it missed the main point, which was made again and again by academic observers in America both before and after the election—namely, that the economic fundamentals had in fact pointed for some time to a victory for a President governing a country whose economy had been growing for a while and whose voters still placed most of the blame for the mess it was in on the previous administration.

Conservative strategists, of course, picked up on this lesson and on Obama's main message, which he first used in a stump speech in the Midwest some two years before facing re-election and which is worth recalling in full:

So basically here's what this election comes down to. They're betting that...
you're going to come down with amnesia. They figure you're going to forget
what their agenda did to this country. They think you'll just believe that
they've changed. These are the folks whose policies help devastate our middle
class. They drove our economy into a ditch. And we got in there and put on
our boots. And we pushed and we shoved and we were sweating. These guys
were standing, watching us, sipping on a Slurpee. And they were pointing at
us saying 'How come you're not pushing harder? How come you're not
pushing faster?' And then when we finally got the car up–and it's got a few
dings and a few dents; it's got some mud on it; we're going to have to do some
work on it—they point out to everybody else and say: 'Look what these guys
did to your car!' After we got it out of the ditch, and then they got the nerve to
ask for the keys back. I don't want to give them the keys back. They don't
know how to drive.

What Conservative strategists did not do, however, was follow the
advice of people on their side who interpreted Romney's failure as a
defeat for the harder-line approach they associated with consultants
such as Australia's Lynton Crosby and America's Karl Rove. Ten days
after the *Telegraph*'s chief political commentator, Peter Oborne,
declared that 'President Obama's subsequent victory is a massive and
humiliating blow to the Rove/Crosby school of politics', the Tories let
it be known that they had hired Crosby to help them win in 2015.[12]

The move made sense. While the assistance Crosby provided to
Michael Howard's campaign at the 2005 election had been controversial and ultimately unable to deliver victory, it had convinced those
working with him, among them Cameron and Osborne, that he had a
talent for focusing on just a few issues and crafting hard-hitting messages on them that were then repeated with a discipline that helped
them cut through to voters. In any case, something had to be done to
assuage the leadership's critics in the media and in the Commons in the
light of Labour's comfortable win in the Corby by-election held right
in the middle of November—a result that was all the more worrying
for the Tories because UKIP's candidate had come from nowhere to
take 14 per cent of the vote, knocking the Lib Dems (whose candidate
lost her deposit) into a poor fourth place. For Labour, the win was the
cause for quiet satisfaction rather than wild celebration. True, it was
the first time the party had taken a Tory seat at a by-election since
February 1997, but the swing of nearly 13 per cent, while impressive,
was hardly earth-shattering. Moreover, polling done in the constituency by Lord Ashcroft suggested that only two-thirds of those who

declared they were going to vote Labour said they would prefer Miliband rather than Cameron as Prime Minister, while the majority of those who had switched from Tory to Labour said they would consider switching back again at the general election.

Labour's victory in Corby was also based around a campaign focused on rumoured service reductions at a local hospital. While this showed that concern about the NHS remained a potential trump card for the party if it could be scaled up at a general election, it could not necessarily be replicated elsewhere. The same could be said for the way the party skilfully exploited the supposed 'desertion' of the seat by a Conservative MP who, before she became the candidate for the 2010 election, had no links with the town. The new Labour MP, Andy Sawston, had not only been selected a year before the by-election but could portray himself, reasonably convincingly, as a local lad, even though, as his opponents pointed out, he had actually spent his adult life after university working in London—first in parliament, then in public affairs and for a think tank.

The argument that the party was becoming dominated by trade-union officials, Oxford PPE graduates, think-tankers, PR people, and former special advisers was also used by its rivals to try to take the shine off victories in by-elections fought on the same night (albeit in safe Labour seats) for Lucy Powell (who had been an MP's assistant and then worked for a pressure group and a quango before becoming Ed Miliband's acting Chief of Staff) and Stephen Doughty (who had been a special adviser to Douglas Alexander before joining the international charity sector). It clearly was not a charge that could be made to stick in each and every constituency where a local party selected a new candidate or a by-election was fought. In the three contests that Labour won a fortnight later, for example, its candidates were a successful local council leader who had earlier worked in publishing (Croydon North), a lawyer specializing in military matters (Middlesbrough), and the chief executive of a children's hospice (Rotherham, where, to the party's great relief, Respect made a poor showing but, to its discomfort, UKIP polled over 20 per cent). Nevertheless, the charge that Labour was turning into an organization run by and on behalf of people who had never done anything outside politics was one that it purported to take seriously, since it was not one made only by its enemies. Somehow, however, it never quite got round to answering it—just like it never really got round to finding out why, just as worryingly perhaps, almost all CLPs that did not use all-women shortlists seemed to select men.

In mid-November 2012, however, Labour was naturally more concerned with making the most of its win in Corby—a seat that since its creation in 1983 had always been held by the party elected to government, the taking of which showed Labour could win outside its strongholds. 'This constituency', Miliband told assembled journalists, 'is at the heart of our country. This constituency has sent a very clear message today. It has sent a message that it is putting its trust in a One Nation Labour party . . . Middle England is turning away from David Cameron and the Conservatives.' On the face of it, there was a grain of truth in all this. However, more detailed opinion research conducted a couple of weeks before the by-elections suggested it needed sprinkling with a large pinch of salt. As was his occasional wont, Tory peer Michael Ashcroft had conducted another one of his mega polls along with focus groups in several marginal seats—Nuneaton, Pudsey, War-rington, Hastings, Watford, and Thurrock. His aim was to take a closer look at those who had switched or would consider switching to Labour in 2015. As usual, there was good news and bad news.[13]

On the positive side of the ledger was the fact that Labour had managed to tempt at least a few 2010 Tory voters into the fold, even if it was only 7 per cent of them. Labour could also take heart from the fact that, when those who had not finally decided and might change their mind were asked which parties they would seriously consider voting for, the Conservatives achieved only 37 per cent to its 43 per cent. Indeed, some 10 per cent of all voters, while not currently intending to vote Labour, would apparently consider doing so. Similarly heartening was the fact that, of every ten people who had voted Labour in 2010, nine of them were planning to do so again, suggesting the party's core vote was holding up well. Moreover, it looked as if well over a third of former Lib Dem voters were still intending to vote Labour at the next election. Labour seemed, albeit predictably, to have a lock on public-sector employees, too: among those working in the private sector its lead over the Conservatives was the same (that is, nine points) as its lead nationally; but, among those employed by the state, local or national, it was twenty-five points (that is, 51:26). Finally, nearly half of those not currently intending to vote Labour but who would consider doing so thought it was the party 'on the side of people like me' compared to just one in ten of those who named the Conservatives.

But there was still ample cause for concern for any Labour politician brave enough to dig deeper into the figures, as well as the comments from the focus groups. A quarter of those who had switched to Labour confessed that they had not decided and might well change their minds, with four in ten of that group saying that one of the concerns they had about the party was that it would spend and borrow more than the country could afford. Those who had not switched to Labour but would consider doing so were much less ready to say that Labour could be trusted to govern again and more ready to believe that, had it won in 2010, the party would have carried on spending and borrowing. Labour's opposition to cuts and what people saw as its refusal to take responsibility for the state of the public finances when it left office only served to reinforce concern that it had failed to learn the right lessons from its time in government. Leadership was also a problem for this group: those who were not intending to vote Labour but might consider doing so had a low to neutral opinion of Ed Miliband; indeed, in Ashcroft's opinion, he was 'a factor preventing some people from switching to Labour. If this were not the case, Labour's poll share would be above 50 per cent.' Even by those who had switched to Labour (and for some who had stuck with the party) Miliband was seen as, to quote Ashcroft again, 'the price to be paid for a Labour government'.

When it came to policies, Ashcroft's polling suggested immigration was still a weakness for Labour, but not as big a weakness as welfare. Over a third of those who had either stuck with or switched to Labour had done so despite their belief that the Conservatives were the best party for 'reforming welfare to stop scroungers and cut dependency'. The same was true of over half of those who would consider but did not currently intend voting Labour, with four in ten of that group believing that 'the problem of people living on benefits when they are able to work' would have been worse had Labour stayed in power. Predictably, then, the party's supposed tolerance of welfare dependency and abuse was a bruise that George Osborne was determined to punch as hard and as often as he could. Coming just days after a humiliating (but politically wise) capitulation to the campaign for much tougher regulation over payday loans companies led by the media-savvy Labour MP Stella Creasy, the Chancellor's Autumn Statement, presented in the first week of December 2012, afforded him the ideal opportunity—and the chance to prove once again that attack is often the best form of defence.

On the face of it, the Chancellor was in trouble. He was having to admit that he had again missed his targets for eliminating the deficit and reducing the debt. But he turned the consequent need to extend austerity further into the next parliament to the Tories' advantage by announcing that, in order to save the Treasury billions of pounds (and because 'fairness is about being fair to the person who leaves home every morning to go out to work and sees their neighbour still asleep, living a life on benefits'), a whole host of working-age social security payments would be uprated by just 1 per cent per annum for three years. Parliament, Osborne added, would be asked in the New Year to vote on legislation enshrining the measure, meaning that Labour would effectively be forced to choose between fiscal rectitude, on the one hand, and, on the other, support for a real-terms cut for millions of people on low incomes, most of whom, even according to the government's own figures, were not the 'skivers' of public imagination but the 'strivers', those doing jobs that simply paid too poorly to allow them to make ends meet. Osborne made it all the more difficult for Labour by once again freezing fuel duty, raising the tax threshold for basic rate-payers, and reducing tax relief on pension contributions for higher earners; this allowed him to argue more or less convincingly that he had hit the rich while doing something for the squeezed middle and even the lower paid. No wonder Ed Balls, whose job it was to reply to the Chancellor in the Commons, had one of his off days in the chamber.

The leadership's initial reaction to Osborne's move was to play for time. Labour, it briefed, would wait to see what exactly its MPs were being asked to vote on before it made up its mind. It was obvious, however, that it needed to decide on a line to take rather more rapidly than that. The argument for swallowing hard and going along with the benefit uprating cap was obvious. This was a classic elephant trap, and, however much it hated it, the party could not allow itself to fall into it. If Labour voted against it, it would be faced again and again with questions about why it thought people on benefits, regarded as feckless and fraudulent by many of their fellow citizens, deserved a bigger 'pay rise' than those in work—and not just those in the private sector (who, according to projections, would soon see their wages rising) but also those in the public sector, for whom Labour had agreed to support not just a 1 per cent cap but a full-on pay freeze. Moreover, resistance was ultimately futile: the government would get its way in parliament; the only way to stop what was happening was to win in 2015, and, if supporting the measure meant that the party avoided being stranded on the wrong side of public opinion in the run-up to the next election, then it was a price worth paying.

Yet, however obvious that argument was, it was not, in the end, one that persuaded many around the top table—and for a number of reasons. First, the sheer range of benefits directly and indirectly affected—jobseeker's allowance, employment and support allowance, income support, housing benefit, maternity pay, working tax credit, child tax credits—was such that literally millions of people would be affected. Even leaving aside the fact that their daily lives would be made much more difficult, there were so many of them that a failure to oppose what was being done to them would not only trigger outrage among Labour's activists and the churches, charities, and pressure groups that it preferred to keep on side, but would actually risk losing votes. After all, the number of people who would feel the pinch as a result of Osborne's decision to cap the rise in benefit levels at 1 per cent was in many marginal constituencies far greater than the Tory majorities in those seats in 2010—a point shown by detailed, constituency-by-constituency research conducted in the next few days.

Secondly, opinion polling conducted in the immediate aftermath of the Autumn Statement did not run equivocally in Osborne's favour. Many more respondents thought the measures outlined would benefit the rich rather than anyone else. On the benefits cap specifically, 33 per cent of respondents agreed with it and a further 19 per cent of people thought it was actually too generous. However, that left 35 per cent of people thinking that benefits should have been allowed to rise in line with inflation. Among those intending to vote Labour, which at that point was 42 per cent of those asked, some 55 per cent were against the cap, and only 17 per cent for it, with a further 16 per cent happy to see benefits frozen altogether. Some of those opposing it were, of course, directly affected. But the party also had to take into account the middle-class progressives (not least those who had switched to it from the Lib Dems since 2010) who, while personally untouched by the measure, regarded it as an unconscionable attack on the less fortunate. Moreover, that view was also the one taken by the vast majority of Labour MPs. Whipping them to vote for, or even to abstain on, the Bill would have proved very difficult indeed.

Thirdly, there was at least a chance that Labour would be able, if it did its research quickly enough and hit back strongly enough, to make a case to floating voters on average incomes that the cap would hit large numbers of 'ordinary, hard-working families', as well as one or two particular groups of people likely to garner public sympathy. This was one reason why, even though the party's attempt to get the media talking about what it wanted to call the 'mummy tax' in the same breath as the 'granny tax' came to naught, Yvette Cooper was probably right to home in on the consequences for maternity pay. If she and her colleagues could find a way dramatically to contrast what was being done to all those affected with what Osborne was doing for his 'rich friends', all the better.

Accordingly, Balls bounced back from the monstering he had received following his poor performance in the Commons the week before and went into bat. First up, he put his name to an article for the *Sun* headlined 'Working Families Paying for Tory Failures', which presaged an attack on what Liam Byrne, at Shadow Work and Pensions, went on to call a 'strivers' tax'—a raid on precisely those people whom the Tories had spent their conference in Birmingham claiming to represent.[14] This was followed a day or two later by Balls confirming that Labour would vote against the cap—unless, of course, Osborne agreed to scrap his lowering of the top rate of tax to 45p and prove that we really were 'all in this together'. This was clever, but whether it was convincing was another matter, especially when it was up against a Conservative Party willing to invest in digital rebuttal ads and leaflets asking voters whether they preferred to help 'hardworking families' or 'people who won't work'—the latter illustrated, not for the first or last time, by a picture of a slob lounging at home on his sofa. This was one of the stock images regularly picked out by focus groups when asked whom they thought Labour represented and so was guaranteed to trigger memories (at least among those who had registered the soundbite in the first place) of Osborne's distinction between, as he had put it at the Conservative Party Conference, 'the shift worker, leaving home in the dark hours of the early morning' and 'their next-door neighbour sleeping off a life on benefits'.

Polling on the uprating cap itself—partly because the responses elicited seemed to depend so much on the wording of the question—was ultimately inconclusive. However, even those companies who found large numbers of people objecting to the measure generally found even larger numbers of people who agreed with it. But this was not just about survey results on an individual item of policy. It was about an underlying narrative—a war rather than a single battle and one that was being waged by Osborne on two fronts simultaneously. Labour, by rejecting the cap, was not just going to be seen as a soft touch for shirkers; it was also bound to be accused of talking about the need for 'hard choices' and 'tough decisions', but, when it actually came down to it, refusing again and again to make them. It was also going to be asked how, if it was going to forgo the billions of pounds saved by the introduction of the cap, where it proposed to get the money to eliminate the deficit and reduce the debt instead. Its failure to fight off those accusations and to answer those questions undermined the steps (like agreeing to a pay freeze, admitting it would be unable to reverse every cut, and promising to carry out a zero-based review) that it had taken to prove it could be trusted with the nation's finances. This was one reason why, following the Autumn Statement, the credibility gap between the Conservatives and Labour on managing the economy, which had been closing, began to open up once again. By the end of the year it was back to double digits.

One obvious solution to this problem, and one that some Blairites called for, would have been for Labour to make it clearer exactly which government cuts it would agree to. Even better, it could come up with alternative cuts of its own, which it could then use to justify its opposition to what it decided were the most egregious cuts (not least those relating to welfare) proposed by the Tories. But this the party refused to do, and for equally obvious reasons. As Balls confided in an interview in December 2012, he had warned colleagues (including, presumably, Jim Murphy at Defence, who had gone ahead and done it in November anyway) against signing up to particular cuts proposed by the government, since their inevitable reluctance to sign up to each and every cut proposed would effectively imply that they intended to reverse all those they refused to endorse—and trigger questions as to how they were going to afford to do it.[15] As for Labour laying out its own alternatives, it risked shattering the hope (some would have said the illusion) that Labour could make a difference and disappointing those directly affected, thereby demotivating many of the people the party was relying on both to vote for it and to encourage others to vote. Cuts capable of raising any serious money, after all, were in budgets that Labour could not openly contemplate cutting—with pensions, healthcare, and education the obvious examples.

Admittedly, there was one big-ticket item that many in the party would gladly have said no to; but the chances of Labour announcing before an election that it wanted to cancel plans for a like-for-like replacement of UK's continuous-at-sea Trident submarine-based missile system were vanishingly small. For one thing, old hands like Admiral Lord West were telling the leadership that the idea that there was some convenient cut-price alternative was a Lib Dem fantasy—a view shared by Shadow Defence Secretary Jim Murphy.[16] For another, whatever their private views on the whys and wherefores of an independent nuclear deterrent, too many people at Labour's top table were simply too afraid of anything that risked returning the party to the bad old days of the 1980s—a decade during which it had been crucified by its Conservative opponents for being soft on defence and sometimes much worse. Finally, the sheer uncertainty of the economic situation, added to the desire not to give hostages to fortune and to preserve the possibility of springing last-minute surprises, meant that, if he could help it, Balls (and indeed Miliband) had no intention of announcing a raft of tax and spending decisions until much closer to the general election—one that those constantly clamouring for more detail seemed to have forgotten was still well over two years away. In Balls's view, the fact that, like those calling on Labour to apologize for its supposed mismanagement of the public finances when in office, so many of those calling for it to declare its hand were Conservatives told you all you needed to know.

The trouble was that none of this made it any easier to deal with Osborne's welfare wheeze, not least because it tapped into long-established and popularly held distinctions between the 'undeserving' and the 'deserving' poor that were easily mobilized and maintained by a print media overwhelmingly supportive of the Conservatives' agenda. YouGov research released in early January 2013, for instance, showed a clear correlation between lack of familiarity with the benefits system and misguided beliefs about it, as well as underlining that those beliefs were widespread. But even the average respondent thought that 27 per cent of the welfare budget was fraudulently claimed and that 41 per cent of the welfare budget went on assistance to the unemployed, when the true figures were under 1 per cent and 3 per cent respectively. Overall, 42 per cent thought benefits were too generous.[17]

Providing respondents with more accurate information did change their opinions quite markedly. The problem, however, was that, when it came to broadcast media—the most important source of news for the majority of the population—that information was not repeated nearly often enough to make a difference. The necessary detail was difficult to convey and just as difficult to take in. In any case, it was nowhere near as memorable as the real-life or larger-than-life characters who periodically appeared on people's screens to confirm prejudices that were also fed by first- (or at least second-)hand familiarity with friends, family, or neighbours who were 'on the fiddle'. When it came to many newspapers, however, that information simply was not made available at all. Moreover, any lingering hopes in Labour circles that they could, by sheer force of argument or weight of well-researched and well-presented press releases, somehow change this situation had, by December 2012, gone up in smoke. The reason? Leveson.

Following his announcement in July 2011 that he was setting up an inquiry into 'the culture, practices and ethics of the press' to be led by Lord Justice Leveson in July 2011, David Cameron had made it clear that he would not countenance a system of press regulation that failed to satisfy victims of gross intrusion like the parents of Madeleine McCann or Milly Dowler. As publication of the Leveson report at the end of November 2012 grew nearer, however, Downing Street was making it clear that Cameron was minded to reject any attempt to underpin an independent regulator by statute—something that an overwhelming majority of owners, editors, and journalists had made clear they objected to. For Ed Miliband, however, the publication of the report, and any attempt by Cameron to wriggle out of its recommendations, offered not only the opportunity for those who had suffered at the hands of the tabloids to ensure that some good came out of that suffering, but also the chance for him to reprise his starring role in Hackgate as defender of the people against vested corporate and political interests. He was spurred on by discussions with Nick Clegg, which suggested that, in common with most Labour MPs, the Lib Dems were prepared to consider legislation—and also by the fact that the public appeared to support it. A poll conducted for the Media Standards Trust found that eight out of ten respondents, seemingly irrespective of where they were on the political spectrum or what their daily newspaper thought, favoured the creation of an independent regulator established by law, with only one in ten actually opposed to the idea.[18] Miliband also knew, because just over forty Tory MPs had made it clear in an open letter to the Prime Minister—one eventually signed by over seventy of them—that there were many on the benches opposite who wanted him to stick to his guns.

When, therefore, Leveson presented his eponymous report, Labour's leader declared that its recommendations should be accepted in their entirety, although he quickly qualified his support for the idea that Ofcom should provide oversight of the legally underpinned self-regulation system proposed for the press. However, the fact that Cameron made it clear that, while not ruling out statutory underpinning, he agreed with the press that it was a step too far, presented the Labour leader with a conundrum. Like Nick Clegg, who disassociated himself and his party from Cameron's (and therefore the government's) position by making a separate speech in the Commons, Miliband knew that the best hope of putting together a workable compromise was some sort of cross-party agreement. He could also see that, notwithstanding snap polls that suggested a majority of people (like the majority of victims of hacking) disagreed with Cameron on the question of legal underpinning, the PM was already being feted as a heroic defender of free speech by many of the best-read titles in the land, not least the *Mail* and the *Sun*. While no one on the Labour side expected those papers to support anyone else but the Conservatives at the next election, the prospect of virtually guaranteeing their unremitting hostility day-in and day-out for the next two-and-a-half years was nevertheless a daunting one. On the other hand, Miliband was concerned lest Cameron try to use the need for cross-party agreement to string the whole thing out until public interest had waned, at which point he would try to implicate Labour in any subsequent failure to arrive at a consensus.

Given this, and given his already strong identification with the cause of the victims, Miliband decided that his only option was to play hardball. And he found a more-than-willing wing-man in Tom Watson, who was happy to volunteer the resources (and the contacts book) of the party to the Hacked Off campaign, which, predictably enough given its role as the voice of the victims, was demanding full implementation of Leveson. Dismissing as ludicrous the government's decision to publish a draft Bill on statutory underpinning simply to show how difficult it would be, Labour published its own draft—with the conditional backing of the Lib Dems—in order to show how easy it would be to do it and, it argued, still protect free speech at the same time. Harriet Harman, in her capacity as Shadow Culture Secretary, also made it clear that, if no progress were made, Labour would try to force a vote on the issue sometime in the New Year.

At the beginning of January 2013, however, Labour had other matters on its mind. One Nation had gained so much traction, at least with the media if not the public, that the leadership had decided to run harder and longer with it than many of those involved had anticipated. But that meant that they were now under pressure to come up with one or two policies to counter criticism (internal as well as external) that One Nation was in reality little more than an all-purpose prefix on the party's press releases—a slogan in search of a programme. It also needed to show, in advance of the parliamentary vote on the benefits uprating Bill, that it, too, could be tough on welfare. Its solution to both problems was now ready to go—a call for a One Nation compulsory Jobs Guarantee not just for young people, for whom Labour had already advocated such a scheme, but for the long-term unemployed too. Those out of work for two years in the first instance would be obliged, on pain of losing benefits, to take a private or voluntary job, paid for by the government and paying the minimum wage, the scheme to be financed by reversing the Coalition's decision to increase the relief on pension contributions for top-rate tax-payers.

The extent to which the scheme, launched by Miliband, Balls, and Byrne and briefed out as 'compulsory work or lose benefits', survived contact with the enemy (and even with friends) was debatable, however. In the wake of the announcement, Labour had to concede that it had previously earmarked the changes to tax relief on pensions that it was proposing to use to fund the scheme in order to pay for another policy, obliging Byrne to admit that said policy—action on tax credits following the Autumn Statement in 2011—had effectively expired. Inevitably, this led to questions about which of its other policies were also past their sell-by dates. Balls was also obliged to explain that the Jobs Guarantee was yet another one of those policies that Labour would be pursuing if it were in government now, not necessarily something it was committing to include in its 2015 manifesto. The wager the leadership was making—and, given how much attention the average voter pays to such things, it may have been a fairly safe one—

was that the vast majority of those who had noticed that Labour was planning to do something that was constructive but also tough on welfare would fail to register the fact that the policy in question was perishable rather than built to last.

According to the Conservatives, of course, and to some of their favourite Blairite stay-behinds in the blogosphere, what Labour was proposing was not tough enough anyway—not compared to their 1 per cent cap on benefits, the legislation for which was now introduced into the Commons, accompanied by a poster that read 'TODAY LABOUR ARE VOTING TO INCREASING BENEFITS BY MORE THAN WORKERS' WAGES. CONSERVATIVES: STANDING UP FOR WORKING PEOPLE' and a press release, faithfully relayed as usual by the *Mail*, to the effect that 'Labour has opposed welfare savings that amount to £83 billion by 2015/16 and would have to raise borrowing or debt by the equivalent of £5,000 per family'. The Bill duly received its second reading, since only three Lib Dems refused to vote for it, although journalists were less interested in the result than in speculating whether David Miliband, despite labelling Osborne's measure 'rancid' in his speech, had issued some sort of challenge to Balls by suggesting Labour work within the spending 'envelope' established by the government.[19] If he was, then he was only calling on the Shadow Chancellor to do now what many people expected him to do eventually anyway—namely, to repeat the trick Gordon Brown pulled off in the run-up to the 1997 election. Moreover, the elder Miliband was not the only one. Behind closed doors, his brother was also coming round to the conclusion that it might be better if Labour accepted some version of Tory spending limits sooner rather than later: could the party really afford to leave it until late 2014 or early 2015 when voters seemed to be craving reassurance about Labour's fiscal probity now rather than eighteen months down the line?

As if to underline that it was clearly a case of when rather than if, a fortnight later the leadership was obliged to intervene in order make it clear that the Shadow Minister of State at the DWP, Stephen Timms, who had just assured the Commons that Labour believed in increasing benefits in line with inflation, had merely been outlining what the party would prefer to happen now rather than pointing to what its policy would be in 2015. All this contrasted markedly with another policy that was announced around the same time and, like the Jobs Guarantee, was also branded as a One Nation measure. At the end of

January, Miliband pledged to do more for the 'forgotten 50 per cent' who were not going to go to university by a new focus on vocational education and on-the-job training achieved by the introduction of a gold standard 'Technical Baccalaureate' qualification and a massive expansion of apprenticeships made possible by obliging firms doing work for government to provide them. But because the spending implications were less obvious, and because (like the proposal he was about to make on establishing a network of business-friendly regional banks) it fitted with Miliband's desire to turn the UK into a Germanic, long-termist, coordinated economy, helping the 'forgotten 50 per cent' seemed to be a solid commitment, not simply one more good intention on an evanescent and therefore worthless wish list.

The same could not be said of the next One Nation policy wheeled out by the party. In the course of a wide-ranging speech on the need to create an economy that grew from the middle out rather than the top down, Miliband called for the reintroduction of the 10 pence tax band scrapped by Gordon Brown, to be financed by the 'mansion tax' on high-value properties known to be favoured by the Lib Dems, most prominently by the Business Secretary, Vince Cable. This one, admittedly, made more of a splash, intended as it was not just to encapsulate the One Nation idea in a single, 'doorstep-ready' proposal but also both to highlight differences with the previous Labour government and to divide the Coalition. But, again, its impact was lessened by Labour having to admit, even as it forced a parliamentary vote on the issue in an effort to embarrass the Lib Dems, that it was an aspiration rather than a promise—and that the party was not ruling out additional council tax bands in order to effect the mansion tax rather than introducing the discrete charge for properties over £2 million originally suggested.

Putting flesh on the bones of One Nation was not, of course, the only thing the leadership needed to achieve in the early part of 2013. At the end of February, a by-election was held in Eastleigh following the resignation of Chris Huhne, a Lib Dem MP later imprisoned for perverting the course of justice. Labour finished a poor fourth, its selection of the comedy writer John O'Farrell as the party's candidate seemingly having done it little or no good. The only consolation—if straws in the wind were to be clutched at—was that constituency polling suggested that well over a third of those who saw themselves as Labour supporters actually voted for the Lib Dem who had successfully defended the seat. This did nothing to help the party argue that it was capable of winning in the south. But, if it were repeated at a general election, the Tories were going to have far more trouble gaining seats from the Lib Dems than they had expected, boosting Labour's chances of at least emerging as the largest party in 2015. The fact that the Lib Dems held on also made it much less likely that they would try to replace Nick Clegg—a huge relief to Labour, since one of its biggest nightmares was that a social democrat such as Vince Cable or Tim Farron might take over and tempt back some of those voters who had switched to Labour immediately after the 2010 election. The most arresting aspect of the contest, however, had been the strong showing by UKIP and the attempt by the Conservative Party to counter UKIP's appeal by doing its best to match its hard line on Europe and immigration—issues on which Labour was well aware it was also highly vulnerable. Realistically, neither issue could be expected to help it win a general election. But it might be possible at least to neutralize them so as to limit the damage they could potentially do to its chances.

On Europe, however, things were not looking too promising. Labour may have scored a tactical parliamentary victory in the autumn by voting with Conservative rebels on Mark Reckless's amendment calling for a cut in the EU budget. However, the decision to do so had exposed divisions within the leadership between those, like Ed Balls, who argued that Labour had to adapt to the fact that the centre of political gravity was moving in a Eurosceptic direction and those, like Douglas Alexander, who were wary of courting accusations of opportunism and doing anything that might threaten the party's reputation as a committed, albeit pragmatic and realistic, supporter of EU membership. Miliband had used the first speech of his leadership on Europe, given to the CBI in mid-November, essentially to reconcile the two concerns by stressing that, while he would not 'allow our country to sleepwalk towards the exit because it would be a betrayal of our national interest', neither would he shrink from a frank assessment of the EU's problems or from articulating people's concerns about them—a sensible thing to say given that polls suggested almost half of those currently intending to vote Labour would vote to leave the European Union in a referendum.[20] Neither this speech, nor indeed the parliamentary game-playing, prevented David Cameron from returning from Brussels a week later as some sort of winner, having worked with other leaders to prevent agreement on a Budget that included the uplift the Commission was asking for. Moreover, it had long been obvious that, under pressure from both his own backbenchers and the right-wing media, as well as from UKIP, Cameron was going to offer the country an in–out referendum, albeit not before the next election and not before making the effort to renegotiate the UK's relationship with the EU, the better to be able to persuade people it should remain a member. As a result, the Shadow Cabinet had to decide soon after Christmas how Labour would respond to what would undoubtedly be a popular move.

There were very few people at Labour's top table calling on Miliband to trump Cameron by demanding an in–out referendum before he did. There were, however, some who argued that, if a vote was not going to be ruled out, it might be better, rather than risk eventually being dragged into supporting one anyway, to call the Prime Minister's bluff (and presumably to split the Tory Party in two) by demanding it be held before rather than after the election. This would be a high-stakes gamble that, if it went right, would see a vote in favour of staying in and therefore avoid saddling a Labour government with the issue but that, if it went wrong, could result in a no vote and a Labour government having to cope with all that entailed. This was simply too risky for the majority, which decided that Labour's best course of action, at least for the moment, was to present itself as a party of principle, and indeed a party of government. Accordingly, it would declare that, while it had no intention of repealing the Coalition's legislation, which mandated a referendum should any further transfer of sovereignty occur, now was not the time to promise such a vote— not least because the ensuing uncertainty would undermine business confidence when the economy was already in such a fragile state.

The problem with this position, as became immediately apparent in the wake of Cameron formally announcing his policy at the end of January, was that it was (a) complicated (so much so that both Miliband and his Minister for Europe, Emma Reynolds, managed to confuse interviewers on the question of whether or not Labour was ruling out a referendum) and (b) inevitably courted the accusation that the party was running scared of democracy. Immediately after Cameron's Bloomberg speech and a session of PMQs at which he not only made a virtue out of necessity but routed Miliband, a YouGov poll suggested just over half of voters thought Labour was wrong to oppose a referendum.[21] Speaking a couple of weeks later, in the wake of the news that Cameron had apparently managed both to secure an EU Budget without an uplift and to protect the UK's rebate, Ed Balls confessed: 'If we allow ourselves either to be the "status quo party" on Europe, or the "anti-referendum party" on Europe, then we've got a problem. But I think we would be pretty stupid to allow ourselves to get into either of those positions.'[22] Many Labour people were now worried that, despite his best efforts, this was exactly what had happened.

When it came to immigration, there was at least the possibility that the government's failure to deliver on its over-ambitious target for reducing net migration from hundreds to tens of thousands would begin to register with the public. And then there were the periodic slip-ups affecting the UKBA, which allowed Yvette Cooper, Shadow Home Secretary, to question the competence of her opposite number, Theresa May, who eventually grew so frustrated with the Agency's performance that she announced (in March 2013) that it would be reabsorbed into the Home Office. Even so, the leadership knew it could not afford to let up in its efforts to tell voters that Labour had got the message they had sent it in 2010 and that it was adjusting its offer accordingly—even if those efforts were met in some sections of the print media with suspicion bordering on contempt. Just before Christmas, for instance, Miliband had given a speech in which he had promised a Labour government would take several steps to encourage immigrants to speak English in order to promote integration. His team could be reasonably confident that the speech would be covered with customary balance by television news programmes. The papers, however, were a different matter. Although accused by some liberals as getting into dog-whistle politics, Labour's media team were not necessarily disappointed with the *Daily Star*'s headline 'SPEAK ENGLISH OR STAY AWAY; Ed U-Turn on Migrants'. Other titles, however, focused more on the fact that Miliband, by omitting a pre-briefed sentence apologizing for the fact that Labour 'did too little to tackle the realities of segregation in communities that were struggling to cope', was still—in their eyes anyway—refusing to face up to the mess in which the Blair and Brown governments had left the country.[23]

In a Party Political Broadcast at the beginning of March, Miliband was therefore in full confessional mode:

One of the things I've done since I became the leader of the Labour Party is understand where we got things wrong in government and change them. One of the things we didn't get right was immigration and that's why I've got a new approach. Millions of people in this country are concerned about immigration and if people are concerned about it, then the Labour Party I lead is going to be talking about it . . . it's not prejudiced when people worry about immigration. We were wrong in the past when we dismissed people's concerns. Low-skill migration has been too high and we need to bring it down.

These sentiments were duly echoed in the speech by Shadow Home Secretary Yvette Cooper, which the broadcast teed up. While eschewing 'an arms race of rhetoric on immigration', Cooper outlined a series of specific new regulations (up to and including sanctions and fines) on employers of immigrants. She even attempted to outflank the Tories on cracking down on illegal immigrants and on EU migrants' access to financial support from the welfare state, in particular claims for job-seeker's allowance and the (to most people ridiculous) law that allowed workers to claim UK child benefit for their offspring living abroad.[24] The problem, of course, was that a Tory-led government concerned to maintain its edge over Labour and, increasingly, to keep up with UKIP was always going to be able to match any offer on this front—which Cameron duly did two weeks later by announcing new curbs on migrants (including, it seemed, EU migrants) claiming welfare benefits.

Cameron's speech was widely interpreted as his latest attempt to halt UKIP's momentum in the run-up to local elections in May. But—in combining two issues that were toxic for Labour (three if you counted Europe)—the Prime Minister was also putting just as much, if not more, pressure on the opposition. Welfare in particular was rapidly becoming something of a 'wicked issue' for the Labour leadership—a problem with multiple, overlapping aspects that seemed impossible to grip and impervious to any overarching solution. The search for the latter was encouraging research by think-tankers and campaigners such as Graeme Cooke, Declan Gaffney, and Kate Bell, picked up on by politicians such as Liam Byrne, Jon Cruddas, and Frank Field before them, about reviving the contributory principle that had once upon a time characterized social security in Britain and that was still going strong in countries such as Sweden and Denmark that had long been regarded as shining examples by social democrats in the UK.[25] As a way of rewiring a sense of fairness and legitimacy back into a system that had become essentially needs-based and therefore detached from the majority of people paying taxes to finance what they increasingly saw as its naive largesse, the logic was compelling. But the implementation challenges were daunting—and certainly big enough to ensure that it was no quick fix. Meanwhile, back in the real world, the party was having to deal with what was being thrown at it by a government that was continually coming up with initiatives that seemed likely to cause genuine hardship but that were nevertheless widely supported by an electorate whose views on welfare (as confirmed by longitudinal research by the British Attitudes Survey and for the Joseph Rowntree Trust) had become markedly less charitable over the previous decade or two.[26]

Sometimes those initiatives were unplanned. In March, the government was forced to introduce legislation following a legal judgment that called into question its ability to dock payments from jobseekers who were deemed not to be actively seeking work. The Labour leadership was worried about being seen to support millions of pounds worth of compensation that would have gone to jobseekers had the court's decision not been overridden by the Bill. It was also true that the government in which most of them had served had made use of similar sanctions. Notwithstanding some concern about the retrospective nature of the corrective legislation, the leadership decided to instruct Labour MPs to abstain rather than vote against it. This triggered a sizeable backlash against the unfortunate Shadow Minister concerned, Liam Byrne, with many on the left weighing in to condemn the decision as if it were some Blairite counterstrike and completely ignoring the sterling work he was doing at the time to expose and exploit the serious problems that were plaguing Iain Duncan Smith's pet project, Universal Credit. The decision also resulted in a sizeable rebellion by Labour MPs (not all of them on the left, it should be said)—an action that earned them praise from none other than Unite's Len McCluskey.[27]

Perhaps fortunately, the vote on the Bill was soon followed by David Miliband's announcement that he would be standing down from parliament and moving to New York to head up the International Rescue Committee. The move occasioned as much relief as disappointment and was almost certainly born out of his frustration that, in Mary Riddell's words, he could 'barely nip out for teabags without inviting visions of a fratricidal score-settler wielding a banana in one hand and a grenade marked Ed in the other'.[28] Being snapped on someone's mobile phone snoozing on the tube at three in the afternoon with his flies undone and then seeing said picture plastered all over the newspapers and the Web was hardly helpful either. In any event, it meant that forty-four Labour MPs rebelling against the leadership did not attract as much sustained media attention as it might have done. The same could not be said, however, of the next move by the Tories to try to put Labour on the wrong side of public opinion.

When Mick Philpott, who had famously fathered seventeen children while living on benefits, was convicted of murdering six of them in an arson attack, George Osborne happened to be visiting a factory in Derby, where the attack had taken place, on the day in early April when sentence was being passed. Asked by a journalist for his reaction, the Chancellor replied: 'I think there is a question for Government and for society about the welfare state and the taxpayers who pay for the welfare state subsidising lifestyles like that and I think that debate needs to be had.'[29] As he must have guessed would be the case, Labour front- and backbenchers, forgetting the way Tony Blair had used the murder of James Bulger in 1993 to condemn the Tories, could hardly contain their fury at his implication. Sadly their words served, once again, only to put Labour on the wrong side of the dividing line that Osborne (when he was not devising schemes like 'Help to Buy' to stimulate the economy through the housing market) spent so much of his time and energy constructing. As with other Tory welfare policies—the so-called bedroom tax, which reduced the benefit going to those in social housing deemed to have more space than they needed or the sometimes questionable reclassification of those previously declared unfit for work because of disability or sickness—the fact that Labour politicians' reactions were wholly understandable and their objections arguably valid made little or no difference. The scapegoating, the stereotyping, and the largely baseless beliefs that they were determined not to connive in promoting were already too powerful, as a rash of polling published in the wake of the Philpott furore attested.[30] Many of the very voters Labour needed to convince, struggling as they were on salaries that sometimes left them worse off than those who were out of work, saw only that the party was, yet again, sticking up for scroungers instead of the people paying out for them to live the proverbial life of Reilly. As professional 'plain-speaking' MPs such as

Frank Field, Simon Danczuk, and Tom Watson all made clear in media appearances over that weekend, Labour would be in trouble unless something changed.

It was at this moment that Tony Blair—to Miliband's obvious irritation—penned an article in the centenary edition of the *New Statesman*, which he used to issue a warning to his old friends in the Labour Party:

> The ease with which it can settle back into its old territory of defending the status quo, allying itself, even anchoring itself, to the interests that will passionately and often justly oppose what the government is doing, is so apparently rewarding, that the exercise of political will lies not in going there, but in resisting the temptation to go there.[31]

Blair was swiftly followed by three Shadow Ministers anonymously assuring journalists that they and many of their colleagues shared 'Tony's' concerns, and by David Blunkett, who, being at the end of his political career, was prepared to go on the record. 'The Blair Bitch Project: Ex-PM and Heavyweight Pals Tear into Red Ed', screamed a delighted *Sun*.[32]

At least some of the pleasure provoked in Fleet Street by Miliband's difficulties could be put down to his having cornered Cameron three weeks previously into agreeing that the Royal Charter proposed by the Prime Minister to oversee press regulation be underpinned by law. But those difficulties were not solely the product of journalists' fevered imaginations. All the polls were now pointing to Labour having lost significant support during the year to date. They also suggested that its leader's personal ratings were declining even further and faster, even if he, like his party, continued to do significantly better among women voters (who, as Yvette Cooper was rightly always ready to point out, had borne the vast brunt of austerity).[33] The slide in Miliband's ratings occurred despite the generally positive reviews he received for his performance during what for the party was an inevitably tricky few days following the death of Margaret Thatcher—a Conservative icon whom many Labour people loved to hate but who was nevertheless something of a role model for Miliband. After all, much like Clement Attlee, she had won by promising radical changes to a failed consensus presided over by a Prime Minister far more popular than she was.[34]

In his campaign for the upcoming local elections, however, Miliband was taking a leaf out of the playbook of Thatcher's successor,

John Major. Standing on a wooden pallet, microphone in hand, doing market square meetings in many of the towns Labour needed to win in 2015, Miliband tried to show that he was listening, that he was not afraid to make his case, and that not all politicians were the same. Given the terrible notices he received for his performance in a BBC radio interview just a few days before voting took place—a 'car crash', a 'Milishambles'—this so-called politics-in-the-raw strategy may not have been such a bad move.[35] Whether, however, it would pay dividends on 2 May, when voters in 35 local authorities would be going to the polls to elect over 2,300 councillors, remained to be seen.

# 7

# Warming up: Spring–Autumn
## 2013

The seats up for grabs at the local elections in 2013 had last been contested in the spring of 2009—pretty much the low point of Gordon Brown's government. Labour had taken just 23 per cent of the vote compared to the Tories' 38 per cent and the Lib Dems 28 per cent, and it had lost control of numerous county councils. Now, four years later, if the opinion polls were anything like correct, the party should have picked up an additional 350 seats. In the event, it gained just 284 and won control of only 2 of the 4 county councils it was aiming to retake—its performance in Lancashire, which had been something of a test-bed for its 'community-organizing' strategy, being a particular disappointment. Just as worrying was the uncomfortably large discrepancy between what it was scoring in the opinion polls—still at that point in the high thirties—and its projected share of the national vote, which at 29 per cent suggested it had made no progress since the 2010 general election. True, the Conservatives had also underperformed on their poll rating, achieving just 25 per cent—something that many analysts put down to its losing votes to UKIP, which managed a stunning 23 per cent, knocking the Lib Dems into fourth place on 14 per cent. Labour could also take some comfort from the fact that it all but matched its 2010 share of the vote in the by-election in South Shields triggered by David Miliband's leaving the Commons for his new job in New York. Labour could also claim to have done sufficiently well in places that were on its list of target seats, having won seventeen of them. On the other hand, this meant that there was still some way to go in twenty-nine others. Moreover, although Nigel Farage and his hail-fellow-well-met confection of nostalgia, xenophobia, and Euroscepticism were routinely presented in the media as a threat to the Conservatives, analysis by academics such as Rob Ford and Matthew Goodwin suggested that Labour needed to worry about UKIP's ability to pick up older, poorly educated white working-class voters that once upon a time might have made up part of the centre-left's 'core vote'.[1]

All in all, for a party that claimed to be able to represent the whole nation and to be on course to win in 2015, it was not good enough, and everybody knew it. The revelation that Ed Miliband had rushed to the aid of a woman in London who had fallen off her bike was not going to change that underlying reality—even if she did gush that 'he was actually attractive and not geeky at all'.[2] Had everything been running smoothly for David Cameron, Miliband might have been in more trouble. Fortunately for him, it was not. The Queen's Speech, which followed a few days after the local elections, had, not unusually, something for everyone: reforms to social care and pensions, reorganization and regulation of the banking system, potential privatization of the probation service, and a renewed commitment to building HS2, a high-speed rail link from London to Birmingham. But it also looked decidedly like an attempt to shore up the Conservatives' right flank against UKIP. Although gay marriage was clearly too much of a done deal now for a retreat, 'politically correct' measures such as a minimum unit price for alcohol or plain packaging for cigarettes were left out—at the urging, claimed Labour (to no very great effect, judging by opinion polls), of Lynton Crosby. More powers were to be taken to tackle crime and anti-social behaviour. And a new immigration Bill was announced, aimed at making life much more difficult for foreigners living in the UK illegally or at the taxpayer's expense. The Prime Minister also announced draft legislation on an EU referendum. If he thought this would calm his backbenchers, however, he was wrong: fully half of them backed an amendment to their own government's Queen Speech expressing regret that it did not include a Bill paving the way for a referendum.

This, and the subsequent announcement that Conservative MPs on both front and backbenches would support a Private Member's Bill that did exactly that, offered Labour an opportunity to reconsider its position on the issue. A bolder leader might have risked declaring that the uncertainty could not be allowed to go on and that he was therefore demanding that a referendum be held sooner rather than later, and certainly before the end of the parliament. Such a move might well have split the Tories (and, indeed the Coalition) so badly that any charges against Labour of opportunism would have been swiftly drowned out by all the shouting. And, if the 'in' campaign—the rapid formation of which would have forced business groups to work alongside Labour instead of sniping away at it—had been successful, then it would have solved what was otherwise promising to be a problem that might plague a putative Miliband government. The downside, however, was as obvious as it was massive. If the 'out' campaign triumphed, then the UK would be set on a course that all but a tiny minority of Labour MPs (the twelve who voted with Tory rebels on the Queen's Speech amendment) believed was at best unnecessary and at worst unbelievably stupid: the *Financial Times*'s Janan Ganesh may well have been right to say that, 'instead of flowing from the heart or the head, Labour's pro-Europeanism is a kind of muscle memory, ingrained in the years when admiring the EU was what members of the respectable left were supposed to do'.[3] But it was still powerful nonetheless. And even had it not been, few wanted accidentally to engineer a situation in which Miliband, presuming he made it into Downing Street in 2015, would have to devote most of his time in office making British withdrawal a reality. So, when the Bill, named for the sponsoring MP, James Wharton, came before the House for the first time in early July, the leadership had little trouble persuading most of its MPs to abstain. That said, neither the Shadow Cabinet nor Miliband himself was quite ready yet to rule out a referendum. Back in the mid-1970s Labour's Jim Callaghan had referred to the device as 'a rubber life-raft'. Maybe it still was, even if virtually everybody sitting at the current captain's table hoped they would never have to use it.

Europe, however, came a long way down Labour's list of key priorities in the early summer of 2013. What mattered most was trying to turn around two perceptions that were clearly inextricably linked and that were still doing the party considerable damage—namely, that it was a soft touch on welfare and that it could not be trusted to look after the nation's finances. The fact that the Chancellor was due to lay out the government's medium- to long-term spending plans at the end of June, however, presented the leadership with something of an opportunity—at least when it came to short-circuiting internal opposition to any radical announcements they might want to make. It was widely predicted that Osborne, knowing full well that most voters thought cuts were necessary but that an increasing proportion of them now believed those cuts were 'about right' or 'too shallow', would be using his statement to paint Labour even further into a corner on tax and spend, as well as on benefits. Miliband could therefore argue that he needed to do something that would effectively spike the Chancellor's guns. If he were to do that, then whatever it was would need to be big—a policy or bunch of policies that distinguished Labour from the Coalition but at the same time reassured voters that its priorities would be achieved by spending differently rather than spending more. This desire for credibility as well as difference, as Miliband was fond of putting it, would almost certainly risk offending the unions. They remained committed to an anti-austerity line, as well as to universal rather than means-tested benefits—a principle that Ed Miliband had previously signed up to but that he increasingly felt was a luxury Labour could not afford, either in opposition or in government. Such a move would also require Ed Balls to move a little further towards declaring Labour's hand sooner rather than later, the better to allow it to do what it had long intended to do when eventually the economy began to grow again. This was to shift the focus away from 'tax 'n' spend' and towards issues (such as the cost of living, the question of whether everybody or just a few would benefit from economic recovery, the NHS, house-building, and perhaps childcare and social care) that would hopefully play to Labour's strengths.

In the event, Balls agreed more readily than many imagined, primarily because he believed 'iron discipline' could still be combined with a growth strategy if infrastructure spending could be clearly distinguished from day-to-day outlays. The result was a two-stage announcement at the beginning of June. The first stage saw Balls declare that Labour wanted to end the payment of winter fuel allowance to pensioners earning over £42,000. The payment was one of a number of universal benefits that Cameron, under pressure from Brown, during the 2010 election campaign had agreed to protect. Its removal would affect well over half a million retired people (most of whom probably voted Conservative anyway) but would result in a relatively small saving of £100 million per annum. What mattered most, however, was not the substance but the symbolism: Labour was proposing to make savings and to make them from welfare; it was also advocating means-testing a benefit that had hitherto been made available irrespective of the beneficiary's income; and the party was signalling that it did not necessarily regard the Coalition's ring-fencing of certain budgets as sacrosanct—a sensible move, given the fact that over half of the total social security budget went to retirees.

It was easy, of course, to overdo how much of a departure this move on the winter fuel allowance was. After all, Labour's commitment to universalism had never been as total as many imagined, and this was hardly a tough choice that impacted on a vulnerable group or the party's core support.[4] Nevertheless, it was enough to grab a few headlines, not least because it dovetailed with what the *Sun* was calling its 'Ditch Handouts to the Rich Campaign.' That said, the paper was not hugely impressed: 'At long last,' it wrote, 'Ed Balls has dipped his little toe into the waters of reality. Sadly that's as far as he's got.'[5] Others observed wryly that, even in an accompanying speech that was supposed to hammer home Labour's commitment to fiscal discipline, the Shadow Chancellor could not resist the chance to argue, once again, that he had called it right on the economy. The Q&A, they noted, was even worse—at least for those hoping Balls might try, if not for an apology, then at least for a touch of humility, given that opinion polls still showed far more voters blamed Labour than the Coalition for the country's economic difficulties: 'Do I think the last Labour government was profligate, spent too much, had too much national debt?', he asked rhetorically. 'No I don't think there's any evidence for that.'[6] Yet the speech was still significant. Balls lashed Labour to a set of fiscal rules that, although they allowed for higher capital spending on projects such as housing and care (which meant it could differentiate itself from the government), would see the deficit eliminated before the end of the next parliament. In the more immediate future he committed the party, outside any growth-promoting capital spending it might undertake, to stick to the Tories' spending plans in the first year of government.

In fact, Balls was also the warm-up act for what was intended as an even more striking intervention by Miliband. In a wide ranging speech, which bore the imprint of both Liam Byrne and Jon Cruddas, the Labour leader confessed that the party would not be able to reverse the Coalition's withdrawal of child benefit from higher-rate taxpayers, and admitted that the claimant count for incapacity benefit had risen too fast under the previous government. He also floated the possibility of a regional benefits cap and of reinforcing the contributory aspect of social security—for example, in lengthening the period people needed to be in work in order to qualify for non-means-tested benefits, which might then be made more generous. Most importantly, however, he committed Labour to a multi-annual cap on welfare spending, albeit one that was balanced by the suggestion that, in government, the party would attempt to shift resources currently devoted to funding benefits to funding programmes that would reduce demand for them: building social housing, for instance, might go some way to reducing the housing benefit bill, although only in the long term.[7]

Again, in terms of garnering headlines, the intervention was a success, although that hardly guaranteed cut-through to the electorate. Indeed, a poll commissioned later in the summer for the website Labour Uncut showed that 54 per cent of voters blamed Labour for the welfare bill being so high, as opposed to only 5 per cent who blamed the Coalition. And, when asked who would do more to prevent welfare spending rising out of control, just 14 per cent named Miliband while 45 per cent said Cameron.[8] It was not just that it was always going to be hard for an announcement on welfare to compete with, say, the marital difficulties of Charles Saatchi and Nigella Lawson, which were soon mesmerizing the public. It was also that the messages were mixed. Labour appeared to be both for and against more borrowing, depending on whether it was for capital or day-to-day-spending (not a distinction that most people understood anyway). It also seemed to be in favour of cutting some benefits but increasing others. More profoundly, Miliband seemed to want to pose simultaneously as the enemy of a failed consensus and as someone who could be trusted to stick strictly to the limits imposed by those who were too blind to see that its time was up.

Inevitably, too, there were doubts expressed—inside as well as outside the party—as to whether all this was not too little, too late. Surely this was the kind of counter-intuitive move that should have been undertaken (following Blair's and Cameron's example) soon after Miliband won the leadership, not nearly three years later, after the opportunity for a serious audit of the New Labour years had passed and public perceptions had hardened. Scepticism only increased after it became clear that Labour, facing what were surely inevitable accusations from the Conservative Party that it was planning 'a raid' on them, was not sure whether pensions would be included in the overall cap or not—a lack of 'bomb-proofing' that suggested the whole thing had been hastily put together rather than, as the pre-speech briefing implied, being the work of many hands over many weeks. Those listening very carefully to Miliband's address to Labour's NPF a couple of weeks later would also have noted that, in insisting that Labour could change things even as it brought the deficit down, Miliband did not rule out a role for 'extra revenue' in helping to do it. Whether this was electorally wise, it was at least realistic—rather more so, perhaps, than George Osborne's continued assertion that, whatever independent analysts like the Institute for Fiscal Studies argued, fiscal consolidation could be achieved by cuts alone.

When Osborne finally delivered his statement on projected spending on 26 June, it soon became clear that he was not going to let Labour off the hook by welcoming its belated conversion to the cause but was instead going to set it yet more tests. Not only did he propose a four-year cap on welfare spending, he also made clear that it excluded pensions, meaning that cuts in other areas of social security would have to be big—probably too big for Labour to match item by item. Moreover, the fact that he had at the very least matched Labour's offer meant that debate during the election could well return to the question of the £26,000 cap imposed on benefits going to individual households. Polling and focus groups suggested this was still very much a winner with the public; but Labour, despite Liam Byrne beginning to try to attack it from the right (by claiming there were still families getting more than £26,000) rather than from the left, refused to commit to it officially. And that was not all: well over a 100,000 additional jobs would end up going in the public sector, while those left were going to lose automatic annual increments; meanwhile, anyone losing his or her job was going to have to wait seven days before being able to make a claim for benefits—a move that would save money but that risked denying people in need help they could previously have counted on straight away.

As usual, the fact that Labour declined to accept all this meant that the savings gained were added by CCHQ to its running total of extra spending and borrowing that Labour was supposedly committed to—a figure of nearly £50 billion, which, it announced later on in the summer, meant a bill of £2,960 for 'every hardworking family' in Britain. The only upside was that, by attacking public-sector jobs and conditions, as well as traditional rights to social security, Osborne ensured that Labour's advocacy of more means-testing and an overall cap on social security spending—a position that would previously have attracted the opprobrium of many activists—now looked mild in comparison. This effectively short-circuited some of the incipient internal opposition to the announcements made a couple of weeks previously by Miliband and Balls, whether that opposition came from the grass-roots left or from trade-union leaders. It was now clearer than ever to both groups that the Tories were the real enemy and that they needed to do everything they possibly could to help Labour stop them in their tracks in 2015. This was extremely fortunate, since the relationship between the two wings of the labour movement—political and industrial—was about to be tested almost to breaking point.

As so often in the build-up to any political crisis, this one first presented as a little local difficulty. Labour's candidates for the European Parliament election were to be shortlisted by regional selection panels composed partly of party members and partly of trade-union representatives. Their shortlists were then voted on by party members, with the candidates who attracted the most votes awarded a higher position on the regional lists, which would eventually be presented to voters in May 2014. In April 2013 reports began to emerge of a supposed 'stitch-up' by the panel responsible for shortlisting in London. A candidate who had done well in 2009 had not made the cut, whereas candidates backed by the Unite and GMB unions, whose officials and their left-wing allies apparently dominated the selection panel, had. It did not take journalists long to find other people in other parts of the country with similar complaints—or to begin to move the story on to what some on the right of the party, including Peter Mandelson, were alleging was also happening in selections for Westminster seats.[9] A simple count, assisted by Conservative Party research, revealed that over a third of candidates so far selected had won with direct support from the trade unions. Really determined diggers could also point to a couple of changes made to the party's rule book in the wake of *Refounding Labour* that arguably shifted the balance in favour of union-backed candidates. The first extended the time (and therefore presumably the money) that candidates had to spend on campaigning for the votes of local party members. The second was that anyone hoping to stand as a Labour candidate without being a member of a trade union would have to obtain the permission of the full NEC, and not one of its subcommittees.

The problem for Ed Miliband was that all this was easily slotted into an existing narrative—one where, in return for help in getting him elected and continuing to fund the party so generously, he was doing trade-union leaders a few favours, even though they were clearly hoping (as leaked documents like Unite's Political Strategy had already made clear) to change the composition of the parliamentary party as part of a wider plan to tilt the party to the left. And Miliband's difficulties were compounded by the fact that some of those trade-union leaders seemed increasingly willing to throw their weight around in public as well as in private. Just as concerns about candidate selection were beginning to bubble up, Unite's Len McCluskey told the *New Statesman*'s George Eaton in an interview that, if Ed Miliband were 'brave enough to go for something radical, he'll be the next prime minister. If he gets seduced by the Jim Murphys and the Douglas Alexanders, then the truth is that he'll be defeated and he'll be cast into the dustbin of history.' And he was no more subtle about Labour's Work and Pensions spokesman: 'Byrne certainly doesn't reflect the views of my members and of our union's policy. I think some of the terminology that he uses is regrettable and I think it will damage Labour. Ed's got to figure out what his team will be.' Whatever his personal views on the merits of some of his Shadow Cabinet, Miliband could hardly let this pass and duly authorized an unusually sharp rejoinder: Len McCluskey's 'attempt to divide the Labour Party', an unnamed spokesman for Miliband told journalists, was 'reprehensible'—'the kind of politics that lost Labour many elections in the 1980s. It won't work. It is wrong. It is disloyal to the party he claims to represent.'[10]

Given all this, when the media broke the story of an apparent attempt by Unite to 'stitch up' the selection of Labour's parliamentary candidate in Falkirk West, Miliband was in no mood—and probably in no position—to let it lie. Under a scheme set up under Tony Blair, trade unionists who wanted to join the Labour Party as individual members, and who would therefore become entitled to vote in selection contests, could have their subscriptions paid in the first instance by their union. The allegation was that Unite, in an attempt to secure additional supporters for its favoured candidate, Karie Murphy (a close friend of McCluskey's who also happened to work for Labour's campaign chief, MP Tom Watson), had used the scheme to sign up over 100 new members, some of them without their knowledge. Labour Party officials at Party Headquarters in Brewer's Green had been worried about the influx of multiple members being paid for by the Union, only to be told—apparently by a 'senior figure'—that the whole thing was above board and they should go ahead and not only approve the memberships but backdate them so that those who had joined would be eligible to vote in the selection contest. When an internal investigation was ordered, Unite was accused of putting pressure on people who had earlier reported having been signed up without consent to retract their statements. Its response was to deny any wrongdoing at any stage and also to point out that one of Murphy's original rivals for the seat, Gregor Poynton (who had worked in field ops for Labour before becoming UK Political Director of Blue State Digital and who was married to a Labour MP), had also been signing up new members. To those defending the union, the whole thing was a witch-hunt whipped up by Blairites, who, through organizations like Progress, had apparently been using any means necessary to parachute favoured sons and daughters into safe seats for years.[11] For their part, those being accused of sour grapes by the left pointed to documents now in the public domain that showed unions such as Unite and the GMB boasting of their various successes in getting 'their' people selected as candidates in winnable seats all around the country. There was dark talk of Blue State Digital having being told by an unnamed senior figure that it stood to lose business from the party if Poynton refused to pull out of the selection—a contest that was eventually decided anyway using an all-woman shortlist.[12] There were even rumours that, before the government's proposed boundary changes had been rejected by the Lib Dems, Unite had been working to ensure that Douglas Alexander would not be selected as the MP for a merged seat in Paisley.

In the last week of June, and in response to the report of its hurried internal enquiry—one that it had decided not to release to the media—the party announced that Falkirk West was going to be put in 'special measures'. This saw it join thirteen other CLPs in a scheme that allowed close supervision from London, up to and including (as in this case) the imposition of a shortlist for a selection in which only those people who were members prior to the various sign-up campaigns could participate. Karie Murphy, who had already stepped aside as a candidate, was to be suspended, along with the Chair of the CLP, a full-time Unite official called Stevie Deans. The union, which condemned the whole thing as 'Kafkaesque', was furious, not least because it had not been given sight of the report and would not, even now, be provided with copies. The Conservatives, on the other hand, had a field day. At the first session of PMQs in July, David Cameron managed to squeeze Unite and Len McCluskey into almost all his replies. More woundingly still, because it tapped into the key concerns about Miliband raised in focus groups and opinion polls, he accused the Leader of the Opposition of being 'too weak to stand up to the Unite union and too weak to run Labour and certainly too weak to run the country'.

It was not pretty but it was effective. Too many more sessions like that one, and concern about Miliband's performance from those on the benches behind him would have led to the renewal of serious questions about his leadership. Something had to give.

The first thing was Tom Watson, who resigned the next day, although not before penning an unhelpful resignation letter that seemed to imply that the Labour leader had practically begged him to stay—which may well have been rather nearer the truth than the spin later put out that he had somehow been told to step down. This, however, was containable, since Watson had his critics as well as his admirers, and even the latter, who valued him as a big character and a good organizer whom trade-union leaders took seriously, acknowledged he was the kind of politician (as one of them put it) who 'gets into a lot of scrapes'.

The second thing to give was much bigger. From the moment he won the leadership, Miliband had been adamant that he would not set out to pick a fight with his party in order to demonstrate to journalists and voters that he was a strong leader—one of the reasons, perhaps, that he had supposedly allowed Tom Watson to run things basically the way he had wanted. Now, however, the Labour leader had little choice but to accept a challenge that, if handled skilfully enough, would give him a chance to show not just that he was willing to stand up to some vested interests of his own but that he could take tough decisions too. Miliband's move against the Murdoch press back in summer 2011 had been painted as a period of inattention, even inaction, suddenly giving way, under pressure, to a very swift but very risky decision. On the union link, the pressure was even greater and the decision even swifter and even riskier.

In a series of briefings and then in media interviews, Miliband declared not only that he would be scrapping the scheme that Unite had 'frankly abused' in order to sign up new members, but that he was 'incredibly angry' about the whole thing and was now determined to review Labour's relationship with the trade unions. Since 'the integrity of my party' was at stake, he said, 'let nobody be in any doubt. There is only going to be one outcome to this.'[13] Exactly what he wanted to do, however, was not immediately clear. McCluskey got his retaliation in first, with an article in Britain's only popular left-wing daily, the *Mirror*, in which he dismissed the party's investigation into events at Falkirk as 'a shoddy fraud' and emphasized that all the union was trying to do was to 'give our democracy back to ordinary working people' so as to prevent it becoming 'the preserve of an out-of-touch elite— Oxbridge-educated special advisers who glide from university to think tank to the green benches without ever sniffing the air of the real world'. Oh, and it was also 'trying to reclaim Labour from the people that bought in to the free-market myth wholesale, who bet the country's future on the City of London—and who sometimes fiddled their expenses while they were at it'. Miliband, on the other hand, could do little more than pen what amounted to a holding article for the upmarket *Observer* in which he argued that the party should 'mend the relationship, not end it'—whatever that meant.[14]

The right-wing media were naturally enjoying the whole thing immensely. Not only had Andy Murray won Wimbledon, but the economy finally seemed to be coming right and Theresa May had at last managed to deport the radical cleric Abu Qatada. CCHQ researchers were also supplying hostile journalists with example after example of Labour candidates and sitting MPs who were sponsored by unions. They also made the most of the fact that McCluskey had apparently taken to calling some of them 'Unite MPs'.[15] They were also routinely citing figures that purported to show that the party was almost entirely dependent on the unions. This perception was wide-spread even if was not entirely borne out in reality: of the £16.84 million that flowed into Labour's coffers in the first six months of 2013, for instance, fees and donations from its fifteen affiliated unions accounted for £4.16 million—not a sum that Labour could afford to do without, obviously, but nonetheless outweighed by money coming in from membership fees and small donations (£4.85 million), fun-draising and commercial activities (£4.20 million), and parliamentary/ government grants (£3.62 million).[16] Still, with Nick Clegg announcing on 4 July that the talks on party funding that had been going on since 2012 had now finally collapsed, it was difficult to imagine that

Labour would sacrifice such a significant source of funding completely, not least because the small post-election boost in its membership seemed not to have lasted: indeed, figures released by the Electoral Commission at the end of July suggested, if anything, that it had declined slightly from nearly 194,000 in 2010 to just over 187,000 at the end of 2013.[17]

Labour's accounts showed that, although it had made a surplus of almost £3 million the previous year, it still had debts of £7.3 million, many of them dating back to the huge amounts spent re-electing Tony Blair in 2005 and being repaid at a much higher rate of interest than currently prevailed. Now that the Co-operative Bank was in dire financial straits, Labour could no longer rely on any favours there, while its only other friend in the financial sector, Unity Trust, was a bank associated with the trade unions themselves. Moreover, Labour people were beginning to realize that unions whose members decided, probably by overwhelming majorities, to pass up the choice of belonging to the party were unlikely to be able subsequently to use their political fund contributions to write a big fat cheque to that party instead. Given all this, would Miliband really be willing, as the historian Peter Clarke put it in the *Financial Times*, to embark on a course of action that could leave him with 'clean but empty hands'?[18] It was hardly surprising, then, that the Labour leader's big speech on the union link, due to take place a few days later, was looked forward to with as much scepticism as anticipation.

Miliband's proposals were simple, but possibly deceptively so. He wanted to select Labour's next candidate for Mayor of London via a primary rather than via the NEC—a big boost for democracy, although one that would still leave Labour behind the Tories, whose Mayoral primary was open to all voters in London, not just those signed up as registered 'supporters' of the party. Miliband also called for a clampdown on MPs having second jobs, albeit one achieved indirectly (and not necessarily that easily) by proposing limits on their outside earnings (which were known to be much higher among Conservative than other MPs). His main proposal, however, was that trade unionists who wanted to support Labour should individually opt in to being full members of the party rather than, as was currently the case, being collectively affiliated by their union as a result of their not actively opting out of paying into its political fund. However, this would need to be implemented voluntarily by the unions rather than regulated by statute. Nor was there any timeframe specified. Unions would also, it seemed, be able to carry on donating to Labour from their political funds, making the party possibly more rather than less dependent than it currently was on the discretion of national executives and general secretaries. Moreover, it was unclear whether the end of traditional affiliation signalled the end of the electoral college (with its affiliated section dominated by trade unionists)—or indeed of the bloc votes wielded at conference or the reserved seats on various panels and committees all the way up to the NEC. Those hoping for swift and definitive answers to such questions, however, were likely to be disappointed. Miliband also announced that he had appointed Ray Collins to prepare a report. A former General Secretary of the Labour Party and also a key figure in the creation of Unite, Collins (who was doing Miliband a massive favour given that he knew he was not even his first choice for the job) was likely to negotiate a deal that included something for everyone, not draw up some kind of *decree nisi*.

According to Miliband, he had 'seized the moment in making the difference and making a big change. I think that's the right thing to do.' And he was not the only one who was impressed. His first pick as Shadow Chancellor, Alan Johnson, who had been a trade-union leader himself and whose working-class credentials were second to none, quickly came out in support, which was helpful. But the real coup, of course, was Tony Blair himself, who declared it was 'a defining moment. It is bold and it is strong, it's real leadership,' he said, even adding: 'Frankly, I should probably have done it as leader.'[19] Given this endorsement from the man so many on the left loved to hate, there may have been a touch of disappointment among the leader's immediate circle that Len McCluskey refused to step straight into the role of pantomime villain. Although as incensed as any other trade-union leader that those writing the speech had made no attempt whatsoever to square (or even share) what was being proposed with him or anyone else, he welcomed the speech, presumably because he could see some advantages in reducing what amounted to the fixed element of the union's contribution to the party in favour of upping the variable amount that he controlled. Other general secretaries, however, quickly obliged, not least the GMB's Paul Kenny, who not only made it clear that the unions were not going anywhere but also declared that he found it hard to imagine many of his 650,000 members opting in to join Labour—something that, he warned, would have major financial consequences for the party.

Other leaders of smaller unions made a similar point, and McCluskey apparently informed his executive that he would expect only 75,000 Unite members to join Labour, as opposed to the one million people the union currently affiliated to the party. McCluskey then hardened his line even further in the wake of Miliband announcing a few days later that any settlement would be put to a vote of a special conference in the spring—the same device that Blair had used to ratify the changes he famously made to Clause IV. In a speech to a Unite audience, its leader agreed to the opt-in. However, with one eye on ongoing talks between his union and the non-affiliated PCS run by the militantly left-wing Mark Serwotka, he also noted that, in return for its continued financial support, Unite wanted a Labour Party that was more than 'a pinkish shadow of the present Coalition'. The union was fed up, he insisted, with being 'taken for granted by people who welcome our money, but not our policy input, who want to use our resources at election time but do not want our members as candidates'. It was time for 'Oxbridge Blairites' to realize that, unless Labour offered 'a real and vivid choice' between itself and the Tories, then it was unlikely to tempt many trade unionists to join its ranks, let alone vote for it—words that were only partially contradicted by a survey of Unite members carried out by the mischievous Michael Ashcroft. Among other things, the poll revealed that over 60 per cent of them felt that neither their union nor 'their' party really represented them, that over 85 per cent of them supported George Osborne's benefits cap of £26,000 per household, and that only 16 per cent of them could put both a name and a face to a photo of McCluskey himself. But it also suggested that three-quarters of Unite members would decline to opt into Labour Party membership, and that quite a lot of the rest were unsure that they would either.[20]

The GMB's Paul Kenny did not need a poll, it seemed, to tell him what his members wanted. Instead, at the beginning of September, his union announced that it intended to cut its affiliation fees to Labour from £1.2 million annually to just £150,000—an amount calculated by multiplying the £3.00 membership levy by the approximately 50,000 GMB members who voted in the 2010 Labour leadership contest. There was a practical logic behind the decision: the membership was due to vote in 2014 on whether it wanted to continue its union's political fund; the executive was concerned that, now its members were perhaps more aware than they had been about how much of it went to a party not all of them supported, let alone wanted to join, they might vote to get rid of the fund altogether, making it impossible for the union to do any campaigning on its members' behalf. But the decision was obviously political too—a warning shot on behalf of the whole union movement of the potentially dire consequences of Miliband's plan. As such, it certainly succeeded in spooking some people. The normally supportive *Mirror*, for example, calculated that, if all fifteen affiliated unions did the same, it would represent a 'financial Ed ache' for Labour totalling £9 million pounds annually, while the 'multi-million pound bungs paid out by tycoons and City Fat Cats' to the Tories would simply continue. As a result, it pleaded that 'Unions thinking of following the GMB, which has slashed funding to Labour, should hold fire to give Mr Miliband an opportunity to explain his move. If necessary, the Labour leader should concede that he acted hastily.'[21]

Given the high stakes, there was no way that Miliband or those around him were going to do the latter— at least not in too obvious a manner. There were also, it had to be said, limits to how far the unions wanted to push things, not least because they wanted to present a united front against the government's plans to use a Bill ostensibly concerned with cleaning up lobbying to limit 'political' campaigning in election years by 'third-party' organizations. Fortunately for both sides, the fact that Ray Collins had been given a few months to come up with his recommendations meant that there was time for tempers to cool and, if necessary, for discretion to become the better part of valour.

In fact, that process began almost immediately. The party had previously gone so far as to submit its report to the police in order to check that what had happened in Falkirk did not involve criminal activity. But in the run-up to the conference season, and on a busy news day, it conceded that it could not prove that its rules had actually been broken rather than just bent. It therefore lifted the suspensions imposed on the individuals involved in the case—a move that removed the threat that Unite might actually boycott Labour's annual meeting in Brighton. And, when Miliband addressed the TUC in Bournemouth (where Unison just happened to announce that it, too, would be cutting its annual affiliation fee to Labour), he made a non-confrontational speech focused mainly on the Conservatives as a common enemy and a promise to take action on zero-hours contracts, which figures recently released suggested affected 250,000 workers. His speech was therefore received politely, albeit with only muted applause, in the aftermath of which his spokesman made clear that Collins would be looking only at how to implement the move towards opting-in: changes to the bloc vote, leadership election rules, and the composition of the NEC were apparently not on the agenda, not-withstanding a YouGov poll of both the general public and trade unionists that showed majority support for such measures.[22] It was hardly a surprise, then, when, at the next session of PMQs, Cameron proved unable to help himself. The Leader of the Opposition, he cried, had 'folded faster than a Bournemouth deckchair!' Miliband had 'completely bottled' what had clearly been missold as a big fight: 'He told us it was going to be *Raging Bull*—but he gave us *Chicken Run!*'

Perhaps because of this, or perhaps because most people were rather more interested in, say, the birth of the royal baby than they were in Labour's link with the unions, Ed Miliband's poll ratings showed no discernible rise as a result of his decision to reform it. On the other hand, that decision could perhaps have helped mitigate the impact of other stories that might have been expected to damage the party. The most obvious of these concerned yet more revelations about poor standards of care in the health service. Like the Prime Minister, Conservative Health Secretary Jeremy Hunt had surprised everyone by initially refusing to make political capital out of February's Francis Report into the appalling events at Mid-Staffs hospital, possibly pre-ferring papers like the *Sun* ('Labour's NHS created a hospital where starved patients drank from flower vases and wallowed in filth while smug managers and bullying nurses callously abandoned them to die alone and in agony') to lead the attack.[23] Within a month, however, he was claiming that 'a lack of interest in patients by ministers had appalling consequences' and demanding an apology and 'a proper account' from Shadow Secretary of State for Health Andy Burnham (who had, of course, been the actual Secretary of State between 2009 and 2010), in the absence of which the public could only 'conclude that similar events could easily happen again if Labour regained power'. Now, under pressure because of mounting evidence of rising waiting times in A&E departments all around the country, he was back in the game, blaming the whole thing not on a shortage of funding but on Labour having allowed GPs to opt out of providing out-of-hours services too easily and on its 'target-at-any-cost culture', which (just in case anyone had forgotten) had 'led to the disaster of Mid-Staffordshire'.[24]

Given this, and given that the atmosphere was already highly charged after an independent inquiry revealed in June that an investigation into shocking shortcomings at Morecambe Bay Trust had been suppressed by the Care Quality Commission, Labour was expecting the Tories to go on the offensive when a review by the Medical Director of NHS England, Sir Bruce Keogh, of fourteen hospitals with high mortality rates was published in the middle of July. Those expectations were fully justified. 'IF FOUNDING THE NHS IS CONSIDERED LABOUR'S PROUDEST ACHIEVEMENT, TODAY IS THEIR DARKEST MOMENT...' was the Daily Mail's front-page screamer, taken straight from Hunt's speech to the Commons. This was backed up by an open letter from Tory MPs with constituents who were affected claiming that 'the last Labour government oversaw thousands of unnecessary deaths', that it 'failed to expose or confront these care scandals', and that 'it would be an outrage if Andy Burnham were ever to return to the role of secretary of state for health'.[25] Keogh was reportedly so furious at what he called the 'political operation' that had been mounted around his report so as to discredit Burnham that he had personally apologized to him.[26] This did not, however, deter the Conservatives. In early October, emails obtained under the Freedom of Information Act were interpreted to suggest that there had been an attempt on the part of the previous government to deter the CQC from informing the public of the dire state of affairs at Basildon University Hospital. After leaving backbench MPs to make the running on the story for a few days, Hunt declared that there was 'now a strong body of evidence that Labour Ministers leant on the hospital watchdog to cover up poor care, leaving hundreds of patients to suffer under a system that put political priorities first'. But it was his reference on Twitter to '@andyburnhammp's attempts to cover-up failing hospitals' that led Burnham's patience to snap, provoking him into instructing Labour's lawyers, Steel & Shamash, to demand Hunt provide evidence or else retract and apologize—a highly unusual step that finally resulted in the Secretary of State writing Burnham a public letter to assure him that he did not doubt his 'personal integrity'.[27]

Interestingly, although not altogether surprisingly given the stickiness of parties' perceived strengths and weaknesses on particular issue, none of this had any permanent impact on Labour's big lead over the Conservatives on the NHS. Straight after the general election in 2010 YouGov put that lead at eight percentage points, rising into double figures by the beginning of 2011. At the beginning of 2013 it was fourteen points—exactly where it was at the end of the year. True there was some fluctuation, but that had more to do with the Conservatives' rating as 'best party' on the issue than with Labour's, which hovered around a consistent average of 36 per cent.[28]

In years gone by this would almost certainly have led the party to spend even more of its time attacking the Conservatives on, say, hospital closures or the mounting difficulties in A&E or, indeed, the 'backdoor privatization' that contracting out of services by GP-led clinical commissioning groups seemed to threaten. However, the dire state of the economy—plus Balls's reluctance to repeat what was widely regarded as Cameron's and Osborne's mistake in ring-fencing any department's budget—inevitably made for awkward questions about what Labour was going to spend in order to put things right. Moreover, the leadership was desperate to avoid the accusation that its default answer to any problem was simply to throw money at it. In addition, while many Labour people remembered how effective the party's 'seven days to save the NHS' campaign had been in 1997, others recalled that it had built up large leads on the issues over the Tory governments that were re-elected in 1983, 1987, and 1992—all to no avail. Burnham may have promised at the 2012 Labour Party Conference to turn the next election into a referendum on the NHS on the grounds that it might not survive another Tory government. But few in the leadership thought they should rely on health trumping the economy in 2015.

Besides, there was an internal discussion still going on at the very top of the party about what exactly policy on the NHS should be. Burnham had been making the case for some time for what he called a 'whole-person' approach that required the effective merger of health and social care. This was an approach that many agreed should be followed in the interest of patients in general and elderly people in particular. However, unless the independent commission set up by Burnham in April and chaired by Sir John Oldham discovered some sort of silver-bullet solution when it reported in early 2014, it was bound to be incredibly disruptive and phenomenally expensive. It might also prove electorally unpopular if the only way that could be found to pay for it was to revive the idea of some sort of charge on estates—a plan that the Tories had successfully branded a 'death tax' before the last election. Concerns about this, as well as the possibility that the Tories' attacks on Burnham's record would help them deflect criticism of their own running of the NHS, led to seemingly informed speculation that the Shadow Health Secretary might be reshuffled in the autumn—a possibility that he chose, riskily but in the end effectively, to try to close down in August by openly implying (in an interview with the *Guardian*) that his dismissal would amount to a failure by Labour's leader to think big:

I'm saying to Ed, I will give you an NHS policy that is one nation to its core, people will say that's what one nation means, all people covered for all of their care needs in a system that is based on the values of the NHS. What better way for Labour to say it's relevant to the 21st century than to bring forward a policy as bold in this century of the ageing society as the NHS was in the last? That's the way that Ed Miliband wins, by having policies that just knock the others off the pitch basically. And, that's what I want to give him.[29]

Andy Burnham was not the only Shadow Minister whose future apparently hung in the balance over the summer. Indeed, he was not even the man most briefed against. That dubious honour went to Stephen Twigg—Shadow Secretary of State for Education and, as Honorary Chair of Progress, someone who was routinely singled out for criticism by left-wing trade-union leaders.

Despite playing a part in forcing his opposite number, Michael Gove, into a humiliating climb-down over a plan to scrap GCSE's earlier on in the year, Twigg had otherwise struggled to lay a glove on him. This was due in part to the latter's skill as a parliamentary and media performer. But it owed even more to Twigg being caught, arguably through no fault of his own, in a virtual no-man's land between, on the one hand, teaching unions who regarded the government's reforms almost entirely negatively and, on the other, a Labour leadership that, whatever the party's default attachment to Local Education Authority control, knew full well it would end up preserving most of those reforms—either because they were too popular and too costly to undo or because it had no fundamental objection to them in principle. It was therefore left to Twigg to oppose what Gove was doing with, say, free schools (particularly their being set up in areas where places were not at a premium). But at the same time he had to insist that Labour supported parental choice and was therefore pragmatic about the issue, thereby making it pretty clear that the free schools were not going to be scrapped should the party regain power in 2015—just as the extension of academy status to almost any school that wanted it would not be changed. And, when he finally made the position on free schools clear in a speech in the middle of June, albeit with the proviso that there needed to be some form of oversight exercised away from Whitehall and some sort of attempt made to avoid 'surplus places', he got little support from the unions— and this in spite of an attempt to sweeten the pill by promising that national pay bargaining would be maintained and that all state schools would be obliged to employ only qualified teachers.[30]

Twigg was not, of course, the only Labour frontbencher needing to steer a course between pragmatism and pressure—both from above and from the unions. Back in 2012, Maria Eagle, the party's transport spokesperson, had welcomed a report, *Rebuilding Rail*, by a group called Transport for Quality of Life.[31] Funded by the main rail unions, it advocated the reintegration of rail operations and infrastructure and the gradual reincorporation into public ownership of rail franchises that were currently held by private train companies, albeit heavily subsidized by the taxpayer. This was understandable given the fact that the current system seemed to be delivering neither efficiency nor value for money—which was why Labour believed it was worth targeting rail commuters in marginal seats around London and why polls consistently showed a surprisingly high level of support for 'renationalization'.[32] On the other hand, any such policy, much like Burnham's plan for integrated health and social care, would take quite some doing. Even if franchises were taken into public ownership as they came up for renewal and along the lines of the not-for-profit company that had taken over the East Coast service, that still left the question of what to do with regional railways. They could perhaps be run by Transport for London-style public boards. But this would be complicated and cost a fair amount of money, too. Not surprisingly, then, this was something that a Labour leadership, wary of being seen as a left-wing throwback or of biting off more than it could chew in government, was bound to worry about.

More worried than most, perhaps, was Ed Balls, although renationalization was actually far from his biggest concern when it came to transport. That honour went to HS2, the planned high-speed rail link, running initially between London and Birmingham, which the government announced it would be legislating for in the Queen's Speech in May. It was not so much the project itself but its escalating costs (and indeed the opportunity costs) that he was beginning to wonder about, even going so far in the last week of August to note that there could be 'no blank cheque' for the project. And he was not alone: although Andrew Adonis, a former Transport Secretary who was now heading up a team for Miliband looking into a national growth strategy, remained passionate about HS2, other veterans of the previous Labour government, notably Peter Mandelson, Alistair Darling, and John Prescott, had all expressed their reservations publicly.

Maria Eagle, whatever doubts she may have had initially, was now, however, in the Adonis camp, believing HS2 was vital to future-proof the network against capacity constraints and hopeful that costs could be contained. Miliband, who earlier in the year had been talking enthusiastically about the tens of thousands of apprentices that the project would employ under a Labour government, was too—at least for the moment. Yet she was still having to have what should really have been a private (if not necessarily a settled) argument in public, and having to make some concessions to the views of those who were less sanguine than she was. She therefore used an interview with the *Sunday Times* at the end of August to make clear that the scheme could not 'start draining money from other vital rail projects' and had to be delivered within the current £50 billion budget—something that would be easier if its management was folded back into Network Rail.[33] Many Conservatives, however, whether they supported HS2 or were against it, remained deeply concerned that the opposition was leaving itself the option of declaring the project unaffordable before the election—a move that might not only make Labour look fiscally responsible but also free up some money for other, more popular promises.

Eagle's intervention may not have convinced everyone, but at least it showed that she was busy—something that could not be said, grumbled some Labour MPs about their front-bench colleagues and even Miliband himself. Most of their grumbling was done in private, although John Prescott felt obliged to use his column in the *Mirror* (which also published some very depressing ICM polling on Ed) to complain in mid-August that the front bench had missed an open goal by disappearing off on holiday and so 'massively failed to get our case over to the public and hold the Tories to account'.[34] He did, however, make an exception for those who had been working through in order to hammer home Labour's message that the squeeze on real wages and changes to tax credits and other benefits meant 'a cost of living crisis' for many middle- as well as low-income families—a campaign fronted by Shadow Chief Secretary to the Treasury Chris Leslie. Anyone paying attention would also have noticed Caroline Flint, Shadow Energy Secretary, beginning to talk an awful lot about 'the big six' energy companies and the £3.3 billion in windfall profits they had made since 2010 by supposedly ripping off both business and residential customers. Miliband, too, was making an effort, using his first appearance after a holiday to remind voters at a market in Elephant and Castle that 'Cameron is out of touch; you are out of pocket'—an intervention rewarded by one of them with a flurry of eggs, which at least guaranteed the Labour leader a place on the television news that evening.

That Leslie, Flint, Miliband, and a few others were not followed into battle by the rest of their colleagues was, in fact, mainly down to the Leader's Office. It was worried about too many voices diluting the message and had therefore declined to put together an elaborate summer 'grid' of announcements. It was also worried about Shadow Cabinet Ministers going off piste and making promises that they—or at least Ed Balls—would be unable deliver. And anyway Miliband, consistent with his tendency to devote an awful lot of the late summer to an annual set-piece speech, believed it was better for the party to keep its powder dry until the conference season, when people were more likely to be paying attention. The perils of doing otherwise were illustrated by what happened in mid-August to Labour's Immigration spokesman Chris Bryant. His attempt to use the political close-season to draw attention to the party's commitment to reducing the influx of low-skilled migrants went off at half-cock when his office put out the draft of a speech that wrongly criticized two of Britain's best-known retailers for their employment practices. The situation was not helped when, ten days later, Diane Abbott appeared to suggest that the party was affecting a tougher stance on the issue not because it really wanted to but because of opinion polling. Among other things, the latter showed majority support even for the government's most recent gimmick—the poster vans going round the streets of London telling illegal immigrants to 'Go Home or Face Arrest'.[35]

Things were certainly getting tetchy. Tessa Jowell (a Blairite but a party loyalist who was also known to be interested in running for Mayor of London in 2016) even took to the pages of the *Guardian* to suggest that those giving Miliband supposedly helpful advice in public might want instead to talk to him in person and in private, or else spend some of their ill-used spare time campaigning on the doorstep.[36] But then came something out of the blue—something that initially wiped all the stories of Labour's and Ed's 'summer crisis' off the headlines only to end up reinforcing the sense of unease.

The civil war in Syria had been going on for over a year. The country's ruler Bashar al-Assad had been accused more than once of barbaric acts against those parts of the civilian population that opposed him. But in August 2013 evidence emerged that he had crossed a line by using chemical weapons. The USA was, it seemed, determined to punish and deter him by launching missile and possibly air strikes, and the UK seemed set to join the operation. Public and political disquiet about 'a rush to war', however, prompted David Cameron to recall parliament on the assumption that, notwithstanding some serious concerns within the parliamentary Conservative Party there would be enough support on both sides of the House to enable the government to pass a motion in support of military action. Labour MPs, however, were torn between, on the one hand, their party's instinctive internationalism, as well as their natural outrage at what had occurred, and on the other, their concerns (which opinion polls suggested were shared by many voters) about getting sucked into another military conflict in the Middle East, particularly without being sure that the case for intervention was watertight and had the backing of the wider international community.

Ed Miliband, on the record as regarding the invasion of Iraq as a tragic error, was equally torn. He was convinced, however, that a way could be found to give the government the option to participate in military action as long as it was legally justified, specifically designed to deter chemical weapons use, had clear goals, and had international support. After meeting the Labour leader in Downing Street, the Prime Minister was convinced that he had secured his agreement to a motion that seemed to cover all these requirements, up to and including the need for a second vote to trigger a strike. Having consulted his colleagues, however, some of whom remained seriously concerned (particularly in the light of the government briefing

journalists that Labour backed military action in principle), Miliband
suddenly contacted Cameron to say that his party would not now
support a parliamentary call for such action until the UN inspection
team that had been sent into Syria had issued its report.

Downing Street was livid—so much so that one unnamed government source went so far as to tell journalists that both Number Ten and
the Foreign Office thought Miliband was 'a fucking cunt and a
copper-bottomed shit'.[37] Despite a furious whipping operation, the
government's motion went down to defeat, thirty Tories and nine Lib
Dems having joined the vast majority of Labour MPs in voting against
it. They did not, however, vote for the opposition's alternative either.
Cameron, to the surprise of many (including many on Labour's front
bench), immediately made it clear that there would be no attempt to
debate the issue again and therefore the UK would not take part in any
operation in Syria—a decision that not only confirmed the nascent
constitutional convention that the executive required legislative
approval for military action but gave the USA pause for thought,
which in turn bought the Russians time to broker a deal based on
destroying Assad's chemical arsenal.

Any elation that Miliband may have felt as a result of defeating the
government and supposedly stopping any 'rush to war', however,
quickly evaporated. Partly as a result of Cameron's precipitate decision, and partly because of the way that Tory spinners somehow
managed to transform his humiliation into a triumph for parliamentary
democracy, a significant number of Labour MPs (and certainly far
more than the handful who had abstained on, rather than voted
against, the government's motion) began to express reservations—
not just about the international ramifications of the vote but also the
message it sent to the electorate about their own party's (and, indeed,
Miliband's) principles, credibility, and firmness of purpose. And those
reservations grew stronger when the leadership appeared to tighten its
criteria for approving military action still further by talking about there
needing to be a threat to the UK's national security and the possibility
of al-Quaeda obtaining chemical weapons. Assurances from Douglas
Alexander and others that this was a decision concerning a particular
case, not a move towards some new, isolationist doctrine, helped some
but not all the doubters, as a critical *Guardian* article by the well-
known Blairite former minister Ben Bradshaw made all too obvious.[38]
Rather than come out swinging, however, and taking to the airwaves

to justify acting in the interests of international law and in line with what the British people seemed to want, Miliband instead seem to lack either the courage of his convictions or else the convictions of his courage—and that was as worrying for those who agreed with him as for those who did not. Perhaps, Fraser Nelson, the editor of the *Spectator*, put it best when he noted wryly:

Were British elections decided by essay competition, Miliband would win hands down. But political battles are decided by darker arts, including whether you are capable of throwing a second punch. Ed isn't. After the One Nation speech, there was no policy to show what he meant. He seemed astonished by his Syrian victory, and to regard the whole episode as an unwelcome and rather embarrassing interruption to his speechwriting...It takes a rather special Opposition leader to halt a prime minister on the road to war, in accordance with the wishes of the majority of the population, and be universally panned. But as Miliband is showing, he is a rather unusual leader.[39]

Nelson was referring, of course, to Miliband's address to the party conference. The previous year's effort had been a triumph, if a short-lived one. But it had been delivered at a time when, relatively speaking, Labour's leader had not been under too much pressure. This year, 2013, in Brighton, was different. Having somehow snatched defeat from the jaws of victory over Syria, Miliband, along with his leadership, were once again the subject of speculation. The chatter may, for the most part, have been about people positioning themselves to take over after the election rather than before it. And of the four people whose willingness to do constituency fundraisers all over the country was attracting attention—Ed Balls, Yvette Cooper, Chuka Umunna, and Rachel Reeves—the latter two were also among Miliband's doughtiest defenders, at least in public, in broadcast studios up and down the land. However, unless he could regain some much-needed momentum, the chatter would only get louder, notwithstanding the fact that the Australian Labor Party's loss of that country's federal election in September should have reminded everyone that a last-minute change of leader is by rarely a silver bullet. As the delegates of its British sister party made their way down to the coast, they were in uneasy, rather than confident, mood.

# 8

# Final Bend: Autumn
# 2013–Spring 2014

Iain Dale has to be one of the most enterprising people in and around British politics. A Tory blogger and talk radio host for London's LBC, he is also a publisher of some of the best-selling political titles in the country. None of them, however, had been as eagerly awaited as *Power Trip*.[1] Its author, Damian McBride, had been Gordon Brown's chief spin-doctor until he had eventually overreached himself and been forced to resign in April 2009. In publishing, as in politics itself, timing is everything, and McBride's head-butt-and-tell memoir was to be released—and serialized in the *Daily Mail*—just as the Labour Party headed down to Brighton for its annual shindig. Since, to coin several clichés, the book was a lurid tale penned by a master of the dark arts who knew where the bodies were buried, there was genuine concern (and, among Labour's opponents, fervent hope) that discussion of its contents would effectively derail conference and drown out any of the policy announcements made there. And certainly, for the first couple of days at least, there was talk of little else among journalists and delegates themselves.

There was also a touch of relief—and even anti-climax. There was nothing in the book that directly linked either Ed Balls or Ed Miliband, both of whom had worked alongside McBride in the Treasury as special advisers, to any of the seriously unsavoury things that had gone on during the time he had spent spinning for their boss, Gordon Brown. Some of those who were in and out of Downing Street at that time find it difficult to believe that the two Eds really did have no idea what was going on: at the very least, they argue, both men must have chosen to look the other way. Yet *Power Trip* provided no smoking gun. This undoubtedly disappointed the *Mail* and other Tory-supporting titles, and left some to wonder whether McBride's Roman Catholicism and residual loyalty to the Labour Party had encouraged him to pull his punches and heap the bulk of the blame for what had happened onto himself rather than his colleagues. However, it did mean things were nowhere near as bad as they might have been.

This was fortunate because, not unusually, the pre-conference polling did not look great for Miliband, whose big speech was once again being routinely referred to as 'make or break'. According to the *Observer*'s survey conducted by Opinium, his net approval stood at −29, while David Cameron's was at −17. Although, 25 per cent of respondents thought the Labour leader was in touch with ordinary people's lives, just 15 per cent thought he was able to make tough decisions. No more than 29 per cent of people could imagine Ed Miliband as a Prime Minister, as opposed to 65 per cent who could not.[2] A poll of Labour councillors for the BBC's *Sunday Politics* revealed that nearly a third of them would prefer him not to lead the party into the next election.[3] The by-now obligatory shots of Miliband walking around the conference city with his wife and children or addressing people in the streets on a raised platform were not going to change that, especially when, as the *Observer*'s Andrew Rawnsley and Toby Helm recorded in a pre-conference profile of the Labour leader, 'critics, friendly and not friendly at all, have been pouring what one colleague calls "10 buckets of shit" over the head of the Labour leader'.[4] Nor were the unions offering much comfort either. Indeed, Unite, still smarting over Falkirk, even passed up the chance to pay for a table at the conference's biggest fundraiser, where Miliband, of course, was the guest of honour.

True to form, Miliband had spent a long time—perhaps too long—preparing his speech. Last year's One Nation effort had gone down well, not least for the way it had been delivered so fluently without notes. But it had been largely devoid of policies that captured its essence and could be sold 'on the doorstep'. This year's would need to demonstrate equal flair but also deliver something more substantial. Fortunately, it did both. Apparently inspired by the work of Cambridge professor Simon Baron-Cohen on the importance of empathy, character, and compassion in leadership, he got in a wounding dig at Cameron, who, he observed, 'may be strong at standing up to the weak' but was 'always weak when it comes to standing up to the strong'. He also lifted fruitfully (although maybe a little too repetitiously) from pre-'97 New Labour by claiming again and again that 'Britain can do better than this'.

All this, together with confirmation of the continuing strength of Labour's commitment to the NHS and its determination to repeal the bedroom tax, helped to ensure the speech went down well with his audience in the hall. However, it also contained several 'signature policies' aimed at potential (but less partisan) voters out in the country. Some of these policies (notably the strengthening of fines on businesses found not to be paying the minimum wage, the reversal of rises in business rates to be paid for by jettisoning a cut in corporation tax, the building of 200,000 new homes per year enabled by radical changes to planning legislation, and votes at 16) had either already been trailed to the media in the build-up to Brighton and/or would be included in Shadow Ministers' speeches. This did not, however, guarantee their success—as illustrated by the plan to insist that businesses hiring skilled foreigners also take on a British apprentice, which was predictably ridiculed as unworkable under EU law, and by the commitment to oblige primary schools to provide childcare between 8 a.m. and 6 p.m., for which, it transpired, no additional funding had been identified. But by far the biggest announcement—one that had first been suggested midway through 2012 by Greg Beales and then extensively tested by the opinion research that he was commissioning on the party's behalf—was both a big surprise and, arguably, an even bigger success. The next Labour government, Miliband revealed, would, as a contribution to resolving the 'cost-of-living crisis' that he had been majoring on since the summer, freeze gas and electricity prices for twenty months so it could 'reset the market' in favour of consumers.

The measure was not, of course, without its risks, as some of the reaction to it—and to Miliband's announcement that developers banking land would be told to 'use it or lose it'—illustrated. 'Red Ed', claimed the Tories and their friends in the media, was lurching left and threatening to take the country back to 1970s-style socialism and the inevitable power cuts that would accompany it.[5] Some on the right even branded his ideas Stalinist, although the *Mail*, for reasons that were soon to become apparent, made do with insisting that they betrayed the malign influence of his Marxist father, Ralph. Even on the centre-left there was considerable anxiety that, by plumping for populism rather than talking (as even Ed Balls had done in his speech) about the continuing need for cutbacks, Miliband had wasted one of his last chances to win back 'credibility' on the economy and instead burnished his 'anti-business' credentials. To the combative New Labourite Philip Collins, previously a speechwriter for Tony Blair and now a regular *Times* columnist, this, just like the old-time religion on the NHS that Andy Burnham, the Shadow Health Secretary, had offered in his speech to conference, was comfort-zone Labour at its worst. There was nothing that was counter-intuitive, only confirmatory.[6] To some, this was no bad thing: the Fabian Society's General Secretary, Andrew Harrop, for instance, had argued in the run-up to conference that the party should concentrate on 'the groups who are naturally sympathetic to Labour but, right now, struggle to say anything about the choice the party offers them'.[7] To Collins, however, not worrying too much about erstwhile Tory voters was a counsel of despair. Cameron's speech to his party conference—a tightly argued reassertion of the Conservatives' commitment to extending opportunity, rewarding hard work, equipping the country to compete, and at the same time protecting the vulnerable—only served to confirm that Miliband's effort was not necessarily the game-changer, let alone the knock-out blow, that some had hoped it might be. And Osborne, notwithstanding his commitment (fully supported by Lynton Crosby) to contrast Miliband's opportunism with the Tories' 'long-term economic plan', had in any case used his speech to match Miliband's offer with a petrol-duty freeze of his own.

Arguably, however, the upsides of Labour's gas and electricity prices announcement trumped the downsides. It was likely, given widespread concern about utility bills on the part of consumers, to be popular with people, whichever party they tended to prefer. In addition, it provided a practical cutting edge to the more conceptual arguments about 'responsible capitalism' that Miliband had been making ever since he became leader. By showing that a Labour government could make a real, immediate difference, it also addressed the argument, often heard in focus groups composed of potential Labour supporters, that there was not much point in voting because the parties were all the same. Moreover, the enthusiasm with which the announcement was greeted by those who were already supporters should not be discounted. When polls suggested that there was precious little traffic between Labour and the Conservatives, giving the faithful a reason to knock on doors or even just to go out and vote could make the difference between winning and losing. Furthermore, as the support coming from, say, Andrew Adonis (who believed that cartels needed breaking up and dysfunctional markets need fixing) attested, not every New Labour veteran was as concerned as Collins or Peter Mandelson (or, indeed, Ed Balls) about Labour being seen as anti-business. In any case, Mandelson's scepticism was quickly dismissed by Labour's 'Blairite' Shadow Energy Secretary Caroline Flint, who, as well as helping to produce a detailed green paper on Labour's ideas for reorganizing the energy market later on in the autumn, fronted Labour's unusually well-executed media effort in the days immediately following Miliband's announcement. Shadow Business Secretary Chuka Umunna also did his best to reassure the commercial world that this was a one-off, sector-specific measure rather than the thin end of the wedge.

The freeze made sense politically, because it both highlighted and offered an easy-to-understand, retail solution to the 'cost-of-living crisis', which remained important to voters in spite of the fact that the economy seemed to have turned the corner. Moreover, it loaded the cost of that solution not onto hard-pressed taxpayers and consumers—the famous 'squeezed middle' whose real incomes had been falling for years—but onto a bunch of companies that (as Labour had been carefully reminding voters for a few months now) had been racking up billions by jacking up bills. Just as importantly, Labour's promise was unlikely to be matched by the Tories, for whom interference in the market was anathema or at least best avoided—a position that risked stranding them on the wrong side of a populist dividing line that pitted them, together with 'the Big Six', against 'the people'. And, if the government did shift its position (as eventually happened when it unsuccessfully attempted to lower bills by shifting the 'green charges' imposed on energy companies to general taxation), then it would be tantamount to admitting that Labour was right. The fact that the utility firms—very much 'predators' rather than 'producers'—walked into a trap by immediately warning of possible blackouts, and the fact that Tory politicians and newspapers decided to join them, was simply the icing on the cake.

The two big criticisms of Miliband's 2012 speech had been that it was too abstract and that there had been no follow-through. This announcement—in common with others promising to extend the

bank levy to pay for more hours of free childcare for pre-schoolers and
to stop rail operators exploiting their customers by less-than-transpar-
ent ticketing—was anything but abstract. And it was clear that Labour
strategists had no intention of letting it drop. For one thing, they had
invested in a clever multiplatform ad campaign put together by TBWA
that featured bills encased in ice cubes. For another, they were convinced (quite correctly, as it turned out) that energy companies would
soon be putting up their prices yet again. The fact that Energy Minister
Ed Davey reacted to the hikes by appearing to suggest people should
join him in putting on a jumper, and the fact that former Tory Prime
Minister John Major criticized the companies for creating a situation in
which 'people are going to have to choose between keeping warm and
eating', made things even better. In the wake of Miliband's price-
freeze promise in Brighton, one of his delighted aides had told the
*Huffington Post*'s Mehdi Hasan, 'The right hates it. The left likes it. The
public will get it. Most importantly, you can't ignore it.'[8] For once,
they were right.

What none of Miliband's people could guarantee, however, was
whether his announcement would cut through to people who were,
by and large, bored rigid by politics. After all, when the announcement
was made, most news programmes were still dominated by the horrific
attack on Nairobi's Westgate shopping mall. Nor could Labour guarantee that, even if voters liked the sound of the policy, they would
believe a Miliband government was capable of delivering it. Certainly,
the polling sent mixed messages. Surveying the public for the *Independent* at the end of October, and therefore after the dust had settled
on the conference season, ComRes found that eight out of ten
voters—including not just nine out of ten Labour voters but also
seven out of ten Tory voters—supported the idea of the freeze.
However, just over half of voters doubted Miliband would be able
to pull it off if elected to office.[9]

The underlying impressions created likewise gave cause for hope
and concern in equal measure. Polling just after conference, ComRes
had found that people believed the Tories would be significantly
more likely than Labour to keep the economy growing and to keep
public spending under control. On the other hand, Labour was seen
as twice as likely as the Tories to keep prices down. Labour also led
by a considerable margin when people were asked about which
party would best ensure their own family was better off. Polling by

Ipsos-Mori suggested Miliband's own satisfaction ratings had improved markedly, especially among Labour supporters, even if they had failed to provide much of a 'conference bounce' for the party as a whole. It also suggested that just over half of voters saw Miliband as left wing or left of centre—about the same proportion who saw Cameron as being right wing or right of centre, but up 10 per cent on 2010. This did not necessarily put people off Labour, however. The party had increased its support among the quarter of the electorate classified by YouGov as 'the squeezed middle' (ABC1 under-sixties who felt they were struggling to make ends meet) by fourteen points since the general election, although less at the expense of the Tories, who had dropped five points, than the Lib Dems, who had crashed from 29 to just 8 per cent.[10]

Miliband's announcement on energy prices also gave Labour a big opportunity to exploit the significant investment it had been making in its digital operation. The greatest value of the latter probably lay in enabling the party to collect and process data in order to be able to identify and contact potential voters, perhaps with the kind of tailored direct mail that went out to some of them in the wake of the price-freeze promise. But one of the sources for those data, of course, was responses to its marketing and advertising, which was itself increasingly built around digital rather than traditional (and traditionally much more expensive) media. Supporters were encouraged to tweet and retweet using the *#freezethatbill* hashtag, and the party reported that a so-called thunderclap—a simultaneous message sent across social media by, in this case, nearly 1,000 supporters—reached 4.5 million people. It also mounted a big push through Facebook and claimed to have reached over a million people in September—at least five times as many as it had reached the month before. Relative to the achievement (and indeed the financial clout) of the Obama campaign on which some of Labour's digital people had cut their teeth, this was small beer. Matthew McGregor of Blue State Digital, which was advising Labour, for example, had been only one cog—albeit a very important cog—in a much bigger machine assembled by the Democrats to fight Mitt Romney. Still, it did suggest that Labour, even if it was not necessarily way ahead of the Tories (who had made something of a splash by hiring Obama's 2012 campaign manager, Jim Messina, as an adviser), might be able to hold its own.

Where Labour was hoping to have its nose in front of its main rival, however, at least in campaigning terms, was in field operations, primarily because, under General Secretary Iain McNicol, it had made a point of ensuring that as many party staff as possible were based on the ground, in the regions and in key seats, rather than back in Brewer's Green in London. Many quite senior and therefore expensive Headquarters staff had been let go early on and the money saved invested in over a 100, frequently younger, more energetic field operatives who were often big fans of the community-organizing ethos brought to the party by Arnie Graf and embraced in no small measure by McNicol, who made a point of getting out and about rather than staying stuck in London. He had, after all, spent much of the early part of his career as an organizer and was convinced that the party, which during its thirteen years in government had simply shrivelled away in many key seats, had to recast and decentralize its relationship with its members and supporters if it were to stand a chance of winning in 2015. Voter identification was one thing, but, for Labour to be able to use the same kind of 'persuasion scripts' that were used by the Obama campaign to convert potential in 2012, it would need not only stalwarts who could carry a clipboard and a tick-sheet but enthusiastic volunteers who felt respected and trusted and who were capable of acting autonomously and spontaneously.

The idea that Labour was beginning to gear up a well-oiled machine may, however, have been a little optimistic. Anyone looking at Ashcroft's occasional polling of marginal constituencies, for example, would have been struck by the fact that Labour's contact rates were not systematically better than the Conservatives'. And among the politicians at the top and the staffers in the Leader's Office, there was clearly less interest and, indeed, belief in the need for a switch from (in the words of somebody deeply involved in training organizers and candidates) 'the politics of broadcast to the politics of conversation'. To them, Graf had little experience converting movement politics into votes where it really counted, and was both a distraction and a threat to their way of doing things, not least because his enthusiasm for radical decentralization dovetailed with the 'new politics' being preached by those who, like Jon Cruddas, wanted to see the party do the same in policy terms—something seen by many in and around the leadership as equally naive and potentially awkward. In any case, right at the top many were far more preoccupied with the vexed question of exactly who should be doing what and who was going to be in charge.

After conference, it was announced publicly that, following the long hiatus after Tom Watson's resignation as Campaign Coordinator in the wake of Falkirk, Douglas Alexander would be running the show as chair of general election strategy. Helping him would be Spencer Livermore. After years of advising Gordon Brown and helping to run Labour's election campaigns, Livermore had left Downing Street, where he had been Director of Strategy, for the private sector not long after 'the election that never was' in 2007—a mess for which he, alongside Alexander, had (unfairly, many thought) copped most of the flak. Now he was back as 'Campaign Director'. Since the number of people in Britain with experience in running campaigns at the highest of levels is incredibly small, this made a certain amount of sense. However, it clearly depressed some (and alarmed others) that, yet again, Miliband seemed to be putting the Brownites back in charge—even when those Brownites were not necessarily the best of friends. The impression that this was the case was only reinforced by the announcement that Shadow Cabinet Minister Michael Dugher, who had been Brown's chief spokesman before being elected to parliament in 2010, would continue to play a part in campaigning—specifically in Labour's 'attack' and rebuttal operations.

What was even more worrying, however, especially to those who believed Miliband had a tendency (like Brown) to avoid decisions by trying to square circles, was that it was not immediately obvious, especially when one factored in all the other players in the Leader's Office and Brewer's Green, who had responsibility for what. More-over, it looked as if, in order to calm fears that Gordon's gang would be running things, Miliband was also keen to involve, even if only peripherally, some Blairite veterans—including not only Alistair Campbell but also Alan Milburn, who many Labour people believed had gone over to the dark side (or the even darker side) by agreeing in August 2010 to become the Coalition's so-called social mobility tsar. All this seemed to leave precious little room for people whose Shadow Cabinet or party positions arguably entitled them to play a bigger role, the most obvious examples being Ed Balls, Deputy Leader Harriet Harman, and the two MPs playing the biggest official roles in policy development, Jon Cruddas and Chair of the NEC Angela Eagle. The fact that virtually everyone mentioned in a document that was leaked

to the press in early December was male rather than female was also a
bone of contention.[11] Aside from the equity issue, surely this made a
nonsense, first, of the party's boast that (albeit thanks largely to all-
women shortlists) it had more female candidates in place than its rivals
and, secondly, of its declared intention to press home its advantage
among younger women voters by making a big offer on childcare? It
was one thing to make the most of the fact that the Coalition was
unable to magic up a single woman on the front bench for a session of
PMQs in early February, and another to ensure that Labour's female
contingent (Mili's 'fillies' as they were inevitably dubbed by the *Sun*
the next day) was as influential behind the scenes as it was visible—
sometimes anyway—frontstage.

The problem, of course, was that the obvious way of dealing with so
many demands for inclusion—particularly for someone with a reputation for preferring to have it both ways rather than make a definitive
choice—was to assure all those concerned that they would be
involved. The consequent formation of a more inclusive general-
election strategy committee would only end up increasing the number
of people who needed consulting before campaigning decisions could
be made—and, as a result, increase the risk of confusion and disagreement as the election drew nearer, at the same time as making it more
likely that only a handful of people would be invested with any real
power.

Reconciling the multiple and overlapping sites of authority represented by his own office, Balls's staff, the Executive Board, Brewer's
Green, the election strategy people, and the Shadow Cabinet was,
however, only one of many things on Miliband's plate as the political
year began in earnest. His most immediate task was to complete and
announce a reshuffle. But before that could take place he had to cope
with an upsetting campaign by the *Mail*, which had decided to mount
an indirect attack on the Labour leader by laying into his late father.
'The Man who Hated Britain: Red Ed's Pledge to Bring Back Socialism Is a Homage to his Marxist Father' ran its headline, after which the
paper asked: 'So what did Miliband Snr really believe in? The answer
should disturb everyone who loves this country.'[12] Miliband junior
was swift to react, taking to social and other media to say, first, that his
father, a Belgian Jew who had fled the Nazis and then served in the
Royal Navy during the war, had loved his adopted country and,
secondly, that he was simply not prepared 'to allow his good name

to be denigrated in this way'. He also demanded and got a right of reply in the *Mail*, although a subsequent article in the paper made it clear it was sticking to its story—something it continued to do despite the revelation that its Sunday team had gone so far as to send reporters to a memorial service for Miliband's late uncle in the hope that they could pick up some juicy gossip.

Miliband also had to cope with speculation by right-wingers that his refusal simply to shrug the whole thing off had as much to do with his hope that the affair would revive memories of the leading role he had taken during Hackgate as it did with any sense of filial duty. As it turned out, any sympathy or admiration for Miliband engendered by the affair did not translate into increased ratings either for him or for his party. That said, the fallout from the affair, along with the appearance of UKIP's Nigel Farage in Manchester, did at least disrupt the media's coverage of the Conservative Party Conference the following week. Fortunately for Labour, the dust had pretty much settled by the time Miliband's reshuffle was announced at the end of the first week of October, although the initial headlines it generated hardly gave cause for celebration. In characteristically cack-handed manner, the demotion of Blairites—Liam Byrne (from DWP to Universities), Jim Murphy (from Defence to International Development), and Stephen Twigg (from Education to Constitutional Reform)—was leaked to the media before the news of the various promotions, helping to ensure that the story was framed far more negatively than it might have been. According to the best-selling *Sun* (never knowingly underpunned) 'Miliband's Revenge' was the 'Blair Ditch Project'—belated payback by Ed for those who had supported David in the leadership campaign and whose heads had been called for by Len McCluskey.[13] Even so, there were enough wise-heads in the lobby for it not to go unnoticed that all three men, rather than leaving the front bench altogether, had chosen to accept lesser roles—a decision that seemed to confirm not only that Miliband's position was secure until the election but also that he was still thought to be in with at least an outside chance of winning it.

What was also interesting, particularly in the days that followed the reshuffle, was that it was not going to be used as cover for any significant shifts of policy. If anything, the reverse was true: in a number of cases people were brought in precisely because it was hoped they were going to be able to tell essentially the same story better than those they replaced. This was perhaps most obviously the case at Education, where the media-friendly Tristram Hunt (whose appointment rather gave the lie to the idea that this was a 'bonfire of the Blairites') continued his predecessor's policy of adapting to rather than simply junking many of Michael Gove's reforms, not least free schools, which Hunt had previously written off as a 'vanity project for yummy mummies' but was now happy to accept as 'parent-led academies'—a euphemism that Ed Miliband himself had come up with.

The same was true of welfare. Although hinting, at least initially, at concerns about the practicality of the return to a more contributory regime, which Byrne had talked about, Rachel Reeves made it absolutely clear that Labour's desire to get the long-term unemployed and young people into work would, in some instances, mean it would need to be 'tougher than the Tories' when it came to benefit rates and conditionality. This triggered public criticism from outraged trade-union leaders.[14] Clearly, the left's distrust and dislike of Byrne (and, indeed, all things New Labour) had been so strong as to blind it to the fact that it was not just him but the leadership more generally who believed Labour had to harden its line on welfare. Byrne, despite his best efforts and his evident expertise, had simply been unable to turn things around. Poll after poll showed that the Tories were much more in tune with the public on the issue—a point reinforced in a leaked private presentation made to a trade-union audience in early October by one of the party's main polling experts, James Morris.[15] Bringing in a bright, voter-friendly fresher face, whose card was not yet marked (or marked so heavily anyway) by opponents of further reform, seemed to make a lot of sense.

Reeves was not the only woman promoted by Miliband in what was clearly an attempt to bring on as many of the best performers of the 2010 intake as possible. Emma Reynolds, for instance, was promoted to Shadow Housing Minister after impressing in the Europe portfolio. Gloria De Piero, who, like Reynolds and Reeves, entered the House in 2010, but whose previous career in television journalism meant she was possibly better known outside Westminster, was promoted to the Women and Equality portfolio—a move that inevitably provoked chatter that Miliband was clipping the wings of Shadow Home Secretary Yvette Cooper, who had occupied the post on a part-time basis and who was, many believed, planning on running for the leadership if and when he departed. Also given a promotion, however, was one of

Cooper's shadow team, Stella Creasy. The MP for Walthamstow was made spokesperson for Competition and Consumer Affairs in the shadow Business, Innovation, and Skills (BIS) team under Chuka Umunna, who (even in advance of his effective harrying of the Coalition over its botched privatization of Royal Mail and its response to the potential takeover of drugs firm AstraZeneca by US giant Pfizer) was also widely tipped as a frontrunner for the leadership should Ed step down. Creasy herself was sometimes mentioned, along with Reeves and De Piero, as a potential future leader, as she had made a well-deserved name for herself not just as a skilled user of social media but as an extremely effective campaigner against payday loan firms. Indeed, so effective was she that the government seemed to be shifting closer and closer to Labour's position—namely, that the industry needed root-and-branch reform and much tougher regulation.

Few other rising stars could claim such an immediate impact, but room was found for some of them nonetheless, with Dan Jarvis, a former soldier who came into parliament only in 2011 in a by-election, probably the pick of the bunch. Room, of course, had to be made by some people moving and others leaving the front bench altogether: Chris Bryant, for instance, was switched from the tricky Immigration portfolio to Work and Pensions, while celebrity left-winger and former leadership contender Diane Abbott returned to the back benches, her usefulness presumably long outlived. There was also a recall for some old warriors, most notably (Lord) Charlie Falconer, who, after contributing mightily to Labour's efforts on press regulation post-Leveson and notwithstanding his reputation as a Blairite, was asked by Miliband to head up a unit working on the party's transition to government—a good idea rendered all the more important by David Cameron announcing in March that Labour would have to wait until October 2014 before it could begin officially sanctioned talks with civil servants about its programme.

There was a move, too, for Mary Creagh, who had been in parliament in 2005 but had particularly impressed after 2010—first, when she had helped lead the successful campaign to force the government to abandon its plan to sell off publicly owned forests in early 2011 and, secondly, with her well-judged performances on the horsemeat-in-ready-meals scandal at the beginning in 2013. In a straight swap, Creagh's job as Shadow Secretary of State for Environment, Food and Rural Affairs went to Maria Eagle, with Creagh stepping into

Eagle's job at Transport. This meant, for the most part, railways and in particular HS2. Renationalization of the rail operators in the sense of re-creating some sort of twenty-first-century British Rail was not on the cards. But the leadership would have to decide over the next year how to respond to calls to take existing franchises back into public hands as they came up for renewal—a decision that could, however, be delayed until the culmination of the policy review in the late summer/early autumn of 2014. HS2, however, had become something of a running sore since the summer, when senior figures, most damagingly Ed Balls, had begun to express their doubts about its costs.

Before she left the Shadow Transport portfolio, Eagle hoped she might have done enough to reassure all sides by stressing both Labour's continuing commitment to the project and its commitment to securing value for money. Clearly, however, she had failed fully to persuade Balls, who had used his conference speech—one presumably signed off by Ed Miliband—to observe that 'the question is not just whether a new high-speed line is a good idea or a bad idea, but whether it is the best way to spend £50 billion for the future of our country'. With a vote coming up in parliament right at the end of October 2013 and Cameron making it clear that, without Labour support, the project could not go ahead, Creagh had to try and ensure that such support would be forthcoming—a task not made any easier by Balls remarking archly to a television interviewer that 'the Millennium Dome was a Conservative vanity project which the Labour government should have scrapped in 1997 and didn't. It was a mistake and I think you should learn from your mistakes.'[16]

That sort of talk inevitably provoked a backlash from the leaders of local authorities such as Bristol, Birmingham, Nottingham, Sheffield, Leeds, Manchester, Liverpool, and Newcastle, who warned publicly (and not perhaps unhelpfully as far as Creagh was concerned) of what they called 'protracted public conflict between the party leadership and the Labour led core cities'. In the event, she was able to assure the Commons that Labour was 'the true friend' of a project that she believed was in the national interest and that it had decided collectively to support, although she also promised to 'continue our scrutiny of these costs and our discipline on the public finances'.[17] On the other hand, Labour asked only those MPs who were in the House anyway to vote (a one-line whip), which meant that, while eleven rebels voted against, only seventy-four of the party's MPs actually voted in favour.

This did not escape the attention of the various unions whose members were employed on the railways, and they later made public a letter to Ed Balls in which they made their feelings about any backtracking on Labour's part crystal clear. Nor, however, did it escape the attention of Conservative MPs, who continued to worry (much to Balls's delight, no doubt) that he might still be tempted to use the cancellation of the project as a £43 billion rabbit that he might pull out of his hat just before the election. When Balls returned to the subject in March 2014, after the recently appointed Chairman of HS2, David Higgins, had completed a report that, it was hoped, might help assuage his concerns, he was, worryingly for many, only slightly less equivocal. However, his less than full-throated support did not—much to many people's relief—prevent Labour voting for the Bill preparing the way for HS2 on its second reading in April.

For the moment, however, the Shadow Chancellor was not having an easy time of it. In mid-November journalists—and those Labour people who enjoyed seeing him taken down a peg or two—had fun with an internal email, accidentally copied to a Tory MP, in which Torsten Bell in the Leader's Office, expressing his frustration at Balls's apparent failure to get on with the programme when it came to Labour's messaging on the economy, used the word 'Nightmare'. Conveniently ignoring the fact that this sort of stuff goes on all the time in workplaces the world over (including, one presumes, newsrooms) without those involved descending into all-out war, the incident was used to stand up a long-running story that 'the two Eds' were permanently at each other's throats/barely on speaking terms/unable to agree on even the basics of Labour's approach to the economy, Europe, and the election (delete as appropriate). As so often, there seemed to be just enough truth in the tales of tension between the two men to mean that, as with the stories circulating about differences between, say, Douglas Alexander and Michael Dugher, they could be recycled or else simply referred to in passing by anyone keen to show they were in the know.[18]

Clearly, there were differences that well-informed, expert analysts could tease out. One example was Ed Balls's concern, prompted by comments coming from the CBI and other organizations, that the private sector was refusing to buy the distinction that Ed Miliband seemed to want to make between small and medium enterprises (which he and his advisers presumably saw as Middle-England's *mittel-stand*) and 'big business' (which they were in danger of caricaturing as the baddies). But for the most part they were differences of degree rather than kind—turf wars rather than a tragic return to the Blair–Brown era by a party unable to help itself. Moreover, as the *Mail*'s hatchet job on Miliband's father and, a few months later, on Harriet Harman's so-called 'links' with the Paedophile Information Exchange in the 1970s proved, any friendly fire paled beside the attacks mounted on Labour's leadership by the other side. And when, towards the end of November, Balls himself came under fire from the Tories and their friends in the media over his supposed association with the disgraced former chairman of the Co-operative Bank, 'Crystal-Methodist' Paul Flowers (a man he barely knew), Miliband, along with Dugher, was notably quick to defend him.

However, it was not the confected kerfuffle over the Revd Flowers that did Balls most damage as the year drew to a close. On 5 December, George Osborne rose to deliver his annual Autumn Statement to the House of Commons. As expected, he made much of the return to growth, brushing off criticisms that it was fuelled by consumer debt and an inflated housing market but stressing that there was nevertheless still some way to go when it came to tackling the deficit. He would therefore be extending cuts until 2018 and 2019 and capping welfare expenditure in particular. He nevertheless found room for a few giveaways, funded, he claimed, by his continued crackdown on spending and a renewed effort against tax avoidance. Osborne also found time to try to adopt or at least adapt a few of Labour's ideas on youth unemployment and benefits, on small businesses, and on rail fares— 'taking the steak and leaving the gristle', as Tory spinners dubbed it in their briefings to journalists. None of this gave much for Balls, who had to make an instant response, to work with, especially as Conservative MPs were more than happy to remind him that his predictions that austerity would result in slow or no growth and mass unemployment had not been borne out in reality.

Expectations were therefore low as Balls rose to speak, but he actually managed to sink so far beneath them that even sympathetic commentators were scathing. Perhaps the best summary, both of the occasion and the problem it arguably illustrated, was provided by the *Guardian*'s Aditya Chakrabortty:

In a day without any big winners, the shadow chancellor was the clearest loser. . . . Balls delivered the same attack lines he has been using since 2010.

'Flatlining', 'slowest recovery for over 100 years', 'tax cut for millionaires': all were present and technically correct, just rather shopworn after three years of constant service. But...Balls has always had the dangerous tendency for a politician of wanting to win an argument, even if it means losing an election...he still wants to prove his point; even though events have moved on, and it's well past time for the argument to do so, too...Over the past couple of years, I have been in meetings with party frontbenchers as they toyed with the idea of setting some benchmarks on what a real recovery would look like: rising wages, businesses investing more, banks lending to the real economy and so on. Everyone agreed it was a good idea, but it never got off the starting blocks. Yet now the recovery is here and Labour is still stuck on what to say about it.[19]

Given this, it was fortunate for Balls that the independent Institute for Fiscal Studies, which was increasingly seen as an infallible guide to all things budgetary by the media, managed to put more of a spoke in Osborne's wheel than he had. In its view, the Chancellor was a touch too confident and a little too vague about his projections, and nothing in what he said could disguise the fact that average household incomes would be 5 per cent lower in 2015 than they had been in 2010; moreover, Labour's argument that this equated to around £1,600 pounds was, it opined, 'pretty consistent' with the data.[20] However, neither this—nor Balls's announcement in an interview with the *Financial Times* a fortnight later that Labour would be launching a stringent 'zero-based spending review'—prevented rumours circulating that he might be replaced as Shadow Chancellor before the election.[21] In the final PMQs before the festive break, Cameron, having to put up yet again with Balls gesticulating as he was speaking, shot back: 'I would have thought that after today's briefing in the papers the hand gesture for the shadow Chancellor should be bye-bye. You don't need it to be Christmas to know when you are sitting next to a turkey.'

By the time parliament reconvened in the New Year, however, the biggest news story was not political; it was the widespread flooding and consequent electricity blackouts that had afflicted parts of England over the holidays and that looked set to continue for some time yet. Those involved in politics, however, had other things on their mind—at least until the flooding got so bad in February that they were practically obliged to don wellies and waders and tour the afflicted areas in order to show they cared. The year 2014 was the last full one before the general election and therefore the last chance to eliminate whatever negatives and accentuate whatever positives might influence voters before the campaigning began in earnest in early 2015. The late spring would also see both local elections and elections to the European Parliament—an opportunity to guage progress and perhaps even pick up some momentum. In truth, few people on the Labour side were expecting much of either. For all the excitement generated by the Brighton conference, 2013 had not been brilliant. As the blogger Dan Hodges, never one to look on the bright side where Miliband was concerned, noted: 'At the end of 2012 Labour's YouGov daily poll average was 11.3 per cent. As 2013 ends it has been halved to 6 per cent. By the end of December 2012, Ed Miliband's personal YouGov approval rating was minus 21 per cent. As 2014 opens it has slumped to minus 34 per cent. If that represents a good year for Labour, it can ill afford a bad one.'[22]

To its critics, Labour's biggest weakness, apart from its leader (and its Shadow Chancellor), remained the economy, with welfare and immigration—in the news again because of UKIP's dire warnings about the expected influx of Romanians and Bulgarians taking advantage of the end of transitional controls—trailing not very far behind. The worry was that, as the economy began to improve, this would eventually feed through into votes for the Conservatives, not so much because of gratitude for a job well done but because Labour itself had not re-established enough trust on the issue to be seen as a sufficiently safe alternative. Miliband, and those around him, however, were rather more sanguine, believing that, while credibility was, of course, vital, victory could be theirs if they could just do two things. First, they had to remind people that, whatever the government's figures said, their household incomes were showing little or no sign of serious improvement. Secondly, they had to persuade them that the British economy, at least as it was currently configured, would be unable, even if it continued growing, to provide them with the security and the opportunities they craved. Never mind Thomas Piketty, the French scholar whose tome on inequality was about to become the must-have adornment for every British progressive's coffee table. Never mind, either, the equally voluminous biography of Theodore Roosevelt, scourge of the robber barons (and assorted wildlife), by Doris Kearns Goodwin, which Miliband had just given as a Christmas gift to some of his staff. No, this was pure James Carville and Stan Greenberg, whose book *It's the Middle Class, Stupid!* provided anyone who read it with a clue to the narrative that ran like a red thread through the Obama 2012 campaign and would do so right through Labour's in the run-up to 2015.[23]

In the middle of January 2014, Ed Miliband gave what was widely billed as his 'big speech on the economy'. Sadly for him, it gained less attention than he had hoped in the wake of interventions by the Governor of the Bank of England, Mark Carney, and the Chancellor of the Exchequer, George Osborne, concerning (in Carney's case) the futility of caps on bankers' bonuses and (in Osborne's) the possibility of raising the minimum wage. But the speech—and the assorted interviews and articles that inevitably accompanied it—was no less important for that. In policy terms, it was about the fact that, if the country were to build a 'One Nation economy', the 'Big Five' banks needed no less reform than the 'Big Six' utility companies. But the big theme was about addressing what he called in an article for the *Telegraph* the 'gnawing anxiety about what the future holds' felt by huge numbers of families—one that had been picked up on not just by systematic opinion research but by frontbencher Gloria De Piero, who had been trying to find out what was preoccupying real people beyond the Westminster bubble. 'The current cost-of-living crisis', he insisted, 'is not just about people on tax credits, zero-hours contracts and the minimum wage. It is about millions of middle-class families who never dreamt that life would be such a struggle.'[24] This squeezed-middle frame also extended to a speech on boosting the housing supply via reforms intended to stimulate small-build and self-build made a couple of days before by Emma Reynolds—a programme reiterated by Miliband himself in mid-February, albeit with the embarrassing addition of an absurd promise to prevent developers selling to overseas rather than domestic purchasers.[25] In a 'big speech' on welfare made a few days after Miliband's intervention on the economy, however, by Rachel Reeves, the main point was to communicate that the party's concern to help people into work would see it pursue what she referred to in interviews as 'tough-love' policies such as bringing forward basic skills tests for those signing on. However, there was also something for those who might not expect to find themselves out of work, as she emphasized her interest in work being done by IPPR on increasing the amount payable to those with long work records newly claiming jobseeker's allowance, even if this meant, in effect, reducing it for those whose work records were less impressive. This backing of the contributory principle—something that IPPR had been talking about for some time—affirmed that Reeves was not departing so very far from the path set out upon by Liam Byrne. It also dovetailed with another message that she was keen to relay. Labour—still understandably desperate not to allow widespread hostility to immigration to undermine its support or, indeed, support for the welfare state itself—would 'look at any practical proposals [the government could] come up with to extend the period new migrants have to work and contribute before becoming entitled to full support and addressing the anomaly that allows child benefit to be paid out for children not living in this country'.[26]

In this, Reeves was again following on from Ed Miliband, who earlier in the month had talked about how people's 'understandable' fears about migration were best dealt with by closing loopholes that encouraged firms to hire cheap labour from abroad to work in an economy 'hard-wired into a cycle of low wages, low skills, insecure jobs and high prices that is tearing into the living standards of ordinary families' rather than erecting a 'fortress around Britain'.[27] For the moment anyway, this appeared to rule out seeking changes at an EU level to somehow limit the right of free movement—something that Chuka Umunna, in an off-the-cuff answer on BBC's *Question Time*, appeared to suggest was, in fact, a possibility. That said, Reeves, in interviews, seemed to be prepared to countenance lengthening the time that EU citizens were required to be in the country before claiming welfare payments, even if she refused to utter the words 'benefit tourism'. Sadly, but not unpredictably, no sooner had Labour expressed support for tougher measures than the government moved to up the ante, announcing in late January, for example, that it would be extending its delay in paying out-of-work benefits to include housing benefit, too.[28]

Maintaining its advantage over Labour on the immigration issue was not, of course, the only reason the government was continually tightening its stance. It was also looking nervously over its shoulder at UKIP. In the wake of Cameron's increasingly evident failure to meet his ambition to reduce net migration 'from the hundreds to the tens of thousands', Nigel Farage's party was trusted by more than twice as many voters in marginal seats as the Tories to control immigration and was now being tipped to finish first at the upcoming European Parliament elections at the end of May.[29] To some Labour people, that prospect was hardly a tragedy: after all, it would lend momentum to a party that was likely to do serious damage to the Tories' chances of an overall majority, or even ending up the largest party, if it were to poll anything approaching double figures at the general elections. But more and more Labour people were beginning to worry about the damage that UKIP might do to their own party's prospects—not just in the longer term but also (as Peter Hain warned publicly in early February) in the short term, especially at local elections in places with high concentrations of poorly educated, older, white working-class voters who had lost any faith they might once have had in Labour to represent their concerns.

To Hain, the answer was 'not to tack to UKIP's anti-Europe, anti-immigrant, anti-almost everything agenda but to rebuild trust among our grassroots base and have clear and radical policies on housing, jobs, investment, growth, opportunities and give disillusioned people hope'.[30] Some of his colleagues, most prominently perhaps the media-friendly backbencher John Mann, argued, however, that attack was the best form of defence—a strategy that the party road-tested, seemingly with some success, during a by-election held in mid-February in the safe Labour seat of Wythenshawe and Sale East, the main aim of its offensive being to point out to voters quite how Thatcherite UKIP's policies were. This, combined with a relentless focus on bread-and-butter issues such as the cost of living and public services, as well as an insistence that a Labour government would do things very differently from the Coalition, was the way forward, according to Douglas Alexander. Other Labour MPs, however, were less than convinced that it was going to be enough. According to people like the Member for Rochdale, Simon Danczuk, who seemed determined to make a name for himself for 'common-sense' criticism of the leadership in the *Mail* and the *Sun*, Labour also needed to talk even more and to talk even tougher than it had already tried to do about immigration.

For all that Danczuk may have made himself every Conservative's favourite Labour MP, he was not as much of an outrider in his own party—at least on this issue—as he seemed to imagine. After all, Labour was not 100 per cent dominated by what he called 'guacamole-dipping, skinny latte-sipping effete types'.[31] Jon Cruddas, for example, had never been afraid to point to 'widespread anger at immigration' as a key part of 'a politics of victimhood and resentment' originating in social democracy's failure to adapt to the fracturing of society brought on by globalization and deindustrialization. And, while Cruddas was busy thinking big thoughts about it, one of his senior colleagues was going ahead and making policy anyway. At the beginning of the European and local election campaign in early April, Yvette Cooper made the latest in a series of speeches she had given on the issue since becoming Shadow Home Secretary, each one of which signalled a slight turn of the ratchet towards restriction. Insisting that she wanted 'an open honest debate that doesn't promote hostility but doesn't ignore concerns', she tried to show how Labour's 'progressive immigration policy' differed both from 'a traditional conservative approach' ('all immigration is bad'/'we can build a wall and hide behind it') and from 'a free-market liberal approach' ('views all migration as good and tries to open all the doors'/'immigrants as a source of innovation, but also as cheap labour to keep wages and inflation low'). She began by going over what Labour had already promised on wages and exploitation (with the addition of a promise of a consultation exercise with business, unions, and communities) and on controls (with the addition of a promise to bring back finger-printing of illegal immigrants caught at Calais). She then made, for the first time, a definite commitment to keep the Coalition's cap on skilled workers (although also to remove students from the net migration target), as well as a pledge that, under Labour, 'all public-sector workers who work directly with the public will have to be able to speak English to a decent standard'. And she finished with two new tough promises: first, there was what now seemed to be a serious commitment to 'pursuing reforms in Europe so that child tax credit and child benefit are no longer paid to families abroad'; and, second, there was a commitment to change the rules so that EU citizens found guilty of assault, burglary, or robbery are deported even if sentenced for less than a year.[32]

How much difference Cooper's words—or, indeed, Ed Miliband's own speech and media interviews on the self-same issue a week out from the European and local elections—actually made is a moot point. Maybe they were simply futile: as John Healey (who, back in 2010, came second in the last Shadow Cabinet elections ever held) observed to the *Spectator*'s Isabel Hardman just after the European and local elections, it might have been better to have concentrated on providing activists with a tried and tested toolkit of responses to UKIP that they could use on the doorstep.[33] Maybe, however, all the speeches and the interviews were actively counterproductive, boosting Farage's party by helping to ensure that immigration remained at the top of the public's list of 'most important issues facing the country'. Certainly, like virtually all Labour's official interventions on the issue since the general election, they reflected the tendency of centre-left politicians to come up with an economic answer to what was, for many of those affected, even those on low incomes, as much a question of identity. Partly as a result, perhaps, they did nowhere near enough to impress the handful of rent-a-quote backbenchers bent on demanding they do more without ever bothering to specify exactly what 'more' should mean. And, if voters' responses bore any relation to the newspapers those MPs were so desperate to appear in, they were not particularly promising either: 'Labour's Yvette Cooper apologises for her party's shameful record', noted the *Sun* the next day. 'She has little choice,' it went on. 'Listen carefully . . . you'll hear the stable door being slammed shut and hooves galloping down the street.'[34]

This was nothing less than Labour had come to expect from the majority of the print media, whose antipathy—ideological in origin but sharpened by a determination to do whatever it took to prevent the election of a government committed to tougher press regulation—it had come to take for granted. Pretty much the same reaction—at least outside the pages of the *Mirror*, the *Guardian*, the *Independent*, and (more unusually these days) the *Financial Times*—had greeted Ed Miliband's announcement in March that the party would not be matching the Conservatives' guarantee of an in–out referendum on EU membership in 2017 but would instead pledge to hold one should 'a further transfer of powers' to Brussels be mooted in the future—something he did not anticipate happening in the next parliament.[35]

The rent-a-quotes and the small band of Labour Eurosceptics aside, this stance made sense to most people in the party, even to those like Ed Balls, Andy Burnham, and Jon Cruddas who might have been tempted to go further but now seemed content to have moved Miliband at least part of the way towards their position. Views within Labour on UKIP may have varied, but there was broad agreement that it would take more than a promise of a precipitate vote on Europe to stop it in its tracks. There was equally broad agreement, too, that such a promise would look opportunistic and inauthentic, and therefore unlikely to sway many voters. In any case, as demonstrated both by opinion polls and by the apathy that greeted Labour's opposition to the

Tories' attempt to enshrine their referendum in law via a Private Member's Bill, most voters, even if they were sceptics, were largely uninterested in the European issue. If the Conservatives, instead of talking up the economy at every opportunity, chose to spend valuable time banging on about Labour's failure to promise a referendum, then they were more than welcome to do so. Polling on what might stop potential Labour supporters voting for the party showed that this issue paled in comparison to, say, the economy, welfare, and Miliband himself. Besides, as most Labour people saw it, even the possibility of Brexit (the UK leaving the EU) would be enough to spook the markets and damage the economy—something that, as a potential government, they wanted to avoid at all costs. Nor, if they became the government, did they want to waste two years fighting a referendum campaign against the combined forces of the Conservative Party, its friends in the media, and the mid-term blues.

Miliband's announcement on Europe was also coupled with a demand for far-reaching reform of the EU—a demand that Ed Balls re-emphasized in a speech in the last week of the European Parliament election campaign.[36] On Europe at least, then, Labour had some hope of gaining the support of business leaders, the majority of whom wanted reform but certainly not exit. And the party's policy was now aligned with that of the Lib Dems—something that could come in handy should another hung parliament cast Clegg (or his successor) as kingmaker once again. In the longer term, since any UK government was now committed by law to holding a referendum on any significant transfer of powers to the EU, it was not necessarily a bad idea to turn that vote into one on whether to stay or to leave: this would deprive Britain's notoriously sceptical voters of what would otherwise be a free hit at Brussels and make it more likely that any such transfer would be approved.

All that, however, was for the future. Right now, Labour had more pressing matters to attend to—and none so pressing as ensuring that plans to reform its relationship with the trade unions could be presented as a win for Ed Miliband at the same time as preserving one of the party's main sources of funding. It had long been apparent that this was going to involve compromise on all sides and that, fortunately, the Labour leader had ended up with exactly the right man for the job. Few could match Ray Collins's contacts right across the movement, and he proved himself a skilful negotiator, putting together an agreement to which all sides were willing, if not necessarily happy, to sign up. He was able to do this, at least in part, because, once tempers had cooled, all those involved were honest enough to admit that the relationship between party and unions as it stood was far from ideal, particularly when one looked beneath the national and the regional to the local, branch level. As one Labour MP from a union background noted, Collins

took the heat out of the debate and got increasingly a focus on 'Does it work in quite the way it should?' And the more you asked that question, the more people said 'Well, no it doesn't.' And therefore we started to move on to the territory of 'Well, alright then, what is it that makes that link more legitimate' . . . but crucially focusing on that local engagement.

In any event, Collins and others from the party who worked to get a deal pulled off little short of a miracle. In an atmosphere poisoned by the political and (not to be sniffed at) personal fallout from Falkirk, and working backwards from a speech that many staffers considered not just unnecessarily rash but a real risk to Labour's financial viability, they were able to stave off the latter and get so much more besides. Because no one really wanted to think about how badly things might have turned out if things had gone wrong, and because war averted is never as interesting as war declared, this remarkable achievement was not perhaps accorded the praise it actually deserved.

Under the package, the unions agreed that they would affiliate to Labour only those members who opted in to paying part of their political levy to the party. However, they would be given up to five years to phase in the system so that it covered not just new joiners but existing members. Only those who opted in would become affiliated supporters, entitled to vote in Labour leadership elections and the London Mayoral primary (although not parliamentary selections), and their contact with the party—including the sending-out of ballot papers—would be direct rather than through their union. Henceforth, leadership elections—which Miliband, few seemed to remember, had not even mentioned when he declared the union link needed reforming—would take place not via the three-part electoral college that had chosen Miliband but on a one-member/supporter-one-vote basis. As a result, Labour MPs (and MEPs) would no longer exercise a disproportionate influence on the vote itself. However, they would continue to have a big say in the contest, since any candidate would have to be nominated by 15 per cent of his or her colleagues—up from the 12.5 per cent needed in 2010 but not as high a threshold as Collins had initially suggested. Meanwhile the unions preserved their voting strength on the NEC, the NPF, and at conference, meaning that whatever formal say they had on policy remained officially intact even if, as many predicted, it might be hard to defend in the fullness of time.

The party, assuming the number of union members who opted in would be considerably less than the numbers currently affiliated on the opt-out basis, was almost certainly going to suffer a drop in its 'guaranteed' income—possibly, in the long term at least, in the order of between £4 million and £7 million a year. In fact, of course, that income had never really been guaranteed because it was up to unions' leaderships to decide how many members they wanted to affiliate to the party. Nor would the resulting reduction occur immediately—and anyway it was still open to unions' executives to make up any shortfall via *ad hoc* donations. This, the Conservatives pointed out, meant Labour was now more, rather than less, reliant on the whims of 'union bosses'—something Len McCluskey seemed happy to confirm when Unite decided in early March to follow the GMB's and Unison's lead and halve its annual affiliation payment. Quite how much discretion he and his ilk really had, however, was a moot point. Talk of eventual disaffiliation and founding a new party on the left was all very well, but right now Labour was the only game in town. And, with the Tories apparently considering Boris Johnson's plea to outlaw strikes where less than half the membership took part in any ballot, getting rid of the current government was as much of a priority as ever.

The party, meanwhile, was likely to do as much as it felt it decently could to keep the unions sweet—and not just because it needed their money and their manpower to fight the rapidly approaching general election. For one thing, Labour's leadership knew that winning in 2015 would cost the party millions because it would trigger the loss of the Short Money granted by parliament to opposition parties. For another, the party was on the verge of transferring its banking business (and therefore any loans and overdrafts) from the troubled Co-operative Bank to Unity Trust, which was part-owned by several unions. None of this meant that Labour was as utterly dependent on the unions as the Conservative-supporting press liked to suggest. The figures from the Electoral Commission that journalists routinely cited did not include the many small donations that the party was not required to report, and Labour had a handful of very generous individuals, such as Andrew Rosenfeld, David Garrard, and John Mills, who were wealthy enough to make much larger gifts. That said, everyone in the party was well aware of the dire financial consequences that might have followed any failure to do a deal that kept everyone on board. If that meant missing out on the opportunity for some sort of 'Clause IV moment', then, as long as said deal could reasonably be sold as Ed Miliband getting broadly what he wanted, so be it.

There were, then, very few objections to the package when it went through the PLP, the Shadow Cabinet, and the NEC in early February. This was the case even though the press had finally managed to get hold of a copy of the party's internal inquiry into Falkirk. Indeed, whoever had leaked it may ultimately have been disappointed by how little sustained media attention it attracted. Perhaps this was because it was now relatively old news. Perhaps it was because the evidence for its main conclusions (that people were signed up and paid for without their really knowing what was going on, that this was done in order to influence the outcome of the selection process, and that those involved had made it difficult for those charged with investigating it) was not quite as incontrovertible as it might have been. Whatever the reason, however, its publication did not poison the atmosphere sufficiently to pose any problems at the Special Conference held on 1 March to ratify the reforms. Delegates voted by 86 per cent to 14 per cent to approve a package backed not just by the unions but by Tony Blair and by Elizabeth Smith, whose husband John had begun the reform process as Labour leader before his untimely death in 1994. The result even prompted David Owen, who famously left Labour back in 1981 to found the SDP, to announce that he was making a donation to the party. Whether many voters remembered him well enough for his gesture to make much of an impact was doubtful. The news, anyway, was dominated, not by Labour's reforms but, first, by Angela Merkel's visit to London and then by Russia sending its troops into the Ukrainian territory of Crimea—a move that some Tory MPs insisted had its origins in Labour's vote against action in Syria, which, in their view, had persuaded Vladimir Putin that nothing would be done to stop him.

Although the Labour leadership joined in the widespread condemnation of Russia's actions, its mind was on other things. George Osborne was due to present the Budget in mid-March, and there was widespread agreement that Labour desperately needed to up its game if it were to stand any chance before the general election of convincing voters that it could make a better fist of the economy and the nation's finances. The year had not begun well for Ed Balls. He could cope with a few nameless Labour MPs telling any journalist who would listen that he seemed to have 'lost his mojo' since his poor parliamentary performance on the Autumn Statement. Indeed, their sniping had an upside, since it had effectively forced Ed Miliband into telling television interviewers that the other Ed was doing a good job and would be Shadow Chancellor going into the election. What was more difficult, however, was the distinctly underwhelming reaction to a major intervention he had made in the third week of January. In a speech to the Fabian Society (dubbed 'Labour's most sanctimonious middle-class redistributionist cabal' by the political commentator Adam Boulton in the *Sunday Times*), Balls pledged that a Miliband government would eliminate the deficit and ensure that debt was falling as a percentage of GDP by the end of the parliament.[37] To those who pointed out that Osborne had promised to do this by 2018/19, Balls pointed out that, unlike his opposite number, he planned to enshrine his commitment to new fiscal rules in legislation. Admittedly, this left Labour free to increase taxation rather than make more cuts, and Balls continued to make clear he was talking about current rather than capital spending, which he believed needed to be maintained or even increased in order to invest in growth-boosting infrastructure. Nevertheless, it was a big deal, not least because it was well known that Balls would have preferred to make Labour's pitch for fiscal credibility rather nearer to the election.

Maybe it was these mixed feelings, or else a desire to curry favour with backbenchers and grass-roots members, that persuaded Balls that it would be a good idea to couple his announcement on the deficit with confirmation that Labour would indeed be hiking the top rate of tax back up to 50p. This—like his announcement a few weeks later that Labour's jobs guarantee would now be financed by a further levy on bank bonuses and a big reduction in tax relief on top earners' pension contributions—provoked concerted condemnation from some of the business world's usual suspects. It was also a massive distraction from his other, strategically far more important, pledge. No wonder people were questioning the quality of Labour's media and campaign operation. Concerns about it had already surfaced periodically—for example, when it failed for days to shut down the *Mail*'s attack on Harriet Harman over the Paedophile Information Exchange's links with the National Council for Civil Liberties in the 1970s. But those concerns only increased with the release of a party broadcast, *The Un-credible Shrinking Man*. Produced by ad agency Lucky Generals (later selected to do the bulk of the party's advertising in the run-up to the general election), it mashed up Ealing Comedy and Harry Enfield's Mr Cholmondeley-Warner in order to poke fun at Nick Clegg's supposedly co-dependent relationship with his preternaturally posh Conservative colleagues.[38]

That broadcast could be defended, more or less convincingly, as a daring bid to grab the attention of voters who were turned off by more conventional formats, as well as an attempt to remind Lib Dem voters who had defected to Labour why they should stick with the party. As one of those involved put it, with characteristic bluntness, 'I've never subscribed to the view that when a man is down you stop kicking him...Your job is to make sure they don't get up again'—streetfighting talk that made sense, given that, in virtually all the Conservative seats the party was targeting, the Lib Dem vote was larger than the Tory majority in 2010. Commentators might sneer, but those responsible, having 'focused grouped the shit out of it', as another of them put it, were relatively unconcerned. That was not so true, however, of another ad (this time a poster) that attracted criticism for purporting to highlight the impact of the government's VAT rise on the cost of living while featuring eighteen out of twenty-four grocery items that were zero-rated, including a jar of white asparagus—not, it was probably fair to assume, a product included in most shoppers' supermarket trolleys.[39] All pretty trivial stuff, of course. Or it would have been if Balls had not made it clear that he had not signed off on the poster and if Miliband, when asked in a television interview just days before European and local elections to estimate his family's weekly grocery bill, had not struggled to come up with a convincing answer. This was rapidly followed by his failure, on a local radio station, to remember the name of the leader of the Labour group in the town where he was campaigning that day, and—most famously of all—his ungainly attempt to eat a bacon sandwich during a photo-opportunity intended to show just what a normal guy he was. Cue another round of stories about Miliband's intrinsic weirdness and about in-fighting and incompetence at the top.[40]

These stories were more than a little irritating, because Labour's media people were hoping that they had managed to change the negative narrative that had taken hold for a week or so after Osborne's Budget in mid-March. The contents of the Chancellor's speech had been difficult enough for Labour: another increase in the threshold at which people began to pay the basic rate; some good news on beer, bingo, petrol, and potholes; yet more help for the housing market and a new 'garden city' in Ebbsfleet; a totally unexpected liberalization of pension regulation that would massively increase the tax-take from pensioners in return for giving them more control of their nest eggs; and the announcement of an additional cap on welfare spending, which the Labour leadership (without, note, encountering too much trouble from backbenchers) had quickly decided that (like the pensions reform) it had little alternative but to support. However, what had caused even more trouble was Miliband's response—or rather the lack of it. Instead of mounting a devastating attack on what he had just heard (admittedly, never an easy task and one made harder by Osborne apparently breaking with the convention of providing a redacted version an hour in advance), the Labour leader had stuck doggedly to wearily familiar attack lines: bankers, the bedroom tax, cost-of-living crisis, falling real wages, tax cut for millionaires, out-of-touch Etonians—pretty much everything got a look-in.

Journalists could, of course, have decided to praise the Labour leader for showing admirable message discipline on the grounds that it is only when obsessive Westminster-watchers are heartily sick of hearing a soundbite that it stands any chance of being noticed by your average voter. Instead, picking up on the disappointment clearly felt by many of his own MPs, they had put it down to Miliband's inability to recalibrate his party's offer to cope with a resurgent Chancellor and a growing economy. This inevitably prompted 'sources' and 'senior figures' to tell reporters how unhappy they were with how things were going. This duly infuriated those working in the Leader's Office, which, according to an eye-opening despatch from the inside by Steve Richards, had a tendency when things got tricky to hunker down, to tell Ed what he wanted rather than what he needed to hear, and to assume the worst of colleagues.[41]

An ill-timed open letter to the *Guardian* from assorted members of what they themselves referred to 'the progressive community' cautioning Labour against the sort of 'safety-first'/'shrink the offer' strategy associated (rightly or wrongly) with Douglas Alexander did nothing to lighten the atmosphere either.[42] Rather than taking an opportunity to kick Miliband when he was down, those involved were mainly hoping to help screw his courage to the sticking post in what some insisted on caricaturing as a battle between managerialist centralizers like Ed Balls and radical devolutionists like Jon Cruddas and Shadow Care Minister Liz Kendall—or even between 'good' and 'bad' Ed Miliband, the first a passionate believer in a 'bold, imaginative transformative offer', the second a cautious ditherer. Even so, it was damaging, partly because it did reflect a degree of genuine irritation— partly policy driven, partly personal. On the policy front, some of those involved were worried that Miliband might talk about moving towards a multi-level, multi-faceted, more responsive 'relational state' (just as he had in his Hugo Young lecture on public-service reform in early February) but that ultimately it would all come to nothing as electoral and Treasury-driven concerns about control of the public finances trumped any incipient enthusiasm for 'localism' and 'people power'.[43] On the more personal front, Alexander, it transpired, had apparently driven the worthy think-tankers to distraction by sup- posedly helping to send their favourite American organizer, Arnie Graf, back across the pond. According to well-sourced newspaper accounts, there was also little love lost between him and Shadow Cabinet colleagues such as Balls and Dugher.[44] Add to all this the publication of polls that, in addition to suggesting the Budget had been reasonably well received, showed the Tories closing the gap and Osborne's reputation recovering along with the economy, and the 'Labour in crisis' stories practically wrote themselves.

Fortunately, however, the wobble did not last too long. The Tories' post-Budget bounce proved short lived, and the media's interest in any troubles Labour was experiencing was soon overshadowed by the long-drawn-out resignation of Conservative Culture Secretary Maria Miller over her parliamentary expenses. That episode acted as a fire- break that allowed Labour to get on the front foot once again by announcing that it was hiring one of the masterminds behind Barack Obama's campaigns, David Axelrod. Although dismissed by some as a desperate attempt to top the Tories' signing of the Obama campaign's Jim Messina and 'Wizard of Oz' Lynton Crosby, it was, at least potentially, a genuinely important development. Labour had been in touch with Axelrod over the previous year, and he was clearly convinced that there were useful parallels between the strategy being pursued by the party and Obama's stress on needing to ensure any increase in national prosperity delivered on both the desire for security and the aspirations of an increasingly anxious blue- and white-collar middle class, not just the detached super-rich. He was also very much someone who believed in combining any air war with a sophisticated ground game based on long-term mobilization of volunteers at the grass roots, which dovetailed with the Arnie Graf/Movement for Change model that General Secretary Iain McNicol was trying to embed in constituencies. Moreover, Axelrod also believed that it was more possible than many imagined to persuade people who had not voted before or did not normally vote, most obviously the young. Labour was already trying hard to target them, not just by the way it campaigned but through what it was offering. Their concerns played a big part, for instance, in the party's announcement (albeit one marred by a failure properly to secure industry cooperation) that it wanted to limit rent rises and improve security of tenure for the millions of households that relied on the private rented sector.[45]

In any case, the six-figure contract Labour signed was with the firm AKPD Message and Media, which meant Labour would be getting strategic and tactical advice—mainly over teleconferences rather than face-to-face—not just from Axelrod himself but from other progressive campaigners such as Larry Grisolano and Mike Donilon. The AKPD team, even though it would remain based in the USA, was expected to help Labour shape, sharpen, and target its message, even down to single sentences that might encapsulate what it stood for and wanted to do. This was clearly something the Leader's Office had always struggled with and would find even harder as, in the words of one person working there, 'we went from being a narrative-heavy, policy-light party to being a policy-heavy, narrative-light party'. One Nation certainly was not going to do the trick unless, as a brand, it could also communicate a message—just as, for example, 'New Labour' had conveyed a conviction that economic efficiency and social justice should and could go hand in hand. AKPD, it was hoped, might help in the search for such a message, particularly on the economy, an issue that Axelrod insisted must not be ducked, even if Labour currently trailed the Tories on it in opinion polls.

Just as crucially, Axelrod and colleagues would also advise on how to present Miliband to his best advantage in an election in which personal attacks on him in the media were bound to feature heavily. Now that Maria Miller's replacement as Culture Secretary, Sajid Javid, had made it clear that he was relaxed about the majority of newspapers refusing to be bound by the Royal Charter negotiated in the wake of the Leveson Inquiry, there was a clear dividing line on press regulation between the two main parties. If the Conservatives needed help in attacking Labour and its leader, they could be even more sure than ever that they would get it. Some in the party claimed to be unconcerned about this in an era of falling circulation, where even the interested public could bypass traditional sources of information and go straight to blogs, Twitter, and Facebook. They recognized, of course, that newspapers helped set the agenda for other media. Indeed, according to one key figure in Miliband's Office: 'Ed's been interviewed by John Humphrys three times and two of the three times Humphrys has had the *Daily Mail* open next to him . . .' But, as the same figure went on to note: 'We know where the papers are going to be at the next election . . . but we also know that they make bugger-all difference: it's an emperor's new-clothes thing. Politicians consistently overestimate the effect of the print media and underestimate the effect of broadcast media.'

Perhaps if Ed Miliband himself were really convinced by it, instead of being as painfully preoccupied by the newspapers as the next politician, then this might have been a more reassuring argument. Likewise if there were any evidence that he had succeeded in upping his game when it came to television and radio. Any number of painfully awkward encounters in broadcast studios over the previous four years, however, strongly suggested that he had not—one reason why Labour at the beginning of April put out an advert for a new post, 'Head of the Leader's Broadcasting', responsible for 'developing fresh ideas for making the best of Leader of Opposition's brand strengths and communicating his message in broadcast medium'. The fact that it was hoping to pay the successful candidate only £45,000 a year, however, suggested to many in the industry (where high salaries are not uncommon) that the party still failed to grasp quite how serious—and how structural—its media problem was. There had been a lot of criticism among Conservatives of Craig Oliver, who had taken over from Andy Coulson at the head of the Downing Street operation. However, as a former BBC man, he at least knew broadcasting inside out, and any such criticism was mild compared to that directed at Labour's operation. As one insider put it:

I've got an idea. Why don't we appoint three middle-aged, middle-class, white men all from broadsheet newspaper backgrounds—none with broadcast experience—and give them all the same job description and then, just to make it even better, why don't we make sure that two out of the three never speak to each other and the only time they speak about the other is to brief the press about how crap the other is?

This may have been an exaggeration, but it was not just insiders who were concerned. Journalists were just as critical and confused. They knew that Tom Baldwin tended to play rougher and tougher than Bob Roberts. But they were unsure of the division of labour between the two men or quite how Patrick Hennessy's role differed from theirs. And why did so much of their time and attention seem to be directed towards the lobby and next day's headlines rather than devoted to, say, 'rolling the pitch' for big announcements by buttering up expert correspondents and op-ed and leader-writers? What journalists did know, however, at least if they were in television, was that the Tories' top media people—especially those around George Osborne—tended to think in terms of 'pictures first, story second', while their Labour counterparts often gave them nothing that they could hope to use or else gave it to them way too late. Nor was Labour as clued up about the whims and preferences of different shows, meaning that the right politician was not always provided for the right audience. Some of the Shadow Ministers' media people were more of a match for their Tory counterparts—as was Labour's digital team, even if much of its effort, because it went through Facebook rather than Twitter, was less familiar to journalists (for whom the latter is the main social media platform) than it might have been. But the party as a whole could not match the relentless message discipline and overarching narrative provided by CCHQ, which seemed to be able to shoehorn mention of the Tories' 'long-term economic plan' and Labour's lack of competence and trustworthiness into each and every press release and media interview. None of this was exactly encouraging, especially when the results of the local and European elections held on 22 May were expected to provide another tough test for Labour's spinners—and, of course, for the party as a whole.

# 9

# Home Straight:
# Spring–Autumn 2014

It was going to be a long weekend—and not in a good way. Results of the local elections were due in the early hours of the morning of Friday, 23 May. Results of the elections to the European Parliament, however, would not be revealed until after the polling stations closed in other EU member states on Sunday evening. The Labour leadership was not expecting to do particularly well in either contest and had therefore been trying to manage expectations downwards for weeks. Rather than the nearly 500 local government gains that would put it on course for a working majority in 2015, the party was forecasting around 200. In the event, it exceeded its unrealistically pessimistic estimate by well over 100 councillors, but, given that opposition parties traditionally do better the year before a general election than they do at the general election itself, this was far from good news. Rather than building on its performances in previous local contests, Labour had, if anything, slipped backwards. So had UKIP, although in its case very few people noticed because of its stand-out performances in several northern towns (where it could now claim to be the main opposition to Labour) and in Thurrock (number two on Labour's list of target seats). The Conservatives, on the other hand, had improved a little, while the Lib Dems had done slightly better than their opinion poll ratings might have suggested.

There were some consolations. UKIP's performance in the West Midlands, where Labour needed to pick up seats in 2015, was a big worry. But its popularity in the east of England suggested it was still more than capable of costing the Conservatives seats in marginal constituencies that could fall to Labour if the right's support was split. Meanwhile, Labour's own performance in London, where it won control of Merton, Redbridge, and Croydon, was impressive—and made all the more so by it taking the Tories' flagship council Hammersmith and Fulham. There was also some cause for hope, if not outright celebration, in a list of target seats outside the capital: Amber Valley, Bradford East, Burnley, Bury North, Cambridge, Carlisle, Colne Valley, Crawley, Dudley South, Harlow, Hastings, Ipswich, Keighley, Lincoln, Norwich North, Pendle, Peterborough, Plymouth Devonport, Reading West, Swindon South, Warrington South, Weaver Vale, and Wolverhampton South West.

Polling released by Lord Ashcroft in the hiatus between the local government and European elections brought slightly more encouraging news, too.[1] Whatever damage UKIP might be doing to Labour, over half of those who had just voted for it had previously voted Tory, compared to just one in seven who had voted Labour last time round. And, although many of them guessed they might desert Farage at the general election, just as many were adamant that they would stick with him in 2015. Moreover, in a mega poll of marginal seats Labour had an average lead of ten points—twelve if voters were prompted to think about their constituency and the candidates who would be standing there. Although it disguised a good deal of local variation, this was a much bigger lead over the Conservatives than Labour enjoyed in national polls and at the local and European elections. If repeated in 2015, it would see Labour make around eighty gains from the Tories, and, even if it were not, Labour at least looked on course to end up as the largest party in what looked likely to be a hung parliament.

Even those Labour people more inclined to see the glass half-empty than half-full—and who pointed to the possibility that a collapse in the Lib Dem vote might disproportionately benefit the Tories—had to concede that there was little sign in Ashcroft's marginals' polling that the Conservatives were about to open up the five-point lead that, at a minimum, they would need to secure an overall majority. Moreover, nearly half of those polled said they would definitely not vote Tory—considerably more than the 38 per cent who ruled out Labour. This suggested that the party had more potential supporters out there than its main rival if only it could win them over and then mobilize them. Less encouraging, though, was the fact that a quarter of those currently intending to vote Labour said they would consider switching to the Conservatives. On the other hand, the majority of those currently intending to vote Labour were doing so despite the fact that they believed the economy would continue to do well both for the country and for themselves and their families. This suggested that Tories who were confident that a recovery would send them back to Downing Street might well be disappointed. The same went for Tories who were sure the slogan 'Vote Nigel, get Ed' would see many of their former supporters return home: only one in seven voters who had defected to UKIP told pollsters that message might put them off.

The media and MPs being what they are, however, none of this seemed to matter much when the results of the European Parliament elections were finally announced. Labour may have improved by ten percentage points on its miserable performance in 2009, but it had been beaten into second place by UKIP, which had won 27 per cent of the vote. Even more worryingly, perhaps, Labour finished only just ahead of the Conservatives. And, as in the local elections, even this was due mainly to the disproportional success Labour had enjoyed in London. Moreover, research suggested that this owed as much to the party's overwhelming support among ethnic minority voters as to the capital's white British residents being somehow more liberal or tolerant than their counterparts in the provinces.[2] Indeed, as further analysis revealed, Labour was going to have to be careful not simply to double down on its support in ethnically diverse cities and among younger, socially liberal voters, while failing to appeal to 'grittier' constituencies with higher concentrations of less-well-educated and less liberal white working-class voters who were tempted by UKIP, as well as to 'leafier' suburban seats where the Conservatives still had cause for hope.[3] The only good news—although not so good if one believed that the Lib Dems needed to defend at least a few of their seats against Conservative challengers in 2015—was that Nick Clegg's party had finished fifth behind the Greens, losing all but one of its nine MEPs. Come the general election, Labour would therefore be in a very good position to win seats directly from the Lib Dems—a possibility confirmed by an Ashcroft poll of some of them published at the beginning of July, which reported an average swing sufficient to produce seventeen Labour gains if repeated across the board in ten months' time.[4]

More worrying in some ways than the results, however, was the willingness of Labour people to pile in and point the finger at who or what was supposedly responsible for the party's poor performance.

Their lack of restraint stood in marked contrast to the discipline demonstrated by the Tories, who, after all, had just as much to worry about but seemed willing to give Cameron the benefit of the doubt in return for him campaigning against the appointment of Jean-Claude Juncker as President of the European Commission—a campaign Labour wisely decided to back (if not very vociferously) so as not to be branded somehow federalist or unpatriotic. For those Labour MPs who were not prepared to criticize Ed Miliband directly, even anonymously, the men with most to answer for were Michael Dugher and Douglas Alexander. They were said to have run a poor, error-prone campaign that, according to some of the usual suspects who were happy to go on the record, had all but ignored the UKIP threat. The solution to the latter, those critics claimed, was to talk louder and tighten policy on immigration. This was an argument to which some Shadow Cabinet members, including Ed Balls and Andy Burnham, seemed to be attracted but which was immediately dismissed by Tony Blair in one of his rare public interventions on domestic (as opposed to international) politics. The former Prime Minister told the *Today Programme* that such a move would simply confuse Labour's own supporters and would not attract any new support. Shifting right had not done the Tories any good, he pointed out. 'The way to deal with UKIP', he insisted, was 'to stand up and take them on'.[5]

Given that this was exactly what Lib Dem leader Nick Clegg had tried to do during two disastrous television debates he had had with Nigel Farage earlier in the year, the chances of Ed Miliband going quite that far were small. Nevertheless, he did decide to make something of a stand by going straight to Thurrock, where Labour had lost control of the council it had won in 2012, in order to make a speech arguing that, while UKIP voters were 'hardworking people' who 'love our country', its take on Europe and immigration was 'not the answer for our country' and would 'never be Labour's mission or policy under my leadership'. A Labour government, he pledged, 'would have controls when people arrive and leave here . . . tackle the undercutting of wages . . . ensure people in public services speak English and people need to earn their entitlements'. But Labour, he declared, would not 'make false promises, or cut ourselves off from the rest of the world, because it would be bad for Britain'.[6]

If Miliband was hoping that his words would put an end to the matter, he was wrong. For a start, it was not just UKIP but the Tories who had an interest in insisting that Labour was still a soft touch, with George Osborne taking advantage of an interview with the *Sun* (which was campaigning to make immigration a 'red line' in any renegotiation of the country's relationship with the EU) to warn that the 'floodgates' would 'swing back open' if Labour were elected in 2015.[7] And then, of course, there were the internal critics. First out of the traps was the small but dedicated band of Labour Eurosceptics who decided to write an open letter to the *Observer* calling on Miliband to protect the 'communities that the Labour Party was founded to represent' by pledging to slap restrictions on the right of free movement granted to all EU citizens—a call backed by ex-Deputy Leader John Prescott, who seemed increasingly willing to use his *Sunday Mirror* column to offer supposedly helpful advice to his successors. Similar sentiments were reflected in a piece for *Prospect* magazine, by, not altogether surprisingly, John Mann, MP for Bassetlaw.[8]

Possibly more worrying, however, was the intervention of John Denham.[9] Although very much an Ed Miliband loyalist, he had become increasingly concerned—prompted in part by what he was hearing on the doorstep of his Southampton constituency—about Labour's positioning on immigration. Writing on the LabourList blog, Denham began by making the (historically accurate) point that 'there is nothing in Labour history, values or traditions that requires us to be in favour, in principle, of unlimited immigration' and that the Blair government had not operated an 'open-door' policy. He moved on to make the point (a controversial but entirely logical one, given the fact that the UK's points-based system makes no room for low-skilled migrants from outside Europe) that 'many of the EU citizens who are entitled to come here are people we would reject if they came from anywhere else'. Next he made the even more controversial point that 'we should work actively to reduce the number of EU migrants coming to the UK, and move closer to the relationship we have with the rest of the world', reminding readers that this was what Labour's 'current policies—clamping down on dodgy agencies, enforcing minimum wage, requiring apprenticeships, tackling unregulated housing—are designed to do', only 'we are so politically correct we cannot admit that's the aim, even though that's exactly what most of our voters want to hear'. Those voters, he asserted, were not so much racist as bewildered by the pace of change, took a common-sense view that more people coming in put more pressure on scarce public resources (especially when it came to housing), and expected Labour—the party that was supposed to be about fairness and rewarding contribution—to be 'on their side'. Leading the fight to change EU rules would not be easy, but it would be worth it. In any case, those who shared his views, argued, what choice did the party have? Could it really ignore the fact that polls were suggesting that, in voters' eyes at least, immigration had for the first time since the spring of 2008 overtaken the economy as 'the most important issue' facing the country—or the fact that, as official figures released at the end of August confirmed, net migration, despite the government's efforts, was rising rather than falling?

Denham's views were promptly attacked by Labour's liberal progressives—and their opinions had to be taken seriously.[10] Labour, after all, claimed to be devoted to evidence-based policy, and its liberals' views reflected those of many of the NGOs and academics who specialized in migration. It was also alive to the risk that, in trying too hard to appease anti-immigration sentiment, the party would strain voters' credulity at the same time as raising the salience of the concerns that UKIP was so keen to tap into. Moreover, at the end of the day, those concerns were much more prevalent among older, poorer, less-educated voters than among the voters of tomorrow. Was it really worth alienating the latter for the sake of the former, especially if it pushed the party into policies that would undermine one of the few advantages it enjoyed over the Conservatives when it came to appeal-ing to the country's wealth creators—namely, that, as well as keeping Britain in the EU, it would ensure it remained 'open for business' and able to compete in the 'global race for talent'? Whatever the private views of some Shadow Ministers, then, 'the line to take' remained the one faithfully repeated by Denham's successor as Shadow Business Secretary, Chuka Umunna, at a Progress event held the weekend after the European election results had been announced. A Miliband government would act to reduce benefits going to EU migrants. It would also carry out its promises to regulate in order to put the squeeze on employers and landlords trying to exploit cheap labour from abroad, and it would insist on tighter English language requirements. But there was no future or point in Labour trying to 'out-UKIP UKIP', nor was there any question of resiling from the fundamental principle of free movement in the EU.[11]

This official line held when, a week or two later, the Fabian Society gave the media an early steer on research overseen by its Deputy

General Secretary Marcus Roberts, who had actively supported Ed Miliband's leadership campaign but was now deeply concerned by the safety-first mindset at the top of the party and the consequent failure to realize the havoc that multi-party politics might wreak in some key constituencies. The research, conducted with the help of elections expert Ian Warren, who was later taken on full-time by the party, suggested that the electoral threat posed to Labour by the loss of blue-collar votes to UKIP was far more severe than previously imagined—a message reinforced when Ashcroft's pollsters revisited Labour–Conservative marginals in July and when the Fabians eventually published their final report in early October as *Revolt on the Left*.[12] The official—'thus far and no further'—line was not, however, quite the whole story, since the *Sun* was (rather conveniently) given to understand in the second week of June that 'a leaked document from shadow home secretary Yvette Cooper says it is vital people know Labour are "listening to their concerns" . . . The 20-page "immigration campaign pack" was sent out to Labour MPs and candidates last week. It suggests they set up "listening events with constituents" to let them know "Labour's approach to immigration has changed".'[13]

Sadly, at least for those who believed it needed pushing a little harder, that message was almost immediately drowned out—at least in June—by the chorus of criticism that greeted Ed Miliband's decision (*a*) to allow himself to be photographed holding a copy of special World Cup souvenir of the aforementioned tabloid, thereby making a mockery of his boast that he had taken a stand against Rupert Murdoch and at the same time offending seemingly every Labour member on Merseyside, and (*b*) to apologize for his error of judgement, thereby provoking the combined ire and mockery of the very same media outlet he had tried to cosy up to in the first place. Nobody ever explained what on earth Miliband and his team thought they were doing, but suffice to say that, whatever it was, and whoever was responsible (some blamed his Political Secretary Anna Yearley, others his Communications chief Bob Roberts), it did nothing to boost confidence either in him personally or in his operation more generally. In any case, taking part in a tabloid marketing campaign—even if it went smoothly—was no guarantee that said newspaper would subsequently give you an easier ride, as David Cameron, who also agreed to pose for the *Sun*, found when (not for the first or last time) he attempted to 'out-UKIP UKIP' by promising at the end of July to crack down on benefits going to migrants. None of the papers that mattered—including the ('IT'S A MIGRANT COP-OUT') *Sun*—seemed in the least bit interested in Yvette Cooper's claim that the Prime Minister was at last implementing Labour policy, choosing to focus instead on the manifest inadequacy of the new measures and making it clear their belief that nothing significant could happen until the UK either threatened (or went ahead with its threat) to leave the EU. That said, the *Sun* did appear to welcome comments made by Shadow Work and Pensions Secretary Rachel Reeves in an interview with its staff a few days later to the effect that 'it isn't right that somebody who has worked hard all their lives and has contributed to the system is entitled to only the same as somebody who has just come to this country, so we need to look at that. It shouldn't be that you can draw on the system without having contributed.'[14] It was also noted that her remarks chimed with those made by Ed Balls in an interview with the *Telegraph*'s Mary Riddell and James Kirkup in which, after expressing his concern about the rise of UKIP and the need for Labour to address people's concerns about immigration, he argued: 'You shouldn't be free to work in Britain and send back tax credits. You shouldn't be free to come to Britain and be unemployed... What I want is fair movement not free movement. It needs to be fair to people who come and work here, and fair to people in this country.'[15]

All well and good perhaps, but whether it would really help limit UKIP's appeal was another matter. Labour was essentially wielding a penknife against an opponent waving a shotgun. Flirting with the renunciation of one of the EU's fundamental freedoms was unlikely to counter the message conveyed, for example, by a UKIP leaflet from the Heywood and Middleton by-election held on 9 October: while the Tories, it declared, had 'stood idly by as immigration has driven wages down, created housing shortages and made the life of ordinary people tougher every day', Labour had 'betrayed ordinary working people through their love affair with immigration, political correctness and multi-culturalism'—a betrayal 'no more apparent than with the young white working-class girls of Rotherham and Rochdale where rather than upset immigrant communities, years of abuse were ignored and complaints swept under the carpet.' It was provocative stuff—and all the more powerful because, in many voters' eyes, it contained more than a grain of truth. If it did not, then why, they could justifiably ask, was Labour so keen to get rid of South Yorkshire's Police and Crime

Commissioner, former Labour councillor Sean Wright, when he refused to accept responsibility by resigning immediately in the wake of the damning report about Rotherham? In fact, the language used in the leaflet was actually pretty mild in comparison to some of the vitriol thrown at Labour by speakers at UKIP's conference held (quite deliberately) in Doncaster, where Miliband's own constituency was located, ten days before the by-election. This did not, of course, stop one or two of Labour's self-appointed tribunes of the white working class piling in to demand Miliband harden the party's line on immigration after it turned out that it had only beaten UKIP in Heywood and Middleton by a mere 617 votes. Exactly what Messrs Mann and Danczuk thought their leader (presuming they still regarded Miliband as such) could realistically do remained unclear.[16] Trying to qualify the right to free movement of EU citizens, perhaps, or maybe stopping benefits being sent home to families living in other EU countries? If so, both of those measures were already Labour Party policy and had been highlighted not just by Balls and Reeves but by Yvette Cooper, too, most recently in her highly regarded platform speech at Labour's conference in Manchester in late September.

Besides, even if the party could have moved toward an even more restrictive stance (which would have been doubly difficult since Cooper's tough talk was balanced by her decision to commit Labour to scrapping the government's nonsensical net migration target), then who exactly was going to sell it—convincingly anyway—to voters in the seats Labour had to win back in 2015? Certainly, if the polling of them done by ComRes for the BBC was halfway accurate, it was not going to be Labour's new cohort of parliamentary candidates, over half of whom, at least if they were fighting marginal seats, were (according to research by the *Guardian*) former special advisers, party workers, researchers, lobbyists, or ex-MPs.[17] Only 15 per cent of Labour candidates polled by ComRes believed current levels of immigration were too high, while 89 per cent thought EU immigration was a good thing for the country and only 7 per cent reckoned the UK was too generous to immigrants.[18] Voters who disagreed (and it was true, there were many of them) would have seen straight through any attempt to talk tougher on their part. Voters who did not (many of them precisely the kind of ex-Lib Dem supporters whom Labour desperately needed to hold on to) might have turned away in disgust. And, while much was made, quite rightly, of Miliband's stupidly forgetting to include a planned passage on immigration in his own speech in Manchester, it remained true that he (and Cooper and a whole host of other colleagues) had spoken on the subject again and again (and again) since 2010, but all to little or no effect on public opinion—a frustration with which all those who had served as ministers in the Home Office when Labour was in government for thirteen years were all too familiar.[19] In short, while it may have been fair to say (as the astute Labour-supporting journalist John McTernan did say after Heywood and Middleton) that the party needed to talk far more about immigration where it really counted—that is, on the doorstep and in its leaflets—anyone thinking that this would be easy or, indeed, solve the problem was almost certainly mistaken.[20]

Given all this, it was hardly surprising that the Labour leadership remained as keen as ever to change the subject. Since the Conservatives enjoyed big leads on 'the economy' in general and public finances in particular, this left it with basically three options. The first, and most obvious, of these was to press on with its attack on the 'cost of living crisis'—an issue that opinion research and real-world data still suggested resonated with the public in spite of the much-trumpeted return to growth. As such, Labour had absolutely no intention of dropping it, believing (not unreasonably perhaps) that the advice of some pundits that it was a wasting asset said more about their short attention spans and high incomes than it did about its continued relevance to ordinary, rather more hard-pressed voters. Any pick-up in the economy would, Labour knew, eventually result in the kind of 'feelgood factor' that would presumably benefit its rivals. But, as academic research by the team responsible for the British Election Study at the last few elections strongly suggested, there was a considerable time-lag involved—one Labour hoped its efforts might prolong. Moreover, the same research showed that even those voters who were becoming more optimistic, both about their circumstances and about those of the country in general, were not giving the government anything like as much credit for the upturn as it claimed it deserved.[21]

Labour's second option was to try to draw attention to Labour's increasingly ambitious plans for a national growth strategy. Embodied in Andrew Adonis's review and Chuka Umunna's *Agenda 2030*, this was built around a radically decentralized (but nevertheless 'enabling') state and a determined effort both to upskill the UK's workforce and to upgrade its infrastructure. Although it could hardly be described as a 'retail offer' to the average voter, it did have the advantage of being taken seriously by specialist correspondents and commentators and, indeed, by business more generally—not least because many of its recommendations went hand-in-hand with reports prepared for the party by respected business figures such as John Armitt (of the Olympic Delivery Authority), George Cox (former head of the IoD), Bill Grimsey (ex-Wickes), Mike Wright (Jaguar Land Rover), Bill Thomas (ex-Hewlett Packard), Norman Pickavance (ex-Morrisons), and Alan Buckle (KPMG). This respect was something the leadership (and particularly Ed Balls) craved—not so much because of residual nostalgia for the New Labour era (although that was not wholly absent) but because of the damage that the party, in spite of polling that revealed widespread antipathy to big business and the banks, feared might be done to its overall credibility by the drip-drip criticism emanating from high-profile business figures and organizations. It was all very well for Labour to hold a summer gala that raised close to half a million pounds and attracted the support of people from the arts such as Antony Gormley, Jason Isaacs, David Morrissey, Grayson Perry, and Stephen Fry. But the leadership knew that, ultimately, voters were much more likely to pay attention to their employers than to a bunch of entertainers, however worthy.

In this respect, the growth strategy, which also had the advantage of being sold by two politicians (Adonis and Umunna) who were well thought of in commercial circles, sat alongside Labour's continued commitment to EU membership as something that a Miliband government could offer that a Cameron government clearly could not. Whether this would be enough to overcome the antipathy to Labour in business circles was another matter. After all, that antipathy had deep cultural and ideological roots. And it was exacerbated by Labour's new-found enthusiasm for higher taxes on the well-off, by its desire to rein in and regulate big business and the banks, by its talk about reforming zero-hours contracts and employment tribunals, increasing paternity leave and raising the minimum wage, and by its scepticism about outsourcing to a small bunch of large companies that all too often ended up doing exceedingly well out of the government. The impression thus created was not going to be turned around by a single policy, such as Ed Balls's promise to ensure that the UK's corporation tax would remain the lowest in the G7, or by earnest collections of essays like *Owning the Future* edited for Policy Network by Chuka

Umunna.[22] Events like Policy Network's 'Inclusive Prosperity' conference, held at the Science Museum's Imax Theatre in mid-July,
could do no harm. But even then the business-friendly message that
Labour (and Balls in particular) was desperate to project was all too
easily undermined by supposedly sceptical comments made by erstwhile supporters like Lord Sainsbury, the Blairite peer who had once
pointedly described Ed Miliband as 'average'. Nor was the situation
helped by what some (including Labour's former City minister Lord
Myners) saw as the sheer ineptitude of the efforts made by Miliband's
personal operation to help their man win the confidence of a private
sector that refused to be impressed by his neat rhetorical distinctions
between small and big businesses or between being 'pro-business, but
not business as usual'.[23]

Labour's third, and in some ways most obvious, option was to move
the national conversation onto an issue on which it enjoyed a seemingly permanent advantage over its Tory opponent—namely, the
NHS. The evidence that the Health Service was under severe strain
had been mounting throughout 2013 and 2014, with targets for waiting times in Accident and Emergency emerging as a particular problem. Cuts to local authority budgets were also, it seemed, slowing
discharge from hospitals back into the community, particularly of the
ever-growing number of elderly patients, resulting in difficulties in
admitting new patients into those same hospitals and therefore in
cancelled operations—a situation compounded not just by a few
years of tight funding settlements but by the fact that the UK, one of
the world's most efficient healthcare systems, already had far fewer
beds per head of population than the majority of its European counterparts. Waiting times in ambulances, for tests, and for cancer treat-
ment were also rising, and people were finding it harder to get
same-day (and in some cases even same-week) appointments with
their GPs. More and more hospital trusts were running deficits—all
this at a time when the new system of commissioning established by
Andrew Lansley's controversial Health and Social Care Act had contributed to restructuring costs put at some £3 billion. Indeed, so
serious were things getting, both clinically and financially, that what
seems striking in retrospect is how little effort—relatively speaking—
Labour had so far put into exploiting the situation. There was an
extent to which this was driven by a desire to keep the party's powder
dry on an issue that it planned to run hard on as the general election got

closer, as well as the knowledge that people's own experiences and media coverage almost did the job themselves. But the leadership's reticence also owed something to the difficulty it was having in coming up with an answer to the obvious next questions that criticism on its part would provoke—namely, what would Labour do differently and where was it going to magic up the money to pay for it?

The answer to the first had been clear for quite some time. Ever since reassuming the health brief he had held in government in early 2011, Andy Burnham, ably supported by Shadow Care Minister Liz Kendall, had been charting a course towards much closer integration between the NHS and the care system that was currently the responsibility of local authorities, the aim being to provide the 'whole-person care' that had been the subject of an independent report into the issue commissioned by the party from Sir John Oldham.[24] Although this made clinical and, at least in the long term, financial sense, it posed a number of political challenges. The first was convincing people—especially those actually working in health and social care—that a move in this direction would avoid precisely the kind of 'top-down reorganization' that Labour had been so keen to criticize during the passage of the government's highly contentious Act. The other was how to pay for it—a debate that was conducted not only within the confines of the party's official policy review, but also, as advocates of various schemes tried their best to build support for them, through the media.

Burnham himself was widely known to be more open than his colleagues to some sort of levy on estates—an idea that the Tories had destroyed as a 'death tax' before it even got off the ground before the previous election and would pounce on again given the slightest opportunity. The second alternative, which was not seen as much more palatable given Labour's stress on easing the cost of living, was some form of earmarked NHS tax, the easiest option (and the most progressive one if ceilings were raised or abolished) being to use National Insurance contributions. This was the solution for which the high-profile backbencher Frank Field was publicly campaigning. It was also one that held considerable attraction for those who believed that Labour needed to combine the proverbial 'bold, transformative offer' with the equally proverbial 'economic credibility': former Number Ten adviser Patrick Diamond, for example, made a strong case in the media for a 'hypothecated insurance fund' on exactly those grounds.[25] Polling on whether the public would be prepared to pay more, however, was mixed. Results varied according to how the question was phrased, and was certainly nowhere near solid enough to reassure those old enough to remember the 1980s and early 1990s, when widespread concern about the NHS did not translate into a willingness to fork out extra to save it, particularly when there were doubts about whether additional funding would be spent wisely.[26]

The third alternative was to hope that the 'zero-based' spending review that Labour had promised to conduct once in power (and Shadow Chief Secretary to the Treasury Chris Leslie was beginning to work on even in opposition) would identify savings in other departments that could be switched to Health. This seemed like a long shot and anyway was not something that could be done with the kind of precision that would be required if the promises thus made were to survive the scrutiny to which they were bound to be subjected during an election campaign. The fourth alternative was simply to muddle through and join the Coalition parties in pretending that, as long as current spending on the NHS were maintained and protected, then, despite the fact that its annual cost of £95 billion was forecast to rise to nearer £130 billion by 2020, somehow everything would be fine. The fifth and final alternative—basically no more than a pledge-card-style twist on the fourth option—was to do little or nothing to plug the yawning funding gap but instead offer a symbolic improvement in provision paid for by a raid not on the general public but on a group or groups that most people (especially Labour supporters and those who had deserted the Lib Dems in 2010) would agree could well afford it.

This last alternative was the one the leadership eventually chose, with Ed Miliband announcing in his conference speech (unfortunately to no one's surprise, since it had accidentally leaked the previous evening) that Labour would fund 20,000 more nurses, 8,000 more GPs, 5,000 more care workers, and 3,000 more midwives via a levy on tobacco companies, a clampdown on tax avoiders, and a mansion tax on properties worth more than £2 million—the latter the cause of such concern among the party's London MPs (and particularly those who were thinking of running for the Mayoralty) that it required a clarification (though not a complete climb-down) by Balls a few weeks later.[27]

Miliband's decision to announce the so-called 'time to care' package himself may have marked something of a slap-down for Andy

Burnham. Some in the leadership believed that the Shadow Health Secretary's much grander plans for the NHS had as much to do with him enhancing his own reputation in preparation for another crack at the top job as it did with a genuine desire for fundamental reform—a degree of cynicism bordering on paranoia that Burnham's bravura conference speech delivered the day after Miliband's own distinctly underwhelming effort did nothing to calm. In fact, though, the policy was more a testament to the enduring power of New Labour and its belief that the party could have it both ways so long as it could come up with a sufficiently clever gimmick to sell whatever it was doing—not necessarily a mistaken assumption, given the overwhelmingly positive response (72 per cent support according to Survation) to the idea by voters across the board.[28] It was also evidence of the power now wielded behind the scenes by a Shadow Chancellor determined above all to demonstrate that Labour's sums supposedly added up. Given that what was being suggested on the NHS was manifestly inadequate to the task at hand, they clearly did not. The obvious retort was that Labour had no more to apologize for than the Tories or the Lib Dems in this respect: Clegg's conference plea to make mental health a priority and Cameron's promise to carry on 'ring-fencing' NHS spending, backed up by another reminder that his family had relied on the service to treat his severely disabled son, were arguably just as disingenuous. What Clegg and Cameron were not, however, was stupid. Neither wanted an election dominated by the NHS and were certain to spend money that the UK supposedly could not afford in order to avoid the kind of 'winter crisis' that would play straight into Labour's hands. Moreover, they were bound to make a virtue of necessity by trumpeting any additional funding in order to show just how much they cared.

In some ways, Miliband's announcement on the NHS put Labour's supposedly inclusive policy process, the culmination of which was the NPF, involving 198 delegates meeting over the weekend of 18–20 July, squarely into perspective. In terms of preserving party unity and ensuring that the membership and the unions bought into the broad direction of party policy, it had been an impressive exercise, even if it remained bewilderingly and sometimes frustratingly unclear to many (even some frontbenchers involved) quite how its conclusions would be married together with the work done by Shadow Teams. Obviously some hard bargaining went on; but, compared to the 2008 equivalent at Warwick, all was sweetness and light. This was thanks in no small part to the effort put in not just by the Leader's Office and by Jon Cruddas (and his chief of staff, Jonathan Rutherford) but by Angela Eagle. As Chair of the NEC, her work behind the scenes to connect and reconcile people was for the most part unsung outside the party but it was nevertheless vital—especially because, now that CLP delegates were elected by OMOV rather than by delegates to the annual conference, a majority for the leadership and the unions (which had thirty delegates between them) was by no means baked in. However, the NPF was by no means the only game in town when it came to policy-making, since Shadow Cabinet Ministers, as long as they had the approval of the leadership, were apparently free to pre-empt it by announcing policy in their area, an obvious example being Tristram Hunt's release at the end of April of a blueprint for policing school standards, which the *Guardian*, perhaps a little breathlessly, called 'the most important statement on Labour education policy for 10 years'.[29]

Nor, it seemed, was the NPF going to be able to lock the leadership into the kind of 'bold, transformative offer' that Cruddas and others had been rooting for, the spirit of which was nicely captured in the pamphlet *One Nation: Labour's Political Renewal* published in September.[30] Instead, at least when it came to what Labour would try to emphasize in the run-up to the election, Miliband and his colleagues— be they politicians such as Douglas Alexander and Ed Balls or staffers such as Spencer Livermore and Torsten Bell—seemed to be reverting to Brownite type. On the one hand, this meant subtly shrinking promises so as to avoid hostages to fortune and accusations of profligacy: for instance, the target of an additional 200,000 homes built every year was now to be reached only by 2020 and achieved mainly through supply-side measures, while Balls (without many people noticing) announced he would not borrow additional funds in order to finance capital investment. On the other, it meant opting for what the *Guardian*'s Patrick Wintour neatly summed up as 'a collation of small-bore policy goodies' that could be put on a pledge card rather than made part of a coherent narrative and a bigger, more inspiring story.[31]

To those paying sufficient attention, this was all of a piece with their muted reaction to the much-trumpeted tome from IPPR on *The Condition of Britain*, which had been launched, by Miliband himself, in a charity arts centre in Shoreditch a month before the NPF met in Milton Keynes.[32] Despite the hype—the report had been billed as something approaching both a blueprint and (as the *Observer*'s Toby Helm put it) 'a bible on how to reinvigorate social democracy in an age of austerity'—it was immediately apparent that Labour was not, in fact, rushing to adopt it wholesale.[33] Much had been made over the last year, for instance, of the possibility that the party would make investment in universal, affordable childcare for pre-schoolers a flagship policy, not least because one of Miliband's former aides, Lucy Powell, was now in charge of the brief. However, even though the idea was a major thrust of IPPR's report and recommendations, the leadership now seemed to have cooled on it—at least in the short term. Indeed, the policy that Labour's media team decided to sell hardest at the launch was a proposal to replace jobseeker's allowance currently paid to unemployed 18–21 year olds with a means-tested payment funded by reducing the tax-free take from well-endowed pension pots and made conditional on the recipients undertaking further training. And it was not only cynical observers who sensed that the cherry-picking of that particular measure had more to do with the party's ongoing attempt to match the Tories as tough on welfare as it did with pointing the way to the sunlit uplands of national renewal. A few days later Jon Cruddas himself was recorded at what he thought was a private meeting bemoaning the fact that IPPR's report (with which he had been intimately involved) had been deliberately condensed into 'a punitive hit on 18 to 21-year-olds', as well as the fact that 'instrumentalised, cynical nuggets of policy' designed 'to chime with our focus groups and our press strategies and our desire for a top line in terms of the 24-hour media cycle' seemed destined to 'dominate and crowd out any innovation or creativity'. Anything more radical, he complained, had been 'parked, just parked' by what he called 'a profound dead hand at the centre'.[34]

Whether it was down to that dead hand or else the buy-in Cruddas himself had worked so hard to achieve is impossible to tell, but July's NPF was characterized not by showdowns or shenanigans but by loyal toeing of the leadership's (surely somewhat misleading) line that, in straitened circumstances, Labour had to be about 'big reform, not big spending'. Indeed, when a vote was forced on the decision to accept the Coalition's spending plans for 2015/16, the leadership won it by 125 votes to 14. Trident renewal did not even go to a vote. And even the issue that looked at one stage as if it might cause a bit of a headache—rail renationalization—was resolved by a compromise that would see public-sector and not-for-profit bidders compete with private companies whenever franchises came up for renewal. That said, even if Milton Keynes had somehow produced more in the way of drama, it seems highly unlikely that anyone would have noticed. Labour's spinners seemed keen to keep it all pretty low key—another reason why some questioned quite how invested the leadership now was in a big, bold, Cruddas-style offer. In any case, the headlines were dominated by news of the shooting-down of a Malaysian Airlines passenger jet by pro-Russian rebels in Eastern Ukraine, killing everyone—including several British citizens—on board. But, even for those more concerned with domestic politics, there were other, possibly more important things to think about, not least, in Labour's case, the Scottish referendum due in a couple of months' time on 18 September.

To say that Labour had been complacent about a 'No' vote would be unfair—but not unduly so. True, in order to assist a Scottish machine that was not what it once was, the party had dispatched both Douglas Alexander (to no great acclaim, especially after a widely panned campaign broadcast for which he was supposedly responsible) and Jim Murphy (who fared much better, especially after taking to the streets with a couple of *Irn Bru* crates). Yet, it was hard to escape the conclusion that the leadership had been lulled into a potentially false sense of security by opinion polls that consistently gave 'Better Together'—the cross-party campaign led by former Chancellor Alistair Darling—a comfortable margin over 'Yes', spearheaded by the SNP's Alex Salmond. As a result, although many of the party's Scottish MPs had been working assiduously to help preserve a union that in 2010 had afforded Labour some forty-one out of fifty-nine Scottish seats at Westminster, they were left by London pretty much to get on with it.

There was some coordination with the efforts of the party's MSPs, but it was highly variable, and there were often quite profound differences not just over tactics but over substantive issues—most obviously, perhaps, the role that the switching of income tax from London to Edinburgh should play in any promises of further devolution made to voters. Ed Miliband and the odd Cabinet Minister had made occasional speeches, most of them designed to remind people of the risks posed by going it alone and to convince Labour voters that they should not make the mistake of voting 'Yes' simply in order to get rid of the Coalition—something they would be able to do, ran the argument, pretty soon anyway. Ed Balls had also decided to join his opponents, George Osborne and Danny Alexander, in a coordinated attack in February on the SNP's assurances that an independent Scotland would be able to carry on using the pound sterling. Some Labour people feared this attack might produce a backlash, but it was generally felt to have done its job—namely, to add to fears that a 'Yes' vote was a risky decision. Not everyone, however, was happy with the way things were going—including Gordon Brown, who, after authoring a well-reviewed book, *My Scotland, Our Britain*, issued a public warning at the beginning of June that a campaign that he considered both negative and patronizing was driving voters into the nationalists' hands.[35]

At least initially, Brown's rumblings were dismissed, not least by former colleagues, as 'Gordon being Gordon'—understandable, perhaps, given a YouGov poll in the second week of August that, just as it had in June, put 'No' at least twenty points ahead of 'Yes'.[36] The decision to focus on the concerns of undecided voters about the economic consequences of independence and the ambivalence felt towards Alec Salmond himself, especially among women, may not have been particularly edifying, but it looked like being highly effective By the end of August, however, and following a much more combative performance by Salmond in the second of his two televised debates with Alistair Darling, nerves were beginning to fray a little, and, at a rally in Dundee, Brown was invited to share a stage with his former Chancellor for the first time. When, a few days later, YouGov recorded the gap between the two sides as having shrunk to just six points, something approaching panic hit the party, not least because the same poll appeared to show a big shift in support among its own supporters.[37] Miliband made a previously unplanned appearance in Lanarkshire to give a speech that appeared to contravene the non-aggression pact between the unionist parties by claiming that Ruth Davidson, the Scottish Conservatives leader, had all but admitted the UK party was not going to win the next general election, allowing him to assure 'his' voters that 'these Tories can be beaten. A Labour government is within our grasp.'[38] Behind the scenes, the word went out to English and Welsh Labour MPs to get up to Scotland and do whatever they could, starting with reminding anyone who would listen that only a couple of the SNP's MPs had turned up to help defeat the Conservatives on a Private Member's Bill promising to dilute the bedroom tax—the one welfare change by the government that Labour had rapidly made up its mind had to be resisted and that it seemed to have persuaded the country against. The party also confirmed that in a few days' time Ed Miliband would be appearing on the same platform as Brown for the first time since he became leader.

To those worried that the last thing Miliband needed was to be associated and, even worse, outshone by a discredited blast from the past, this move might have appeared unnecessarily desperate. Until, that is, a YouGov poll on 7 September suddenly gave the 'Yes' side a two-point lead over 'No'—a bombshell that prompted Brown, with the eventual blessing of Cameron, Clegg, and Miliband (who later jointly published a last-gasp 'vow' to Scotland) to declare that proposals for 'home rule' would be presented to parliament by Burns Night, 25 January 2015.[39] The former Prime Minister then followed up with an evangelical defence of the union in an eve-of-poll speech that not only became a minor sensation on YouTube but left even some of his critics breathless in their admiration. No such luck for Miliband, who suffered the indignity of being bundled out of a shopping mall by minders for his own protection when the crowd turned ugly—not a good look, especially on the evening news bulletins, for a man already routinely dismissed as weak in focus groups and opinion polls alike. At least, however, Miliband could console himself with the fact that most surveys seemed to indicate that the 'No' side was back in the lead and heading for the victory that those at its heart, like its manager, Labour's Blair McDougall, had always anticipated.[40] So, when the result became obvious in the early hours of Friday, 19 September, it came as more of a relief than a surprise.

The same, however, could not be said for what happened next. David Cameron knew that he was not going to go down as the leader who lost Scotland. But he was now under pressure from colleagues who felt he had been too willing to give away what one minister called 'financial party bags' to the Scots in order to persuade them to stay. As he began making a statement in Downing Street just after 7 a.m., it quickly became apparent that, rather than issue a clarion call for national unity, he had decided to pull a fast one. The government would keep its promise to Scotland, but it was also time to hear 'the voices of millions of English people' and in particular to clear up the anomaly (known as the 'West Lothian Question') whereby Scottish MPs could vote on legislation on matters that affected the other parts of the union when MPs who represented the countries affected had no equivalent say on the same matters in Scotland. The most obvious solution (albeit one that constitutional experts like Cameron's old Oxford tutor Vernon Bogdanor soon pointed out was fraught with problems) was English Votes for English Laws (EVEL)—in other words, barring Scottish MPs voting at Westminster on legislation that supposedly did not affect their constituents since the matters it covered were, in Scotland, the sole responsibility of the Holyrood parliament.[41] The consequences for Labour if this were to happen were, of course, potentially catastrophic. The party would do well to win in the UK as a whole in 2015 but the chances of it winning in England were very slim indeed. If EVEL were in operation, it faced the prospect of trying to run a government—perhaps even a majority government—that would find it impossible to pass legislation on, say, health, education, and even taxation. On a more personal level, it would be incredibly difficult to hand Scottish MPs UK ministerial responsibility for any portfolio covering issues that had been devolved to the Scottish Parliament. None of this could hide the fact, however, that defending the status quo—or pretending that the anomaly at its heart could be resolved by the kind of devolution to cities and regions that Labour was currently contemplating—essentially meant defending the indefensible.

Yet this was essentially what Labour found itself doing for several hours on the morning of the 19 September—until, that is, the leadership managed to cobble together a commitment to some sort of constitutional convention to be held (surprise, surprise, said its opponents) after the general election. There were excuses aplenty, of course. Everyone—including the Director of Policy and Rebuttal Torsten Bell—had been so focused on making sure the referendum went the right way in Scotland that they had not had a moment to think about anything else. David Cameron had never once mentioned it in talks he held during the campaign with Ed Miliband, who, after all, was spending every waking hour touring Scotland or writing his conference speech. And who could possibly have guessed that the Tory leader would (as his Labour opponents saw it anyway) demean the office of prime minister by acting in such a cold, calculating, and partisan manner, even going so far, initially anyway, as to suggest that the vow made to Scotland could be honoured only 'in tandem' with settling the English question?

But those excuses were pathetic. For one thing, there were MPs and left-leaning think tanks, most notably John Denham and IPPR, who had been warning for years that the English question was getting more and more pressing.[42] For another, EVEL had featured in the last three Tory manifestos and had been extensively debated by the McKay Commission into 'how the House of Commons might deal with legislation which affects only part of the United Kingdom, following the devolution of certain legislative powers to the Scottish Parliament, the Northern Ireland Assembly and the National Assembly for Wales', which had reported in March 2013.[43] More to the point, anyone reading the newspapers on the day before the vote and on the day itself would have seen numerous reports that this was exactly what the Conservatives were intending to do. And, even had they not, the leadership should, long before then, have tasked someone to game the 'what ifs' and the 'what nexts'. Indeed, a variety of people at a variety of levels had brought up the need to do exactly that. Somehow, however, it had never got done. Understandable perhaps—it is easy to forget, especially in hindsight, quite how much political parties have on their plates—but unforgivable all the same.

Miliband was genuinely furious at what Cameron had done. His argument that EVEL, as he put it in a television interview, was a simplistic, 'back-of-the-envelope, fag-packet' solution to a complex conundrum of multi-level governance was equally genuine. However, while it may have convinced the constitutional *cognoscenti*, it was immediately obvious that it was going to struggle in the court of public opinion. As both polling and Miliband's embarrassingly evasive appearance on the BBC's flagship *Andrew Marr Show* demonstrated, the simple logic of EVEL was all-but-unanswerable.[44] Rejecting it was tantamount to admitting that Labour would not be able to win in England, where 84 per cent of the UK population lived and where Labour had captured more seats than the Tories in all the elections it had won with a convincing majority in the post-war period. It also made the party look every bit as nakedly partisan as its opponents—for the simple reason that it was. The alternative that Miliband eventually proposed after a few hours of frantic phone calls and embarrassing radio (and TV) silence—some sort of constitutional convention—might perhaps have afforded sufficient cover, especially if it had been sold as a democratic, people-powered initiative in contrast to some sort of stitch-up in a smoke-filled room in Westminster. But that could only have happened had Labour been smart enough to introduce the idea before rather than after Cameron had seized the initiative—and only if it had avoided throwing in a load of foreign-sounding nonsense about 'a Senate of the Nations and Regions' for good measure.

Still, Labour was now stuck with the idea—and with its 'see no EVEL, hear no EVEL, speak no EVEL' stance—ensuring that Cameron's chutzpah, and his proposal, would not only dominate the first day or two of Labour's conference in Manchester but provide a stick with which he could beat Miliband whenever he felt like it between now and the general election. It was also possible that Cameron's flirtation with the idea of making home rule for Scotland conditional on a settlement in England might, notwithstanding the fact that it was quickly rejected by Nick Clegg, lead Labour supporters north of the border to suspect they had be tricked, driving them to vote SNP in the general election and making it even harder for Labour to win in May 2015. As it was, the referendum campaign itself had driven up support for the Nationalists and had apparently seen them treble their membership: indeed if the figures were correct, then the SNP now had six members for every one who belonged to the Scottish Labour Party.[45] All this raised the possibility that the party's meagre resources would be needed to defend previously impregnable seats rather than being employed in the marginals—one that later became horribly real when, in the wake of Johann Lamont's embittered resignation as Labour's leader in Scotland in October, polls suddenly showed Labour facing something close to electoral meltdown north of the border.[46]

That said, Labour strategists—before that shocking news at least—were not completely disconsolate. Just as they had been forced to acknowledge earlier in the year, when Miliband had tried and failed to skewer Cameron over the criminal conviction of his former Director of Communications Andy Coulson, the Conservatives seemed not to realize that English home rule, while no doubt fascinating to politicos inside the Westminster bubble, was of little interest to most ordinary voters out in the country. As with Europe, it was perfectly possible for pollsters to elicit some pretty strong responses on the English question without it making a significant impact on people's decisions about which way to vote at a general election. And, as with

Europe, all the time the Tories spent talking about EVEL was time not spent talking about the bread-and-butter issues (the economy, public services, and maybe immigration) that probably did decide elections—one reason why the Labour leadership took the decision in mid-October simply to boycott the 'talks' on the subject offered by William Hague. Labour could also take some comfort in the fact that the last couple of weeks of the referendum campaign suggested that its much-vaunted ground game really could make a difference once it cranked into gear. This was important. Behind the scenes, the party, although it would have struggled without the £6.9 million Short Money it received from the state every year, had achieved big cost savings. The annual report it issued in the summer of 2014 showed its net liabilities now stood at £2.6 million (down from £24.5 million in 2006) and were on course to be eliminated by 2016; meanwhile its annual surplus was £5.5 million compared to £1.8 million for the Tories and just £228,000 for the Lib Dems.[47] This was achieved, however, as part of a programme that had seen the party switch resources away from London (and away from direct mail and expensive poster campaigns) and spend money instead on regional field operations and on recruiting and training paid organizers at constituency level. It had also spent heavily on digital—with the latter playing a big part in leveraging the efforts of the former, and vice versa. And, while the community-organizing model championed by Arnie Graf may have attracted a degree of scepticism in some quarters, it had actually done a great deal to inform and energize the way the party worked on the ground to build up its banks of contacts and volunteers.

While it remained true, then, that Labour was likely to be outspent by the Conservatives, both at a national and a local level, its professional staff and indeed many of its MPs and candidates who had first-hand experience of canvassing remained hopeful that it could compete. That said, there remained more than a degree of scepticism about the political operation of the campaign. In early July, its nominal head, Douglas Alexander, announced that frontbenchers Gloria De Piero, Jonathan Ashworth, and Toby Perkins were being added to the campaign team and would be 'liaising with prospective parliamentary candidates, maximizing performance from field operations, and broadcast'. While the three MPs concerned were generally well thought of, the move did not fill everyone with optimism: according to many insiders, it was hard enough to know who was in charge and who was supposed to be doing what already; was expanding the team really going to make things better?

Exactly the same complaints were made about the Leader's Office and about the party's media operation, and were often picked up by journalists. A column penned by Isabel Hardman in July summed up the concerns:

The trio [of Tom Baldwin, Bob Roberts, and Patrick Hennessy] might be impressive individually, but just as three good chefs can spoil a broth if they try to make it together, the three spinners have very different approaches... These three former journalists do not get along particularly well, and have been known to blame one another for party mishaps—or at least to distance themselves from initiatives they disagreed with after they bombed... It's not just the press operation: the same happens in Miliband's private office. There is always someone else to blame, and never an attempt to ask whether it's the team itself that's making a mess of things.[48]

These criticisms of Miliband's press and personal operation subsided a little over the summer. Indeed, there was a degree of praise offered for the way Shadow Cabinet Ministers were lined up to make a series of speeches billed us a 'summer offensive'. Stressing the tangible improvements the party was offering and delivered by media-friendly frontbenchers such as Tristram Hunt, Liz Kendall, Emma Reynolds, Mary Creagh, and Caroline Flint, they were designed to highlight what Labour insisted on calling 'The Choice' at the next election. They were designed, too, to show (along with a bunch of morale-boosting 'Seaside Express' trips to coastal marginals led by Gloria De Piero and Jon Ashworth) that the leadership was not going to let things slide in the way that it had so obviously done the previous August. However, the criticism was renewed, and if anything grew even louder, in the wake of the Labour Party Conference, which began a couple of days after the result of the Scottish vote was declared.

Many of those who travelled to Manchester were exhausted from the effort they had put into the referendum campaign. They had also been thrown off balance by David Cameron's post-referendum demand for English Votes for English Laws. But they were plunged further into gloom when Ed Miliband's attempt to repeat his signature no-notes trick saw him forget to mention, of all things, the deficit and immigration in his leader's speech. The speech was, in any case, a mediocre mishmash of largely reheated policy announcements and cringeworthy references to real people designed both to dramatize Miliband's 'together we can'/'six-point plan' message and to show he was in touch with the 'working people' Labour was clearly homing in on. Fortunately, however, when chopped into soundbites for the evening news on television, it looked and sounded better than it had in the hall, and both focus groups and polling suggested the policies it showcased were popular with the public.[49] Equally fortunately for Labour, what with the US beginning air strikes on the Islamic State (which Miliband agreed the UK should participate in as long as they were confined to Iraq) and the conviction of a former Radio 1 DJ for historic sex offences, it was an unusually busy news day. Less fortunately, the fact that Labour's press operation contrived to put out copies of the speech as it was supposed to be delivered rather than as it actually had been delivered meant that Miliband forgetting to mention the deficit became a big story the next day and, worse still, something that the Tories would be able to mention again and again in the course of what promised to be one of the longest election campaigns in British political history. It was clear that the party's new broadcast head, Matthew Laza, a former Labour Students activist who had gone on to become a producer on the BBC's *Politics Show* and (perhaps suitably, given Miliband's continued focus on the cost of living) *Rip-Off Britain*, was going have his work cut out.

To make things worse, Miliband's dire speech contrasted poorly with Cameron's address to the Conservative Party Conference in Birmingham a week later. The Prime Minister was, if anything, under even more pressure than the Labour leader, having by this stage lost two of his MPs to UKIP. He nevertheless produced one of his best performances, as did George Osborne, who, by announcing further cuts and freezes in benefits in order to free up money for the tax cuts floated by Cameron, was clearly determined to continue the dividing lines he had established earlier on in the parliament. But even if the the Prime Minister and the Chancellor had not had a good week, Miliband would still have had to cope with the fact that he had been shown up in Manchester by two of his own colleagues who were widely rumoured to be positioning themselves for a crack at the top job if it were to fall vacant. Both Andy Burnham and Yvette Cooper had made highly effective speeches, notwithstanding the insistence by the Leader's Office that Shadow Cabinet Ministers should keep their speeches brief—an edict that many felt smacked not just of control freakery but of a degree of paranoia about Miliband being upstaged. This, plus the narrowness of the party's victory over UKIP in Middleton and Heywood and the fact that the Tories temporarily took a lead over Labour in opinion polls, prompted his critics to go even further than they had before.

To those who were happy to speak (anonymously of course) to journalists like *The Times*'s Sam Coates, this was all of a piece with the 'dysfunctional' and 'chaotic' operation that was the Leader's Office.[50] According to one of them: 'The office has been fucked from the start and still is. No one has been able to bring any semblance of order.' Worse, particular people were singled out for criticism. Chief of Staff Tim Livesey was one of them: 'For someone to arrive in that job not knowing anything about the Labour Party and the way politicians work, having never worked in parliament either, is ... a massive disadvantage. I don't think he's ever overcome it. Also, I think he's a massive pussy.' Campaign Director Spencer Livermore was supposedly not a fan of Livesey's either and may even have been after his job. Another problem, apparently, was Miliband's Political Secretary Anna Yearley, who, according to Coates, was seen as 'divisive, playing up to the Labour leader's love of gossip'. And then there was Douglas Alexander, 'whose clipped style sparks strong emotions among colleagues yet who is treated with almost brotherly respect by Mr Miliband' and who was said to be 'barely speaking' to Chris Bryant, the frontbencher responsible for by-elections. Nor did Miliband himself escape criticism, even if, by emphasizing that his closest counsellors were Oxford academics and that it was maddeningly difficult to get a decision out of him, that criticism ran along very familiar lines.

Whether all this was payback for rumours flying around in mid-October that Miliband was desperate to get rid of Ed Balls as Shadow Chancellor, who can say? It is hard to believe that Labour's leader had never considered the possibility. After all, the party seemed to be slipping even further behind the Tories on the economy: for instance, when YouGov polled voters in the wake of the Tory Conference, 28 per cent of people expected to be better off and 37 per cent worse off if the Conservatives were to win in 2015; if Labour were to win, only 17 per cent expected to be better off and 42 per cent worse off.[51] And Miliband could certainly have done with a game-changer—and maybe even a scapegoat. Certainly, it would have been in Balls's interest to get the rumours out into the open, forcing Miliband's office to issue a denial from which there was then no escaping. Whatever, the Labour leader was neither decisive enough, nor strong enough, to do the deed—one that would (unless Miliband really had wanted blood on the carpet) almost certainly have required Balls's wife, Yvette Cooper, to consent to a straight swap. Instead, he opted for a mini-reshuffle that was barely noticed save for the return of the Blairite former minister Pat McFadden as Shadow Minister for Europe. The appointment of the latter suggested that the leadership, notwithstanding the Tories' bluster on limiting the influence of the European Court of Human Rights and standing up to the EU, believed Labour's pro-European position could be turned from a potential liability into a useful asset. Just as importantly, however, it also suggested that not all those initially unimpressed by Miliband had given up hope that the party he led could nevertheless make it back into Downing Street in 2015.

# Conclusion: Mission Accomplished?

One term opposition is a tough job, but that is my task. That's my mission. I'm confident and optimistic, but it's a tough ask.

Ed Miliband, *Daily Telegraph*, 24 March 2012

There is nothing like polling to put politics into perspective—as long, that is, as you read the small print. Labour supporters depressed by their leader's poor performance at the party's 2014 conference in Manchester might have been plunged even further into despair when they learned that more than three times as many people polled by Lord Ashcroft a couple of weeks later recalled that Miliband had forgotten to mention the deficit than recalled Labour had been talking about the NHS. But if they had looked a little more closely they would have seen that those who remembered his slip-up made up just 15 per cent of those surveyed. An even closer look would have revealed that only 20 per cent of respondents—just one in five—had even noticed that Labour had held a conference at all.[1] Such events, then, inasmuch as they impact at all on most of us, seem merely to confirm rather than transform our impressions of the parties competing for our favours—impressions that are based on deep-seated brand images and on political leaders for whom we have increasingly little time. How much those parties and those leaders can actually do to affect their fate is therefore pretty questionable. Indeed, one of the most perceptive members of the guild charged with observing and commenting on their activities at close quarters, Janan Ganesh, even goes so far as to assert: 'The first law of politics is that almost nothing matters. Voters barely notice, much less are they moved by, the events, speeches, tactics, campaigns or even strategies that are ultimately aimed at them. Elections are largely determined by a few fundamentals . . . The role of human agency is not trivial, but it is rarely decisive either.'[2]

He could well be right; but his use of the word 'almost' is important. Tracing and analysing human agency remains a worthwhile pursuit—not simply because some of us find it intrinsically compelling but because it may yet make a material difference to electoral outcomes that ultimately affect the lives and life chances of literally millions of people. Trying to work out what counts and what does not is all the more fascinating because of the sheer uncertainty involved. One of the pioneers of American retailing, John Wanamaker, is reputed to have observed: 'Half the money I spend on advertising is wasted; the trouble is I don't know which half.' The same applies to the effort put into politics both by those intimately involved in it and by those trying to understand what they do from the outside in.

For all that it has done since 2010, Labour is still seen by voters as the party that, leaving aside its tendency to be too soft on scroungers, immigrants, and recipients of overseas aid, has its heart in the right place but that is none too good with money. Spending on front-line services would, they believe, be better protected by a Labour administration than by a Conservative government, but at the cost of higher taxes and borrowing. That this is the mirror image of the Tory brand is neatly captured by a YouGov survey from June 2014 that found that 48 per cent of respondents said Labour was 'nice', against 26 per cent who said the same about the Tories. When, however, it came to being 'smart', some 40 per cent thought the label applied to the Tories but only 20 per cent thought it applied to Labour. Partly as a result, and partly because the common sense surrounding the need to 'balance the nation's books' is so powerful, voters were also inclined to believe that government cuts, even if only 19 per cent thought they had been handled fairly, were not just necessary (by a ratio of 54:28) but (by 44:37) good rather than bad for the economy. Asked who they most trusted to run it, Cameron and Osborne beat Miliband and Balls every single time.[3]

Yet none of this was necessarily inevitable. For most of its time in government between 1997 and 2010 Labour had enjoyed huge leads over the Conservatives on economic competence. Clearly, that had

been insufficient to shift its historic disadvantage on the issue, especially in the wake of the crash—partly, perhaps (as commentators like
Polly Toynbee have long argued), because Blair and Brown never
really dared, as Margaret Thatcher dared, to use their time in office to
undermine the prevailing consensus, choosing instead to practise social
democracy by stealth rather than trumpet it from the rooftops.[4] Yet the
party might still have rescued something from the wreckage had Ed
Miliband not been so desperate to distance himself from New Labour
that he effectively threw out the baby with the Blairite/Brownite
bathwater. Alternatively, had Miliband's decision to forgo a robust
defence of Labour's record been part of a thoroughgoing effort to
'concede and move on' by admitting that it had indeed spent and
borrowed too freely—and had he insisted that his Shadow Chancellor,
Ed Balls, do the same—then the party might have earned a little more
credit from a sceptical electorate when, eventually, it did manage to
come up with some specific (if largely symbolic) measures to cut the
deficit. It may even have been the case that being more open about
Blair's and Brown's mistakes, in particular their willingness to borrow
even in the good times, would have allowed Labour's leader to recall
their very real achievements more easily. It might also have provided a
more solid foundation of credibility from which to present what
Labour wanted to offer the electorate in 2015. Indeed, it might have
allowed that offer to be bigger and bolder, in much the same way as the
Tories, after four-and-a-half years of banging on (if not actually doing
that much) about the deficit, were able to dangle the possibility of
£7.2 billion's worth of unfunded tax cuts in front of voters at their
2014 conference without being laughed out of court.

Whether David Miliband would have done this, and therefore done
better, who knows? His supporters, holding up his acceptance-speech-
that-never-was as proof, certainly think so.[5] In reality, however, he
might have found it just as difficult as other members of the previous
Labour government to confess to economic crimes that, whatever the
Tories and their friends in the media had persuaded the public to
believe, they knew they had not committed. And he, too, would
have had to think long and hard before opting to counter the charge
of 'deficit denial' with an apology that would undoubtedly have been
used by the Conservatives as a stick with which to beat Labour—and
not just in 2015 but for years before and decades afterwards. Besides,
even if he himself had been prepared to take that risk, any victory he

might realistically have won in the 2010 Labour leadership contest would not have been so sweeping that it would have permitted him to ride roughshod over his colleagues' sensitivities—particularly if the price of said victory had been to make Ed Balls Shadow Chancellor in return for the second preferences of his loyal supporters in the PLP. And, as even some of those who wish the elder rather than the younger Miliband had won that contest acknowledge, anyone who thinks David Miliband would have proved a model of decisiveness and a master of political timing probably did not work very closely with him in the Brown government.

We cannot know for certain, either, whether David's personal ratings would have been that much better than Ed's, although, admittedly, it is hard to imagine they could have been much worse. By 2014 the younger Miliband was polling so badly that Jeremy Paxman, demob-happy on his last night presenting the BBC's *Newsnight* programme, claimed polls showed 'he hasn't much more appeal than a flatulent dog in a lift'.[6] Asked by YouGov what they thought of him a little less than a year out from the general election, voters were scathing. Just 11 per cent of them described him as strong, whereas 51 per cent saw him as weak. A mere 16 per cent thought he was an asset to his party compared to 43 per cent who considered him a liability. Asked if he was up to the job, only 21 per cent agreed while 60 per cent said no. Only 14 per cent of respondents thought he looked and sounded like a Prime Minister, while 70 per cent disagreed.[7]

It has to be remembered, of course, that Ed Miliband is not facing an unbeatable opponent. David Cameron may look and sound like a Prime Minister, and he outscores Miliband on all the dimensions listed above, as well as on intelligence, competence, and the ability to take tough decisions. But he does not score that highly himself either. Moreover, he has serious problems of his own: in July 2014, for instance, YouGov found that, by a margin of 72:20 per cent, people agreed that the Prime Minister did not 'really understand the problems faced by normal people in their everyday lives'; and he has long been running scared of the Conservative Party's Eurosceptic, populist right. It is also worth recalling, as many Labour optimists routinely point out, that Margaret Thatcher famously trailed Labour Prime Minister Jim Callaghan in 1979—the year in which she ejected him from Downing Street and ushered in eighteen consecutive years of Tory government.

That said, it has been little consolation to Labour people to be told by YouGov's Peter Kellner that Miliband is actually less of a drag on his party's fortunes than Mrs Thatcher was on hers—not when Kellner went on to note that, when Miliband's name was attached to the standard voting question, 'Labour's lead generally slips by 2–4 percentage points'.[8] The picture in the all-important marginals has been no less bleak, with a ComRes survey of forty of them at the end of September 2014 finding 59 per cent saying Miliband put them off voting Labour, compared to just 18 per cent who said he encouraged them to do so.[9] Just as disheartening has been the fact that, far from Miliband growing on people, familiarity with him seems to have bred contempt. In the middle of 2012, when everything seem to be going wrong for the Tories, he had at least managed to be no more unpopular than Cameron, YouGov giving both men a net-approval rating of −21. By November 2014, the Prime Minister had moved up to −5, but Miliband had seen his net score plummet to −55, lower even than the notoriously 'toxic' Nick Clegg and way worse, six months out from an election, than any of the other leaders of the opposition (Foot, Hague, Howard, and Kinnock) who have gone on to lose.

Possibly, if televised leaders' debates really are held during the election—something that may happen only if the media threaten to stage them irrespective of whether David Cameron deigns to take part—all this may put the Labour leader at some sort of paradoxical advantage: expectations of him are so low, runs the argument, that he is almost bound to exceed them, not least because he is probably at his best doing Q&A's with relatively small crowds. To his most determined critics, however, this is just whistling in the dark—which is why, at the beginning of November 2014, there was a determined, if not exactly concerted, attempt by a number of MPs and ex-MPs to whip the media and the party into a state of anxiety sufficient to tempt or force current or former frontbenchers to question the settled wisdom that Miliband should (or at least would) remain leader until the election. That others were prepared to grumble more loudly than usual and, more importantly, to grant those involved a few days to see if they could get a bandwagon rolling, was down not just to Miliband's dreadful numbers. Yes, the Scottish polling had undoubtedly come as a shock; but his personal ratings had been woeful for what seemed like for ever.[10] What mattered just as much was his reaction to the renewed pressure he was under.

The so-called Bonfire Night plot (if it can be said to deserve the name) actually followed a Bonfire Night reshuffle carried out by Miliband. Its ostensible purpose was to adjust the Shadow Cabinet to take account of Jim Murphy's decision to stand for the leadership of the Scottish Labour Party. But, by moving Mary Creagh to replace him at International Development and promoting Michael Dugher to Transport, Miliband strengthened the hand of his trusted campaign chief Douglas Alexander. What was even more alarming for those worried that the Labour leader's main aim was, as the political commentator John Rentoul put it, 'to make the bunker walls thicker', Miliband also brought his former Chief of Staff, Lucy Powell, into the Shadow Cabinet as Vice Chair of Campaigns and brought one of his most loyal adherents, John Trickett, already in the Shadow Cabinet, into the Leader's Office.[11] It looked, to coin a phrase, like *déjà vu* all over again. The party's activists might be signing petitions and tweeting #webackEd in their thousands. Labour councillors might be telling researchers the same.[12] But, in the eyes of Miliband's infuriatingly anonymous critics, what his supporters failed to grasp, in their understandable anger that half the PLP seemed to be colluding with the media to do the Tories' dirty work for them, was that they were supporting a loser with no idea of how to turn things around other than to try more of the same and to surround himself with old friends whose only achievement was to get him the job in the first place.

Had Labour operated under the same rules as the Conservative Party, which allows for a vote of confidence in its leader to be triggered by just 15 per cent of its MPs writing (confidentially and individually) to the Chairman of its backbench 1922 Committee, then Miliband might have found himself out of a job—and perhaps well before the autumn of 2014. But Labour's constitution makes it so much more difficult for Labour than for Tory malcontents to topple and replace an incumbent—requiring 20 per cent of MPs openly to back a challenge in order to trigger a card vote at an annual or special conference on whether a contest should even be held. As a result, there has, in reality, been, as one frontbencher put it, 'consistently zero prospect' of Miliband being removed. Indeed, even if the rules could somehow have been short-circuited—say by a delegation of Shadow Cabinet colleagues persuading him to step down in favour of a pre-anointed successor—such a move has never been seriously on the cards. As one MP who might have been prepared to get involved in an attempt to oust him noted, it could probably only have been done during the short window of opportunity between people telling themselves 'he'll get better; he'll grow into the job' and then admitting to themselves 'it's too close to the election'. Sadly, at least for Miliband's detractors, that window was shut almost before it opened by Osborne's 'omnishambles' budget midway through 2012.

Whether one can argue, therefore, that an event universally judged at the time to have badly damaged the Tories may, ironically, have ended up doing them an enormous favour depends, however, on one being able to identify someone on the Labour benches capable of providing a convincing and consensual alternative—something those who actually sit on those benches day-in, day-out, have patently failed to do. This is partly because the most obvious contender, Alan Johnson—as he stressed once again when the prospect was raised with him both publicly and privately in October 2014—has remained frustratingly (for his fans anyway) unwilling to step up to the proverbial plate. His refusal to do so has left Labour, for all practical purposes anyway, with a choice between Yvette Cooper and Andy Burnham, neither of whom commands universal respect and/or affection in the PLP and both of whom in any case seem content (in common with the rest of the party's 'Medium-Sized Beasts', as columnist Rafael Behr labels them) to wait on the result of the general election.[13] The only other option would have been to turn to one of the new intake. However, none of them was deemed ready, whether they were recognizable rising stars like Chuka Umunna (whose claims were undoubtedly strengthened by polling done during the Bonfire Night crisis) and Rachel Reeves—or darker horses like Dan Jarvis, editor of the 2014 version of *Why Vote Labour?* and already a frontbencher despite his entering the Commons as recently as March 2011.[14] In any case, what happened to Labour's sister party in Australia, which replaced its leader just seventy-two days before the 2013 federal election serves as a warning to anyone who thinks such a move would solve all the party's problems in one fell swoop. It is also worth remembering that the Conservatives' relatively swift replacement of Iain Duncan Smith by Michael Howard in 2003 made little difference to how well they did in 2005. None of these home truths, however, has prevented people wasting valuable time and energy on thinking and talking about who is best placed to take over if (some say when) Ed Miliband loses the general election. Those who think, incidentally, that Miliband stands any chance whatsoever of staying on (except in some sort of caretaker capacity) should Labour be condemned to another term in opposition are utterly deluded.

All this might be slightly less depressing for the party's members at Westminster and beyond were it thought that those around the Labour leader are either capable of helping him to raise his game or else have one or two additional tricks up their sleeve that might at least help make the best of a bad job. However, it seems clear to most insiders that they have already shot their bolt in this respect—and in such a way as to reveal, at least in their critics' eyes, everything that is wrong with Miliband's personal operation. Towards the end of July, Ed finally secured a much anticipated 'brush-by' meeting with Barack Obama in the White House—an occasion marked by some fairly unprepossessing photos of the two of them sitting round a small table with assorted colleagues, which in Miliband's case meant Douglas Alexander, Tim Livesey, and Stewart Wood, who (much to the amusement of journalists) brought with them a plastic shopping bag full of DVDs as a gift to their host. Only a few days later, however, there was Miliband, now back in the UK, declaring, in a speech supposedly intended to deal head-on with his critics:

If you want the politician from central casting, it's just not me, it's the other guy. And if you want a politician who thinks that a good photo is the most important thing, then don't vote for me. Because I don't. But here's the thing: I believe that people would quite like somebody to stand up and say there is more to politics than the photo-op . . . I am not trying to win a photo-op contest in the next 10 months. And I wouldn't win it if I tried. But I offer something different. Something which seeks not just to defeat the Tories but to take on cynicism.[15]

This inevitably brought forth a rash of stories from hostile journalists on the hypocrisy of Miliband's claim, given what he had evidently just flown halfway round the world to secure—and given the fact that he had supposedly been receiving coaching from voice and body-language coaches. It also obliged even normally sympathetic commentators (including those who could probably see the sense in the recommendation by experts like Simon Baron-Cohen that the Labour leader make the most of his natural empathy) to point out that Miliband's speech, as the *Observer*'s Andrew Rawnsley put it, 'was not really an attempt to abolish the politics of perceptions, but to change the terms of it to his advantage'.[16] In any case, as Rawnsley went on to note, Labour's problems ran rather deeper than 'its leader's resemblance to Wallace or his struggles with bacon butties'. He was not the only one. As Stephen Bush (then at the *Telegraph*, now at the *New Statesman*) observed a day or so later: 'To the extent that [the speech has] changed the conversation at all, it seems to have had the effect that every critique of him now begins with some variation on "Ed Miliband thinks his problem is that he's a weirdo. Actually his problem is..."'.[17]

The answers to that question proffered by insiders vary considerably. This is partly, one suspects, because they reflect an inevitable if deeply depressing desire to ensure that, if Labour loses, it will be seen to have lost for reasons that suit one of the candidates, real and imagined, who would be in the running to replace him or else the strategy that they should supposedly pursue. Hence, Miliband is either too left wing in the first place or held back by hide-bound colleagues. Or he is too much of a North London policy wonk and not enough of a natural communicator. Or he is too New Labour rather than Blue Labour. That is not to say, however, that all explanations are as good as each other—or that there are not other, rather more prosaic but equally pointed criticisms that one could make. For instance, in an era of 'valence politics', where voters place good management way above ideological consistency, it is amazing that Labour has somehow allowed Cameron and his colleagues to miss so many targets and waste so much public money in such a wide variety of fields (prisoner escapes, passports, Royal Mail privatization, the introduction of Personal Independence Payments and universal credit, the bizarre goings-on at the 'Big Society Network', not to mention deficit reduction itself) without doing far more than it has to try to weave their failures into a wider narrative of government incompetence. After all, the latter may well have done the Conservatives far more damage than Labour's routine allegations of heartlessness, which for many voters is, rightly or wrongly, a characteristic already, as they say, priced into the Tories' reputation.

Of the more profound explanations for Miliband's (and therefore his party's) problems, however, one in particular stands out, not just because it is consistent with so much of the story traced in these pages but because it is rooted in something that is said about the Labour leader by insiders whose views run right across the party's ideological spectrum. This is the assertion that he is at one and the same time arrogant (or at least 'intellectually self-confident') and yet chronically prone to indecision—someone who thinks he knows best yet continually consults others, who always listens but never really hears. These flaws, if flaws they are, may well have preceded his time working for Gordon Brown but were almost certainly exacerbated by that formative political experience. Those who knew him then and know him now sometimes express this in terms of Ed as two people. There is the Ed who genuinely thinks Blue Labour was onto something, who really does want radical reforms to the governance and the economy of the UK, who is absolutely convinced of the merits of an elected senate and a private sector more like Germany's, who longs to unlock the elusive 'progressive consensus' supposedly denied us by short-sighted centre-left politicians and an outmoded electoral system, who believes in standing up to Israel and even, on occasions, the United States itself, and whose belief in a more empathic, emollient style of leadership comes over as completely sincere to people who meet him, or see him speak, in person. Then there is the Ed who was Gordon Brown's apprentice, who, for all his denials, is as anxious as Brown was about what the papers are saying, who almost relishes a crisis because that is when many people think he is at his best, who, if truth be told, really values the opinion only of insiders rather than outsiders, professionals rather than insurgents.

According to this view, Ed Number One wants to let a thousand flowers bloom and have IPPR write a grand, sweeping *Condition of Britain* report that recasts social democracy for the post-crash era. Ed Number Two, however, wants to make sure it says nothing he cannot defend in the *Sun* or on *Marr*. Like Brown, it is said, he tends to play for time, is reluctant to close down options lest he make the wrong choice, and so will always try to have his cake and eat it too. The greatest manifestation of this, perhaps, is in personnel. He appoints Jon Cruddas to think big thoughts about what a Labour Party that valued contribution as much as fairness, the local as much as the global, would look like. But he relies on Torsten Bell, a Treasury man and special adviser to Alistair Darling, as his Head of Policy to ensure nothing too ambitious makes it into the manifesto. He tasks Arnie Graf with turning Labour into a community-organizing movement as well as a political party. But he appoints a consummate insider to head up field operations and then looks on, apparently powerless, as Graf, to quote one insider, is 'nobbled' and returns to the States. He gets Stewart

Wood to envision an economy that, instead of favouring a financial sector willing to surrender some of its stupendous profits to the state only if it turns a blind eye to its dodgy dealings, delivers long-term, sustainable growth. But he keeps Ed Balls there to tell him—and the party—to get real.

Miliband, then—and by extension the party under his leadership— has ambitions to be radical, but, not necessarily unreasonably, fears the consequences. Labour claims to want debate and to promote people capable of thinking outside the proverbial box while simultaneously favouring the old guard, prioritizing unity, and avoiding conflict. Labour also craves credibility at the same time as wanting to signal, not least to its active members and to voters who became deeply disillusioned with it after 1997, that it can make a difference. As a result, Labour has spent most of its time in opposition not so much stuck in its comfort zone as trying to square circles. Partly as a consequence of this, it has struggled, just like its leader, to find a voice that sounds authentic—hence its continual resort to the 'devices and verbal tics', the 'empty slogans and the odd bit of fake folksiness', which, according to the *Guardian*'s John Harris, ordinary people find so offputting.[18] This is paralleled—and to some extent generated—by the mismatch between Labour's apparently wholesale reappraisal of the UK's Anglo-Saxon model of capitalism and the distinctly retail offer it now looks intent on offering voters. There is bound, of course, to be a disjunction between the two—between what some call 'pamphlet Labour' and 'leaflet Labour'. But, under Miliband, ideologically inclined towards the former but temperamentally inclined towards the latter, it is arguably especially glaring.

Yet, the squaring of circles has obviously brought with it one huge dividend. Labour, to quote Matthew D'Ancona, author of a fine book on the Coalition, has 'defied political tradition by stubbornly refusing to split into a thousand scarlet shards'.[19] Clearly this is not all down to Miliband. Cameron's abandonment of his modernization project, as well as the failure of the Conservatives to establish a convincing opinion poll lead, means that even those who would have preferred his brother as leader have long believed that, as long as it holds itself together, Labour has at least a chance of winning—even with Ed at the helm. Had the Coalition pursued the consensual, 'compassionate Conservatism' that Cameron made so much of when he first became Tory leader, then things might have been different. However, as it is, to quote one Labour frontbencher who is no great fan of Ed Miliband's:

There is an absolute determination to get back into office ASAP because the communities that we serve are getting shafted. If you have to go and do the surgeries that we have to do at weekends, when you have to comfort people because they've been thrown out of their house because of the bedroom tax, you're pretty fucking motivated to get back into power.

Just as crucial is the universal desire to do whatever it takes to avoid a repeat of the 1980s—something mentioned by Labour people right across the spectrum. Moreover, with the decline (if not the complete defeat) of the Labour left achieved by Kinnock, Smith, and Blair, that spectrum is now much narrower than it was back then, meaning, quite frankly, that there is less to fight about. Associated cultural change may also have helped: one veteran even talks about 'a "feminization" of the Labour Party. Everybody used to go in for very aggressive, brutal language and people just don't do that anymore. It's much *nicer*.'

Miliband's own conflict avoidance has nevertheless played a big part in Labour's absence of war. And it is not entirely true to say, to quote one of his critics, that 'he's got everyone to sing from the same hymn-sheet but he's done that by ensuring that they're all tunes people are really, really familiar with'. True, what Labour has lacked under Miliband is a bunch of counter-intuitive initiatives or even just visual images, which, especially if they had been launched early on (in much the same way as Cameron launched them in the first year of his leadership), might have encouraged voters to register that change was being made and lessons learned. True, too, that this had a great deal to do with Miliband insisting that he was not going to copy Cameron or Blair and define himself against his party—a stance that he seemed to think would earn him plaudits rather than the total lack of interest with which, rather predictably, it was actually met. Yet, it is also true that the party has been obliged under his leadership to reconcile itself to things that in 2010 it would have rejected out of hand. As one of Miliband's most loyal supporters in the PLP rightly notes:

People can now look at what somebody like Rachel is saying about welfare and say that is a *Labour* story. Three years ago they would have said to anybody—and they did to Liam—if you're talking about not spending so much on welfare you must be telling the *Tory* story. So now, on that issue, there's a Labour story about welfare but we're still going to spend less money.

Clearly, the extent to which that has happened varies across issues. On education, Labour has managed to oblige its members, however unenthusiastically, to commit to tweaking rather than unwinding Michael Gove's reforms. On immigration, too, there has been considerable movement. This, at least in part, was prompted by the leadership, even if it is fair to say, as do some of his MPs, that Miliband (who, as one of his advisers notes, 'didn't come into politics to bang on about immigration') has been too inclined to signal such shifts via the occasional speech rather than, say, getting Brewer's Green to produce publicity material that would hammer the message home by being handed out 'on the doorstep' week-in, week-out. On the NHS—and arguably on public service reform more generally—there has been less progress, although to pin that solely on the Shadow Secretary of State's desire to keep party members and the trade unions sweet in preparation for a post-election leadership bid is probably unfair to Andy Burnham: why would Labour want to mix its messaging on an issue that is by far its strongest electoral suit?

This is not to say, however, that unity has had no downsides. Perhaps most importantly it has made it both easier and more imperative to split differences, to delay decisions, and to promise more to some than realistically the leadership was ever going to deliver, prompting disappointment (and the distinct feeling that they had been strung along) among those who were probably always going to be let down. Most obviously, this group includes those who had high hope of the bottom-up, movement-oriented, communitarian, nation-building project embodied in the NPF, in Arnie Graf's organizing, and in IPPR's focus on retooling social democracy by switching spending and devolving power. As one of them reflected, the 'triangle' comprising 'Ed, Torsten, Douglas (with Spencer attached)' could 'never really incorporate it into their way of thinking which is policy-focused, tactical, instrumental. They always see the trees and not the wood.' Too influenced by the snapshots produced by polling, Ed's operation, according to the same critic, is 'constant stop–start, stop–start, always trying to catch up, defensive, reactive and, when the big things hit it, totally incapable of responding'. Challenging it, however, is impossible, because it is like arguing with 'jelly or blancmange', ensuring that the leadership's approach wins by appearing to take criticisms and suggestions on board but ignoring and eventually subtly excluding those who make them: 'You know how these things happen in institutions and organizations: information that's given and not given, meetings you're invited to and not invited to; events that happen that are incorporated into it or kept outside of it.' According to this view anyway, because there are no factions to speak of and because Labour's loss of seats in 2010 was bad enough to depress people but not bad enough to spark some sort of combustion, the prevailing mood has too often been one of 'quiescence, impotence'. 'There's no energy. Where's the energy going to come from? It comes from a bit of conflict, and argument, and definition. There's none . . . Ed's prided himself on the unity but it comes at an enormous cost.'

Whether things would have been very different under David—someone who might have generated more conflict than he avoided—is something nobody will never know. What we do know, however, is that, unless things change mightily between now and polling day, Labour's strategy will be in the hands, not of those who, to quote Jon Cruddas's words to a fringe meeting at Manchester 2014, believe Labour's only hope is 'to come out with a big bold re-imagination of what social democracy is' but in the hands of those, to quote him again, who think 'if we keep our mouth shut we might get over the line. Less is more, dodgy 1–0 away win.' Seen from the other end of the telescope, this means Labour will go into the general election with a disciplined approach delivered by mostly familiar faces, backed up by a much-improved party organization, and based on a few well-tested messages that attempt to minimize the negatives and play up the positives, namely: you can trust us with the economy and the public finances; we hear your worries about immigration and welfare, and we will never let them get out of control again; we will take concrete action to raise your standard of living by making work pay and, where appropriate, taking action to cap price rises; we will help, within reason, to build more houses; and we will look after the NHS. To anyone who knows their political history, and therefore knows how slowly defeated parties change—at least in the absence of a truly galvanizing, charismatic leader—then none of this is particularly sur-prising. Indeed, after just five years, what has happened lies somewhere between par for the course and pretty good going.

To many observers, however, even Cruddas's 'dodgy 1–0 away win' looks increasingly unlikely. Traditionally, the main opposition party in the UK tends to lose rather than gain support as an election approaches, and these days there are more competitors hoping to make gains at its expense. The threat posed to Labour by UKIP has already been discussed, but there are also indications that it could lose voters—possibly in sufficient numbers to damage its chances of winning a few seats in places with high numbers of student voters—to the Greens, who have on occasion polled higher than the Lib Dems. Many of these will presumably be left-wingers who voted Lib Dem in 2010, then abandoned the party when it went into coalition, telling pollsters that they had switched to Labour. As such, they were a key component of the electoral coalition that Miliband was hoping to build, whether or not he was following the much-maligned (if mythical) '35 per cent strategy' or, indeed, the rather more ambitious *Labour's Next Majority: The 40% Strategy* devised by the Fabian Society's Marcus Roberts.[20] Given the fact that Miliband (who made something of a reputation for himself on the issue as a minister) has said and done very little on the environment since 2010, and given his willingness to sanction the rushed passage of the Data Retention and Investigatory Powers Act in the summer of 2014 (despite all his fine words early on about civil liberties), this drift to the Greens may not be altogether surprising. The news that Shadow Justice Minister, putative London Mayoral candidate, and Miliband campaign manager Sadiq Khan was supposedly tasked by the Labour leader in the autumn of 2014 to set up 'a strategy unit' to help counter the threat from the Greens looked very much like the kind of thing parties put out to reassure their members rather than anything that could possibly make a difference. It could be that some voters tempted by the Greens may ultimately vote Labour for fear of letting in another Tory-led government—in much the same way as some voters on the other end of the spectrum may end up switching from UKIP to the Tories in the hope that it will prevent Labour winning. But whether the odd article in the left-liberal press by Khan turns out to be responsible for them doing so is a moot point.[21]

Labour, in other words, is now fighting on as many as five fronts—against the Conservatives and the Lib Dems (and now the SNP) for seats, and against UKIP and the Greens for votes that may, in turn, cost it seats. This fractured communications and campaign environment is made all the more complex because actions on one front are likely to impact on the others. It is easy, for instance, for Labour MPs to call for tougher talk and action on immigration but to forget that there are voters out there whose hearts sink at any hint that Labour (as left-wingers like Diane Abbott claimed was happening in the wake of

Ed Miliband's speech on immigration in Rochester in October) is trying to fight on 'UKIP's turf'. It is equally easy to dismiss those people as 'the chattering classes' or 'metropolitan liberals'—the kind of people who looked on in despair as a panicked Ed Miliband, in the wake of the Rochester and Strood by-election, sacked a loyal Shadow Minister for tweeting a photo widely interpreted as mocking 'White Van Man', the England-supporting skilled worker who constitutes (or at least symbolizes) electorally precious C2 voters.[22] But, as Tory modernizers can attest, it is difficult, if not impossible, to win an election without at least some of those dismissed as *bien-pensant* bleeding hearts on board. The same, of course, goes for those voters, C2 or otherwise, who cringe when they see Miliband posing in a *This is what a feminist looks like* tee-shirt or tossing coins into the cup of a 14-year old Romanian beggar who lives with her aunt, a mother of nine, reportedly in receipt of £550 a week in welfare benefits.

It is not, however, impossible for Labour to win in 2015, or at least to emerge as the largest party in a hung parliament—something that must now have to be the height of its ambition unless Jim Murphy, elected Leader of the Scottish Labour Party in mid-December 2014 despite trade-union opposition, can pull off a minor miracle and, by stressing he does not take orders from London, stave off heavy losses to the SNP in Scotland. Indeed, several factors still favour the party. First and foremost there is the electoral system: because boundary reform has trouble keeping pace with population movements, and because Labour's vote is spread more efficiently than the Tories', then Labour is almost certain to win more seats than the Conservatives on any given share of the vote. Secondly, Labour's strategists, while nowhere near as unconcerned about UKIP as some imagine, are probably correct in continuing to bet on it costing the Conservatives more seats than it will cost Labour, particularly if voters in Tory-held marginals begin to think (however mistakenly) that voting for the self-styled People's Army is not necessarily a wasted vote.[23] Certainly, polling suggests that 'Vote Farage, get Miliband' does not have the kind of magical power to send people scurrying back to the Tories with which some seem to imbue it. Thirdly, when it comes to issues, healthcare is rising up the agenda and, unlike immigration, which is very often mentioned as the most important issue facing the country but not as one facing people's immediate family and friends, it is as much a tangible as an abstract concern.

Fourthly, and by the same token, while the Tories have established a big lead on 'the economy' as an overarching concept, Labour can cling to the fact that, when it comes to those aspects of the economy that people notice in their daily lives, things are not quite so rosy. Unemployment is, as the government claims, dropping. However, many of the jobs created in the upturn are not well paid and many of them offer fewer hours than those taking them would ideally like. Moreover, official figures show that far more people than previously imagined seem to be on the infamous zero-hours contracts that Labour has spent time highlighting over the last couple of years. Official figures also show that the country has suffered the biggest fall in wages since the 1870s, and that 2015 will be the first year since the 1920s in which voters will, on average, be worse off at the end of a parliament than they were at the beginning. Polling also suggests that, in spite of inflation falling, Labour's attack on 'the cost of living' still has resonance. True, the party can be criticized for providing, in the words of one Labour veteran, 'an analysis, not a solution'. But the same could be said of the Conservatives in 1970 when they won a surprise victory (with, note, a less-than-inspiring leader) fighting a campaign rooted in Labour's failure to tackle the cost of living.

Ed Miliband, then, presuming televised debates do end up taking place, will almost certainly be able to ask David Cameron the question that Ronald Reagan famously asked of President Jimmy Carter in 1980: 'Are you better off now than you were four years ago?' Moreover, it looks as if his opponent will have just as much trouble convincing people he understands and cares about them as Mitt Romney did in 2012. And, while the Chancellor's Autumn Statement, delivered at the beginning of December 2014, was by no means a disaster for the Conservatives—'giveaways', after all, included reductions in stamp duty, additional spending on roads, and the promise to clamp down on aggressive tax avoidance by big companies—Osborne came under severe pressure for, on the one hand, continuing to maintain that the Conservatives could somehow deliver tax reductions in the next parliament while, on the other, insisting that the spending cuts required (assuming they were even achievable) were not as 'colossal' (to quote the independent think tank, the IFS) as they plainly were. All this at least raised the possibility that Labour could at least stake a plausible claim to the hallowed centre ground by promising that its plans to reduce the deficit (while still not as detailed as some would have liked) were 'tough but balanced' rather than being ideologically driven, unfair, and a serious risk to key public services. Labour was also fortunate that both Balls and Miliband—Balls immediately and Miliband a few days later in a setpiece speech—responded much more effectively than they had the previous year.[24] This would not be enough, of course, to eliminate Cameron's and Osborne's lead on the economy, not least because few voters seemed to believe they would be much better off under Labour, even if they had no great confidence in the Tories.[25] Moroever, another Eurozone crisis would undoubtedly provide the Chancellor with yet another excuse both for his tough targets and for his conspicuous failure so far to meet them. But, for Labour, it was considerably better than nothing.

Finally, although Labour people may be far too sanguine about the superiority of their 'ground game'—volunteers count but so, after all, do the less visible phone banks in which the Tories have invested—their organizational efforts may have something to do with the fact that polls consistently showed Labour doing better in many marginal seats than nationally.[26] Moreover, while there is always a lot of talk about how poorly it is performing in the south, typified for some critics by its reduced share of the vote in November's Rochester and Strood by-election, the key to victory actually lies in other regions and in particular the swathe of 'suburban towns', most of them in the Midlands, that it lost in 2010. The fact that the government ignored advice from the Electoral Commission and increased the amount parties can spend on the so-called long campaign, running from a week before Christmas to polling day itself, will clearly advantage the Conservatives, since they have by far the biggest 'war chest'. But, while money helps, in the UK at least, it is not everything.

As to what victory—or at least a victory of sorts—would bring, that depends partly on the parliamentary arithmetic. Although many Shadow Ministers shudder at the prospect of coalition and would prefer a single-party minority government if they thought they could get away with it, a deal with the Lib Dems remains a possibility, assuming, of course, that the Lib Dems do not perform so poorly that they cannot supply Labour (or indeed the Conservatives) with enough additional seats to secure a majority coalition.[27] Relationships with Clegg and other so-called Orange Bookers have yet to recover from what most of those on the Labour side regard as the attempt to play them for fools in 2010, since when, as they see it, the Lib Dems have signally failed to prevent the Tories from doing pretty much whatever they wanted. The dismissive private briefings and public sneers directed at Miliband during the Lib Dems' last conference before the election did nothing to help matters, although some of that posturing is discounted (if not by Miliband himself) as 'just business'. After all, inasmuch as the phrase 'Lib Dem policies' means anything these days, there remains a considerable degree of overlap between the two parties' programmes. And their willingness to work together to make changes to the bedroom tax from 2014 onwards, notwithstanding the fact that Labour initially criticized Clegg's *volte face* on the issue as 'unbelievable hypocrisy', is clutched at as a straw in the wind by those who believe an arrangement is possible. According to Labour insiders, however, coalition with the Lib Dems is not an option that anyone in the Leader's Office or the Shadow Cabinet can be seen to be seriously discussing. If there is a group at the very top working out the details of Labour's negotiating stance—something that would surely be sensible, given the party's lack of preparedness in 2010—then it is operating under very deep cover indeed. If that is the case, it would be entirely understandable, not so much because the Lib Dems are electorally toxic or because imagining a deal with them would incur the wrath of trade-union leaders like Len McCluskey, but because the very existence of such a group would risk shattering the illusion that Labour is gunning for an overall majority—one deemed to be important to maintain the morale of activists.

That is not to say, however, that the party is unprepared for government. Beyond the much-hyped 'zero-based' spending review conducted by Shadow Chief Secretary Chris Leslie—intended to 'scare the shit' out of his colleagues, said one of them—there has been a lot of very detailed work done behind the scenes.[28] Much of it is being conducted with the help of private-sector management consultants working pro-bono and under the supervision of Lord (Charlie) Falconer and Alan Buckle, former CEO and Deputy Chairman of consulting and accountancy group KPMG.[29] With varying degrees of cooperation from Shadow Ministers (some of whom consider themselves old hands and therefore do not like to be second-guessed; some of whom are relative newcomers and therefore happy to accept help), it has been thinking seriously about the implementation of Labour's policies at the departmental level, but also about how it would run Number Ten differently from David Cameron (and, indeed, Gordon Brown and Tony Blair).

Whether all that preparation will help much, given the enormity of the fiscal challenges and the inordinate power afforded to parties' 'awkward squads' by small or non-existent majorities, who knows? Many observers have their doubts. Janan Ganesh, quoted at the start of this concluding chapter, is far from alone in predicting that 'a Labour government fronted by Ed Miliband will writhe like a tortured animal for five years as it tries to reconcile beliefs it cannot afford with spending cuts it cannot avoid' and, as a consequence, 'could end in the kind of shambles that takes a generation to live down'.[30] There are some in the party who agree with him—most of all those who have never once wavered in their belief that five years ago Labour elected the wrong brother. Others are less pessimistic, prepared to entertain the possibility, however unlikely it has sometimes seemed, that Ed Miliband may yet surprise everyone. If the five-year mission Labour set out on back in 2010 is finally accomplished in May 2015, we will very soon get the chance to find out.

# Notes

## INTRODUCTION

1. For a blow-by-blow account of Brown's premiership, see Anthony Seldon and Guy Lodge, *Brown at Ten* (London: Biteback, 2011). See also Andrew Rawnsley *The End of the Party: The Rise and Fall of New Labour* (Harmondsworth: Penguin, 2010)—a masterful account of the party under both Blair and Brown.
2. See Andrew Rawnsley, 'The New Prime Minister is Master of his Universe', *Observer*, 1 July 2007.
3. See Steve Richards, *Whatever it Takes: The Real Story of Gordon Brown and New Labour* (London: Fourth Estate, 2010), and William Keegan, *Saving the World? Gordon Brown Reconsidered* (London: Searching Finance, 2012).
4. See Tim Bale and Paul Webb, 'The Conservative Party', in Nicholas Allen and John Bartle (eds), *Britain at the Polls 2010* (London: Sage, 2010).
5. The best account, particularly from Labour's perspective, of the frantic post-election negotiations is Andrew Adonis, *5 Days in May: The Coalition and Beyond* (London: Biteback, 2013).
6. See James Cronin, George Ross, and James Shoch (eds), *What's Left of the Left: Democrats and Social Democrats in Challenging Times* (London: Duke University Press). See also the regularly updated 'State of the Left' blog by Policy Network's array of correspondents <http://www.policy-network.net/content/392/State-of-the-Left>. This and all other URLs that follow were correct as of December 2014.
7. Paul Goodman, 'Ed Miliband is a Pale shade of Tony Blair', *The Times*, 21 August 2013. <http://www.thetimes.co.uk/tto/opinion/columnists/article3848431.ece>.

## CHAPTER 1. STRANGERS AND BROTHERS: SPRING–AUTUMN 2010

1. For a detailed explanation of the main parties' rules for selecting their leaders, and how they have changed over time, see Tim Bale and Paul Webb, 'The Selection of Party Leaders in the UK', in Jean-Benoit Pilet and William Cross (eds), *The Selection of Political Party Leaders in Contemporary Parliamentary Democracies: A Comparative Study* (Abingdon: Routledge, 2013).
2. Amber Elliott and Caroline Crampton, 'Ed Balls interview', *Total Politics* (December 2011).

3. For a taste of what it was like for the volunteers, see Emma Burnell, 'Ed's Leadership Campaign: Perspective from the Coalface', *Scarlet Standard*, 3 July 2011 <http://scarletstandard.co.uk/?p=770>.

4. For a sense of the febrile political and journalistic atmosphere at the contest's climax, and for much else on Ed besides, see the excellent biography by James Macintyre and Mehdi Hasan, *Ed: The Milibands and the Making of a Labour Leader* (London: Biteback, 2012).

5. For YouGov's surveys of members and trade-union members in July, see <https://d25d2506sfb94s.cloudfront.net/today_uk_import/YG-Pol-Sun-LabMembers-290710.pdf> and <https://d25d2506sfb94s.cloudfront.net/today_uk_import/YG-Pol-Sun-LabTUmembers-290710.pdf>. For September, see <https://d25d2506sfb94s.cloudfront.net/today_uk_import/YG-Archives-Pol-YouGov-LabourLeaderPartyMembers-100910.pdf> and <https://d25d2506sfb94s.cloudfront.net/today_uk_import/YG-Archives-Pol-ST-LabourLeadTradeMembers-100910.pdf>.

6. Chris Bryant, *The Politics of 'Tidy Britain'—Why Labour Lost and How We Win Again* (London: Smith Institute, 2010); Liam Byrne, *Why Did Labour Lose and How Do We Win Again?* (London: Progress, 2010); Michael A. Ashcroft, *Smell the Coffee: A Wake-up Call for the Conservative Party* (London: Ashcroft Publishing, 2005).

7. Ann Black's invaluable reports of NEC meetings can be found at <http://www.labourblogs.com/public-blog/annblack>.

8. See Richard Jobson and Mark Wickham Jones, 'Reinventing the Block Vote? Trade Unions and the 2010 Labour Party Leadership Election', *British Politics*, 63/3 (2011), 317–44, and Hugh Pemberton and Mark Wickham-Jones, 'Brothers All? The Operation of the Electoral College in the 2010 Labour Leadership Contest', *Parliamentary Affairs*, 66/4 (2013), 708–31.

9. Unions are facing major challenges all over Europe, although their strength and membership vary considerably between countries. Their position in the UK is nowhere near as weak as it is in Southern and Eastern Europe, but nor is at anywhere near as strong as it is in Northern Europe, especially Scandinavia. See Rebecca Gumbrell-McCormick and Richard Hyman, *Trade Unions in Western Europe: Hard Times, Hard Choices* (Oxford: Oxford University Press, 2013).

10. For YouGov's surveys of members and trade-union members in July, see note 5. See also Andrew Sparrow, 'Return to Politics of New Labour would Put off Voters—Poll', *Guardian*, 4 September 2010.

11. John Rentoul, 'No One to Replace Ed Miliband? Try Yvette Cooper', *Independent*, 3 January 2012.

12. Magnus Linklater and Sam Coates, 'Ed's Route is a Dead End, says Mandelson', *The Times*, 30 August 2010.

13. See Nicholas Watt, 'David Miliband is the Voters' Choice, Says Poll', *Guardian*, 3 September 2010. See also Andrew Sparrow, 'Return to Politics of New Labour would Put off Voters—Poll', *Guardian*, 4 September 2010.

14. Ed Miliband, 'I'll Make Capitalism Bend to the People's Will', *Guardian*, 29 August 2010.

15. Mark Ferguson, '"Do we Have the Courage to Change?": The Ed Miliband Interview', *LabourList*, 26 August 2010 <http://labourlist. org/2010/08/do-we-have-the-courage-to-change-the-ed-miliband-inter view/>.

16. Ed Miliband's essay, along with those of the other candidates, was published in an online-only pamphlet by the Fabian Society in August 2010 <http:// www.fabians.org.uk/wp-content/uploads/2012/04/TheLabourLeadership. pdf>.

17. Jenni Russell, 'Labour must Check this Bandwagon before the Wrong Miliband Takes over', *Guardian*, 25 November 2009.

18. Ed Miliband, Speech, 28 September 2010 <http://www2.labour.org.uk/ ed-miliband—a-new-generation>.

CHAPTER 2. NO HONEYMOON: AUTUMN 2010–SPRING 2011

1. Ed Miliband, 'My Vision to Rebuild Trust', *Sunday Telegraph*, 26 September 2010.

2. Gavin Kelly and Nick Pearce, 'Wanted: an Old, New Left', *Prospect*, August 2010 <http://www.prospectmagazine.co.uk/features/wanted-an-old-new-left>.

3. See Patrick Hennessy, 'A Party Waiting for Miliband to Start Leading', *Sunday Telegraph*, 28 November 2010.

4. Lord Ashcroft Polls, 12 December 2010 <http://lordashcroftpolls.com/ wp-content/uploads/2012/01/lib-dem-voters-results.pdf>.

5. David Marquand, *The Progressive Dilemma: From Lloyd George to Blair* (London: Weidenfeld and Nicolson, 1999).

6. See Ed Miliband, 'These Education Proposals Risk Setting back Social Mobility for a Generation', *Observer*, 5 December 2010, and Mary Riddell, 'Alan Johnson Interview: I'd be Delighted if David Miliband Decided to Join us', *Daily Telegraph*, 4 December 2010.

7. Alan Johnson, '£9,000 is Too Much: A Graduate Tax Is the Only Fair Way', *The Times*, 8 December 2010.

8. See Steve Richards, *Whatever it Takes: The Real Story of Gordon Brown and New Labour* (London: Fourth Estate, 2010).

9. For full details of the case, see the Standard Note provided by the House of Commons Library in December 2010 <http://www.parliament.uk/brief ing-papers/SN05751/election-petition-oldham-east-and-saddleworth>.

10. What Ed Balls really thinks of Miliband's intellect compared to his own, no one but he himself can really know, but it is widely assumed by those who served with both men in government that one reason for the tension between the two is, as one of them puts it, that, at least in the Shadow Chancellor's view, 'for all those years, Ed Miliband was the office boy and

Ed Balls was the brains'. See also James Macintyre and Mehdi Hasan, *Ed: The Milibands and the Making of a Labour Leader* (London: Biteback, 2012), 60–8.

11. Andrew Grice, 'Miliband Sets out Charm Offensive he Hopes will Woo "Lost" Lib Dems', *Independent*, 26 January 2011.

12. Philip Gould, *The Unfinished Revolution: How New Labour Changed British Politics Forever* (London: Abacus, 2011).

13. George Eaton, 'Labour's Growing Dependence on the Unions', New Statesman Blog, 23 February 2011 <http://www.newstatesman.com/blogs/the-staggers/2011/02/unions-donations-labour-2010>.

14. Ed Miliband, Speech, 26 March 2011 <http://www.newstatesman.com/blogs/the-staggers/2011/03/ed-miliband-hyde-park-speech>.

15. Bagehot, 'Labour's Flat-Earthers Demand the Cuts Go away', *Economist Blog*, 25 March 2011 <http://www.economist.com/blogs/bagehot/2011/03/ed_miliband_0>.

16. Labour Party, *Refounding Labour: A Party for the New Generation* (London: Labour Party, 2011).

17. YouGov, 8 May 2014 <https://d25d2506sfb94s.cloudfront.net/today_uk_import/yg-archives-pol-sun-results-060511.pdf>.

18. See Ipsos Mori <https://www.ipsos-mori.com/researchspecialisms/socialresearch/specareas/politics/trends.aspx#partyleaders1>.

19. Allegra Stratton and Patrick Wintour, 'Ed Miliband—no Huskies, no North Pole, but he's in for the Long Haul', *Guardian*, 22 November 2010.

20. See Tim Bale, *The Conservative Party from Thatcher to Cameron*, 2nd edn (Cambridge: Polity, 2011).

21. Maurice Glasman, Jonathan Rutherford, Marc Stears, and Stuart White (eds), *The Labour Tradition and the Politics of Paradox* (London: Lawrence and Wishart, 2011), free to download at <http://www.lwbooks.co.uk/ebooks/labour_tradition_politics_paradox.html>.

22. Robert Philpot (ed.), *The Purple Book: A Progressive Future for Labour* (London: Biteback, 2011).

23. Rowenna Davis, *Tangled up in Blue: Blue Labour and the Struggle for Labour's Soul* (London: Short Books, 2011).

24. James Macintyre and Mehdi Hasan, *Ed: The Milibands and the Making of a Labour Leader* (London: Biteback, 2012), 287.

25. Robert Philpot, 'Labour Isn't Working', *Progress*, May 2011 <http://www.progressonline.org.uk/2011/04/19/labour-isnt-working/>.

26. Mary Riddell, 'Labour's Anti-Immigration Guru', *Daily Telegraph*, 18 July 2011.

27. Matthew Parris, 'No Cheek by Jowell: I'm One of the Unsmooched', *The Times*, 29 September 2011.

28. See Jacob S. Hacker, 'The Institutional Foundations of Middle-Class Democracy', Policy Network, 6 May 2011 <http://www.policy-network.

net/pno_detail.aspx?ID=3998&title=The+institutional+foundations+of +middle-class+democracy>.

29. Peter A. Hall and David Soskice (eds), *Varieties of Capitalism: The Institutional Foundations of Comparative Advantage* (Oxford: Oxford University Press, 2001).

30. Conservative Party, *Ed Miliband's 100 Days of Dithering and Disarray* (London: Conservative Party, 2011) <http://conservativehome.blogs. com/files/100-days-of-dithering-and-disarray.pdf>.

CHAPTER 3. PREDATORS: SPRING–AUTUMN 2011

1. See James Robinson, 'David Cameron, Ed Miliband and Co Flock to Pay Homage at Rupert Murdoch's Summer Party', *Guardian*, 20 June 2011.

2. See Peter Watt, *Inside out: My Story of Betrayal and Cowardice at the Heart of New Labour* (London: Biteback, 2010).

3. Dan Hodges, 'Just who is Refounding Labour', *New Statesman Blog*, 2 June 2011 <http://www.newstatesman.com/blogs/dan-hodges/2011/ 06/labour-party-zentrum>.

4. Labour Party, *Refounding Labour to Win: Summary Report* (London: Labour Party, 2011) <http://www.leftfutures.org/wp-content/uploads/2011/ 10/Refounding-Labour-to-win.pdf>.

5. IPPR poll, 25 September 2011 <http://www.ippr.org/news-and-media/ press-releases/new-poll-shows-labour-has-biggest-pool-of-potential- voters-but-electoral-mountain-still-to-climb>.

6. Patrick Diamond and Giles Radice, *Southern Discomfort: One Year On* (London: Policy Network, 2011) <file:///C:/Users/Owner/Downloads/ Southern%20Discomfort%20-%20One%20year%20on%20(1).pdf>.

7. Populus Poll, September 2011 <http://www.populus.co.uk/uploads/down load_pdf-160911-The-Times-The-Times-Poll—September-2011.pdf>.

8. Lord Ashcroft Polls, 'The Leadership Factor', September 2011 <http:// lordashcroftpolls.com/wp-content/uploads/2011/12/the-leadership- factor.pdf p.16>.

9. Mehdi Hasan, ' "I'm Ripping up the Rule-Book" ', *New Statesman*, 22 September 2011.

10. Steve Richards, 'Too Much Pessimism Is Self-Fulfilling', *Independent*, 27 September 2011.

11. Graeme Cook, Adam Lent, Anthony Painter, and Hopi Sen, *In the Black Labour: Why Fiscal Conservatism and Social Justice Go Hand-in-Hand* (London: Policy Network, 2011) <http://www.policy-network.net/publications/ 4101/-in-the-black-labour>.

12. Simon Hoggart, 'Enter the Panda—the Man they Want to Love', *Guardian*, 28 September 2011.

13. Benedict Brogan, 'Ed Miliband's Shift to the Left is a Gift for the Tories', *Telegraph Blogs*, 27 September 2011 <http://blogs.telegraph.co.uk/news/

benedictbrogan/100107683/ed-miliband%E2%80%99s-shift-to-the-left-is-a-gift-for-the-tories/>.

14. Stanley Greenberg, 'Why Voters Tune out Democrats', *New York Times*, 30 July 2011.

15. Philip Collins, 'The Last Gasp of Vintage Social Democracy', *The Times*, 30 September 2011.

16. Daniel Finkelstein, 'Ed can do Nothing about his Two Fatal Flaws', *The Times*, 28 September 2011.

17. Michael White, 'Ed Miliband has Escaped the Circular Firing Squad', *Guardian*, 28 September 2011.

18. Quoted by the *Guardian*'s rolling blogger Andrew Sparrow, 'Labour Party Conference Live—Thursday 29 September 2011' <http://www.theguardian.com/politics/blog/2011/sep/29/labour-conference-2011-live-coverage>.

CHAPTER 4. OMNISHAMBLES: AUTUMN 2011–SPRING 2012

1. See 'Ed Miliband Revealed', *Mirror.co.uk*, 21 December 2011 <http://www.mirror.co.uk/news/uk-news/ed-miliband-revealed-at-home-with-the-labour-98444>.

2. Rob Hutton, *Romps, Tots and Boffins: The Strange Language of News* (London: Elliot and Thompson, 2013).

3. See, e.g. those quoted in Dan Hodges, 'Ed's a Washout, but his Party's Stuck with him', *Daily Telegraph*, 16 December 2011.

4. Maurice Glasman, 'Ed Miliband must Trust his Instincts and Stand up for Real Change', *New Statesman*, 5 January 2012.

5. See Tim Shipman, 'Ed is not Doomed like IDS, insists Labour's Spin Chief', *Daily Mail*, 6 January 2012.

6. For details, see Haroon Siddque, 'Ed Miliband Dismisses Critics and Promises New Direction for Labour', *Guardian*, 10 January 2012.

7. Patrick Wintour, 'Ed Balls: George Osborne's Plan Is Failing but Labour cannot Duck Reality', *Guardian*, 13 January 2012.

8. Katie Allen, 'UK Unemployment Hits 17-Year High', *Guardian.com*, 14 December 2011, which also includes video of PMQs <http://www.theguardian.com/business/2011/dec/14/uk-unemployment-hits-17-year-high>.

9. Gavin Kelly, 'Labour Needs an Argument about the State not just the Deficit', *New Statesman Blog*, 8 January 2012 <http://www.newstatesman.com/blogs/gavin-kelly/2012/01/labour-tax-spending-deficit>.

10. Len McCluskey, 'Ed Miliband's Leadership Is Threatened by this Blairite Policy Coup', *Guardian*, 17 January 2012.

11. Prentis, quoted on LabourList, 18 January 2012 <http://labourlist.org/2012/01/miliband-panicked-says-unison-leader/>.

12. See Mark Ferguson, 'GMB to Consider Affiliation to Labour?', Labour-List, 17 January 2012 <http://labourlist.org/2012/01/gmb-to-consider-affiliation-to-labour/>.

13. See Andrew Grice, 'Miliband Vows to Back Public Sector Cuts—even if Union Backers Withdraw their Cash', *Independent*, 18 January 2012.

14. Alan Johnson, 'The Unions' No-Cuts Agenda Is Delusional', *Guardian*, 18 January 2012.

15. Liam Byrne, *The New Centre Ground* (London: Progress, 2012).

16. David Miliband, 'Time to Rethink, not Reassure', *New Statesman*, 2 February 2012.

17. Robert Winnett and Mary Riddell, 'Ed Miliband Goes to War on "Rip-off Britain"', *Daily Telegraph*, 18 January 2012.

18. Ed Miliband, 'Our Toxic Blend of Capitalism and Short-Termism', *Financial Times*, 18 January 2012.

19. Resolution Foundation, *Essential Guide to Squeezed Britain* (London: Resolution Foundation, 2012) <http://issuu.com/resolutionfoundation/docs/squeezed_britain>.

20. Stephen Timms, *Job Guarantee: A Right and Responsibility to Work* (London: Smith Institute) <https://smithinstitutethinktank.files.wordpress.com/2014/10/wealth-of-our-nation-rethinking-policies-for-wealth-distribution.pdf>.

21. BBC, 'Harriet Harman Struggles with Bank Bonus and Job Figures', 16 March 2012 <http://www.bbc.co.uk/news/uk-politics-17401158>.

22. See Transcript, *Andrew Marr Show*, 8 January 2012 <http://news.bbc.co.uk/1/hi/programmes/andrew_marr_show/9673749.stm>. Shiv Malik, 'Peter Mandelson Gets Nervous about People Getting "Filthy Rich"', *Guardian.com*, 26 January 2012 <http://www.theguardian.com/politics/2012/jan/26/mandelson-people-getting-filthy-rich>.

23. Ed Miliband, 'A New Economy', speech to the Social Market Foundation, 17 November <http://www.newstatesman.com/economy/2011/11/term-business-government>.

24. *Daily Mirror*, 21 March 2012. Its cover can be viewed at <http://politicalscrapbook.net/2012/03/mirror-nhs-gravestone-front-page/>.

25. Simon Hoggart, 'Budget 2012: A Grand Day for Wallace and Gromit', *Guardian*, 22 March 2012.

26. See <https://d25d2506sfb94s.cloudfront.net/cumulus_uploads/document/yp5s1ymci9/YG-Archives-Pol-Sun-results-220312.pdf> and <http://www.comres.co.uk/polls/Political_poll_Indy_27thMarch12.pdf>.

27. See James Ashton, 'Dressed for Success, Spread-Betting Tycoon who's Walking Tall Once More', *Evening Standard*, 31 October 2014.

28. See 'It's Dav's Army', *Sun*, 29 March 2012, and Nigel Morris, 'Parties Unite in Outrage at Union Threat to Games', *Independent*, 1 March 2012.

29. See, e.g. <https://d25d2506sfb94s.cloudfront.net/cumulus_uploads/docu ment/6r8ioygkzi/ST_Results_120331.pdf>.

30. Ed Miliband, 'Get Back to the Commons and Tell us: Who do you Really Serve, Mr Cameron', *Mail on Sunday*, 29 March 2012.

31. BBC, 'MP Dorries Calls PM and Chancellor "Arrogant Posh Boys"', 23 April 2012 <http://www.bbc.co.uk/news/uk-politics-17815769>.

32. Ultimately, in 2013, the Office for National Statistics decided that there had been no double-dip recession: see BBC, 'UK Double-Dip Recession Revised away', 27 June 2013 <http://www.bbc.co.uk/news/business-23079082>.

33. See <http://www.icmresearch.com/data/media/pdf/OmBPC-Apr12.pdf>.

34. <https://d25d2506sfb94s.cloudfront.net/cumulus_uploads/document/viupxgwx31/YG-Archives-Pol-ST-results-23-250312.pdf>.

35. Patrick Wintour, 'David Cameron's Mask has Slipped, Says Labour Leader', *Guardian*, 21 April 2012.

36. Ben Jackson and Gregg McClymont, *Cameron's Trap: Lessons for Labour from the 1930s and 1980s* (London: Policy, 2011) <http://www.policy-network.net/publications_detail.aspx?ID=4113>, and Duncan Weldon, 'The Tory "Feelgood Factor"', *Fabian Review*, Spring 2012 <http://www.fabians.org.uk/wp-content/uploads/2012/03/Fabian-Review-Spring-2012.pdf>.

37. See Tom Clark, 'Eurozone Crisis: Guardian/ICM Poll: Voters Think Euro will Break up—but Remain Unsure who to Blame', *Guardian*, 22 May 2012.

38. See Martin Bright, 'Ken Livingstone: Jews Won't Vote Labour because they are Rich', *Jewish Chronicle*, 21 March 2012, and Hélène Mulholland, 'Ken Livingstone Pays Every Pound of Tax he Owes, Says Ed Miliband', *Guardian*, 13 March 2012. See also BBC, 'Ken Livingstone Campaigning for Non-Labour Candidate', 18 October 2010 <http://www.bbc.co.uk/news/uk-england-london-11569758>.

39. Matthew D'Ancona, 'Cameron Needs to Capture Some of Boris's Sunshine', *Sunday Telegraph*, 6 May 2012.

40. See Lewis Baston, *The Bradford Earthquake* (London: Democratic Audit, 2012) <http://www.jrrt.org.uk/publications/bradford-earthquake-full-report>.

41. See Helen Pidd, 'Bradford Spring Turns Wintry as City's Respect Councillors Quit', *Guardian*, 26 March 2013.

42. Andrew Rawnsley, 'David Cameron Needs to Keep his Headless Chickens in the Coop', *Observer*, 6 May 2013.

43. David Miliband, 'We are Losing our Balance: A Left Hand will Steady us', *The Times*, 8 May 2012.

CHAPTER 5. ONE NATION: SPRING–AUTUMN 2012

1. Steve Richards, 'Queen's Speech—a Ragbag of Eye-Catching Measures Worthy of Tony Blair', *Independent*, 10 May 2012.
2. Matthew D'Ancona, 'Ed Miliband: "Tony Blair Gives me Good Advice"', *Sunday Telegraph*, 20 May 2012.
3. Ed Miliband, Speech to Progress, 13 May 2012 <http://www.politics.co.uk/comment-analysis/2012/05/13/ed-miliband-progress-speech-in-full-v>.
4. See Mary Riddell and Tim Ross, 'Ed Balls is Ready for a Run-in with Unions and the IMF', *Daily Telegraph*, 21 May 2012, and Ed Balls and Peter Mandelson, 'We Agree about Europe', *Guardian*, 14 May 2012.
5. See Patrick Wintour, 'Unions Fight Labour's Blairite Faction "in Struggle for Party's Soul"', *Guardian*, 16 June 2012.
6. BBC, 'GMB Union Warns Labour on Funding', 11 June 2012 <http://www.bbc.co.uk/news/uk-politics-18392440>.
7. Patrick Wintour, 'Unions Fight Labour's Blairite Faction "in Struggle for Party's Soul"', *Guardian*, 16 June 2012.
8. See Jane Merrick, 'Ed Miliband: "Cameron is the Last Gasp of the Old Guard"', *Independent*, 17 June 2012.
9. See Hélène Mulholland, 'Labour Pressure Group Progress Announces Shakeup after Union Attacks', *Guardian.com*, 3 July 2012 <http://www.theguardian.com/politics/2012/jul/03/labour-pressure-group-progress-shakeup>.
10. Ed Miliband, Speech to IPPR, 22 June 2012 <http://www.politics.co.uk/comment-analysis/2012/06/22/ed-miliband-s-immigration-speech-in-full>.
11. Michael Savage, 'Miliband Admits Mistake over Flood of Migrants', *The Times*, 23 June 2012.
12. Ed Miliband, speech to Fabian Society Summer Conference, 2 July 2012 <http://www.fabians.org.uk/ed-milibands-speech-at-fabian-society-summer-conference-full-text/>.
13. BBC, 'Osborne: Balls not Personally Involved in Libor Scandal', 5 July 2012 <http://www.bbc.co.uk/news/uk-politics-18716828>.
14. *MailOnline*, 3 October 2012 <http://www.dailymail.co.uk/news/article-2212261/Labour-conference-Builders-plumbers-urged-join-Ed-Milibands-class-war-Conservatives.html>.
15. See <http://classonline.org.uk/>.
16. Kevin Schofield, 'Union's Ed Plot', *Sun*, 21 July 2012. For Quayle's original piece, see <http://www.workersliberty.org/story/2012/07/11/how-unite-plans-change-labour-party>.
17. <http://www.populus.co.uk/Poll/The-TimesPopulus-poll-September-2012/>; see also Sam Coates, 'Labour may Hold Lead but Voters Still Prefer Tories on Economy', *The Times*, 18 September 2012.

18. Mark Hookham, 'Union Boss: We'll Seize Back Labour', *Sunday Times*, 30 September 2012.

19. James Forsyth, 'Labour's Lady in Waiting', *Spectator*, 29 September 2012.

20. Patrick Wintour, 'Labour will Examine every Penny of Public Spending, Ed Balls Promises', *Guardian*, 28 September 2012.

21. Graeme Cooke, Patrick Diamond, and Steve Van Riel, *The Purple Papers: Real Change for Britain, Real Choices for Britain* (London: Progress, 2012) <http://www.progressonline.org.uk/wp-content/uploads/2012/10/The-Purple-Papers.pdf>.

22. Geoff Teather and Joe Murphy, 'I Blame Ken for Losing to Boris: He Paid a Deserved Price for the Errors he Made', *Evening Standard*, 28 September 2012.

23. Rafael Behr, 'Douglas Alexander: "It's Time to Take Boris Seriously"', *New Statesman*, 26 September 2012.

24. Matthew D'Ancona, 'What's the Point of Labour when the Coffers are Empty?', *Sunday Telegraph*, 20 September 2012.

25. For a transcript of the speech, see <http://labourlist.org/2012/10/ed-milibands-conference-speech-the-transcript/>.

26. See, e.g. 'That's One Giant Leap Forward', *Daily Mirror*, and 'Fluent, Adroit . . . Yet Profoundly Dishonest', *Daily Mail*, both 3 October 2012.

27. See 7 October 2012 <http://ukpollingreport.co.uk/blog/archives/6260>.

28. See <http://lordashcroftpolls.com/wp-content/uploads/2012/10/BLUE-COLLAR-TORIES.pdf>.

29. Janan Ganesh, 'Miliband Needs to Give Labour a Shock', *Financial Times*, 2 October 2012.

### CHAPTER 6. BENEFITS OF THE DOUBT: AUTUMN 2012–SPRING 2013

1. Mary Riddell, 'Supersonic Ed Miliband is about to Give Labour the Shock of its Life', *Daily Telegraph*, 18 October 2012.

2. Jane Merrick, 'Ed Miliband Exclusive: "We'd Name and Shame Low-Payers"', *Independent on Sunday*, 4 November 2012.

3. Peter Kellner, 'Labour's Lost Votes', *Prospect* (November 2012) <http://www.prospectmagazine.co.uk/features/labour-voters-election-europe-immigration>.

4. Tim Montgomerie, 'Conservative HQ Briefs Tory Members on its Battleground Strategy', *ConservativeHome*, 12 October 2012 <http://www.conservativehome.com/majority_conservatism/2012/10/conservative-hq-briefs-tory-members-on-its-battleground-strategy.html>.

5. Andrew Rawnsley, 'A Tip for Labour about Planning for Power: Listen to the Tories', *Observer*, 28 October 2012.

6. See Tim Bale, 'Definitely Mature, not Necessarily Mad: Party Members', in Philip Cowley and Robert Ford (eds), *Sex, Lies and the Ballot Box* (London: Biteback, 2014), 229–33.

7. See Lord Ashcroft Polls, 8 March 2013 <http://lordashcroftpolls.com/2013/03/what-are-the-liberal-democrats-for/#more-2040>.

8. John Rentoul, 'Things Must Be Bad when even Gove Disagrees', *Independent on Sunday*, 18 November 2012.

9. Ed Balls and Douglas Alexander, 'Standing Still isn't Enough: The EU Needs Cuts', *The Times*, 29 October 2012.

10. YouGov, 4 November 2012 <https://d25d2506sfb94s.cloudfront.net/cumulus_uploads/document/hqayq9eo9d/YG-Archives-Pol-ST-results%20-%2020121102.pdf>.

11. Jane Merrick, 'Ed Miliband Exclusive: "We'd Name and Shame Low-Payers"', *Independent on Sunday*, 4 November 2012.

12. Peter Oborne, 'A Good Day for Cameron, but a Rout for the Tory Right's Vision', *Daily Telegraph*, 8 November 2012.

13. Lord Ashcroft Polls, 21 November 2012 <http://lordashcroftpolls.com/2012/11/project-red-alert/#more-1818>.

14. Ed Balls, 'Working Families Paying for Tory Failures', *Sun*, 9 December 2012.

15. Roland Watson, 'Tough but Fair: That's our Pledge on Welfare, Says Balls', *The Times*, 21 December 2012.

16. Lord West, 'Alternatives to Trident are Illogical and Dangerous', *Independent*, 27 February 2013.

17. See <https://d25d2506sfb94s.cloudfront.net/cumulus_uploads/document/xzmltcdt5i/YG-Archive-results-TUC-121212-welfare-benefits-knowledge.pdf>.

18. See <http://cdn.yougov.com/cumulus_uploads/document/c9321abal2/Media%20Standards%20Trust%20121123.pdf>.

19. See <http://www.politics.co.uk/comment-analysis/2013/01/08/david-miliband-benefits-speech-in-full>.

20. See <http://www.politicshome.com/uk/article/66147/one_nation_in_europe_%E2%80%93_ed_miliband_speech.html>.

21. YouGov, 26 January 2013 <https://d25d2506sfb94s.cloudfront.net/cumulus_uploads/document/2dyt3nf221/YG-Archive-Pol-Sunday-Times-results-25-270113.pdf>.

22. Jack Blanchard 'Don't Be Stupid on Euro Referendum, Balls Warns Labour', *Yorkshire Post*, 9 February 2013.

23. See Gary Nicks, 'Speak English or Stay away: Ed U-Turn on Migrants', *Daily Star*, 15 December 2012. See also Jason Groves, Tim Shipman, and Gerri Peev, 'How Ed Dropped Plan to Admit Labour's Immigration Failures', *Daily Mail*, 15 December 2012, and, for the speech itself <http://www.politics.co.uk/comment-analysis/2012/12/14/ed-miliband-immigration-speech-in-ful>.

24. See <http://www.politics.co.uk/comment-analysis/2013/03/07/yvette-cooper-s-immigration-speech-in-full>.

25. See Tim Bale, 'Concede and Move on? One Nation Labour and the Welfare State', *Political Quarterly*, 84/3 (2013), 342–52 <http://www.politicalquarterly.org.uk/2013/09/one-nation.html>.

26. See <http://www.bsa-29.natcen.ac.uk/read-the-report/welfare/introduction.aspx> and <http://www.demos.co.uk/files/Demos_Ipsos_Generation_Strains_web.pdf?1378677272>.

27. See Mark Ferguson, 'Welfare Sanctions Vote—the Fallout Continues', *LabourList*, 22 March 2013 <http://labourlist.org/2013/03/welfare-sanctions-vote-the-fallout-continues/>.

28. Mary Riddell, 'Great Expectations? No. Hard Times? Yes. Enter Miliband Snr', *Daily Telegraph*, 7 February 2012.

29. BBC, 'Mick Philpott Case: George Osborne Benefit Comments Spark Row', 5 April 2013 <http://www.bbc.co.uk/news/uk-politics-22025035>.

30. See, e.g. the polling cited in David Wooding, 'Six out of Ten Voters Think State Handouts Are Far Too Generous', *Sun on Sunday*, 7 April 2013.

31. Tony Blair, 'Labour Must Search for Answers and not Merely Aspire to be a Repository for People's Anger', *New Statesman*, 11 April 2013.

32. Kevin Schofield, 'The Blair Bitch Project: Ex-PM and Heavyweight Pals Tear into Red Ed', *Sun*, 12 April 2013.

33. See Anushka Asthana, *The Women Problem: Who is Winning the Battle for Britain's Female Vote?* (London: Mumsnet/Ipsos-Mori, 2013) <https://www.ipsos-mori.com/researchpublications/publications/1591/The-Women-Problem.aspx>.

34. Miliband's House of Commons tribute to Thatcher can be read in full at <http://www.theguardian.com/politics/2013/apr/10/margaret-thatcher-tributes-ed-miliband-speech>.

35. See Patrick Wintour, 'I Blundered over VAT Cut during Interview, Admits Miliband', *Guardian*, 1 May 2013.

## CHAPTER 7. WARMING UP: SPRING–AUTUMN 2013

1. Robert Ford and Matthew Goodwin, *Revolt on the Right: Explaining Support for the Radical Right in Britain* (Abingdon: Routledge, 2014).

2. P. Amara, '"Action Hero" Ed Miliband Goes to the Rescue of Kentish Town Crash Cyclist who Flipped over Handlebars', *Camden New Journal*, 8 May 2013 <http://www.camdennewjournal.com/news/2013/may/%E2%80%98action-hero%E2%80%99-ed-miliband-goes-rescue-kentish-town-crash-cyclist-who-flipped-over-hand>.

3. Janan Ganesh, 'Even the British Left is Turning against Europe', *Financial Times*, 2 July 2013.

4. See Tim Bale, 'Concede and Move on? One Nation Labour and the Welfare State', *Political Quarterly*, 84/3 (2013), 342–52 <http://www.politicalquarterly.org.uk/2013/09/one-nation.html>.

5. 'Sun Says', *Sun*, 4 June 2013.

6. Comment, 'Labour's "Iron Discipline" should be Put to the Test', *Daily Telegraph*, 4 June 2013.

7. Ed Miliband, Speech on 'A One Nation Plan for Social Security Reform', 6 June 2013 <http://labourlist.org/2013/06/full-text-ed-miliband-speech-a-one-nation-plan-for-social-security-reform/>.

8. See Kevin Meagher, 'Uncut Poll Reveals Public Blame Last Labour Government, not Tories, for Today's Benefits Bill', *Labour Uncut*, 12 September 2013 <http://labour-uncut.co.uk/2013/09/12/uncut-poll-reveals-public-blame-last-labour-government-not-tories-for-today%E2%80%99s-benefits-bill/>.

9. See Patrick Wintour, 'Labour Warned on Selection Panel Procedures', *Guardian*, 13 May 2013. For a spirited riposte from the left, see Mark Seddon, 'The Chutzpah of Peter Mandelson', *LabourList*, 22 May 2013 <http://labourlist.org/2013/05/the-chutzpah-of-peter-mandelson-and-why-we-need-more-trade-unionists/>.

10. See George Eaton, 'If Ed Miliband is Seduced by the Blairites, he'll be Consigned to the Dustbin of History', *New Statesman*, 29 April 2013, and BBC, 'Ed Miliband Attacks Unite Leader Len McCluskey's Comments', 25 April 2013 <http://www.bbc.co.uk/news/uk-politics-22283127>.

11. See Mark Seddon, 'The Chutzpah of Peter Mandelson', *LabourList*, 22 May 2013 <http://labourlist.org/2013/05/the-chutzpah-of-peter-mandelson-and-why-we-need-more-trade-unionists/>.

12. Simon Walters and Glen Owen, 'Miliband Caught in "Blackmail" Storm over Dirty Tricks in Safe Labour Seat', *Mail on Sunday*, 23 June 2013.

13. Nicholas Watt and Rajeev Syal, 'Miliband to Explore Break with Unions', *Guardian*, 6 July 2013.

14. Ed Miliband, 'The Falkirk Scandal Shows that Labour Needs to Mend, not End, Union Links', *Observer*, 7 July 2013.

15. See Billy Kenber, 'McCluskey's Olive Branch for Miliband', *The Times*, 8 May 2013.

16. See BBC, 'GMB Cuts Funds it Gives Labour from £1.2m to £150,000', 4 September 2013 <http://www.bbc.co.uk/news/uk-politics-23955577>.

17. For Labour membership relative to that of other parties, see House of Commons Research Note, 24 September 2014 <file:///C:/Users/Owner/Downloads/sn05125%20(3).pdf>.

18. Peter Clarke, 'Labour Realised that Parties Need Recruits, not Conscripts', *Financial Times*, 13 July 2013.

19. Tony Blair, Sky News, 9 July 2013 <http://news.sky.com/story/1113175/miliband-vows-to-reform-labours-union-ties>.

20. See Oliver Wright, 'Union Boss Demands More Say in Labour's Policy Making', *Independent*, 25 July 2013. See also Lord Ashcroft Polls, July 2013 <http://lordashcroftpolls.com/wp-content/uploads/2013/07/Unite-members-poll-Results-summary1.pdf>.

21. Editorial, 'Financial Ed Ache . . .', *Daily Mirror*, 5 September 2013.

22. YouGov, 9 September 2013 <https://d25d2506sfb94s.cloudfront.net/cumulus_uploads/document/jgtl8j1iz8/YG-Archive-Labour-Uncut-results-090913.pdf>.

23. 'Sun Says, "Name & Shame"', *Sun*, 7 Feburary 2013.

24. See Oliver Wright, 'Hospitals Freeze A&E Targets—because they Can't Hit them', *Independent*, 22 May 2013.

25. 'Thousands may have Died because of Labour NHS Failings, Tory MPs Claim', *Telegraph.co.uk*, 15 July 2013 <http://www.telegraph.co.uk/health/healthnews/10181220/Thousands-may-have-died-because-of-Labour-NHS-failings-Tory-MPs-claim.html>.

26. See Daniel Boffey, 'NHS Boss "Sorry over Attacks on Labour's Record": Bruce Keogh "Furious" after Tories' Assault on Burnham over Hospital Trust Death Figures', *Observer*, 21 July 2013.

27. See Patrick Wintour, 'Health Chief Apologises to Burnham for Email "Lapse"', *Guardian*, 9 October 2013.

28. YouGov's 'Political Trackers' <https://yougov.co.uk/publicopinion/archive/?category=political-trackers>.

29. Decca Aitkenhead, 'The Saturday Interview: "We've Lost the Art of Thinking Bigger"', *Guardian*, 10 August 2013.

30. Stephen Twigg, Speech to the RSA, 17 June 2013 <http://archive.labour.org.uk/no-school-left-behind>.

31. Ian Taylor and Lynne Sloman, *Rebuilding Rail* (London: Transport for Quality of Life, 2012) <http://www.transportforqualityoflife.com/u/files/120630_Rebuilding_Rail_Final_Report_print_version.pdf>.

32. See Survation, 'Would Nationalising Railways Help Labour? New Poll of "Commuter Marginals"', June 2014 <http://survation.com/would-nationalising-railways-help-labour-new-poll-of-commuter-marginals/>.

33. See Mark Hookham, 'Labour Puts £50bn Cap on HS2 Scheme', *Sunday Times*, 25 August 2014.

34. John Prescott, 'Come on Ed, Kick 'em out', *Daily Mirror*, 18 August 2013. See also Jason Beattie, 'Ed Alert: Poll Crisis for Miliband', *Daily Mirror*, 20 August 2013.

35. See BBC, 'Diane Abbott: Polls Swaying Labour's Immigration Stance', 21 August 2013 <http://www.bbc.co.uk/news/uk-politics-23784368>. See also YouGov, 13 August 2013 <http://cdn.yougov.com/cumulus_uploads/document/fupsj8wpnk/YG-Archive-immigration-van-results-120813.pdf>.

36. Tessa Jowell, 'Ed Miliband's Labour Critics are a Boon to the Tories', *Observer*, 25 August 2013.

37. See Toby Helm, 'In Focus: How Cameron Lost the Battle with his Party and the Country', *Observer*, 1 September 2013.

38. Ben Bradshaw, 'The Prism that Distorts', *Guardian*, 6 September 2013.

39. Fraser Nelson, 'Even Labour Supporters don't Think that Ed Miliband's up to it', *Daily Telegraph*, 13 September 2013.

CHAPTER 8. FINAL BEND: AUTUMN 2013–SPRING 2014

1. Damian McBride, *Power Trip: A Decade of Policy, Plots and Spin* (London: Biteback, 2014).

2. Opinium, 17 September 2013 <http://ourinsight.opinium.co.uk/sites/ourinsight.opinium.co.uk/files/vi_17_09_2013.pdf>.

3. ComRes, August–September <http://comres.co.uk/polls/Sunday_Polit ics_Councillors_Survey_September_2013_Labour.pdf>.

4. Andrew Rawnsley and Toby Helm, '"It is Going to be a Tough Fight. But I am Absolutely Confident"', *Observer*, 22 September 2013.

5. For a choice selection of the press coverage, see Roy Greenslade, 'Red Ed and the Tory Press—Newspapers Hark back to the 1950s', *guardian.com*, 25 September 2013 <http://www.theguardian.com/media/greenslade/2013/sep/25/edmiliband-national-newspapers>.

6. Philip Collins, 'Ed can Win from here. But he can't Govern', *The Times*, 27 September 2013.

7. Andrew Harrop, 'For Miliband, Steady, Safety-First Politics Is no Longer an Option', *Huffington Post*, 22 September 2013 <http://www.huffingtonpost.co.uk/andrew-harrop/for-miliband-steady-safet_b_3970480.html>.

8. Mehdi Hasan, 'Mehdi's Morning Memo', *Huffington Post*, 25 September 2013 <http://www.huffingtonpost.co.uk/2013/09/24/ed-miliband-speech_n_3985332.html>.

9. ComRes, 29 October 2013 <http://comres.co.uk/polls/Independent_Political_Poll_29_October_2013.pdf>; Ipsos Mori, Political Monitor, October 2013 <https://www.ipsos-mori.com/Assets/Docs/Polls/PolMonOct2013_charts.PDF>; and YouGov, 4 November 2013 <http://d25d2506sfb94s.cloudfront.net/cumulus_uploads/document/lox9cfjwcz/YouGov-Progress-Survey-Results-131011.pdf>.

10. See ComRes, 29 September 2013 <http://comres.co.uk/polls/IoS_SM_Political_Poll_20th_October_2013.pdf>.

11. Toby Helm, 'Secret Memo Shows Key Role for Blairites in Election Team', *Observer*, 8 December 2013.

12. Geoffrey Levy, 'The Man who Hated Britain', *MailOnline*, 27 September 2013 <http://www.dailymail.co.uk/news/article-2435751/Red-Eds-pledge-bring-socialism-homage-Marxist-father-Ralph-Miliband-says-GEOFFREY-LEVY.html>.

13. Kevin Schofield, 'Ed's Revenge is the Blair Ditch Project', *Sun*, 8 October 2013.

14. Heather Stewart and Toby Helm, 'Trades Union Chiefs Slam Rachel Reeves for "Tougher than Tories" Welfare Pledge', *Observer*, 20 October 2013.

15. Joe Murphy, 'Tories Winning on Welfare, Says Labour Pollster', *Evening Standard*, 9 October 2013.

16. See Brendan Carlin, 'New Threat to HS2 as Balls Compares it to Dome Disaster', *Mail on Sunday*, 27 October 2013.

17. See Adam Sherwin, 'Miliband Risks Support in North over Stand on HS2', *Independent*, 30 October 2013.

18. For details of the email trail, see Mark Ferguson, 'Senior Miliband Staffer Brands Ed Balls' Messaging a "Nightmare"—but this Row is Bigger than that', *LabourList*, 17 November 2013 <http://labourlist.org/2013/11/senior-miliband-staffer-brands-ed-balls-messaging-a-nightmare-but-this-row-is-bigger-than-that/>. On the other 'feud', see Simon Walters and Brendan Carlin, 'Ed's Don't Panic Call in Tatters after Bitter Feud Rocks his Election Team', *Mail on Sunday*, 30 March 2014.

19. Aditya Chakrabortty, 'On a Frustrating and Fascinating Day without Big Winners . . .', *Guardian*, 6 December 2013.

20. See Paul Johnson, Institute for Fiscal Studies, 6 December 2012 <http://www.ifs.org.uk/budgets/as2013/openingremarks_AS13.pdf>.

21. See George Parker and Jim Pickard, 'Ed Balls Aims to Identify Spending Cuts in Labour Review', *Financial Times*, 19 December 2013. See also Kevin Schofield, 'Ed on the Block', *Sun*, 18 December 2013.

22. Dan Hodges, 'If that Was a Good Year for Ed Miliband, he can't Afford to Have a Bad One', *Telegraph.co.uk*, 31 December 2013 <http://www.telegraph.co.uk/news/politics/ed-miliband/10544733/If-that-was-a-good-year-for-Ed-Miliband-hecant-afford-to-have-a-bad-one.html>.

23. James Carville and Stan Greenberg, *It's the Middle Class, Stupid!* (New York: Plume, 2013).

24. Ed Miliband, 'Only Labour can Rebuild our Middle Class', *Daily Telegraph*, 14 January 2013.

25. Emma Reynolds, Speech to National House Building Council, 13 January 2013 <http://press.labour.org.uk/post/73194565182/speech-to-national-house-building-council>.

26. Rachel Reeves, Speech to IPPR, 20 January 2014 <http://press.labour.org.uk/post/73937630140/rachel-reeves-a-one-nation-approach-to-social-security>.

27. Ed Miliband, 'We're too Reliant on Low-Wage Labour', *Independent on Sunday*, 5 January 2014.

28. Nicholas Watt, 'Labour Toughens Migrant Benefits Stance', *Guardian*, 13 January 2014.

29. ComRes, 19 May 2014 <http://comres.co.uk/polls/ComRes_Battlebus__The_Independent_Marginal_Seats_Political_Poll.pdf>.

30. Andrew Grice, 'It's a Four-Party Fight: UKIP is Hoovering up the Anti-Politics Vote', *Independent*, 7 Feburary 2014.

31. Simon Danczuk, 'Memo to Ed: We've Got to Stop Treating UKIP like Swivel-Eyed Lepers', *Mail on Sunday*, 25 May 2014.

32. Yvette Cooper, Speech, 10 April 2014 <http://labourlist.org/2014/04/yvette-coopers-immigration-speech-full-text/>.

33. Isabel Hardman, 'Labour MP Warns on Party's Failure to Equip Activists for Battle with UKIP', *Spectator, Coffee House*, 23 May 2014 <http://blogs.spectator.co.uk/coffeehouse/2014/05/labour-mp-warns-on-partys-failure-to-equip-activists-for-battle-with-ukip/>.

34. 'Sun Says, "Migrant Chaos"', *Sun*, 11 April 2014.

35. See, e.g. Tom Newton Dunn and Emily Ashton, 'Eur Being a coward, Ed', *Sun*, 13 March 2014.

36. Ed Balls, Speech to Greater Manchester Chamber of Commerce, 15 May 2014 <http://press.labour.org.uk/post/85849337069/we-need-real-change-to-make-the-eu-work-better-for>.

37. Ed Balls, Speech to Fabian Society New Year Conference, 25 January 2014 <http://labourlist.org/2014/01/full-text-ed-balls-commits-labour-to-budget-surplus-and-announces-50p-tax-rate-plan/>. See also Adam Boulton, 'Now we Know the Difference between Red and Blue: 50p', *Sunday Times*, 26 January 2014.

38. The broadcast can be watched on YouTube <http://www.youtube.com/watch?v=IIH-2lZF2yw>.

39. See Matthew Holehouse, 'Splits at Top of Labour as Ed Balls Disowns Vegetable Poster', *Telegraph.co.uk*, 14 May 2014 <http://www.telegraph.co.uk/news/politics/labour/10832062/Splits-at-top-of-Labour-as-Ed-Balls-disowns-vegetables-poster.html>.

40. See Matt Chorley, 'Is this the Moment...', *MailOnline*, 21 May 2014 <http://www.dailymail.co.uk/news/article-2634977/Is-moment-Ed-re alised-man-sold-bacon-sandwich-voting-Tory-Labour-leaders-nationwide-tour-gets-difficult-start.html>.

41. Steve Richards, 'The Mood around Ed Miliband is one of Paranoia and Suspicion', *New Statesman*, 10 April 2014.

42. 'Labour Must Adopt New Principles', letter to the *Guardian*, 23 March 2014 <http://www.theguardian.com/society/2014/mar/23/labour-must-adopt-new-principles>.

43. Ed Miliband, Hugo Young Lecture, 10 February 2014 <http://labourlist.org/2014/02/ed-milibands-hugo-young-lecture-full-text/>.

44. See, e.g. Gerri Peev, 'Labour's Poll Chiefs Go to War...on each Other', *MailOnline*, 31 March 2014 <http://www.dailymail.co.uk/news/article-2592977/Labours-poll-chiefs-war-Senior-party-figures-fall-ratings-tumble.html>.

45. Nicholas Watt, 'Surveyors Reject Labour's Plan for Private Sector Rents Ceiling', *Guardian*, 2 May 2014.

CHAPTER 9. HOME STRAIGHT: SPRING–AUTUMN 2014

1. Lord Ashcroft Polls, Post European Election Poll, 24 May 2014 <http://lordashcroftpolls.com/wp-content/uploads/2014/05/LORD-ASHCROFT-POLLS-Post-Euro-Election-Poll-Summary-May-2014.pdf>, and Conservative-Labour Battlegrounds, May 2014 <http://lordashcroftpolls.com/wp-content/uploads/2014/05/LORD-ASHCROFT-POLLS-Marginals-report-May-2014.pdf>.

2. Trevor Phillips and Richard Webber, 'Superdiversity and the Browning of Labour', *Political Quarterly*, 85/3 (2014), 304–11.

3. Robert Ford and Ian Warren, 'UKIP has Torn up the Map', *Telegraph.co.uk*, 26 May 2014 <http://www.telegraph.co.uk/news/politics/ukip/10857198/Ukip-has-torn-up-the-map.html>.

4. Lord Ashcroft Polls, *Labour–Liberal Democrat Battleground*, July 2014 <http://lordashcroftpolls.com/wp-content/uploads/2014/07/LABOUR-LIB-DEM-BATTLEGROUND-JUNE-2014-FULL-TABLES.pdf>.

5. See Adam Bienkov, 'Blair Warns Labour not to Lurch to Right on Immigration', *politics.co.uk*, 27 May 2014 <http://www.politics.co.uk/news/2014/05/27/blair-warns-labour-not-to-lurch-to-right-on-immigration>.

6. Ed Miliband, Speech in Thurrock, 27 May 2014 <http://press.labour.org.uk/post/86997808779/britain-needs-real-change-not-false-promises-ed>.

7. Craig Woodhouse, 'Labour will Relax British Borders if they Win... we'll Tighten them up', *Sun on Sunday*, 1 June 2014.

8. 'Immigration: "We Urge you to Constrain the Free Movement of Labour"', *Observer*, 1 June 2014; John Prescott, 'Time to Put our Border in Order', *Sunday Mirror*, 1 June 2014; and John Mann, 'Lessons for Labour', *Prospect*, 12 June 2014 <http://www.prospectmagazine.co.uk/politics/lessons-for-labour>.

9. John Denham, 'Home Truths on Migration', *LabourList*, 2 June 2014 <http://labourlist.org/2014/06/home-truths-on-migration/>.

10. See, e.g. Atu Hatwal, 'At Least UKIP's EU and Immigration Policies are Consistent.', *Labour Uncut*, 3 June 2014 <http://labour-uncut.co.uk/2014/06/03/at-least-ukips-eu-and-immigration-policies-are-consistent-john-denham-cant-even-manage-that/>.

11. See Joe Jervis, 'Ways to Win in 2015', *LabourList*, 6 June 2014 <http://labourlist.org/2014/06/ways-to-win-in-2015-5-lessons-from-chukas-progress-speech/>.

12. Marcus Roberts, *Revolt on the Left: Labour's UKIP Problem and how it Can Be Overcome* (London: Fabian Society, 2014) <http://www.fabians.org.uk/wp-content/uploads/2014/10/RevoltOnTheLeft-Final4.pdf>. See also Lord Ashcroft Polls, Con–Lab Battlegrounds, 22 July 2014 <http://lordashcroftpolls.com/wp-content/uploads/2014/07/CON-LAB-BATTLEGROUND-JULY-2014-FULL-TABLES.pdf>.

13. Kevin Schofield, 'Labour's Answer? Coffee Mornings!', *Sun*, 11 June 2014.

14. See Craig Woodhouse, 'Labour in Benefits Euro Curb', *Sun on Sunday*, 3 August 2014.

15. See Mary Riddell and James Kirkup, '"Anyone who Rises up Gets Knocked down"', *Daily Telegraph*, 2 August 2014.

16. Jeremy Cliffe, 'Whatever the Truth', *Economist Blighty Blog*, 11 October 2014 <http://www.economist.com/blogs/blighty/2014/10/labour-and-immigration>.

17. Rowena Mason and Aisha Gani, 'Labour Picks Westminster Insiders for Key Seats', *Guardian*, 18 June 2014.

18. ComRes, Labour Candidates Survey, September 2014 <http://comres.co.uk/polls/Sunday_Politics_PPC_survey_results_Labour_September2014.pdf>.

19. See Tim Bale, 'Putting it Right? The Labour Party's Big Shift on Immigration since 2010', *Political Quarterly*, 85/3 (2014) <http://onlinelibrary.wiley.com/doi/10.1111/1467-923X.12091/abstract>.

20. John McTernan, 'For Fox Sake', *Progress*, 10 October 2014 <http://www.progressonline.org.uk/2014/10/10/for-fox-sake/>.

21. Paul Whiteley, Harold D. Clarke, David Sanders, and Marianne C. Stewart, 'The Economic and Electoral Consequences of Austerity Policies in Britain', *Parliamentary Affairs*, Advance Access.

22. Chuka Umunna, *Owning the Future: How Britain can Make it in a Fast Changing World* (London: Policy Network, 2014).

23. See, for an example, Jenni Russell, 'Ed and his Team would be a Disaster at No. 10', *The Times*, 3 July 2013.

24. Independent Commission on Whole Person Care, *One Person, One Team, One System* (February 2014) <http://www.yourbritain.org.uk/uploads/editor/files/One_Person_One_Team_One_System.pdf>.

25. Patrick Diamond, 'Promising a New Health Tax is Brave', *Guardian*, 14 September 2014 <http://www.theguardian.com/politics/2014/sep/14/labour-nhs-health-tax-ed-miliband>.

26. Contrast ComRes, July 2014 <http://comres.co.uk/polls/Incisive_Health_Poll_of_the_public_on_tax_and_the_NHS.pdf>, and Populus, September 2014 <http://www.populus.co.uk/wp-content/uploads/Reform-Populus-NHS-tax-tables.pdf>.

27. Ed Balls, 'A Mansion Tax will be Fair, Simple and Pay to Save the NHS', *Evening Standard*, 20 October 2014.

28. Survation, 23 September 2014 <http://labourlist.org/wp-content/uploads/2014/09/Tables-for-Ed-Miliband-Speech-Reactions-Poll.pdf>.

29. See Patrick Wintour, 'Labour Vows to Rub out Gove Era in Education', *Guardian*, 30 April 2014.

30. Jon Cruddas and Jonathan Rutherford, *One Nation: Labour's Political Renewal* (London: One Nation Register, 2014) <http://b.3cdn.net/lab ouruk/7d780d9fb7f25e85bd_1rm6iywub.pdf>.

31. Patrick Wintour, 'Labour is Producing the Policies but not yet a Vision, say Party Strategists', *Guardian*, 5 July 2014.

32. Kayte Lawton, Graeme Cooke, and Nick Pearce, *The Condition of Britain: Strategies for Social Renewal* (London: IPPR, 2014) <http://www.ippr.org/assets/media/publications/pdf/the-condition-of-britain_June2014.pdf>.

33. Toby Helm, 'Labour Fights Itself in Struggle to Find Winning Solution to the "Ed Problem"', *Observer*, 22 June 2014.

34. See Tim Shipman, '"Dead-Hand" Miliband Blasted by Top Adviser', *Sunday Times*, 29 June 2014.

35. Gordon Brown, *My Scotland, our Britain: A Future Worth Sharing* (London: Simon and Schuster, 2014).

36. YouGov, 19 August 2014 <https://d25d2506sfb94s.cloudfront.net/cumulus_uploads/document/jvzzealgmj/Times_Scotland_Results_140815_Tuesday.pdf>.

37. YouGov, 2 September 2014 <https://d25d2506sfb94s.cloudfront.net/cumulus_uploads/document/vt3dw4u8k5/Scotland_EndofAug_Times_Sun_Website.pdf>.

38. Ed Miliband, Speech, 4 September 2014 <http://labourlist.org/2014/09/lets-make-that-change-happen-together-ed-milibands-speech-against-scottish-independence/>.

39. YouGov, 7 September 2014 <https://d25d2506sfb94s.cloudfront.net/cumulus_uploads/document/ywzyqmrf2u/Scotland_Final_140905_Sunday_Times_FINAL.pdf>. See also Roy Greenslade, '"The Vow" and the Daily Record—Creative Journalism or Political Spin?', *Guardian.co.uk*, 31 October 2014 <http://www.theguardian.com/media/greenslade/2014/oct/31/daily-record-scottish-independence>.

40. See Blair McDougall, 'Fight your own Campaign', *Progress*, 29 October 2014 <http://www.progressonline.org.uk/2014/10/29/fight-your-own-campaign/>.

41. Vernon Bogdanor, 'Why English Votes for English Laws is a Kneejerk Absurdity', *Guardian*, 25 September 2014.

42. See, e.g., Richard Wyn Jones, Guy Lodge, Ailsa Henderson, and Daniel Wincott, *The Dog that Finally Barked: England as an Emerging Political Community* (London: IPPR, 2012). See also Philip Johnston, 'After Devolution, the Boot's on England's Foot', *The Times*, 8 March 2010.

43. *Report of the Commission on the Consequences of Devolution for the House of Commons* (2013) <http://webarchive.nationalarchives.gov.uk/20130403030652/http://tmc.independent.gov.uk/wp-content/uploads/2013/03/The-McKay-Commission_Main-Report_25-March-20131.pdf>.

44. James Chapman, 'Ed Refuses to Back English Home Rule 13 Times!', *Daily Mail*, 22 September 2014.

45. Figures quoted in Robbie Dinwoodie, 'Labour Face Battle to Save Heartlands from SNP Surge', *Herald*, 13 October 2014. For figures on party membership more generally, see Richard Keen, Membership of UK Political Parties, House of Commons Standard Note SN/SG/5125, 24 September 2014 <file:///C:/Users/Owner/Downloads/sn05125%20(4).pdf>.

46. See Cara Sulieman, 'STV Poll: SNP at 52% as Labour Face General Election Meltdown', 30 October 2014 <http://news.stv.tv/scotland-decides/297729-stv-poll-labour-would-annihilated-if-general-election-held-tomorrow/>.

47. See Jim Pickard and Claer Barrett, 'Old Debts Put UK Labour Party Still Deep in the Red', *Financial Times*, 29 July 2014.

48. Isabel Hardman, 'Labour's Team Spends More Time Squabbling than Selling Miliband', *Daily Telegraph*, 11 July 2014.

49. Survation, 23 September 2014 <http://labourlist.org/wp-content/uploads/2014/09/Tables-for-Ed-Miliband-Speech-Reactions-Poll.pdf>.

50. Sam Coates, 'Too Clever by Half: Inside the Troubled World of Team Ed', *The Times*, 18 October 2014.

51. YouGov, 3 October 2014 <https://d25d2506sfb94s.cloudfront.net/cumulus_uploads/document/ij56ls8hol/TimesResults_141002_Cameron_policies_Website.pdf>.

## CONCLUSION: MISSION ACCOMPLISHED?

1. Lord Ashcroft Polls, 12 October 2014 <http://lordashcroftpolls.com/wp-content/uploads/2014/10/Post-Conference-Poll-Full-tables-Oct-2014.pdf>.

2. Janan Ganesh, 'Even Great Political Strategists Barely Affect Elections', *Financial Times*, 5 August 2013.

3. See Peter Kellner, 'The Trouble with Ed', YouGov, 23 June 2014 <https://yougov.co.uk/news/2014/06/23/trouble-with-ed/>.

4. See, e.g. Polly Toynbee, 'Labour's Spending Worked: Why Don't they Defend It?', *Guardian*, 2 July 2013.

5. David Miliband, Draft Acceptance Speech <http://www.theguardian.com/politics/2011/jun/10/david-miliband-speech-that-never-was>.

6. See 'Jeremy Paxman Shows he's Still Got it', *Huffington Post*, 19 June 2014 <http://www.huffingtonpost.co.uk/2014/06/19/jeremy-paxman-ed-miliband-flatulent-dog_n_5510342.html>.

7. See Peter Kellner, 'The Trouble with Labour leader Ed Miliband', *Prospect*, July 2014 <http://www.prospectmagazine.co.uk/features/the-trouble-with-ed-miliband>.

8. Peter Kellner, 'What Miliband Needs to Learn from Thatcher', YouGov, 1 October 2014 <https://yougov.co.uk/news/2012/10/01/what-miliband-needs-learn-thatcher/>.

9. ComRes, 28 September 2014 <http://comres.co.uk/polls/ITV_News_Marginal_Constitencies_Political_Poll_Sept2014.pdf>.

10. STV, 30 October 2014 <http://news.stv.tv/scotland-decides/297729-stv-poll-labour-would-annihilated-if-general-election-held-tomorrow/>.

11. John Rentoul, 'Ed isn't Paranoid but they're Unlikely to Get him', *Independent on Sunday*, 9 November 2014.

12. On the petition, see Mark Ferguson, 'Anonymous Labour MPs. Seriously. You need to Put up or Shut up', *LabourList*, 9 November 2014 <http://labourlist.org/2014/11/anonymous-labour-mps-seriously-you-need-to-put-up-or-shut-up/>. For a survey of councillors, see <http://www.anglia.ac.uk/ruskin/en/home/microsites/labour_history_research/news_and_events/labour_leadership_polling_data.Maincontent.0001.file.tmp/labour_leadership_polling_data_november_2014.pdf>.

13. Rafael Behr, 'Ed, you Can't Remain a Medium-Sized Beast', *The Times*, 9 August 2014.

14. For a summary of the polling done on how much various alternative leaders might help Labour, see Anthony Wells, 'Sunday Polling and Alternative Labour Leaders', UKPollingReport, 9 November 2014 <http://ukpollingreport.co.uk/blog/archives/9057>. See also Dan Jarvis (ed), *Why Vote Labour* (London: Biteback, 2014).

15. Ed Miliband, Speech, 25 July 2014 <http://labourlist.org/2014/07/the-choice-of-leadership-read-the-full-text-of-ed-milibands-speech/>.

16. Andrew Rawnsley, 'Ed Miliband's Lack of Popularity Is Nothing to Do with his Photo-Ops', *Observer*, 27 August 2014. See also Mary Riddell, 'Ed the Human Cannonball has those Nasty Tories in his Sights', *Daily Telegraph*, 30 July 2014.

17. Stephen Bush, 'Ignore the Message and Look at the Messenger', *Telegraph. co.uk*, 29 July 2014 <http://blogs.telegraph.co.uk/news/stephenkb/100281705/ignore-the-messenger-and-look-at-the-message-what-if-damian-mcbride-is-right/>.

18. John Harris, 'Sounding Strange is a Sign of Labour's Terminal Malaise', *Guardian*, 3 June 2014.

19. Matthew D'Ancona, 'What's the Point of Labour when the Coffers are Empty?', *Sunday Telegraph,* 30 September 2012. See also Matthew D'Ancona, *In It Together: The Inside Story of the Coalition* (Harmondsworth: Penguin, 2014).

20. Marcus Roberts, *Labour's Next Majority: The 40% Strategy* (London: Fabian Society, 2013) <http://www.fabians.org.uk/wp-content/uploads/2013/09/LaboursNextMajority_web.pdf>.

21. Sadiq Khan, 'Waste your Vote on the Green Party—or Choose a Green Labour Government', *Independent*, 25 November 2014.

22. See Matt Chorley, Tom McTague, and Martin Robinson, '"I want an Apology" says White Van Man' , *MailOnline* <http://www.dailymail.co.uk/news/article-2842783/Labour-MP-accused-outrageous-snobbery-tweeting-photo-remarkable-house-flying-St-George-s-flags.html>.

23. Geoff Evans and Jon Mellon, 'All Roads lead to UKIP?', British Election Study Blog, 9 December 2014 <http://www.britishelectionstudy.com/bes-resources/all-roads-lead-to-ukip-by-geoff-evans-and-jon-mellon-university-of-oxford/>. Labour's level of concern about UKIP can be gauged by a confidential candidates' briefing leaked to the press on the eve of yet another 'big speech' on immigration by Ed Miliband in mid-December 2014—an intervention that itself followed hot on the heels of a speech by Cooper and indications by Rachel Reeves that Labour would do even more to limit benefits to EU migrants than the government. See <http://i.telegraph.co.uk/multimedia/archive/03138/CampaigningAgainst_3138005a.pdf>.

24. Ed Miliband, speech on the deficit, 11 December 2014, <http://press.labour.org.uk/post/104918318074/speech-by-ed-miliband-mp-on-the-deficit>.

25. YouGov, 5 December 2014 <https://d25d2506sfb94s.cloudfront.net/cumulus_uploads/document/zkoqdsou1a/TimesResults_141204_better_or_worse_off_Website.pdf>.

26. ComRes, 26 November 2014 <http://comres.co.uk/polls/ITV_News_Marginals_Poll_November_2014.pdf>.

27. Research by the British Election Study suggests that the Lib Dem's confidence that they will win more seats than suggested by their woeful position in national opinion polls may be misplaced. See Stephen Fisher, 'What the BES Suggests about Constituency Variation in Party Performance', British Election Study Blog, 7 December 2014 <http://www.britishelectionstudy.com/bes-resources/what-the-bes-suggests-about-constituency-variation-in-party-performance-by-stephen-fisher-university-of-oxford/>.

28. See Andrew Rawnsley, 'Labour Needs to be Candid about Painful Cuts it will Have to Make', *Observer*, 15 June 2014.

29. UK opposition parties routinely take advantage of seconded staff from consultancy firms. For more detail on how much such services have been worth to Labour since 2010, see James Ball and Harry Davies, 'Labour Received £600,000 of Advice from PwC to Help Form Tax Policy', *Guardian*, 12 November 2014.

30. Janan Ganesh, 'Britain's Next Election Carries a Fiendish Winner's Curse', *Financial Times*, 30 September 2014.

# Index